THE FIERCE **URGENCY** OF NOW

Improvisation, Community, and Social Practice

A new series edited by Daniel Fischlin

Books in this new series advocate musical improvisation as a crucial model for political, cultural, and ethical dialogue and action—for imagining and creating alternative ways of knowing and being in the world. The books are collaborations among performers, scholars, and activists from a wide range of disciplines. They study the creative risk-taking imbued with the sense of movement and momentum that makes improvisation an exciting, unpredictable, ubiquitous, and necessary endeavor.

DANIEL FISCHLIN, AJAY HEBLE, AND GEORGE LIPSITZ

THE FIERCE URGENCY OF NOW

Improvisation, Rights, and
the Ethics of Cocreation

Duke University Press

Durham and London

2013

Typeset in Charis by Tseng Information
Systems, Inc.

Library of Congress Cataloging-in-
Publication Data
Fischlin, Daniel.
The fierce urgency of now : improvisation,
rights, and the ethics of cocreation / Daniel
Fischlin, Ajay Heble, and George Lipsitz.
pages cm — (Improvisation, community, and
social practice)
Includes bibliographical references and index.
ISBN 978-0-8223-5464-2 (cloth)
ISBN 978-0-8223-5478-9 (pbk.)
1. Improvisation (Music) 2. Human rights
movements. 3. African Americans — Political
activity. 4. Politics and culture. I. Heble, Ajay,
1961– II. Lipsitz, George. III. Title. IV. Series:
Improvisation, community, and social practice.
MT68.F54 2013
781.3′6 — dc23   2013003137

Duke University Press gratefully acknowledges the
Social Sciences and Humanities Research Council
of Canada for its support of the Improvisation,
Community, and Social Practice (ICASP) project,
at the University of Guelph, which provided funds
toward the publication of this book.

CONTENTS

ACKNOWLEDGMENTS

The experience of working on this collaboratively authored book has been genuinely inspirational for all of us. We've benefited greatly from the opportunity to learn from one another and to savor the ways our friendship and our many common interests have been deepened by the conversations that are played out in these pages.

Opportunities for such collaboration, unfortunately, tend to be all too rare, and we're hugely grateful for all those who've made the writing of this book possible. We'd like to acknowledge the support of the Social Sciences and Humanities Research Council of Canada, through the Major Collaborative Research Initiatives program, for providing generous funding for the Improvisation, Community, and Social Practice (ICASP) project. Our work with ICASP has become more than just a research project: it is in so many ways an exemplary instance of what a vital, resilient, and socially engaged community can be. Special thanks to ICASP's amazing project manager, Kim Thorne, for her ongoing advice and support, for her behind-the-scenes work in making it all happen, for being such a crucial part of our community. We'd also like to express our gratitude to the many friends, colleagues, research-team members, and research assistants who've worked with us on related projects, including the Guelph Jazz Festival Colloquium and ICASP's peer-reviewed journal, *Critical Studies in Improvisation / Études critiques en improvisation*. In particular, we acknowledge Rebecca Caines, Elizabeth Jackson, Eric Lewis, George Lewis, Jesse Stewart, and Rob Wallace. Thanks also to ICASP's various partners and institutions. We'd especially like to acknowledge the support of Kevin Hall, and the generous funding we've received from the Office of the Vice-President, Research, at the University of Guelph.

Our heartfelt thanks go out to Rachel Shoup, our amazing research assistant, for all her extraordinary work in helping us with this project.

Her dedication, focus, attention to detail, and initiative played a key role in enabling the preparation and completion of this manuscript. We're grateful, too, to have benefitted from the support of Christie Menzo, who worked with us as our research assistant during the very early stages of this project.

And we've benefited from ongoing dialogue with our own local communities of musicians, scholars, and friends, many of them exemplary practitioners of improvised musicking. These include Jane Bunnett, Dave Clark, Lewis Melville, Joe Sorbara, and Ted Warren, among many others.

Thanks to the superb staff at Duke University Press, especially to our wonderful editor, Ken Wissoker, for his commitment to our work, and to Editorial Associate Leigh Barnwell.

Thanks to the anonymous readers who made truly constructive and thoughtful suggestions on how to improve our work.

Thanks to our friends at the Guelph Jazz Festival, especially to Julie Hastings, for her dedication to the music.

Thanks to all the amazing musicians whose creativity, passion, and commitment have inspired us to write this book.

Daniel wishes to recognize George Doxas and Andrew Homzy, two truly inspirational teachers and musicians from his early days in Montreal, people who set him on his way, probably unbeknownst to them.

Ajay would like to extend a deep personal thank-you to Dr. Eric Schnell for *being there.*

George acknowledges with deep gratitude the instruction and inspiration he has derived from conversations with Ruben Guevara, George Lewis, Susan McClary, Russell Rodriguez, Sunni Patterson, and Rob Walser.

Finally, and most important, thanks, as always, to our amazing families and the other people with whom we share our lives—Martha Nandorfy, Sheila O'Reilly, and Barbara Tomlinson. This book has been made possible by your wisdom, your patience, your friendship, your guidance, and your love.

Improvisation is a human right.

MUHAL RICHARD ABRAMS, THE GUELPH JAZZ FESTIVAL,
SEPTEMBER 10, 2010

Improvisation is neither a right nor a necessity; it is our natural state of being. It is the way of acting without thinking. This applies equally to music and life.

JOHN MCLAUGHLIN (QTD. IN DANIEL FISCHLIN,
"SEE CLEARLY . . . FEEL DEEPLY")

"THE FIERCE URGENCY OF NOW"

Improvisation, Rights, and the Ethics of Cocreation

A book linking improvisation with rights of any kind—civil, human, environmental—may seem like an improbable endeavor, no more plausible than a book exploring the connections between, say, strawberries and electromagnetic plating. Improvisation and rights seem to belong to completely incommensurable areas of human endeavor. The term *improvisation* connotes artistic activities and practices that are spontaneous, personal, local, immediate, expressive, ephemeral, and even accidental. *Rights*, by contrast, refers to formal standards of acceptable human conduct, rules that are permanent, impersonal, universal, abstract, inflexible, and monumental. Yet in this book, we follow the lead of the artists and activists we study to move strategically across these seemingly impermeable categorical divides. We believe not only that improvisation and rights can be connected but also that they must be connected, that improvisation is at its heart a democratic, humane, and emancipatory practice, and that securing rights of all sorts requires people to hone their capacities to act in the world, capacities that flow from improvisation.

Both rights and improvisation call into being what we call an ethics of cocreation, an understanding that all things are interconnected cocreatively. The permutations of interconnection that bind people together enable a multitude of potential practices that can give rise to new lived, embodied, material realties. Those cocreated realities, insofar as they may be said to possess, invoke, or embody an ethic, emerge from the "relational contingencies" that arise out of being.[1] Improvisation is an important social, musical, and ethical practice for understanding and generating the potential forms of cocreation—deeply relational, profoundly contingent—without which our collective relation to each other and to all things would be unthinkable.

Through our shared work as researchers and coinvestigators with the international Improvisation, Community, and Social Practice (ICASP) initiative headquartered at the University of Guelph, we have come to conceive of musical improvisation as a generative yet largely unexamined model for political, cultural, and ethical dialogue and action. Improvisation for us is more than an artistic conceit, more than the spontaneous creation of notes by musicians or words and gestures by actors. In its most fully realized forms, improvisation is the creation and development of new, unexpected, and productive cocreative relations among people. It teaches us to make "a way" out of "no way" by cultivating the capacity to discern hidden elements of possibility, hope, and promise in even the most discouraging circumstances. Improvisers work with the tools they have in the arenas that are open to them, in order to imbue the world with the possibility of making right things happen. Without a written score or script, improvisers envision and enact something new together, and enrich their experience in the world by acting upon it and changing it, in the process creating things that would not have otherwise come into existence.

Our collaborative writing process for this book might itself be seen as part of an effort to model our own ethics of cocreation, to use a cowriting-as-inquiry approach to illuminate unexpected themes and exciting new areas of inquiry. Driven by a set of principles that are akin to those we associate with much of the music we discuss in this book—an openness to unexpected outcomes, to developing themes or ideas that might not have been predicted on the basis of any one participant's starting point, a willingness to surrender our (in this case, written) contributions to one another as we engage in the process—we've used collaborative authorship not only to see beyond the assumptions and perspectives associated with our own home disciplines, but, in the process, and via a consultative and consensual approach taken in an environment of mutual respect and trust, to allow new methodological paradigms to emerge as well, in short, to create something that would not have otherwise been possible.

In a world filled with paths we can or must take, improvisation compels us to think about the paths we can make. It requires an open attitude toward other people as well as a creative disposition toward art. Improvisation is a manner of speaking that requires listening, a collective conversation that turns great risks into splendid rewards. By definition, it invokes collective interchange that is potentially transformative. Improvisation turns opposites into dialectical syntheses. It balances competing claims and interests. Improvisers need to counterpoise imagination with discipline, ego with empathy, and self-assertion with self-effacement. Improvisation references enduring continuities from the past while calling new collectivities into being in the present. It situates itself at the crossroads of historical specificity and sonic experimentation. It calls into being an experimental, alternative community in which individualism does not have to degenerate into selfishness and where collectivity does not have to dissolve into conformity. Indeed, improvising jazz artists "have discursively transcoded the hard facts of slavery, migration, industrialization, and urbanization in U.S. history into aesthetically rich and complex creations. Their harmonious balance between individual solos and collective improvisation provides a metaphorical solution to one of the recurrent dilemmas of social life in the United States: how to encourage individuality without selfishness and how to encourage collective consciousness without totalitarianism" (Lipsitz, *Footsteps* 91). In the context of the arguments in this book, this is more than a metaphorical solution: it is an embodiment of the very lived agency that improvisation engenders in its most achieved forms, especially in terms of the ethics of cocreation.

The qualities that improvisation cultivates have never been needed more than they are now. In selecting *The Fierce Urgency of Now* as the title of this book, we emphasize that the "now" in which we live is no ordinary time. We write this book in the midst of a global rights emergency, at a time where calculated cruelty and brutality seem to have the upper hand everywhere. We live in a world that seems to be falling apart. The people who control corporations and governments cannot fix the things they have broken. They cannot repair the terrible damage that their policies have inflicted on people and the planet. The cumulative consequences of neoliberalism entail the organized abandonment of entire populations. They have generated seemingly endless cycles of war, worsening economic inequalities, and interrelated environmental catastrophes. The evisceration of the social wage, practices of mass incarceration, and the transformation of public institutions and spaces into sites for private investment and speculation spread misery everywhere. In the educational institutions where we work, relentless pressures toward vocationalization, virtualization, and fiscalization corrupt the learning environment, undermine the quality of teaching and research, and imperil the development of the kinds of critical, creative, and contemplative thinking on which democracy depends (Quinn, *Learning* 17).

Yet as Naomi Klein and others have demonstrated, for neoliberal elites, nothing succeeds like failure. Each catastrophic failure becomes further justification for the implementation of even more draconian measures. A succession of moral panics about terrorism, immigration, and the alleged nonnormative behaviors of aggrieved groups become justifications for the systematic violations of rights that sacrifice core rights principles and create deep-seated, pathological structures of response to difference, structures based on fear. Leaders of advanced industrialized nations have abandoned centuries' old principles of habeas corpus and due process. They have given official approval to waterboarding and other forms of torture for criminal suspects. Armed combatants, soldiers, paramilitaries, and hired mercenaries around the world target civilian populations for destruction. The media pay more attention to the ravings of celebrities than to the scandalous, morally bankrupt behavior of stockbrokers and market-makers. Multinational corporations and international agencies promote starvation by privatizing the agricultural commons. Masculinist power around the globe denies reproductive rights to women and compels women and children to remain in abusive, disempowered relationships.

No one will solve these problems for us. We have to learn to solve them ourselves. The terrible lack of engaged democracy in our society pressures us constantly to think of ourselves in passive terms, as spectators rather than actors, as consumers rather than producers. The reigning structures of feeling of our time encourage us to long for rescue, to believe that our problems can be solved for us by some charismatic politician or some new technology or some underlying demographic or social transformation.

But, in truth, no one can do for us what we must do for ourselves. As the U.S. civil-rights and labor-rights activist A. Philip Randolph used to say, too many of us are relying on a "wishbone" when what we really need is some backbone. Things will not get better unless we make them better. We believe that cultivating the capacity for action, a capacity inculcated by improvisation, and channeling it toward meaningful, embodied rights outcomes is one of the ways we can make things better.

Improvisation provides important training for life. In a world where our cultural practices are often more democratic than our political institutions, improvisation can serve as a key crucible for human rights activism. Improvisation promotes personal confidence and makes people accustomed to taking action, to activating their agency publicly and in relation to others. Improvisers have to be aware of the needs of others. They must recognize problems rapidly and invent solutions immediately: they must do so here and now, or, as we pun later in the book, hear and now. They need to prepare themselves for the inevitable conflicts, ruptures, obstacles, and disappointments that occur in human interactions, yet remain committed to working things through with others and solving problems together. Improvisation can cultivate dispositions, attitudes, and traits with enormous applicability to rights struggles of various sorts. But improvisation is not merely an artistic practice that can be adapted for the purposes of social justice. As example after example in this book reveals, the kind of improvisation we champion depends on breaking down distinctions between life and art, to cultivate a view of art as a practice firmly implanted in and connected to the political and social life of communities. "The improviser is at the focal point of multi-directional energies that occur at the interstices of creative potential. These energies are both embodied in the creative gestures that make the music occur and in the reception gestures that continue to make meaning of that music once it has been played" (Fischlin, "Wild Notes . . . Improvisioning"). Improvised musicking is a critical form of agency, of embodied potential that is inseparable from other social practices that call upon us to be purposeful agents of our cocreated, lived reality.

Without serious shared purpose and collective responsibility, expressive culture runs the risk of becoming little more than a trivial form of self-indulgence. Without firm grounding in and accountability to the life and death issues of human dignity and decency central to rights discourses, improvisation surrenders its epistemological power and squanders its moral potential. Improvisation is not merely an artistic form potentially useful to civil-rights activism, but is also an artistic, political, social, and moral practice that cannot succeed on its own terms unless it does meaningful work in the world. As Sun Ra repeatedly warned his musicians: "Be careful what you play . . . every note every beat, be aware that it comes back to you" (qtd. in Szwed 236).

Improvisation teaches people to enact the possibilities they envision. It emerges from communities whose members have been compelled to look beyond surface appearances, to imagine how what "can be" lies hidden inside "what is." Slaves in the United States who were given starvation rations discovered ways to cook the fatback and intestines of pigs, discarded as garbage by slave owners, and mix them with collard greens to create nutritionally balanced meals. Colonial subjects in Trinidad who were forced to let multinational mineral-extraction companies loot their national resources took discarded metal oil canisters and transformed them into musical instruments perfectly suited for blending Western tonal, functional harmony with Afrodiasporic polyrhythms. Native Americans participating in powwow ceremonies in Minnesota turned poison into medicine by taking discarded Copenhagen tobacco tins and deploying them as ornaments on "jingle dresses" worn in healing ceremonies. Adaptability, improvisation, and invention are the weapons of the weak.

In music, improvisation creates new kinds of art and new kinds of artists. In his important study of the Association for the Advancement of Creative Musicians (AACM), George Lewis shows how the seemingly simple act of breaking with dominant ideas of instrumentation and orchestration opened up new possibilities, how playing triangles and tuned garbage cans created new sonic inventions, how encouraging musicians to play more than one instrument produced a wider range of orchestrations and enabled new multiplicities of timbre that gave the group a sound that "exceeded the sum of its parts" (*Power* 362). Unconventional orchestration and instrumentation interrupted old habits and conventions, forced musicians out of comfort zones, and compelled them to discover things about themselves and their music they did not know they knew. This made them better improvisers, for as Lewis explains in a felicitous phrase, "Chance favors the prepared mind" (*Power* 364). Changes in instrumentation and orchestration also encourage new attitudes about the relationships between music and other forms of expressive culture. The AACM had affiliations with other arts groups, including the Organization of Black American Culture, which created a twenty-by-sixty-foot mural about black heroism on the wall of a Chicago tavern. The painting of the wall became an arts event in itself as activists, tourists, and artists flocked to see the mural evolve. Musicians, poets, and dancers came to the site to inspire the painters. Once completed, the mural became known as the Wall of Respect, a site for political rallies and meetings as well as an inspiration for similar projects in other cities.

In Los Angeles, Horace Tapscott's Pan Afrikan Peoples Arkestra sometimes featured five bass players and four drummers. The experimental nature of the ensemble promoted new arts collaborations as well as new sonic imaginings. Tapscott later recalled in his oral history memoir, "After we had developed a piece of music, somebody would create a dance to it or we'd have some words or some poems written for the tune. Everyone had a shot at creating something in this particular composition. A poet might write a beautiful line for a certain spot in the composition and we'd add it. A dancer might develop a nice step for it and we'd utilize that in presenting the tune. We'd try to present all faces of the composition" (*Songs of the Unsung* 99).

The active and open stance toward art, encouraged by improvisation, drew from and contributed to a broader sense of self-activity in the world. Tapscott's group, in Los Angeles, and the Black Artists' Group (BAG), in St. Louis, did especially important work using art as a vehicle for expanding the sphere of politics. Tapscott made an album with Elaine Brown that featured songs central to the organizing activities of the Black Panther Party. He played benefit concerts for political prisoners and draft resisters. The Black Artists' Group assisted rent strikers in public housing projects in St Louis. The saxophone player and BAG cofounder Julius Hemphill claimed that the BAG's music was "a sounding board for social issues," noting that "unsatisfactory conditions" affect everything in a person's life and therefore have to affect the music too (qtd. in Lipsitz, *Footsteps* 117).

In Chicago, John Shenoy Jackson drew on personal and collective traditions to do important work with the AACM as an administrator, organizer, and publicist. Born in 1923 in Hot Springs, Arkansas, Jackson was raised by Garveyite parents who believed that their own actions had meaning for other black people around the world. "My father didn't wear diamonds," Jackson once told an interviewer, "because he knew if he wore a diamond some Black family was suffering in Capetown" (qtd. in Lewis, *Power* 132). Jackson came to music late in life, first picking up the trumpet as a man of forty, when he purchased instruments for his sons to play. Yet he immersed himself in the challenges of the instrument, noting at one point, "I firmly believe if I'd started when I was a child I'd be one of the giants in the field" (qtd. in Lewis, *Power* 133). Jackson had no intention of becoming a professional musician, however. Instead, he used administrative talents he had accumulated in the military and in social services to organize and deploy the work of others.

Just as improvisation needs a connection to basic rights and attendant struggles for social justice, rights activism desperately needs a more fully realized sense of the importance of culture in promoting mutual respect and collective responsibility. Civil rights cannot be produced merely by endless recitations of rules for good conduct. Civil rights require active constituencies capable of deciding fit standards of human conduct through democratic deliberations, debates, and decision making. Yet as we argue in chapter 1 of this book, the prevailing Western understanding of "human" rights as the personal possessions of individual rights-bearing subjects may itself be a constraint on more expansive notions of rights: human rights in this sense is a parochial construct emanating from the history of Europe, which now functions falsely as a universal norm. This formulation defines human rights in a negative sense through a series of specific prohibitions against practices by nation-states. It is, of course, important to ban torture and genocide, to guarantee free movement and free speech, to protect the religious and cultural rights of minorities, and to promote elections—among many other things. But rather than augmenting the actual agency, dignity, and decency of humans, these prohibitions too often simply serve the self-interests of power, alerting governments and corporations to the minimum standards they must maintain to avoid culpability as violators of human rights. They prohibit torture, but allow starvation wages. They require elections, but do not guarantee people meaningful access to decision-making processes. They ban genocide, but allow companies to concentrate toxic waste hazards in minority communities, to patent seeds and privatize water supplies in a world where people are dying of hunger and thirst. Capital is free to move across borders, but workers may not. As the human rights scholar Catherine Albisa maintains, "To be free only to suffer deprivation and exclusion is no kind of freedom at all. Freedom inherently includes the ability to exercise choices, and that ability is fully dependent on a protective, effective, and rational social infrastructure" (173). The ability to exercise choices also depends on mutual recognition and responsibility, on cultural inclusion and belonging. Without concrete, self-active constituencies deciding democratically the contours of acceptable human conduct, human rights can become a tool of capital's desires for predictability, stability, and security, a discourse that regulates human suffering rather than prevents it. Just as improvisation needs to speak to human rights issues, human rights discourse needs to promote the culture of collective responsibility, dispersed authority, and self-active democracy embedded in improvisation as a social and musical practice.

In this book, we conflate categories in order to study improvisation and rights in concert. In the process, we go against the grain of centuries of academic and popular knowledge, which have taught us to create bounded categories and to honor the borders that divide them. Music and politics are studied in separate departments in universities. Books about these subjects are placed in different sections of bookstores and on different floors of libraries. Even inside these disciplines, the musicologists who study improvisation are generally divided from those who study formal composition, notation, and transcription, while the social scientists and legal scholars who examine human rights rarely become knowledgeable about performance and expressive culture. There is, of course, a certain utility to this division of labor; specialization often produces depth and complexity. Yet outside and beyond classrooms, course syllabi, libraries, and bookstores, improvisation and rights struggles inhabit the same world. Their fates are linked in ways that are hidden when we relegate them to separate realms and categories. Duke Ellington repeatedly warned that fidelity to prefabricated categories inhibited understanding. "The category is a Grand Canyon of echoes," Ellington explained. "Somebody utters an obscenity and you hear it keep bouncing back a million times (38). Even worse, in Ellington's opinion, categories exaggerate differences and prevent us from seeing similarities. "In order to have a category," Ellington argued, "one must build a wall, or two, or more" (360). The practical work of achieving meaningful outcomes for social justice requires us to tear down walls, to cross boundaries, and to see how the categories that contain and constrain us might be turned into vehicles for liberation. This is not a simple matter of rejecting categories, but of finding the right tools for the right jobs.

Many of the categories that we inherit, that build walls artificially and unnecessarily, do not serve our interests. When we learn to think about culture and politics as discrete and mutually exclusive spheres of existence, we neglect the political work performed by culture and ignore the inescapably cultural dimensions of political mobilizations and identities. Yet academic disciplinary boundaries encourage musicologists and political theorists to inhabit separate spaces. People working inside disciplinary categories do not always inhabit fully the identities by which they are hailed, but, over time, socially constructed separations like the ones dividing music from politics come to seem natural, necessary, and inevitable.

This book, then, is written out of the space of what Boaventura de Sousa Santos, the sociologist and rights scholar, calls the ecology of knowledges, in which "the logic of the monoculture of scientific knowledge and rigor, must be confronted with the identification of other knowledges and criteria of rigor that operate credibly in social practices pronounced nonexistent" ("A Critique" 168). De Sousa Santos has theorized the "abyssal line" that divides dominant structures of sanctioned thought from other ways of viewing the world.[2] The abyssal line is an adjunct to hegemony. The line creates profoundly dysfunctional effects in the ecology of knowledges by reinforcing monocultural spaces that exclude forms of knowing that exist beyond the abyssal line. Separating the globe into First and Third World, or developed and underdeveloped nations, is one aspect of this abyssal line, whose specious and value-laden worldview is severely put to the test when one substitutes for Third the term *majoritarian,* or *over-developed* for developed. In such a frame, the primacy of the First World is undone by understanding that it is, in fact, in the global minority. Likewise, construing the space of the overdeveloped challenges how the developed is privileged over the underdeveloped. Thinking beyond the abyssal line is profoundly tied to the capacity to integrate difference into one's scheme of things. Other ways of knowing, other ways of being, other ways of coming to knowledge generate a richer ecology of knowledges. Moreover, in accepting this, there is a profound tie to social justice and rights issues, whose equitable outcomes often are unthinkable without precisely this sort of capacity to cross over the abyssal line, to integrate difference and other ways of knowing into a more expansive sense of what knowledge means. In many ways improvisation and even alternative concepts of rights remain beyond the abyssal line or have been set to the margins of ossified epistemological structures. They present potentially radical, oppositional, and critical forms of knowing that challenge us to imagine a much broader worldview beyond the abyssal line.

This sort of thinking is precisely that described by Dr. Martin Luther King Jr. in his Massey Lecture "Conscience for Change," delivered in November 1967 on CBC Radio, just six months before his assassination on April 4, 1968. There King takes great pains to point out how "difficult it is to exaggerate *the creative contribution of young Negroes* [to the spirit of resistance inherent in the civil rights movement]. They took non-violent resistance, first employed in Montgomery, Alabama, in mass dimensions, and developed original forms of application—sit-ins, freedom rides, and wade-ins" (195; emphasis added). But King saw these strategies as resonant within an even wider context: "The Negro freedom movement would have been historic and worthy even if it had only served the cause of civil rights. But its laurels are greater because it stimulated a broader social movement that elevated the moral level of the nation" (196). Worth noting in King's analysis is the creative power of the freedom movement insofar as it came from the application of a knowledge drawn from across the abyssal line. Young African Americans were able to deploy creative strategies that not only gathered force in the localized civil-rights contexts of the United States but that led to wider national and global impacts as well. The resistant strategies born of African American youth culture and its affiliation with other global sites of resistance (think of Gandhi's use of ahimsa to achieve the independence of India from British imperial culture) located themselves in an expansive notion of the ecology of knowledges. In this instance, rights, resistance, and creativity located in a specific cultural moment came to produce one of the most notable social movements in the twentieth century's struggle with dominant culture. The silo mentality of academic disciplines, then, which resists or prohibits thinking of music as a form of social practice with wider implications and that imagines rights struggles as being disaffiliated from creative forms of expression, is something we challenge throughout this book.

We conceive of things differently. We see politics as cultural and culture as political. In our view there will not be better works of art unless we build a better society, but we cannot build a better society unless works of art expand our imaginations and our aspirations. We work in the tradition of C. L. R. James, who argued, "A revolution is first and foremost a movement from the old to the new, and needs above all new words, new verse, new passwords—all the symbols in which ideas and feelings are made tangible" (qtd. in Ransby 374). In this book, we explore music and politics as mutually constitutive elements in our shared social life. To do this, we need to challenge prevailing categories, rethink fundamental questions about the bounded confines of space and the linear progressions of time. Of course, we are grateful for all good work and we respect all that we have learned from previous paradigms. Scholars across the disciplines have often done honorable and generative work by studying the particularities of place and the meanings of change over time. Ethnomusicologists, for example, have drawn skillfully on principled commitments to understanding the rich relations that connect cultures to particular places. At its best, ethnomusicology has been a site of generative thinking about the dynamics of difference. In the face of scholarly and civic ideologies that fear difference and promote uniformity, ethnomusicology teaches that universality is rich with particulars, that contingencies of time and place matter, that we can learn as much from the things that divide us as from the things that unite us. Ethnomusicology helps us see which differences make a difference.

What ethnomusicology does for place, social history does for time. Accurately locating our inquiries about culture inside the long arc of history, with its cumulative legacy of events, ideas, and aspirations, helps us see that part of what things are in the present is how they came to be in the past. Archives of the past expand the discursive spaces of the present, populating them with perspectives no longer accessible from the common-sense and quotidian experiences of everyday life. Social history promotes social projects by enabling us to perceive what the literary scholar Ramón Saldívar calls "the present signs of the incompletion of the past" (189).

Yesterday's victories, however, can become today's problems. In our time, the assumptions about the isomorphism of culture and place that have been central to the traditional practices of scholarship in the social sciences and the humanities are complicated by mass migrations and new media forms that transmit ideas, images, and sounds across the globe, rapidly and even instantaneously. The focus on linear temporalities and grand narratives endemic to cultural history promotes the perception that history is something that happens to people, not something they create. It promotes passivity and obscures agency. The monumental arc of linear history can persuade people to believe that short-term problems are insignificant because they always get resolved in the long run by long-term solutions, an optimism that is difficult to support responsibly in the face of today's growing environmental, economic, and educational catastrophes.

The Fierce Urgency of Now examines new spatial and temporal imaginaries of politics and culture. Improvisation serves as a focal point in our effort because it can create performance spaces that transform physical places. It can produce performance times that interrupt and redirect historical times. The scholarly categories favored by disciplinary knowledge teach us that there is a time and a place for everything—that people need to be on time and to stay in their place. That is exactly the kind of thinking that improvisation at its best can help us overcome.

Improvisation has a lively and well-chronicled history as a practice prevalent in music, theater, dance, poetry, performance art, and even sculpture all around the world. Through our shared work with the Improvisation, Community, and Social Practice project, we have learned that improvisation is a social practice that goes beyond the arts, that physicians, teachers, community organizers, and athletes also improvise. In the ICASP project, and in this book, we explore musical improvisation as a model for social change. Our examples generally focus on the links between the rich traditions of Afrodiasporic improvisation and the dynamic forms of social critique and social-movement mobilization attendant to them. Much of the music that we discuss gets classified as jazz in generic discourses, but we view the vital forms of improvisation that emerged among jazz musicians in the post–Second World War period as nodes in a network that spans generations and encompasses musics known by other names, including blues, ragtime, swing, gospel, rhythm 'n' blues, and hip-hop. For us, ragtime from the 1890s is a form of jazz, even though the term jazz was not used in print as a generic marker until the 1910s; blues forms and sensibilities pervade jazz and gospel compositions and performances; chords associated with jazz (like augmented ninths) appear in gospel songs sung by Sam Cooke; and hip-hop inherits and incorporates elements of all previous genres of black music (Woods, "The Challenges"). As the late Christopher Small demonstrated so clearly, the Afrodiasporic tradition in its many different incarnations coheres around the idea of music as an integral and essential part of everyday life, as a mechanism that facilitates both social interactions and self-realization (Small, *Music of the Common Tongue* 24).

We believe that these examples demonstrate the value of thinking about improvisation as a model for social change. Our examples are meant to be illustrative but not exhaustive. Contemporary listeners to Western art music recognize improvisation in compositions by John Cage and Pauline Oliveros and in the interpretive performances of baroque music by Glenn Gould. They may have forgotten, however, that Handel, Mozart, and Beethoven improvised, that Bach did not expect his scores to be played the same way in every performance, that opera singers often gain distinction by inventive embellishments of the written scores they sing. Indian classical music expressly requires improvisation from its musicians.

We do not adhere to the formalism that would dictate that any form of improvisation is automatically democratic, egalitarian, and emancipatory. Female musicians often discover that the world of improvisation is as resistant to their inclusion as any other. Dana Reason, a pianist, composer, and musicologist, points out that experimental and cutting-edge female improvisers do not get their work reviewed, and do not receive invitations to participate in improvised-music festivals. On the rare occasions when they do receive attention, Reason argues, they find themselves described mainly by their physical features (62). Similarly, the singularly accomplished composer and performer Pauline Oliveros notes that a distinctly gendered "invisible barrier" marginalizes her inside improvisatory groups, because "males bond strongly around music and technology and leave women out of their conversations and performances" (54).

Some of the improvisational practices most effective in advancing the interests and ideas of black men have contributed to the repression and suppression of black women. The gospel singer Marion Williams and the jazz singer Betty Carter deployed their voices the way advanced improvisers used instruments, yet rarely received critical or commercial recognition for their achievements (Heilbut 222; Bauer 27–30, 94). Male musicians deeply resented Carter's leadership style even though men who led ensembles routinely treated their musicians in similar fashion (Bauer 153). Horace Tapscott and his fellow musicians built an extraordinary improvisational community in Los Angeles in the mid-twentieth century, a community in which women played key roles. The flutist Adele Sebastian, the composer and multi-instrumentalist Linda Hill, the vocalist Amina Amatullah, and the guitar player known as Avotcja made important, if unrecognized, contributions to the ensemble. Gender bias posed a huge problem for them. Adele Sebastian observes that it was not Linda Hill's musical brilliance but rather the willingness and ability to care for the men in the ensemble that earned Hill appreciation in the group. Sebastian felt she could not follow that path. "As much as I loved Horace," she recalls, "I wasn't the follow the leader kind of sister. And those were the kinds of sisters they wanted. I didn't sleep with them. I was just interested in music" (Isoardi 58). Tapscott lived off the earnings that his wife, Cecilia, brought home from her job at the Los Angeles County Hospital during this time, and other men in the aggregation had similar arrangements. "We hung out together all the time," Al Himes remembers. "Horace wouldn't get no job and I wouldn't get no job. Our old ladies were running us crazy because we wouldn't do nothing but play" (Isoardi 52). We do not know what the history of improvised music would have been if sexism had not continuously and artificially constrained the participation of women within it. Improvisation is a tool that can be used for many different purposes. The same medicine that can cure can kill if used in the wrong ways. Yet for all the inevitable flaws that come from its immersion in the social relations of a hierarchical society, improvisation is the right tool today for a very difficult job that needs to be done.

This book is not an encyclopedic and exhaustive survey of either improvisation or social movements, but an argument about the benefits of breaking down walls and transcending the categories that relegate music and politics to discrete and mutually incommensurable realms of existence. It is easy to overlook the limits of conventional categories in ordinary times. Today, this is no longer possible. As Immanuel Wallerstein argues, we are in the midst of a major systemic crisis, not just a period with many economic, social, and political problems. Our time is a time of chaotic disintegration, a period when the traditional mechanisms used to restore social equilibrium no longer work. The question is no longer whether there will be a radical transformation of social institutions and social relations, but rather what kind of institutions and relations will emerge from the upheavals of the next quarter century (Wallerstein). In a hierarchical, exploitative, and unjust society, a period of systemic crisis leaves us without good short-term options; our only choices entail deciding which evils are the lesser evils. The chaotic consequences of systemic breakdown also make it impossible to plan for the long term, to design blueprints in the present for the kinds of social relations and political institutions that we hope will emerge out of the protracted struggle we are certain to see in the years ahead. This unavailability of short-term or long-term options makes the middle term crucially important. Wallerstein explains that in this middle term—the next five to ten years—we need to develop new forms of political education and practice that will deepen the democratic strata of social life, that will help people become accustomed to deliberative talk and face-to-face decision-making, that will sharpen our senses of solidarity and teach us to work together democratically and productively.

The work that we seek to do in *The Fierce Urgency of Now: Improvisation, Rights, and the Ethics of Cocreation* addresses this middle term by calling for new understandings of politics, new understandings of music, and new understandings of the dialectical and dialogic relationships between them. We have found that work of this kind is easily misunderstood. Cultural critics satisfied with the conventional categories of humanities and art generally do not want to see the walls come down. They read our arguments about the importance of the political contexts in which music is created, performed, and received as an unwarranted intrusion on the autonomy of art. Educated to make fine distinctions about musical figures and devices, these critics are often "tone deaf" to politics. They view the political realm as bounded by the voting booth, as an activity that takes place at the ballot box for five minutes once every two or four years. But for us, the political realm includes the time between elections: the three hundred and sixty-four days and twenty-three hours and fifty-five minutes that we spend every year outside the voting booth. For most people, in fact, even the exercise of the franchise is a ritual structured in dominance, a selection between unsatisfactory alternatives, and a moment of choice with no real agency. The political realm that interests us is broader than the ballot box. It pervades practices not usually considered to be political that permeate everyday life.

We remind readers of a complex set of interrelated histories involving music and rights as a concrete instance of this argument. Following the Civil Rights Act of 1957, President Eisenhower introduced yet another civil rights bill in late 1958 that was not to become law until 1960. The new bill was a response to an extended streak of bombings against African American churches, schools, and communities in the South, though the infamous bombing of the 16th Street Baptist Church, in Birmingham, Alabama, on Sunday September 15, 1963, that killed four young girls had yet to occur. That bombing spawned memorable musical tributes by both John Coltrane (the song "Alabama," on Coltrane's *Live at Birdland*, recorded on November 18, 1963, was an elegy for the young girls) and Nina Simone (whose song "Mississippi Goddam" was written in reaction to the racially motivated bombings). The event caused widespread revulsion and radicalized a generation of young African American activists, including people like Angela Davis, whose family not only lived in Birmingham in the area known as Dynamite Hill (because it was so frequently the target of Ku Klux Klan bombings), but who was also friends with one of the victims and whose mother had taught another one of the young girls killed at the 16th Street Baptist Church (Davis interviews that appear as part of the film from 2011 written and directed by Göran Hugo Olsson, *The Black Power Mixtape, 1967–1975*).

The bombing of the 16th Street Baptist Church proved to be a turning point for the civil rights movement in the United States, giving rise to the passage of the landmark Civil Rights Act of 1964, which outlawed discrimination against blacks and women (including racial segregation in schools, the workplace, and public-service facilities) and ended irregularities in the voter registration process that discriminated against minorities. It is worth remembering, though, that integrationist arguments were deemed to be denigrating by activists like Stokely Carmichael, who in 1966 argued, "Integration speaks to the problem of blackness in a despicable way. As a goal, it has been based on a complete acceptance of the fact that in order to have a decent house or education, blacks must move into a white school. This reinforces among both black and white the idea that 'white' is automatically better and 'black' is by definition 'inferior'" (qtd. in Panish xxi). Jon Panish shows with acumen how this attack on normative whiteness was echoed in some of Cecil Taylor's (and others') pronouncements in the same year: "There should be a boycott by Negro musicians of all jazz clubs in the United States. I also propose that there should be a boycott by Negro musicians of all record companies . . . We're no longer reflecting or vibrating to the white-energy principle. The point is: we know who we are. We have a whole history of music in this country" (qtd. in Panish xxi).

Guerino Mazzola and Paul Cherlin, scholars focusing on this period in jazz history, also note that the

> situation with jazz in the early sixties was the impression that this music had been stolen from its mostly black creators by white companies, white intelligentsia, and white organizers. Archie Shepp commented . . . that "Jazz" had become a commercial brand like "Coca Cola." According to him, free jazz was also an attempt to liberate the music and its creative expression from packaged commercialism. In a *DownBeat* interview in 1965, he argued that "jazz is one of the socially and esthetically most significant contributions to America . . . it is against war; against Vietnam; for Cuba; for the liberation of the peoples of the world. This is the nature of jazz . . . Why? Because jazz is itself born from oppression, born from the subjugation of my people." The community of jazz musicians progressively felt miserable and exploited. Ornette Coleman sums this up with his comment: "I am black and a jazzman. As a black and a jazzman I feel miserable." (4)

These voices were part of a much broader alliance of African American artists whose work was explicitly political. Poets like Abiodun Oyewole, of the Last Poets, and poet-musicians like Gil Scott-Heron (along with others like the Watts Prophets) "operated at the nexus of Black America's two most radical art forms: poetry and jazz" (Lynskey 181). In the case of the influential Last Poets it is worth remembering that they had taken their name from the South African revolutionary poet Keorapetse William Kgositsile and his poem "Towards a Walk in the Sun," which argued that the time for poetry was over in the fight against oppression, that poetry was to be replaced by the spearpoint. Kgositsile had a radically active sense of the place of art in a world capable of apartheid and systematic racism, stating, "There is nothing like art—in the oppressor's sense of art. There is only movement. Force. Creative power. The walk of Sophiatown totsi or my Harlem brother on Lenox Avenue. Field Hollers. The Blues. A Trane riff. Marvin Gaye or mbaqanga [a Zulu style of music that origi-nated in the 1960s and led to a South African version of jazz]. Anguished happiness. Creative power, in whatever form it is released, moves like the dancer's muscles" (qtd. in Ro 569). Kgositsile shifts the terms of art from that of a static, inert object to that of an active agent in creating social mo-mentum, movement: art, in short, as the embodiment of agency and social practice—art as aligned with the same sense of movement to be found in the term *civil rights movement*.

Here, as in the other comments from prominent African American art-ists cited throughout this book, explicit connections are said to exist be-tween civil rights struggles and the explicit content of the art produced by African Americans. It is worth remembering that these artists faced real systemic challenges to producing their work and getting it disseminated. These challenges were posed by formidable surveillance and interven-tions from government agencies and operations like COINTELPRO and the disruptive operations carried out by the FBI (1956–71) that explic-itly targeted for the purposes of "neutralization" (in FBI director J. Edgar Hoover's words) everyone from King to the NAACP, the Congress of Racial Equality, various African American nationalist groups, and the American Indian Movement (to name only a few). It is also worth remembering, as the music critic Dorian Lynskey points out, that even after COINTELPRO was dissolved in 1971, "the government continued to monitor black art-ists in other guises throughout the decade" (193). Darthard Perry, an FBI informer code-named Othello who infiltrated the Watts Writers Work-shop (and by extension the Watts Prophets), "revealed [in a TV interview] how much importance the bureau placed on art in the black community.

'You can take their culture and use it against them,' he said, emphasizing that the FBI's archive of African American books, magazines, videos, and records exceeded that of a well-stocked Harlem library. His white FBI supervisor . . . 'could name some jams of Miles Davis that I hadn't even heard of'" (Lynskey 193–94).

In such contexts bringing together momentous rights histories with the specific experience of musicians battling oppression, how is it possible to disassociate some of the most prominent improvisers and their music in the so-called jazz idiom (and, we hasten to add, this improvised music was radical even in jazz terms) from the political contexts to which they were responding, both musically and verbally?

To apolitical culturalists, any mention of politics seems dogmatic and orthodox. They are especially wary of political arguments that threaten their claims about their own innocence, that trouble their certainty that they are not accountable for the hierarchies of class, race, gender, sexuality, and national citizenship that give them privileged lives. Willing to accept a discussion of politics only as a gloss aimed at better interpretation and appreciation of the music, they reject arguments that take music seriously as a social and cultural force. Any politics strikes them as dogmatic orthodoxy, because it intrudes on their fun. These critics sometimes consider themselves to be politically progressive because they are against censorship and oppose intrusions on the rights of artists, but they reflexively reject efforts like ours that show how musical practices both reflect and shape macrosocial, political inequalities, how they permeate the micropolitics of everyday life. These critics want to live more comfortably in this society as it exists. They are embarrassed by its injustices and inequalities but do not believe they have anything to gain by helping to build fundamentally new ways of knowing and being. We argue, on the other hand, that doing principled research about cultural life requires political engagement and action, that we do not understand culture unless we recognize its political dimensions. Too much is at stake in the work we do to surrender the terrain of the political to the politicians. As Toni Morrison maintains, "Excising the political from the life of the mind is a sacrifice that has proven costly. I think of this erasure as a kind of trembling hypochondria always curing itself with unnecessary surgery" (12). We view political analysis as a necessary part of principled cultural analysis and critique, but we also think that focusing on culture makes it possible to rethink politics in useful and generative ways.

Conventional categories also shape and constrain the ways politically minded critics respond to our work. Accustomed to defining the political sphere as a series of public competitions among individuals and interest groups battling over the creation and implementation of government policies, music often strikes these critics as a realm that is too private, too personal, and too small to be thought of politically. Yet we know that politics is an embodied activity, an affective and emotional endeavor, a sphere of life that revolves around desires for collective association and reciprocal recognition, as well as for rights and resources. Political thinkers outside the academy who have been immersed in popular struggles have long understood the importance of culture to democratic and egalitarian social change. For example, writing from within the ferment of the Algerian anticolonial struggle, Frantz Fanon explained how cultural change prefigures political change. "Well before the political fighting phase of the national movement," he noted, "an attentive spectator can thus feel and see the manifestations of a new vigor and feel the approaching conflict" in "unusual forms of expression and themes which are fresh and imbued with a power which is no longer that of an invocation but rather of the assembling of the people, a summoning together for a precise purpose" (243). Similarly, reflecting on radicalism in Italy in the years immediately following the First World War, Antonio Gramsci attributed working-class insurgencies to "a new social group that enters history with a hegemonic attitude, with a self-confidence which it initially did not have." In his view, this group "cannot but stir up from deep within it personalities who would not have previously found sufficient strength to express themselves fully in a particular direction" (98).

Yet acknowledging the dialectical and dialogic relationships linking culture and politics is not enough. Scholars studying the politics of culture and the culture of politics have become attached to conventions and categories that substitute feelings for actions, that resort to moral condemnation rather than cultural analysis that leads to social action. Bored by the everyday suffering of ordinary people, they seek out sensational images of human degradation and debasement. The abject for them is not a potentially generative site of critique and struggle, but proof of the immorality of capitalist culture and of their moral superiority to it. To borrow the apt phrase coined by Felice Blake and Paula Ioanide, they "feel good about feeling bad." They aestheticize their own alienation and seek solace in the scholarly version of residential gated communities where others believe exactly what they believe. They give their readers plenty of things to feel, but no actual work to do. They craft eloquent descriptions of other people's suffering and promote melancholy resignation in response to them. They savor what Raymond Williams discerned in Bertolt Brecht's plays of the 1920s, "a raw chaotic resentment, a hurt so deep that it requires new hurting, a sense of outrage which demands that people be outraged" (100). Like Williams, we disagree with this approach to culture, even though we understand the logic of it. It reflects the disillusionment that many people feel with past efforts at social change, what Williams called "the discovery in ourselves and in our relations with others, that we have been more effectively incorporated into the deepest structures of this now dying order than it was ever, while it was strong, our habit to think or even suspect" (98). There is an undeniable element of truth in this perception, and we fault no one for feeling discouraged or demoralized, given the increasingly indecent social relations that prevail in our society. Yet we believe that this radical negativity is ultimately a form of collaboration masquerading as critique.

Improvisation appeals to us because it is work that makes a difference in the world. It compels us to leave our comfort zones, to forge meaningful interactions with others across categories and social identities, to deepen the democratic strata of society through cultural activities that resonate fully with the contradictions and possibilities of our time. Improvisation in both expressive culture and social-movement mobilizations can keep us attentive to our responsibility to build the world we hope to inhabit. As the civil rights worker Willie Ricks used to say about the activities of the Student Nonviolent Coordinating Committee in the 1960s, "Mr. Say ain't the man, Mr. Do is the man" (qtd. in Jeffries 190). Our work in *The Fierce Urgency of Now* challenges political and cultural orthodoxies, not for the sake of novelty, but in solidarity with and in the spirit of the improvisers whose work we believe points the way to a new and promising path.

When categories collapse, creative community-making begins. This idea is a baseline precept for understanding the ethics of cocreation. In her indispensable book *Black Noise*, Tricia Rose reveals how many of the core categories of hip-hop emerged directly out of the confusing contradictions, conflicts, and crises of African American life in New York City in the 1980s. Young people in the inner city found themselves trapped in inadequate vocational schools, learning soon-to-be obsolete technological skills of the industrial era, like hot-type printing, blueprint making, and repairing electronic equipment. But seeing possibilities where others might only see obstacles, they attached themselves to new technologies in off-centered ways. Futura, a graffiti artist, abandoned the technologies of print, taking up the spray-paint can, while DJ Red Alert and DJ Kool Herc took out their frustrations with obsolete blueprint and auto-repair technologies by pioneering new ways of transforming the digital sampler from recording device to an expressive instrument. These artists used their knowledge as consumers to transform themselves via improvisation into cultural producers, and turned street corners into impromptu theaters and youth centers. Displaced from Brooklyn and Manhattan by urban renewal projects, they created new communities in the South Bronx through rapping, sampling, break dancing, and graffiti writing.

Drawing on the insights of Arthur Jaffa, Rose explains how these youths created improvised art organized around the aesthetic principles of flow, layering, and rupture. Their art equipped them with important training for life. The geometric flowing lines of graffiti echoed the musical lines flowing from the turntables of DJs, establishing and maintaining feelings of continuity and circularity. The layering of sounds, images, and even clothing added to these sensations of continuous movement, yet "break" beats in songs and physical breaks in graffiti lines constructed a unity of opposites between flow and rupture. Rose notes that these aesthetic devices resonated with their creators' experiences of social dislocation and rupture—that they produced a blueprint for social resistance and affirmation by instructing participants to "create sustaining narratives, accumulate them, layer, embellish, and transform them, but be prepared for rupture, find pleasure in it, plan on social rupture, when ruptures occur use them in creative ways that prepare you for a future in which survival will demand a sudden shift in ground tactics" (39). More than mere recreation, the diverse practices promoted by hip-hop came from and spoke to the conditions of an aggrieved community battling dislocation and dispossession.

Improvisation requires renegotiation of the social charter between individuals and groups, but it also enhances and augments the capacities of individuals. A perhaps unexpected but nonetheless powerfully illustrative example of this appears in a rumination of Ken Dryden, a Canadian professional hockey player turned federal politician, on the qualities that made Guy Lafleur a special hockey player. Conceding that Lafleur's inarguable physical gifts as an athlete had much to do with his success, Dryden nonetheless identified Lafleur's ability to improvise as the key to his special status in the hockey world. Dryden noted that unlike most players trained in organized suburban youth leagues, Lafleur spent long hours alone on rivers, ponds, and rinks. Unlike his contemporaries, who developed their skills in organized competitions, Lafleur drew on these long hours of what Dryden calls "time unencumbered, unhurried, time of a different quality, more time, time to find wrong answers to find a few that are right" (157). This time made Lafleur different from other players.

Athletes trained by structured play in competitive leagues are described by Dryden as "student[s] cramming for exams." Their skills are developed by rote and remain remote and uncoordinated. When unexpected circumstances demand more of these athletes, they cannot move beyond their training. They have knowledge of the game, but not understanding. They lack the capacity to invent remarkable solutions in response to challenges for which they are unprepared. Lafleur, on the other hand, had a scope and culture in his skills, according to Dryden, that enabled him "to set higher limits, to settle and assimilate and become fully and completely yours, to organize and combine with other skills comfortably and easily in some uniquely personal way, then to be set loose, trusted, to find new instinctive directions to take, to create" (157). What Dryden saw in Lafleur, we see in artists trained by improvisation's networks of apprenticeship and instruction, artists trained to deploy the challenges of free play in ways that activate one's unique agency in relation to others.

If the people of this planet ever needed to cultivate the ability to carve out new instinctive directions, we need to do so now. We cannot study, teach, learn, play, sing, or dance without recognizing what time it is. The communities we care about are confronting increasingly harsh and indecent social conditions. The beautiful music that compels our attention emerges directly out of ugly realities, out of both old and new social conditions emanating from the long and still unresolved legacies of slavery, conquest, and colonialism, but also out of new forms of work and worklessness, new regimes of mass incarceration and austerity, new suppressions of free citizenship and social membership. The times we face today bear direct resemblance to those facing Martin Luther King's during the last year of his life. In 1967 and 1968 King's speeches took on a new tone of immediacy and urgency. "We are now faced with the fact that tomorrow is today," he argued, adding, "We are confronted with the fierce urgency of now. In this unfolding conundrum of life and history there is such a thing as being too late" ("Beyond Vietnam").

King called on his followers to move past indecision to action. He observed that men and women around the world, our brothers and sisters, were watching the United States and waiting to see action for social justice. "Shall we say that the odds are too great?" he asked. "Shall we tell them that the struggle is too hard? Will our message be that the forces of American life militate against their arrival as full men, and we send our deepest regrets? Or will there be another message, of longing, of hope, of solidarity with their yearnings, of commitment to their cause, whatever its cost?" In times of ferment and upheaval, such as this one, victories can bring about rapid changes that alter the future meaningfully, while defeats can consign us to decades and even centuries of suffering. King called on his listeners to choose to rededicate themselves to what he termed "the long and bitter—but beautiful—struggle for a new world." In words that apply as much to our day as to his, he explained, "The choice is ours, and though we might prefer it otherwise we must choose in this crucial moment of human history." Or, to put it in the words of Sun Ra: "The possible has been tried and failed; now I want to try the impossible" (qtd. in Szwed 192).

DISSOLVING DOGMA

Improvisation, Rights, and Difference

We're all connected; we're all one. I'm concerned about my world—I'm concerned with the Africans in Rwanda, and I'm concerned with what happens in Ireland. Any artist should be. I've seen the suffering of my people, the murder of Palestinians in the Middle East, the murder of Iraqis. Look at America today. There are more and more homeless, and George Bush wants $87 billion for [the war in] Iraq. You don't have to be a musician to be sensitive to these things. Politics is about people. I don't think that it's unusual that I am committed to this. As an artist, I feel obliged to do this, it is part of my destiny to do this . . . Music doesn't change things, but in my own small way, it makes a statement.
—Archie Shepp, "What Inspires You to Compose/Perform Music That Has Political Overtones?"

This book tells a portion of an emergent narrative that links forms of improvised musical expression with global and local struggles to achieve social justice. Analyzing complex social practices at the best of times is risky business. This analysis is especially risky when, as in music, formal and ideological content relies on nonverbal means of expression in conjunction with multiple, overlapped contingencies and histories. Moreover, in music, the nonverbal, instead of being a reduced mode of signifying that can only be self-referential, as it is sometimes argued, may well be an alternative strategy for conveying ideas that circumvent the limitations of spoken or written discourse. Interpretation often works on a lowest-common-denominator logic of reduction. And its methodologies and outcomes are frequently driven by ideologies that remain occluded, not part of a self-reflexive process that makes transparent the driving forces behind a particular analysis. This tendency to reductive interpretation is especially so when describing surpassingly large areas of human activity. Musical improvisation, for instance, is an inescapable aspect of what it means to be human; it is ubiquitous across cultures, national sites, and differing histories. Inescapable too are emergent rights and social-justice discourses that represent manifest global tendencies, discourses that refuse to be silenced as they struggle into being. The epigraphs at the beginning of this book assert improvisation as a human right (Muhal Richard Abrams) and recognize its underlying embeddedness in all aspects of being human (John McLaughlin). These two positions, however seemingly at odds with each other, are not inimical and outline the scope of what we argue in this book. It is our right to be who we are—to enact a "natural state of being" that is cocreative and ethical at once. This natural state, the capacity to express it in contingent relation to others, is at the heart of what it means to have rights. But it is also at the core of what it means to improvise as a way of being in the world, to activate key aspects of this basic form of human agency. So we argue from a cautionary position here, not only in relation to the assertions that follow, which can only tell a version of a more complete story that will come out in its fullness as others continue to elaborate the story, but also in relation to how we've come to this moment in the scholarship associated with improvisation, scholarship in which rights are interposed as a necessary concern.

Imagining Rights, Figuring and Refiguring Improvisation

How is one to understand Archie Shepp when he says we're all "connected" and that he is worried by the state of the world, when he articulates the limits he sees for music as an agent of change? Is he not saying that music, and especially the improvised musicking he has extraordinarily advocated for so many years, does in fact matter, even if only as an iteration, a statement? And if music is only an iterative statement that connects to a worldview in which social justice and equity issues are profoundly at stake, what in fact does it tell us? How does that "statement" operate on and in the larger world to which it contributes? Shepp, as he has been doing since his outspoken critiques of the Vietnam War in the 1960s, asks that we delve deeper into how music, his music, makes connections, how it articulates a worldview that may be powerless in some arenas but powerful in others.

So how then do rights and musical improvisation relate as iterations of complex social practices? Why is their relationship of any importance? What can improvisation teach us about rights, and what can rights teach us about improvisation? Are there core elements in rights and improvisatory utterances that connect the two together at some basic level? This book is a provocation to further thought on these topics.

In the *Grove Music Online* resource, the self-proclaimed "premier authority on all aspects of music," no entries exist on human rights and music, civil rights and music, or, for that matter, rights and music generally. Censorship and music also receive short shrift in the *Grove* article on censorship, with absolutely no attention paid to jazz, free jazz, improvised musickings, and the like. And yet, *censorship* is one of the key terms in which music and rights issues have traditionally been linked. The opening lines of the *Grove* article affirm this: "Censorship is not readily practised on music, because music does not as a rule convey a precise statement such as persons in authority might wish to tone down or ban. Censorship has in the main affected forms that ally music to words, in particular music theatre (opera, ballad opera, and musical comedy) and music with openly political associations (marches set to revolutionary or nationalistic texts, or cabaret songs). Such forms appeal directly to a large public gathering—a possible fount of subversion or violence" (Rosselli). The *Grove* article neglects to mention the work of Freemuse: The World Forum on Music and Censorship, an outgrowth of the first World Conference on Music and Censorship, held in Copenhagen in November 1998. The Freemuse secretariat was formally established in 2000 and "advocates freedom of expression for musicians and composers worldwide" (Aidt) using as its guideline the Universal Declaration of Human Rights of 1948 (hereinafter referred to as the UDHR). Moreover, Freemuse extensively documents the multiple ways music and musicians are repressed, sanctioned, censored, abused, and tortured globally.[1] Indeed, one of Freemuse's publications, *Shoot the Singer! Music Censorship Today* (Korpe), contains an extensive set of studies documenting global practices of musical censorship, from the Americas and Europe, through to Asia, the Middle East, and Africa. Alenka Barber-Kersovan's essay in the collection argues that music is a "sensual instrument of power" because of its affective potential not only to move people and to "transmit values and stabilize political systems" but also to challenge state power—as in the case of Jimi Hendrix's infamous rewriting of "The Star-Spangled Banner," via improvised feedback imitating the bombs falling in Vietnam.

Musical censorship gets at key rights issues often associated with freedom of expression, the freedom to assemble, and the freedom to access divergent forms of thinking. In many of these rights situations a key trope is improvisation: improvisation as a means to speak free of constraint; improvisation as a means to assemble alternative forms of community; and improvisation as a critique of dominant structures of thought. Michael Drewett and Martin Cloonan note that only "recently has the history of music censorship been written about in the west in any systematic way" (3), while pointing to the "range of censorial agencies that serve to highlight the multifactored nature of music censorship" in Africa (3). And elsewhere, in *Policing Pop*, Cloonan and Reebee Garofalo take pains to indicate that censorship "goes beyond the suppression of content to include issues of access, ownership, and the use of popular music and other forms of popular culture" (3). Censorship, in short, is an important, obvious site where music and rights, and improvisation as a radical experimental practice within music, are located as oppositional and even dangerous discourses that need policing.

The extent to which censorship is aligned with corporate interests in the commercial value of music, and especially the value of black musical practices, needs careful attention. Corporatizing music inevitably imposes constraints on freedom of expression. The market value of music is driven by other imperatives—especially profit. These imperatives are at odds with creative-commons musicking generated out of aggrieved communities in the name of resistance to oppression, community solidarity, and identity narratives. It is increasingly difficult to dream outside of the spaces of corporate control, where the commercial and the dominant culture's interests align. Black musical practices no longer fly below the corporate radar as they once did, whatever their genre. The transition from the critical, liberatory, and freedom-seeking forms of expression associated with black improvisatory musicking (and with the many genres of music ineluctably tied to that underlying form of expression, such as blues, R&B, soul, jazz in its many forms, and more recently turntabling and hip-hop) to commercial contexts that vitiate or efface the music's association with resistant politics may well reduce the vision, openness, and opportunities afforded the next generation to the improvisatory musics we align with struggles for social justice. The forms of corporate control that deny improvisatory music its presence as a compelling expression of public common spaces are directly related to the constriction of the human and creative rights this book addresses.

Robert Petti, multimedia scholar and producer, argues that one of the most powerful and monopolistic arbiters of what people actually listen to, Clear Channel, as of the 1996 Telecommunications Act, was "able to purchase over 1,225 radio stations within the United States . . . It owns and operates over two hundred radio stations abroad and it 'controls more live-music venues than any other company.'. . . As one of the most prominent gatekeepers in the radio industry, 'Clear Channel has designed itself as a self-contained, nationwide feedback loop, calibrating the tastes of its listeners and segmenting them into market-proven "formats"' . . . This monopoly proves to be very useful and powerful for corporate profit but does very little for musical innovation and aspiring artists" (25). The corporatization of music in such a pervasive "feedback loop" of condoned taste is a destructive new form of censorship. It shapes our listening and musical learning landscapes in ways that can either utterly marginalize the experimental practices associated with improvisatory black musicking or that can wholly appropriate it to new contexts that eradicate the complex histories and engagements of that music with creative struggles against oppression and injustice. Keith Negus, a scholar examining the work of the writer Nelson George, observes that "tracing the fate of rhythm and blues throughout the twentieth century, George . . . has emphasized the rationalization and restructuring of the record industry [that] gained momentum in the late 1960s. This has been decisive. It has ripped apart the connections that were being established between black musicians, independent black and white businesses and the black community. In their place it has instituted the 'conglomerate control of black music' in which black artists are forced into adopting a 'crossover mentality' to reach a mass white audience" (41). Such a mentality, a form of market-dictated aesthetic choices, amounts to a kind of censorship when it undercuts how "blues singers, regardless of their ethnic background, recognize the historical connection between blues music and black experience" arising from injustice and mistreatment (Davis 114).

Censorship, in its multiple forms, has always been an aspect of how black music that has political content is received. In many cases this censorship took the form of physical violence, especially when music and rights contexts came together. Dorothy Cotton, an activist in the civil rights movement, recalls how in St. Augustine, Florida, she and her fellow activists suffered "forty-five straight nights of beatings and intimidation." She remembers, "We marched regularly at night. We kept being ordered not to march especially at night because it was so dangerous. We sang every night before we went out to get up our courage. The Klan was always waiting for us—these folk with the chains and bricks and things—Hoss Manucy and his gang. After we were attacked we'd come back to church, and somehow always we'd come back bleeding, singing 'I love everybody'" (qtd. in Sumera, liner notes). Here the black historical experience of struggling against racism via public marches in which music played an important role is pitted against physical intimidation, the coarsest form of censorship. Blood and songs about love were used against chains and bricks. The black experience of this historical context ineluctably ties music to protest and community solidarity.

Crossover forms that negate or ignore that connection, or reshape it to more comfortable, uncritical historical contexts (as so often happened when the blues was appropriated to white rock culture), dilute and reduce the potent aesthetics of the music in ways that serve dominant interests. Angela Davis's extended discussion of the politics of the blues, as in the work of Ma Rainey, Bessie Smith, and Billie Holiday, reminds us that "art may encourage a critical attitude and urge its audience to challenge social conditions, but it cannot establish the terrain of protest by itself. In the absence of a popular mass movement, it can only encourage a critical attitude. When the blues 'name' the problems the [black] community wants to overcome, they help create the emotional conditions for protest, but do not and could not, of themselves, constitute social protest" (113). Yet when the social force of the music is overwritten by market conditions that eliminate these affective ties to community expression and critique, both the music and the social-justice potential embedded in the music suffer. And, as Keith Negus notes, "Not everyone has equal access to the means of creating and distributing music. The ability to control access to production facilities, manufacturing plants and distribution networks means that the larger corporations have far more influence than the smaller companies or enterprising individuals" (50–51).

These complex circumstances are very much part of the censorship discussion when it comes to improvised musicking in black culture, whether in the debates over who gets programmed at Wynton Marsalis's corporate-affiliated Jazz at Lincoln Center (JALC), discussed at length later on in the book, or the critical work done by people like William Banfield, who argues, "There is across the board a real suspicion of market forced, corporate-dictated stuff, the need for an American jazz re-education among the masses, concern about the dislodging of jazz from Black identity and the need for musicians to rise up and take back the music" (181). In the case of JALC, the rhetoric of corporate outcomes is familiar. Patrons can attend "Dizzy's Club *Coca-Cola*" where the "Dizzy Ethos," as it is called on the JALC website, gets formulated, somewhat shockingly, as follows: "'Dizzy's Club *Coca-Cola* is designed to entertain people in the spirit that Dizzy had . . . very welcoming,' Mr. Marsalis explains. 'We just want people to have a good time. We want the musicians to feel comfortable to play'" ("The Dizzy Ethos").

The comment reduces Dizzy Gillespie's complex situatedness as a black, improvising musician with a politics to a comforting ethos associated with entertainment. And it overwrites his identity in the name of a powerful, globally ubiquitous corporate brand, effectively piggybacking that brand's name recognition onto his. In short: "Have a good time. Don't think critically. Drink Coke." Gone is the memory of Gillespie's run for president of the United States, in 1964, even if it was partially conceived of as a PR stunt, of which Gillespie has said, "Anybody could [have] made a better president than the ones we had in those times, dilly-dallying about protecting blacks in their civil and human rights and carrying on secret wars against people around the world. I didn't think there was any choice. I had a real reason for running because the proceeds from the sale of the buttons [that said "Dizzy Gillespie for President"] went to CORE [the Congress of Racial Equality] and SCLC the Southern Christian Leadership Conference, whose president was Dr. Martin Luther King, Jr., and I could threaten the Democrats with a loss of votes and swing them to a more reasonable position on civil rights" ("Dizzy Gillespie for President").

The Dizzy ethos in the JALC context effectively censors and dehistoricizes Gillespie's lifelong advocacy of civil rights and battles against endemic racism in the United States, while offering up an anodyne context for listening to music, a context far removed from the civil rights struggles to which Gillespie was so attuned. Even the website instructions on how to get to JALC situate the music in a web of corporate affiliations: "Frederick P. Rose Hall, home of Jazz at Lincoln Center, is located in the Time

Warner Center, Broadway at 60th Street. Frederick P. Rose Hall can be accessed using the JAZZ elevators located on the ground floor of The Shops at Columbus Circle across from Hugo Boss" ("Getting Here"). The politics of such alignments are complex and controversial, and something to which we return elsewhere in the book. But it is clear that corporatized structures that appropriate improvised music in the name of their own "ethos" pose a real threat, refashioning the cultural contexts of the music in ways that dramatically realign its politics and efface its original cultural contexts.

Randy Weston's experience with *Uhuru Afrika* in 1960 is telling. Robin Kelley, jazz scholar and historian, notes how the album was a "manifesto, a declaration of independence for Africa and mutual interdependence between the continent and its [diasporic] descendants" (*Africa* 61). Weston's landmark album, with global rights implications, focused on (African) independence from (Occidental) colonial structures of oppression and on resistance to racism and injustice, appeared in the same historical moment as Max Roach's *We Insist! Max Roach's Freedom Now Suite*. Both used improvisatory structures to create compelling musical statements with significant political and aesthetic valences, much like the *Ten Freedom Summers* suite, released in 2012 by the American improviser, composer, and trumpeter Wadada Leo Smith as an exploration of key moments in the civil rights movement in the United States. In the case of *Uhuru Afrika*, Weston recalled, "Out of the rhythmic fervor engendered [in the recording sessions for *Uhuru Afrika*], waves of spontaneous creativity rose on the pulse of a common musical emotion to break against the microphones in sprays of exciting sounds—and all this within the basic pattern of an overall conception" (cited in Kelley, *Africa* 62).

The response to *Uhuru Afrika*, with its use of the Swahili word for "freedom," was decidedly cool. White fans were turned away by the politics, and Weston's label, Roulette, to whom he had refused to give the publishing rights to the music, failed to promote the album properly. As Kelley notes, "Ironically, *Uhuru Afrika* and [the] *Freedom Now Suite* received a great deal of publicity in [apartheid] South Africa: the government banned both LPs. The South African Board of Censors minced no words—they vowed to censor all records by African American artists, 'particularly any that use "Freedom" in the title'" (Kelley, *Africa* 63–64). Between corporate control and governmental censorship (let alone how African American musicking that explicitly tied itself to rights outcomes was received by a conservative public) both Weston and Roach faced an uphill battle, much like that faced by the civil rights activists with whom they aligned. Moreover, systemic, indirect ways of making sure that politically nuanced musical practices involving improvisation and rights activism were securely in place both as a function of corporate and governmental practices, including choices associated with programming for mainstream jazz festivals. It is worth noting the role that mainstream jazz festivals have played and continue to play in reinforcing institutionalized versions and interpretations of history that reflect corporate interests, especially in terms of the ways these festivals (somewhat like the Clear Channel example described earlier) are shaping the listening landscapes based on what sells, what is "hot," or what is being pushed by major label interests.

Even more ironic than South Africa's ban on LPs with the word "freedom" in the title, and other contexts shaping access to and the dissemination of major African American artists' work, was the fact that black American culture was being used as a diplomatic tool by the American state department during the height of the Cold War, from 1956 to the 1970s, as documented at length by Penny Von Eschen. Major stars like Louis Armstrong (playing with an integrated band), Earl "Fatha" Hines, Dizzy Gillespie, and Dave Brubeck were all involved in this program, with Brubeck's rueful blurb on the back of Von Eschen's book noting, "My quartet was one of the first jazz groups to participate in the U.S. State Department's 'people-to-people' program. We understood, of course, that we played a role in Cold War diplomacy, but unfortunately, we were unaware of the part we played in the overall strategy" (Von Eschen, n.p.). Von Eschen argues that there has since been a shift from "state sponsorship of the jazz ambassadors to predominantly market-driven and corporate images" (258). Citing the "indispensable role of Colin Powell's global tours on behalf of the Bush administration," Von Eschen concludes that present U.S. officials "continue to depend on blackness to legitimate global agendas, even as they have reverted to an empty politics of racial symbolism, devoid of any relation to the vibrant egalitarian movements that animated the jazz tours of the 1960s. In the 1950s and 1960s tours, the unprecedented global scope of the government sponsorship of the arts enabled the musicians to travel, perform, and collaborate independent of the competitive logic of commodity capitalism and even state control" (258). So even when corporate or governmental control are exerted to neutralize, ignore, or manipulate the message associated with African American improvising musicians, the message they were carrying still got out, albeit in circumstances that were often challenging and far from ideal.

In the case of artists like Milford Graves and Don Pullen there was clear pushback against attempts to control improvised black musicking. Eric Porter describes how "in a January 1967 article for *Liberator*, [the percussionist] Graves and pianist Don Pullen linked black intellectual, cultural, and economic self-reliance, as they discussed what they termed [the] 'New Afro-American Cultural Revolutionary (NAACR)'" (199). Graves had "blamed white control of the music industry for the lack of mass black interest in the new music" (E. Porter 199) with which he was associated. Porter maps out how

> Graves and Pullen called for a "self-reliance program," emphasizing that one of the major mistakes [black] artists had made was to forsake the production end of music. Taking a cue perhaps from Charles Mingus Enterprises, they announced the recent release of a self-produced album, *Don Pullen, Milford Graves in Concert at Yale University*, which was available only by mail order. They called for abandoning "Western thought" as a means of understanding black music and advocated creating new instruments and recording techniques that would do a better job of facilitating black self-knowledge than existing technologies, which were products of white society. (E. Porter 200)

"Western thought" in this context exercised control over creative expression as well as the means of production, a key linkage that Graves and Pullen saw as a threat to the music and to freedom of cultural expression. The reproduction in corporate musical culture, then, of the same structures of marginalization and exclusion (let alone of profitability) associated with the very injustices (slavery and racism) that played such a key role in black musicking in the Americas was and continues to be a serious problem in terms of how to reconcile notions in the public commons of improvisatory musicking with "conglomerate control." The struggle to sustain experimentalist, improvisatory spaces of musicking where new forms of musical and social practice can be incubated in the face of imperatives pushing music into the realm of commercial economies of scale cannot be separated from other policing forces that we associate here with censorship. These forces define creative, improvised musical practices as irrelevant, dangerous, or disruptive of neoliberal logics associated with profitability and ownership models of the creative commons. Such practices are eliminated, ignored, or forced to conform to a Clear Channel vision of the musical universe.

In short, the multiple ways different forms of policing are aligned against experimentalist music have a great deal to do with the potential social, political, and affective power music possesses. As Petti argues, "Music has always been a driving force throughout society and it is increasingly becoming used as a tool for economic exploitation. Le Cocq states 'commercialism in the music business is merely looking for what sells, and trying to reproduce it as closely as possible to maximize sales' . . . Fantasy becomes packaged with the intention of priming and transforming society into a collective web of receptive consumers [that entices] people into accepting and believing an ideal rendition of reality rather than having artistic integrity reflect and shape culture and society" (27).

The power of improvised music is to articulate and embody an event horizon of what is creatively possible and thus gives voice to a fundamental right to speak freely, to speak in compelling ways about the human condition. In the history of black musicking, this power cannot be dissociated from improvised music's connection to civil rights struggles. The censorship of music in such a context, whether through limiting access to corporate channels or through direct restrictions on access to the means of production and dissemination, is clearly something to which we must pay a great deal more attention. What are the rights implications for improvisatory musics profoundly tied to aggrieved communities when corporatization, commercialism, consumerism, and the inherent conservatism of these become the norm—or at the very least a dominant force shaping the music and its political contexts?

The perplexing *Grove Music Online* assertion that censorship is not "readily practiced on music" is contradicted by even as conservative a publication as the *Economist*, which in an article from 1998 on banned music stated unequivocally, "Music is probably the most censored of all art forms" while simultaneously musing, but "isn't music too abstract and intangible to corrupt the innocent or threaten the mighty" (Berger 91). These examples indicate the disjuncture between how musical scholarship treats rights issues and the material realities facing musicians the world over. Censorship seems to define the ways music generally relates to rights discourses, even for an organization like Freemuse. That is, music is defined by a negative relationship in relation to rights as a cultural practice under various forms of attack from censors, corporate culture, and other strategies of cultural policing in which race is a factor.

Jazz, in its various manifestations as an expression of improvisatory explorations arising from the social and historical circumstances of African American diasporic cultures, has had a long history of being associated with various forms of censorship and social opprobrium. As is documented by Peter Blecha in *Taboo Tunes*, since the early twentieth century jazz has been designated a "musical impurity," associated with a "virulent poison which, in the form of a malarious epidemic, is finding its way into the homes and brains of youth to such an extent as to arouse one's suspicions of their sanity" (17, citing *Etude*, a magazine published in 1900). Ragtime was associated with the "horrors of war or intemperance and other socially destructive evils" and was deemed a "polluting nuisance" (17). And the discourses attacking jazz often resorted to inherently racist language, bridling at the "syncopated savagery," the "return to the primitive," and immorality (17). Blecha cites a Cleveland city ordinance from 1925 (No. 20456-A) that states, "Vulgar, noisy Jazz music is prohibited. Such music almost forces dancers to use jerky half-steps and invites immoral variations" (18). The battle lines here are clear: any music that liberates the body and that allows for variation (that is, improvisation) is a challenge to moral civic discourse, as opposed to an invitation to throw off repression and restrictions that limit one's expressive freedoms.

In 1933, the Washington state legislature was presented with a "Jazz Intoxication" measure as part of house bill 194, by Representative William A. Allen: "The intention was to establish a five-man statewide commission 'to survey the havoc being wrought on society as a result of jazz intoxication'" (Blecha 23). If the commission found evidence of this, it "should recommend that the governor act to bring about immediate cessation" with all "persons convicted of being jazzily intoxicated [to] go before the Superior Court [to be] sent to an insane asylum" (Blecha 23). In Hitler's Germany, equally despicable moves were made from 1930 on, with the rise of National Socialism. Early elected representatives who were National Socialists "instituted the Ordinance Against Negro Culture with the goal of ridding the land of 'all immoral and foreign racial elements in the arts.' One result was that jazz music was outlawed (a move that Mussolini made in Fascist Italy as well)" (23).[2] So censorship and censoriousness in multiple forms, from early restrictions on how slaves could make music through late forms of fascist incursion, have always been present in the history of improvised music. Cultural marginalization and restrictive ordinances disallowing musicians from playing in specific venues (national and international) have also been an ongoing part of the way censorship has been employed against the music. These restrictions are profoundly linked to general rights affirmations that have to do with freedom of expression.

But what we argue for in this book is that the censorship view tells only part of the story that brings improvised musicking together with rights discourses. By getting at why music is deemed worth attacking, does not another story emerge? Perhaps the story tells of the rather extraordinary and exemplary powers embedded in music as a social practice that resists and critiques other more limiting, less creative stories that shape our relations to each other. And this understanding of the exemplary powers of music may be especially pertinent in thinking about improvisation as a fundamental aspect of all musical endeavor, found everywhere, in all musical forms of expression. No child learning an instrument can evade learning how to play as a function of an improvised relation to the instrument as he or she gains mastery over it (and in fact "mastery," as so many of the greatest improvisers have shown us, will require an extended relationship to the instrument that is only made possible as a function of improvisatory practices). No composer can create without "playing" with musical materials, a play that is always a function of improvised relationships that eventually become more "stable." No community of music-making that starts from scratch can come into being without passing through multiple forms and phases of improvised experimentation.

So musical improvisation, however unrealized or misunderstood, is a key element in how music is created. And if improvisation is such an important component of music, what might focusing on it tell us about why music, as a general social practice found virtually everywhere, is under attack, a crucial site in which contested views of how the world is ordered are articulated, experimented with, and remade? As a universal, generalized practice that is articulated in a myriad of distinctive and specific ways, and as a fundamental response to how we encounter the world around us, improvisation has something to teach us about other such social practices. This is so, even as comparisons to other practices are fraught with the risk of oversimplification and interpretive strategies that reduce the expansive signifying potential inherent in improvisation as a generative creative practice. Rights discourses putatively get at underlying principles shared by all humanity. In our view, a key element in a more expansive understanding of rights would involve explicating how specific musical practices like improvisation relate to rights. What can thinking about rights through the prism of improvised musicking teach us, not only about the general relations between the two, but also about specific aspects of each that need to be better understood?

The *Grove* article on censorship opens with the extravagant and unsubstantiated claim that "censorship is not readily practiced on music," associating this difficulty with music's putative imprecision as a signifying practice that is nonverbal and extradiscursive. The affirmation is highly debatable. Music and musicians are frequently the objects of repression, and they are so precisely because the content of music, both in its formal qualities and in its ideological connotations as a cultural practice, can be highly charged and potentially subversive. It is instructive to remember the comment by Hans Werner Henze, the German composer, that "today music that truly wishes to speak, to be open, virtually resembles an esoteric cult: under attack, sometimes even persecuted, in flight from the dangers of mass society and standardization under dictatorships, and elsewhere from the platitudes of aesthetic slogans . . . Music ignores theoretical correctives, and dissolves dogma whenever it wishes" (123–25).

Henze's comments get at music as an alternative space and form of discourse: one that "dissolves dogma" and is therefore a challenge to the conservatism and ideological agendas associated with dogma. Music becomes an alternative form of discourse that always has the potential to break free of "theoretical correctives" (for example, the tritone as the *diabolus in musica*, the devil in music). Music stands apart from standardization and mass society (as in the music of the early punk movement or the free jazz avant-gardists) and attacks moribund aesthetics (think of the music of Charles Ives or Frank Zappa).[3]

In what follows, we lay the groundwork for a specific vocabulary that addresses the sites in which improvisation as a musical and cultural practice intersects with rights and social-justice discourses. Though many examples of sites where music and rights discourses align are to be found globally, we are specifically interested in improvisation as a form of musical discourse whose ideological underpinnings and historical contexts resonate in particularly interesting ways with the ideals and aspirations enunciated by rights and social-justice discourses. In order to imagine the potential of rights discourses more fully, we need to refigure improvisation as a musical force that is also a social force, a creative practice that calls into question how we think of community, freedom of expression, integration, identity, and alterity.

Improvisation and Freedom

Improvised music and the political location of the musician playing it bear a complex relationship to each other, as the above examples show. Improvisation can be, and largely has been as it emerged out of black diasporic musicking, both a symbolic and an embodied representation of human potential and freedom, whatever one may wish to argue about how "free" any improvisation really is.[4] If Derek Bailey is correct in affirming (and we think he is) that "historically, [improvisation] pre-dates any other music—mankind's first musical performance couldn't have been anything other than a free improvisation" (*Improvisation* 83), then every act of improvisation may invoke this originary moment from which all music was to come. Improvisational utterances, seen in this context, relive this moment of creative potential, however unknowable it will ever be, at the same time as improvisation embodies the freedom enacted in the moment.

Improvisation is both deeply historical (diachronous) and profoundly here and now (synchronous) in its symbolics, both a remembrance of past freedoms and of human potentialities set to erupt in the present moment. Improvisation is a locus where such energies and potentialities, territorializations and reterritorializations, knowledge and embodied content occur. They occur in the performers, as a function of performative utterance. But improvisation always has the potential to transfer this knowledge, intangible as it may be, to the community of listeners it addresses. Inspiration by example is one of the registers in which improvisation embodies itself as a cultural practice. Though difficult to trace in quantitative terms, the influence of improvisation as a model for liberatory, experimental, and self- and community-enabling action cannot be separated from its roots in the African diaspora's musical response to the conditions of its existence.

Olu Alake, a member of the Equality and Human Rights Commission in the U.K., in a fascinating discussion of cultural rights, identity, and citizenship entitled "A Long Way Gone," tells the story of the former Liberian child soldier Ishmael Beah [from whose memoir he takes the title of his essay]. In this [memoir], the shred of humanity that the young boy held on to in very difficult situations and in the face of various atrocities he was witness or party to, was reggae music. Indeed music was to play a significant role in his eventual rehabilitation and today many child soldier rehabilitation centres utilise the arts as a means of empowering the youths to confront and expunge their past demons. This is not just a tale of the redemptive power of music, but also indicative of a need for cultural rights to be enshrined in the psyche of all. Moreover, the assertion of this cultural right to access culture served as a catalyst for reconnecting Beah to his higher self and [for the] assertion of a new identity and sense of citizenship. This right (to access culture) is a core Cultural Right within the human rights framework.

Reggae was born in the 1960s (as was free jazz) of African diasporic musical experimentations that were heavily reliant on improvisation, whether in their rhythmic accompaniments or in the vocal styles known as "toasting," in which the DJ improvises along with dub tracks. Alake's narrative shows how Beah's rehabilitation from child soldier to citizen is mediated by reggae's inspirational force, leading Alake to argue for the fundamental right to access culture as a positive strategy for asserting and developing citizenship. The sublimated role of improvisation here is not to be forgotten, for it remains deeply tied to innovative musical forms that can only emerge out of the conjunction of sonic experimentation and historical specificities (in this case located in how Jamaican musicians linked their own political consciousness of materialism, apartheid, and social criticism generally with new forms of musical expression in which improvisation is implicated, without which reggae could not have been created).

Beah's example demonstrates what Panagiotis A. Kanellopoulos, the scholar of music education, has described as the "political character and the political role of improvisation as a vehicle for constructing particular modes of human agency, of human relationship, and of relationships among children, music, and knowledge" (97). That is to say, improvisation is both a musical and a cultural discourse with political implications, especially in how it functions epistemologically. As such, improvisation is a fundamental aspect of the cultural rights associated with the music discussed earlier. Improvisation is vital because it enacts these rights in a public sphere; it enacts the very origins of these rights embedded in the impulse to improvise that generates specific acts of agency and cultural identity.

Alake's essay ends with productive suggestions with regard to cultural rights generally: "There should be increased support for cultural cooperation programmes as a vehicle for promotion of rights . . . There needs to be a keener sense of cultural responsibility . . . Alliances for the development of cultural creative industries are important and need to be fuelled by cultural diversity, in terms of both the diversity of cultural products and also diversity of human existence." Alake further points to very different notions of rights operative in Africa and the Occident: "In the West, rights are deemed 'inalienable,' natural and inherent in every person, as this concept arises from ancient Greek and Roman ideas of natural law and democracy and [is] strengthened by liberalism and Enlightenment thinking. Many African languages do not have a translation for human rights, but concepts of cultural belonging and responsibility abound in many traditional knowledge systems and cultural understandings."

The distinction is important for our argument about the relationship between the emergence of the improvised musical practices associated with jazz and the civil rights movement. Cultural belonging and responsibility are active concepts opposed to the passive notion of individual inalienability. When something is said to be always already inherent, does it lose its political agency? Is there a problem with static definitions of rights and their provenance when apposed with more active, mobile definitions of rights in which defining how and why one belongs via responsible action is the norm? Are these differences enacted in the moment of improvisation as a function of its emergence from the hybridized musical discourses and cultural practices of the African diaspora? To each of these we would answer a qualified yes. The public spaces in which improvisation occurs demand agency over passivity, demand voicing and countervoicing, demand that group dynamics be freely, cocreatively embodied in both consonance and dissonance. As Kanellopoulos argues,

> Improvisation creates a "public space" where freedom may appear, where players and audience search for ways of musical communications under "no-rule." In improvised music, not only is there no ready-made form awaiting realisation, but "there is nothing to co-ordinate or synchronise the intentions of the musicians as the music unfolds" (Hodgkinson 2000, 30). What remains endlessly open is the determination of the musicians to work on

the basis of what Prévost (1995) calls "heuristic dialogue" and "dialogical heurism" (3). Heuristic dialogue . . . refers to acts of discovery within improvisational contexts that take the form of continuous dialogue between the human body as a thinking mechanism—and producer of sounds—and their investiture with meaning. It is the "inner debate" (Prévost 3) experienced by every improvising musician. Dialogical heurism denotes the struggle between differing personal musical intentions of partners in improvisation. Thus, "Inner debate meets outer debate" (Prévost 3). The irrevocable character of musical acts creates a special sense of listening-in-action. (110–11)

The freedom that appears in improvisation, in Kanellopoulos's reading (derived from the political theory of Hannah Arendt), is an action with no intrinsic value, a performance whose *telos* is the performance and nothing more (102):

At the same time, a life may be termed human only to the extent that it creates a free space for this "useless" and utterly distinctive form of activity. This is the only possible locus of freedom. In Arendt's (2006/1968b) words, "Freedom does not appear in the realm of thought at all" (144). Arendt "conceives [of] *freedom* not as a mysterious inner capacity (the "free will" of the philosophers) but as the act of *being free* manifest in the performance of action within a context of equal yet diverse peers. Freedom truly exists—has the fullest phenomenal reality—only during action's performance" (Brunkhorst 2000, 181). Arendt's conception of freedom centers "on the universal human capacity for initiation" (Kanellopoulos 188). Being free to make new beginnings is what marks her notion of "natality," which is "the existential condition of possibility of freedom."

These ideas associate improvisation as an embodied performance practice of what freedom may mean with the realization of human potential, the capacity to make new starts "within a context of equal yet diverse peers." The enacted freedom in the moment does not have a context (before and after the moment of improvisation) that may impose a telos, that may associate the thing in itself (the improvised performance) with an intention or an exemplarity, as is the case with the musicians we have examined who explicitly associate the telos of free improvisation with spiritual and ethical signifying. If this is the case, then improvised music is more the sublime object of ideology (as a function of how it gets interpreted) rather than the sublime object of nonideology (in Arendt's sense).

Improvisation may entail the conjunction of irreconcilables, like pur-
poselessness and intention, spontaneous moment and diachronous context, individual and community agency, and regulatory hierarchies and
the pleasure taken (and differential political agency achieved) in enacting freedom from these (remember that Nietzsche considered improvisation to be the "pinnacle of pleasure" [qtd. in Peters 141]). In all these,
improvisation functions as a maker, and marker, of difference, an emergent, collective, processual, and modulatory agency in which freedoms
are at stake, freedoms predicated on creation and expressive gestures that
test the capacity of the commons to change, self-critique, and evolve new
forms and social practices.

Paul Hegarty, author, musician, and lecturer in philosophy and visual
culture at University College Cork, argues in *Noise / Music: A History* that
the "freedom of free jazz does not go away, but dissolves into other areas
(including itself as a genre); the freeness is caught within sets of paradoxes that not only do not prevent its existence, but are the reasons for
it. The freeing up of playing, like the freeing up of 'all sound,' filters into
many musics, spreading noise even as they lose their initial moment as
noise in their own right" (54). Hegarty is thinking here of improvisational music's relations to other forms of music and to itself as it resolves
into new forms, say, in the influence of free jazz on the experimentalist
(for want of a better term) rock musicians Captain Beefheart and Frank
Zappa.

But what if we were to suggest that music is not only self-referential
in the way Hegarty's analysis suggests, but also has wider reference as a
form of cultural practice that resonates with and disturbs other forms of
being social, being in culture? So when Albert Ayler talks about "freedom"
as a function of his music, his term also carries with it wider points of
reference. When he talks about "spiritual unity," referencing the ethics of
collective improvisation, that concept has metonymic relation to broader
cultural and political practices that have bearing on community and rights
discourses. What if, in fact, improvisation as a musical practice filters into
other cultural practices, virally spreading its aesthetic and ethical challenges in as yet misunderstood or unstudied ways? Our focus here is on
the link between the performative symbolics of improvisational music
and embodied rights struggles, both framed as a function of the performance of community. Regarding rights struggles, Hegarty points to John
Zorn's notions of improvisatory communities, stating,

There is a widely held belief in improvised music that it is a highly communal activity. John Zorn offers a slightly more anarchist version of a society working as a collective moderation of conflicts: "I basically create a small society and everybody finds their own position in that society. It really becomes like a psychodrama. People are given power and it's very interesting to see which people like to run away from it, who are very docile, and just do what they're told, others try very hard to get control and more power. So it's very much like the political arena in a certain kind of sense" (qtd. in Bailey, *Improvisation* 78). We might not agree or like the sound of all Zorn says, but it shows key elements of how improvisation is not anarchic, but anarchistic, in that de facto power exists—it is open to all, and is transitional (if the society is working). Like Foucault, Zorn does not pretend power can be dissipated, but recognizes that it is a creative force. (56)

Hegarty recognizes the provisional nature of community dynamics, a strategy made explicit in improvisatory practices that perform and explore the contingent nature of all human relations.

Power and its effects are present as aspects of creation, which can entail destruction, anarchy, and disturbances of the norm. In these aspects, improvisation and rights discourses have significant overlap. Both are confrontations with mediated ways of being in relation to each other as a function of power relations that emerge when communities are formed. Again, we want to situate the notion of improvisation as it relates to free jazz squarely in relation to this dynamic of group-power relations and how they are articulated, enforced, challenged, critiqued, and overturned. Ornette Coleman's album *Free Jazz* (1960) "changed the concept of how jazz could function. It supplies a method to improvised music across an increasing range of genres (for convenience sometimes later labeled 'improv'). Instead of a soloist working out variations and tangents from themes, the aim was to have a group improvisation" (Hegarty 45).

Of interest here is that in the very album that names the so-called free jazz phenomenon (and in a sense births it), the key aesthetic is the group's capacity to generate improvisatory utterances. The radical thing about *Free Jazz*, in this context, is how it demonstrates a musical aesthetic tied to a deep-rooted communitarian ideology of cocreation. The individual-centered notions of virtuosity, soloing, voice, and the like that had played such a key role in defining jazz's musical values were giving way to something else, a radical critique of how creative communities generate their own agency. Whether one cares for the music or not, the musical practice here was pointing to a larger cultural critique of communities obsessed with the individual as the prioritized locus of cultural production, something that had never been quite true, since, as we have argued earlier, the individual gains his or her individuality as a function of community, a co-dependent, cocreative, contingent relationship that is, in a sense, always up for grabs, always in need of definition and redefinition. This situation parallels that confronting rights discourses, a state wherein meaning must be made anew as social justice, itself a function of community contingencies, struggles into being against forces seeking to limit, reduce, or eliminate it.

Here it is useful to remember that "free jazz occurs in a particular historical context, that of the demand for civil rights for blacks, and then Black Power and associated movements" (Hegarty 47). As the French improviser Joëlle Léandre argues in her book *À voix basse,*

> Improvisation necessitates a group, collective confidence . . . In the end, it's social, without law, without leader, without king, without score, without music stand. There's just the passage, the play, and imagination and, evidently, the instrumental work that is its principal driver. Three musicians meet, for example. It's a microcosm, a little society with its stakes, its tensions, its courtesies, its harshnesses, its silences, its fears, its powers. It's a game but it's also about the "I" in the collective . . . improvisation, in the best of cases, is the utopian realization of "being together." (76–77, our translation)

Léandre's observations nicely synthesize this sort of pervasive discourse of community to be found in association with free improvisation in all its forms. There is no idealization of what it means to "be together" here, and in fact the community aspects of improvisation necessitate *frottements* and *rudesses*, the dissonances that occur at both the musical and the social level. To not acknowledge their presence is to be hopelessly naive and ill-informed, not only about musical process but also about the sometimes cacophonic processes by which being together is elaborated as a necessary aspect of being human. But for Léandre, improvisation, in its most accomplished forms, is a utopian realization, one that represents its exemplary potential as an alternative cultural practice that must come to grips with other less-than-ideal realizations of community. Improvisation instantiates what George Lewis, in his study of the AACM, calls the recognition of a "mobile, heterophonic notion of the possibilities for unity" (*Power* 214), an idea that Lewis locates in Muhal Richard Abrams's notion that "there are different types of black life, and therefore we know that there are different kinds of black music. Because black music comes forth from black life" (214).

Even within the so-called jazz community, the rise of free improvisational structures and playing in the 1960s led to a rethinking of the traditional spaces in which musical interventions could be made. Lewis documents the musician-run "Newport Rebels" festival, which occurred on the fringes of the Newport Jazz Festival in 1960, as a result of efforts made by Charles Mingus and Max Roach: it provided "an alternative to what they saw as the commercialization, racism, and economic exploitation that the mainstream festival displayed. The alternative event, which took place alongside a riot that caused the cancellation of several concerts, featured young radicals Randy Weston and Ornette Coleman" (Lewis, *Power* 90). And just a few years before he died, John Coltrane, along with Babatunde Olatunji and Yusef Lateef, was working on creating an alternative performance space and booking agency, which had the goals of creating an equal partnership among the three, forcing other promoters to book all three musicians and not just one of them as an aspect of their group solidarity, and exploring "the possibility of teaching the music of our people in conservatories, colleges and universities where only European musical experience dominates and is being perpetuated" (91).

Challenging Orthodoxies

Remarkable in these examples is the sense of solidarity and of enacted, alternative community formation gathering around the musical aesthetics these musicians espoused as improvisers. And in the particular case of the community-driven AACM, as the composer and saxophonist Anthony Braxton states, the group was paradoxically "not tied to any one ideology." Braxton recalls, "At no time during my whole involvement with the AACM did anyone ever tell someone else what to think" (qtd. in Lewis 214). Here the point is that it is possible to be in a community in which association does not mean conformity and in which directive, authoritarian ideologies are not the social glue that binds. This was the radical challenge of the AACM, as it was of other free jazz and improvising collectives, to norms and orthodoxies associated with more Eurocentric governmental and state-driven notions of community that idealized the individual.

Furthermore, in the specific case of Coltrane, who had effectively "made clear the power of non-European music, both in terms of music itself as well as the place of music in the society," the technical and artistic innovations he unleashed, involving the "use of African, Indian, and Arabic musics made it clear that they were not 'primitive' forms as opposed to European music's 'sophistication'" (Nisenson 269). In globalizing the particular form of improvisatory discourse he made thinkable, Eric Nisenson argues that Coltrane was challenging cultural as well as musical orthodoxies:

> The idea of improvisation means that every night a musician plays he can redefine himself, and has one more chance to discover the beauty within. It is perhaps not as ironic as it may outwardly seem that the people, African Americans, who have been the least free in our society have had the greatest understanding of what freedom is . . . Jazz in its synthesis of African and European musical elements is a cultural phenomenon that could only have taken place in the "melting pot" of America. Unfortunately, that melting pot has been too often an ideal rather than a reality in American life, but in jazz, at least, one can hear the musical fruit of that wonderful idea. (269)

Although a fair bit of critical pressure, we would contend, needs to be put on Nisenson's assumption that the melting pot of America represents any kind of "ideal" situation, these comments show how Coltrane represents a high-order example of throwing off the shackles of slavery and oppression, while recognizing global communities of otherness that destabilize limiting and degenerative notions of cultural purity. The music, highly improvisatory in its formulation and execution, enacts creative hybridities that point to musical freedom as a metonymy of greater cultural and spiritual freedoms, what Coltrane called "the life side of music" (Nisenson 122).

Jazz critic Leonard Feather, to his everlasting discredit, dismissed Coltrane's and Dolphy's ostensibly good musical intentions, saying "even Hitler was sincere" (qtd. in Nisenson 119). This reaction was evidence of both the profound ideological threat inherent in improvised experimentations that were also experiments in new social orderings and of the inherently racialized discourses perturbed by a musical culture that was also challenging white imperial culture.[5]

The criticism of the new music as "just noise" can be seen as a holdover from antebellum days, when the music of black slaves, as historian Jon Cruz notes, "appears to have been heard by captors and overseers primarily as noise—that is, as strange, unfathomable, and incomprehensible." As Cruz points out, for slave owners to hear only noise is "tantamount to being oblivious to the structures of meaning that anchored sounding to the hermeneutic world of the slaves." To hear only noise is to "remain removed from how slave soundings probed their circumstances and cultivated histories and memories." Similarly, the noisy anger of the new musicians seemed strange, surprising, and unfathomable to many critics, along with the idea that blacks might actually have something to be angry about. (Lewis, *Power* 44)

Improvisation in this diasporic context serves as an index or register for musical and cultural otherness at the same time it replays a hermeneutic world that is intensely familiar to its makers. The very act of sounding *in* that supposedly universalist, hermeneutic context but *out* of the specific, oppressive cultural situation is profoundly political, profoundly symbolic of a kind of freedom that extends beyond just the music. One person's "noise" is another person's sophisticated signifying system. And the act of sounding discordant, nonnormative musical discourses in a culture dominated by orthodox notions of conventional (commodified) music is, in this instance, an act of critique, courage, resistance, and liberation.[6]

Albert Ayler, saxophonist and composer, articulates the distinctions in an astute observation about free jazz: "It's really free, spiritual music, not just free music . . . we're listening to each other. Many of the others are not playing together, and so they produce noise. It's screaming, it's neo-avant-garde music. But we are trying to rejuvenate that old New Orleans feeling that music can be played collectively and with free form. Each person finds his own form" (qtd. in Hentoff, "Albert Ayler," 16–18). Collective free-form improvisation is historically associated here with the roots of jazz in ensemble playing in New Orleans, but it is also located as an important form of self-agency within a collective context, a context in which listening to each other leads to the spiritual unity so important to Ayler's overall philosophy of improvising. The rights implications could not be clearer. Musical discourse in this context is akin to public declamations of community solidarity and dissent, all buttressed by a strong sense of historical injustice, the very kinds of discourse situated at the heart of the civil rights movement (whether in the thinking of Frederick Douglass, Rosa Parks, Martin Luther King Jr., or Malcolm X).

Improvised music reinforces, both in its aesthetics and its politics, expressions of solidarity with civil rights ideals even as its symbolics enact dissent with repressive orthodoxies rooted in cultural norms from which it strays. George Lewis cites Coltrane's requiem tune "Alabama," "dedicated to the children murdered in the infamous bombing of Birmingham's 16th Street Baptist Church," as an example of how Coltrane's music was directly politicized in opposition to the resistant "universalist" rhetoric with which Coltrane masked his politics for strategic reasons related to his position as subaltern (*Power* 44).

The point is that for Coltrane the bombing of the 16th Street Baptist Church by the Klan, on September 15, 1963—a bombing that killed four young girls and injured twenty-two other children in attendance at the church to hear a sermon entitled "The Love That Forgives"—was a localized act of barbarity "whose symbolism directly threatened not only the lives of all black people, but the humanity of all" (*Power* 44). The visionary rights perspective inherent in such a view, one that is neither narrowly parochial nor driven by limited contingencies, points to the remarkable political valences embedded in the improvisatory musickings associated with Coltrane, music that comes out of a history, that responds to historical circumstances, and that anticipates visionary alternatives rooted in universalist, integrationist, and communitarian principles.

When asked by the historian Frank Kofsky about the relationship between the so-called "new music" associated with the free jazz of the 1960s and Malcolm X's political ideas, Coltrane responded: "Well, I think that music, being an expression of the human heart, or of the human being itself, does express just what *is* happening. I feel it expresses the whole thing—the whole of human experience at the particular time that it is being expressed" (qtd. in Kofsky 225). Whatever Coltrane meant by this, and he was always careful never to limit or reduce the potential expressive power he saw in musical creativity, it is clear that he understood music to reference more than just itself as a cultural practice rooted in "the whole of human experience." He comments, "When there's something we think could be better, we must make an effort to try and make it better. So it's the same socially, musically, politically, and in any department of our lives" (227).

Coltrane's rhetoric is similar to that of Albert Ayler, who suggests, "We are the music we play. And our commitment is to peace, to understanding of life. And we keep trying to purify our music, to purify ourselves, so that we can move ourselves—and those who hear us—to higher levels of understanding. You have to purify and crystallize your sound in order to hypnotize" (qtd. in Hentoff, "Albert Ayler" 17). Inherent in this sort of thinking are ideals of peace involving basic rights, understanding, and the attempt to move beyond impediments to achieving these. Music is seen as a critical tool in making manifest these outcomes, and Ayler's was a particularly eloquent and disturbing (some critics have called it "terrifying") voice among many making similar declamations.

Improvisation, Noise, Civil Rights

Members of the Art Ensemble of Chicago, for instance, were contemporaries of Ayler who "protested both America's war in Vietnam and ignorance of a legitimate free jazz revolution within its borders. (On their great album *A Jackson in Your House*, they openly mock the American military and white America's paranoid fear of blacks.) In 1969 the group embarked on an extended residency in Paris with a team of players (including Ayler's frequent drummer Sunny Murray) who would record a torrent of now-legendary obscurities for the French label Actuel. The European subculture the musicians found themselves in embraced their new brand of music—one made with gongs, toys, noise guitar, non-instruments, silence, grunting, preaching, singing and chanting, as well as the more conventional saxophone, trumpet, bass and drums" (Stillman).

David Toop, an English musician and author, notes the symbolic political content associated with choices of instrumentation and acceptable sounds to be included in an improvising context, or indeed in a generalized musical context:

> For black American improvisers such as Don Cherry and the Art Ensemble
> of Chicago, and at roughly the same time [as] their European and white
> counterparts in AMM, Musica Electronica Viva, Joseph Holbrook, Music Improvisation Company, Nuova Consonanza and the Spontaneous Music Ensemble, a partial move away from the major instruments of jazz and classical music performance was an expression of politics as much as music.
> From the mid 1960s into the disillusioned 1970s, little instruments and non-

instruments (transistor radios, contact microphones amplifying tiny sounds or surface noises extracted from tables, beards, cheese graters, etc.) became symbols of the drive to democratize music, to allow access to unskilled players (including children), [to] draw sounds from instruments rather than subjugate them to systems, [to] open the music up to chance events and create a sense of collectively organized community as an attempted break from hard professionalism, particularly the star system that afflicted both jazz groups and classical performers. (133–34)

The aesthetics and politics, then, of some of the most sophisticated improvising collectives of this period actively took up the problem of noise, not only as a term used to denigrate diasporic musickings by the slave owner and later by the musical establishments associated with white hegemonic culture, but also in the promotion of musical forms whose values were rooted in democratizing, communitarian, and anticommercialization ideologies. We note how these strategies undo the rhetoric of heroism and individuality so often misaligned with improvisatory musickings and their interpretations. They also point to the weakness of any argument that does not account for the subtle interplay between universalist intentionality (the desire to make the world a better place) and the specific performative and historical contexts giving rise to that intention. And we note how these strategies are a remarkable incidence of the reappropriation of demeaning stereotypes by improvising communities in constructive ways that subvert historical misunderstanding and racist ignorance.

Ingrid Monson's well-taken caveat about the degree to which "the jazz artist as the iconoclastic hero, the nonconformist, the transcendent and self-determining subject, and the social critic is so tied up with the symbolic legacy of the music" is not to be ignored here (*Freedom Sounds* 5). The discourses and aesthetic choices made by these improvising collectives, in addition to the historicity of their marginalization, made them the object of heroism and universalist narratives, a way of converting radical specificity into a familiar, controllable narrative form. But these narratives were always profoundly undercut by the extent to which community narratives were foregrounded, as were narratives that spoke to disempowerment, poverty, marginalization, and the specific contexts affecting the agent making the music. And they were undercut by the way the musicians themselves were extraordinarily careful in their comments about the music (and we have seen this at some length already) to avoid reductive and limiting affirmations that undermined the signifying poten-tial of the medium. That these discourses simultaneously pointed toward the possibility of enacting self-determination, achieving transcendent spiritual goals, while offering a critique of hegemonic cultures is one of their great achievements.

The pattern is familiar in rights narratives, too, wherein participants in rights struggles, who by dint of adhering to their agency and their politi-cal purpose, are frequently elevated to heroic status. Think of Gandhi, King, Rosa Parks, and Angela Davis (and any number of rights activists known globally)—where significant energies have been invested in culti-vating their heroic images in what then becomes a comfortable narrative at the expense of the radical challenges these people posed to oppres-sive regimes. This elevation is an imposition that convenes to normative strategies that attempt to contain the progressivist ethical positions of rights agents in familiar and reassuring ways. But these narratives have little to do with the content and the agency of the people being heroized. In the case of so-called heroic figures from the canon of great African American improvisers, Albert Ayler's grinding poverty and suicide, the vicious attacks (physical and critical) on Ornette Coleman and Cecil Tay-lor, and the similar stories involving segregation, marginalization, tragic death, quotidian struggle associated with any number of the most distin-guished practitioners of improvised musickings hardly denotes the life of heroes, though frequently post facto interpretative discourses make these people the object of such narratives.[7] These narratives are radically at odds with the tenor of what improvisers were actually saying about the content of their music in relation to its larger social purposes.

It is important to remember that Coltrane was only the tip of the iceberg in terms of improvising musicians who specifically located their musical discourse in direct relation to civil rights struggles for freedom:

> With regard to the Civil Rights Movement[,] which challenged a system of racial caste and racism, jazz artists such as Tony Bennett, Miles Davis, Ella Fitzgerald, Abbey Lincoln, Jackie McLean, Oliver Nelson, Oscar Peterson, Sonny Rollins, Archie Shepp, and Nina Simone offered musical and personal support. Similarly, in the summer of 1960, Max Roach and Oscar Brown, Jr. recorded "We Insist! Freedom Now," which was written in honor of the four freshmen who, in February of the same year, staged a sit-in at Wool-worth's "Whites Only" lunch counter in Greensboro, N.C. 1960 was also the

year Charles Mingus performed "Prayer for a Passive Resistance" and "Freedom." The following year, drummer Art [Blakey] recorded "Freedom Rider" in support of groups that tested desegregated interstate bus travel . . . In August of 1963, prior to the March on Washington, Duke Ellington staged his protest-oriented musical, "My People," as a theatrical celebration of African-Americans and the Civil Rights Movement. (J. Coleman)[8]

To this partial list may be added jazz musicians from before the 1960s who had used music as a platform to express outrage at social injustice. Billie Holiday's "Strange Fruit," a poignant condemnation of lynching and racism in the South, began as a poem written by Abel Meeropol, a Jewish high school teacher from the Bronx who likely had seen the horrifying photograph by Lawrence Beitler of Thomas Shipp and Abram Smith hanging from a tree in Marion, Indiana, after they had been lynched by a mob (with the cooperation of the police) on August 7, 1930. Meeropol, who, with his wife, adopted the two sons of Julius and Ethel Rosenberg after their execution for espionage in 1953, published "Strange Fruit" in 1936 in the *New York Teacher*, a union magazine, as if to confirm the links among pedagogy, art, and discourses of social justice. Holiday heard the song in 1939 and it fast became a staple in her repertoire (and her best-selling recording) in spite of the anguish it caused her and her constant fear of retaliation for singing it.

As part of the same continuum as Coltrane's "Alabama," "Strange Fruit" is a classic example of the ways jazz and improvised musickings were able to align themselves with discourses of social justice and civil rights over an extended period of time. Recorded performances of Holiday's singing Meeropol's poem show her singular ability to improvise melodic lines in relation to the affect of the lyrics, and part of the song's surpassing emotive power was, no doubt, a direct function of Holiday's artistic capacities as an improviser of affective melodies.

The significant number of improvising musicians affiliated with civil rights initiatives is one form of thinking the relation between improvisatory and rights discourses, that is, as direct commentary, and as widespread expressions of critique and dissent. But the other important trend associated with the cultural practice of improvisation, and one that had a significant impact on sophisticating the political implications of the music, was the integration of other musical forms that were non-Western, disaffiliated from the cultural norms in the West that were being challenged. The transnationalist impetus, what the jazz drummer Milford Graves calls "cultural transmutation" (Austerlitz 179), seeks integrative and reconciliatory affiliation with otherness, whether that otherness is an aspect of one's own roots or of cultures to which one is drawn. That impetus is an important feature of Coltrane's musical philosophy (and the philosophy of others associated with the free jazz movement of the 1960s), and it is intimately tied with the forms his improvisations explored. But it is also a fundamental precondition for addressing global rights contexts in which global communities linked by shared assumptions about equity and justice struggle into being. Scott Saul, a cultural critic and English professor at Berkeley, argues that Coltrane's composition "Liberia" (the third track on *Coltrane's Sound*, originally recorded in 1960, but released in June 1964) heralds "a new black aesthetic, one that aimed to convey the intensity of freedom in a world where it was up for grabs. The cultural roots of blackness were ripe for rediscovery, a new world coming into being in the reinvented image of a much older one, and Coltrane's imagination was working excitedly in the service of this project, which also meant reevaluating bebop and its assumptions about musical irony, technical ingenuity, and ensemble interplay" (210). As Saul argues, Coltrane "was framing his music as an act of transnational imagination" and clearly understood the wider cultural symbolics associated with his musical innovations (210).[9]

Our purpose here is to draw wider connections than are usually made between the symbolic force of music in a rights and social-justice context, and to point to an emergent shared language associated with improvising musicians of the free jazz movement that brought together in the 1960s crucial concepts of freedom, community, agency, and self-identity as a function of cocreative improvisatory utterances.

Elsewhere in *The Other Side of Nowhere* Daniel Fischlin and Ajay Heble have drawn attention to the argument of Tzvetan Todorov, the Franco-Bulgarian critic and philosopher, that what allowed European culture to triumph over indigenous culture in that early modern colonial encounter was the ability of Europeans to improvise more efficiently than indigenous peoples.[10] Rights are predicated on the fact that so many of the encounter models deployed in the world are essentially failed, a function of militarized, violent, and imperial responses to intercultural contact. That is, rights discourse is preventative and curative, a way of addressing the inequities and injustices produced by situations of oppression and aggression, before and after they have occurred.

What are the alternatives to failed encounters? How does improvisation, as a form of dynamic encounter narrative, figure in relation to rights discourses?

We would hope that some of the arguments and case studies we advance in this book give at least the beginnings of possible answers to these questions. Rights discourses, like improvised musickings, are essentially, unalterably communitarian in spite of the deforming focus on individualist contributions. Rights, like improvisations, entail a material, ongoing practice of negotiated community. And creative, improvised musickings that reflect on and enact the formation of alternative communities have a great deal to tell us about how successful, meaningful encounters not predicated on violence, oppression, or inequity can be achieved. These alternative forms of engagement that improvisation makes available as part of its aesthetic and political legacy provide a larger-scale understanding of the communitarian stakes that are so high in rights conflicts, so central to the ways improvisatory creations achieve their ends as a function of asymmetrical, cogenerative, dynamic experimentation. It is to further specific examples of the links among community practice, improvisation, and rights that we now turn our attention.

CHAPTER 1

SOUNDING TRUTH TO POWER

Improvisation, Black Mobility, and

Resources for Hope

In his remarkable book on the influential musicians' collective, the Association for the Advancement of Creative Musicians (AACM), the African American scholar and trombonist George E. Lewis tells us that "the insistence by blacks that music has to be 'saying something' [is] part of a long history of resistance to the silencing of the black voice. Indeed," Lewis argues, "as might be expected from a people whose genetic, historical, and cultural legacies were interrupted through sustained, systematized violence, every effort was made by the musicians to recover rather than to disrupt historical consciousness" (*Power* 41). Lewis is writing about African American experimental musical practices, and, in such a context, his reminder that "black musicians felt that music could effectuate the recovery of history itself" serves as a vital corrective to some widely held and oft-institutionalized assumptions about improvised forms of music-making (42). After all, despite being the most widely practiced (and perhaps the oldest) form of music-making in the world, improvisation, as numerous critics have noted, is also the least understood and most maligned: its cultural significance, in particular, tends to be ignored or in dispute both in the academy and in the broader public understanding.[1] Think, for example, about how, in the context of pedagogies, criticism, arts funding policies, and support structures, improvisative music is often looked at askance, seen as involving adherence to neither convention nor protocol, as tolerating no system of constraint, as requiring no prior thought, as coming out of nowhere, simply being made up on the spot. Think about the fact that since improvisational musical practices are central to many marginalized communities, the resultant failure of scholars to pay serious and sustained attention to improvisation has led to a broader failure to recognize the extent to which improvisation provides a trenchant model for flexible, dynamic, and dialogical social structures that are both ethical and respectful of identity and difference. And think about the fact that, in Lewis's words, "improvisative discourses disclose the extent to which musicians have a vital stake in the ongoing dialogue concerning the future of our planet. Music becomes a necessity for existence, rather than merely a pleasant way to pass time" ("Teaching Improvised Music" 98).

Improvisation as Social Practice

A necessity for existence, the future of our planet, the recovery of history: large claims, these, we admit. These remarks from George Lewis, whose own stewardship of improvisative musicality has done so much to generate new critical perspectives, signal a profound shift in long-held assumptions about improvised music, and they offer a provocative commentary on how musical practices in which improvisation figures prominently are, indeed, social practices, a commentary central to our book's focus on key sites of creative activity, sites in which improvisation as a musical practice intersects with rights and social justice discourses. They point, moreover, to what's at stake—culturally, socially, institutionally— in a music that so many anointed narratives of jazz history would have us summarily dismiss as inconsequential, elitist, eccentric, or incomprehensible. One of the most enduring lessons in Lewis's work is precisely this: particularly for music-makers whose explorations question settled habits of response and judgement, improvised music has the potential to inform and transform contemporary cultural debate. It can do so by deepening and reinvigorating our understanding of the role that improvising artists can play in activating diverse energies of critique and inspiration, and of the difference they can make (and have made) in their communities by using modes of working together to voice new forms of social organization, to "sound off" against oppressive orders of knowledge production, and to create opportunities and develop resources for disadvantaged people. In short, the working models of musical improvisation developed by creative practitioners have played a powerful role in recasting the identities and histories of aggrieved populations and in promoting self-representational counternarratives that enable an enlargement of the base of valued knowledges.

There is a long and illustrious (if too often underrepresented) history, especially within the context of African American creative practice, that links jazz and improvised music with struggles for civil rights and social justice. Much can be learned from performance practices that accent and embody real-time creative decision-making, risk-taking, and collaboration. Robin Kelley, a historian and scholar focusing on black culture and radical social movements, has done important work on the role that hope and the imagination play as revolutionary impulses for social betterment. Key strands of jazz and improvised music-making might be understood in this context. In an era when diverse peoples and communities of interest struggle to forge historically new forms of affiliation across cultural divides, the participatory and civic virtues of engagement, dialogue, respect, and community-building inculcated through improvisatory practices take on a particular urgency.

Lewis's claim about black musicians and the recovery of history does more than simply counter long-standing myths and assumptions about improvisation. It should perhaps also put us in mind of Frantz Fanon's argument in *The Wretched of the Earth* about how imperial powers sought to manipulate and eradicate the subject people's past in an effort to instill feelings of inferiority. For Fanon and many of the black cultural nationalists who followed his arguments, especially during the 1960s, what was critical in countering such institutionalized systems of erasure, what was particularly germane to such efforts to reclaim the past, was the need to develop a sense of self-worth. Iain Anderson, a jazz scholar, suggests in his book *This Is Our Music: Free Jazz, the Sixties, and American Culture* that "this 'revolution of the mind' required a positive reevaluation of blackness in order to shatter the hold of white psychological and cultural oppression" (97).

Kelley, too, reminds us in his book *Freedom Dreams: The Black Radical Imagination* that this "idea of a revolution of the mind has always been central . . . to black conceptions of liberation" (191). However, he is absolutely forthright in his insistence that a revolution of the mind is "not merely a refusal of victim status." Instead, he tells us "about an unleashing of the mind's most creative capacities, catalyzed by participation in struggles for change" (191). Addressing "anyone bold enough still to dream," Kelley argues that "the most radical ideas often grow out of a concrete intellectual engagement with the problems of aggrieved populations confronting systems of oppression" (7, 9). Attracted to a model of artistic practice that, in his words, "invites dreaming, urges us to improvise and invent, and recognizes the imagination as our most powerful weapon," Kelley encourages us to see (and, picking up on his lead, we would add to hear) "life as possibility" (159, 2).

Life as possibility: isn't this, after all, one of the most enduring lessons embodied in, and exemplified by, improvised music? Isn't there more than a little allure in the snap of the new and untried, in the sparkle of provocation, in the itch and prod of a relentless spirit of inquiry, of intuitive knowing, in the right to dream, in the right to embody improvisatory creativity publicly? And if oppositional politics often takes as one of its most salient manifestations an allegiance to forms of artistic practice that cannot readily be assimilated or scripted using dominant frameworks of understanding, then to what extent might improvisatory performance practices themselves be understood as activist forms of insurgent knowledge production? To what extent might improvised music be understood in the context of aggrieved communities struggling for access to representation, legitimacy, social recognition, and institutional visibility, let alone to real access to resources with the potential to transform material realities?

Improvised music, at least in some of its most provocative historical instances, ought to be seen and heard in precisely such contexts. Musicians' collectives such as the Association for the Advancement of Creative Musicians (AACM) and music curators and festival organizers who present and promote improvised music have a vital role to play in the development of new theoretical and organizational models and practices for the creation and nurturing of alternative pedagogical institutions. By providing alternatives to the taken-for-granted course of things, by creating new knowledges and opportunities, by generating alternative ways of seeing and hearing the world, such organizations have much to teach us. They too, in other words, should be understood to be part of Kelley's argument about radical ideas emerging out of "concrete intellectual engagement with the problems of aggrieved populations."

Life as possibility: the creation of new opportunities, the nurturing of new sources of hope for disadvantaged peoples, these have long been hallmarks of the AACM. The flautist and president of the AACM Nicole Mitchell suggested in a keynote talk for the Improvisation, Community, and Social Practice (ICASP) project, under whose auspices this book was written, that a central context for understanding both the musical and social impact of the AACM is the role that improvised and experimental music has played in creating a kind of utopia in sound for African Americans, during a time when they couldn't have it in reality. In an interview with the music scholar and flautist Ellen Waterman in *Critical Studies in Improvisation / Études critiques en improvisation*, Mitchell speaks explicitly about musical improvisation as a form of social practice that allows her to dream of "other worlds." Riffing on a phrase in a poem written about her by Kalamu ya Salaam and included in the liner notes to her recording *Black Unstoppable*, Mitchell suggests that the line "I dreamed of other worlds" suggests the ability "to take blankness or nothingness and create a combination of what's familiar and what's unknown, or what's never existed before, with creativity." She explains, "That's why I love to improvise. Because improvisation is a practice that allows you not to be focused on the smallness of who you are and your reality, but to actually experience the greatness of possibility and surprise and spontaneity."

The greatness of possibility and surprise and spontaneity: there is an activist edge to this assertion, a belief that improvisation can teach us to enact the possibilities we envision. The activist edge is there in Mitchell's belief that music can be transformative, even visionary; it's also there in the title of her recording *Black Unstoppable*, the phrase itself suggesting a strength and determination of purpose. But the activist slant is also registered, perhaps most profoundly, in her belief that hope (a term that comes up throughout the interview) resides in the capacity, indeed in the power, to dream. Again, we're put in mind of Kelley's comments: "We must remember," he writes in *Freedom Dreams*, "that the conditions and the very existence of social movements enable participants to imagine something different, to realize that things need not always be this way. It is *that* imagination, that effort to see the future in the present, that I shall call 'poetry' or 'poetic knowledge'" (9).

Social movements play a crucial role in generating new ways of knowing, new ways of being. The AACM has been a vital social movement that has given rise to a wide range of emancipatory hopes and practices. Now, if Mitchell is particularly attracted to improvised music-making because it enables an expression of utopia in sound, because it allows aggrieved peoples a place for the sounding of unscripted futures, then it's also worth noting that, for her, as for George Lewis and other members of the AACM, improvisation can also be a vehicle for the rehistoricization of minoritized communities: "I also reflect on history and reality in my work," Mitchell tells Waterman in their interview. One pertinent example she gives has to do with her understanding of her own role as a female jazz improviser in what she acknowledges is a "male dominated field." She explains that this understanding has shaped her own practice of using her voice in playing the flute: "I sing into the flute. I sing with the flute. I sing and then I just play the flute. So I have all of these combinations of the relationship be-tween the voice and the flute. Part of that comes from the desire to leave evidence that a woman was here. Because, you know, it is a very male dominated field. Even without a video or picture of that music, I want to leave that mark, that aesthetic of whatever is coming through me as a woman, as a channel for that feminine energy" (qtd. in Waterman). Mitchell's insistence on leaving evidence, on embedding traces of history and forms of memorialization into her improvisatory musical practices, is part of a project of sounding truth to power, of supplying a dissenting voice in a field that "has not exactly been known for its gender equity" (Tucker 260).

In evidence here are musical strategies that might contribute to our understanding of how improvised musics play a role in the so-called poli-tics of hope, which is so often deemed a key aspect of struggles for rights. By invoking the controversial phrase "politics of hope" in the context of improvisation as a social practice, we underline the degree to which hope is often predicated on the possibility of real, lived alternatives to hope-lessness. Is it possible to think of improvisation as embodying the public expression of multiple forms of alternative expression, multiple forms of creative enactment that instantiate and restore the possibility of hope to the everyday?

Changing the Stories We Live By

If the conventions associated with fixed genres "contribute to an ahistori-cal view of the world as always the same," and if the "pleasures of predict-ability encourage an investment in the status quo"—indeed, if the fixity of genres has often functioned as a locus of racialized and gender-based forms of power—then the use of extended techniques in music, the use, that is, of unfamiliar performance techniques on familiar musical instru-ments to expand the sonic vocabularies conventionally associated with

those instruments, may be indicative of improvisation's insistence on finding new kinds of solutions to familiar problems and challenges (Lipsitz,
American Studies 185). The extended technique of Nicole Mitchell's using
her voice as part of her flute playing becomes a way both of engaging with
histories of struggle (in this case, engaging questions of gender equality
and women's agency in improvised music) and of changing the stories we
tell about those histories.[2]

After all, as the Nigerian storyteller Ben Okri puts it, "if we change the
stories we live by, quite possibly we change our lives" (46). Other writers,
such as Kay Schaffer and Sidonie Smith, have written wisely and eloquently about the role that stories and testimonies have played as essential catalysts "to affect recourse, mobilize action, forge communities of
interest, and enable social change" in relation to rights and social justice
claims (3). But what is improvisation for? What's at stake in the stories we
tell about improvised music, and for whom is it at stake? How might the
stories that are told and circulated about improvised music make a difference in relation to pressing matters of public interest and consequence?
Why, in short, does improvisation matter?

In asking such questions, we've discovered loosely connected but coherently focused strands of an emergent narrative about powerful and
historically resonant ways to unsettle orthodox habits of response and
judgment, and we've seen how such a narrative has had (and will continue to have) a profound impact on a wide range of pressing matters
for scholarship, critical pedagogy, and activism related to civil rights,
alternative-community formations, and transcultural understanding. The
profoundly interconnected discourses of improvised musicking and social
justice ought to be understood as complex and multidimensional fields of
endeavor that intersect in ways that have energized new networks of possibility, and inspired resources for hope.

Institutionalized narratives about human rights and social justice seem
to indicate that rights receive their most legitimate, perhaps even their
most profound, expression in legal documents and instruments, in treaties,
laws, covenants, international declarations, and so forth. But this is an impoverished and restricted rendering of a far more nuanced set of realities.
Numerous instances exist globally of localized solidarity networks and
community groups who achieve significant rights outcomes through their
own political agency, as opposed to their using actual rights instruments:
as cited by Daniel Fischlin and Martha Nandorfy in a discussion of global

water-rights struggles, local communities, indigenous groups, women's groups, and concerned citizens have successfully fought the privatization of water (in opposition to treaties enforced by the World Trade Organization and NAFTA that treat water as a "commodity") in Chile, Bolivia, and Kerala, India (*The Concise Guide* 61–63). Similarly, the American civil rights movement came into being without any of the civil rights acts actually being in place, and in fact it was precisely the movement's agency and pressure on institutional inertia that eventually led to the creation of legal rights reforms in the United States, none of these necessarily a guarantee of equitable treatment or of positive rights outcomes—and all a reminder that one of the most pressing rights problems is the enormous gap between rights instruments' ideals and the actual, material implementation of these ideals in day-to-day life. In the case of one of the worst environmental and industrial disasters ever, the 1984 Bhopal disaster in India, in which thousands have died as a result of both the immediate and ongoing contamination, a basic right to "security of person" enshrined in the Universal Declaration of Human Rights of 1948 (UDHR; article 3) was massively infringed upon, again a sad reminder of the material realities of rights implementation. It is important to remember that institutional rights discourses are no guarantor of rights implementation in the material, day-to-day realities of oppressed and aggrieved peoples. And as the eminent legal rights scholar Upendra Baxi argues, rights are not conceded without struggle, often against the very institutions that will later go on to "defend" the same rights they denied: "The whole history of the labour movement . . . testifies to the fact that while initially the state and the law considered the right to liberty of association and assembly of the workers as causing unjustified 'harm' to the pursuit of the general interests of the whole society, in course of the centuries the right of labour to associate, to form unions and even to strike has been conceded. So was the political franchise to women" ("From Human Rights" 194). In too many instances to recount, the idea of rights has existed before the legal and institutional instruments and covenants that supposedly enshrine them.

As the work associated with the artists and cultural and community-based activists discussed in this book should make clear, there is another story, or set of stories, about human rights that needs to be told, one that's too often encoded in unstressed and undervalued sites far from the reaches of legal and institutional discourses that have sought to associate rights with reductive neoliberal concepts of being human as a function (almost solely) of economic realities. There is an abyssal line separating validated forms of knowledge associated with dominant institutional formations from marginalized or disenfranchised forms. Improvisation, as a key aspect of creative agency across multiple disciplines, is an important aspect of an ecology of knowledges. Part of what's at stake in telling the story of improvisatory discourse in relation to emergent rights struggles is the need to rethink the very places and spaces where we look for knowledge, to understand that the creative practices associated with aggrieved peoples confronting systems of oppression are vital repositories of history and memory, and enduring documents of hope, resilience, and determination.

If insufficient attention has hitherto been given to the role that cultural and community-based artistic and performance practices have played in the drive to imagine and to implement a more robust conception of human rights, it is perhaps worth bearing in mind that the United Nations' "human" rights program is founded conceptually upon a three-way relationship among legislation, implementation, and information or education (see Martenson 928). In the context of that three-way relationship, education surely plays a critical (if sorely understudied) role, as do the stories and histories that are promulgated and institutionalized through pedagogical processes. Even the concept of "human rights" tells only part of a much more complex story that elides the multiple contingencies (like the environment, the public commons, the relations of humanity to nonhuman being, and the like) that allow the human to exist.

As the former diplomat and former director of the International Centre at the University of Calgary William Warden writes in his essay "From Analysis to Activism," "the challenges for those promoting human rights are . . . formidable" (985). He argues that "in the struggle for human rights the principal agents of protest and progress will not be governments or institutions . . . Rather the main instruments will be individual activists moved to action by the abuses of the oppressors and energized by the grassroots" (988). The focus on individual activists is not necessarily well placed, but analysts must rethink the places where they look for knowledge about rights as an expression of the full creative and social potential of what being human can mean. Activists can't rely primarily on government policies or on institutionally sanctioned models of knowledge production to advance awareness about rights issues, let alone to prevent suffering and atrocities. After all, public discourse is, as

Edward Said has aptly noted, densely saturated "with interests, authorities, and powers whose extent in the aggregate is literally unimaginable in scope and variety, except as that whole bears centrally on the acceptance of a neoliberal postwelfare state responsive neither to the citizenry nor to the natural environment, but to a vast structure of global corporations unrestricted by traditional barriers or sovereignties" (*Representations* 124). Said is quick to remind the reader, moreover, that the very language of human rights has largely been co-opted by some of those very same interests, powers, and authorities, as when the "State Department or the president," for example, "say that they are for human rights and for fighting a war to 'liberate' Iraq" (*Representations* 132). Upendra Baxi makes a similar observation when he tells us that "unsurprisingly, the more severe the violation of human rights, the more the orders of power declare their loyalty to the regime of human rights" (*Future of Human Rights* 87).

A wariness about the language and rhetoric of human rights is also expressed by numerous other activists and critics. There are huge areas of justice and human dignity that the historical and neoliberal human rights framework not only neglects, but actually undermines.[3] Others have commented on the specialized and elitist nature of human rights discourse. In an essay entitled "Why More Africans Don't Use Human Rights Language," the lawyer and activist Chidi Anselm Odinkalu writes, "Instead of being the currency of a social justice or conscience-driven movement, 'human rights' has increasingly become the specialized language of a select professional cadre with its own rites of passage and methods of certification. Far from being a badge of honour," he tells us, "human rights activism is, in some of the places I have observed it, increasingly a certificate of privilege."

The AACM offers an enlivened alternative to the neoliberal, institutionalized framework and rhetoric of human rights critiqued by Said, Baxi, Odinkalu, and others. Building on a grassroots, community-based, on-the-ground, and localized approach (rather than on the prioritizing of individual freedoms that characterizes a neoliberal human rights agenda), the AACM has sought to extend its activist initiatives "to embrace far-reaching social ambitions aimed at bringing cohesion, pride, and self-determination to South Side [Chicago] neighborhoods through the regenerative potential of the arts" (I. Anderson 143). In this sense, they provide a compelling illustration of the ways, as Edward S. Herman and Noam

Chomsky argue in their landmark study *Manufacturing Consent*, "the organization and self-education of groups in the community . . . and their networking and activism, continue to be the fundamental elements in steps toward the democratization of our social life and meaningful social change" (307). While the phrase *human rights* doesn't explicitly show up in the organization's mandate or statements of purpose, the AACM's teachings and priorities constitute something of a largely untapped resource with much to contribute to narratives of community-based arts activism as a powerful model for meaningful social change.

The nine purposes of the AACM, as outlined in the organization's charter in 1965, with its emphasis on phrases such as "spiritual growth," "high moral standards," and "uplift[ing] the public image of creative musicians," alert the reader to the fact that the organization has always been driven by social and ethical impulses as much as it has been by musical ones, and that, as George Lewis suggests, their key principles could "be easily read as an attempt to counter . . . widespread stereotypes about black musicians that had infected not only the academic world, but the dominant culture generally" (*Power* 116). From its inception, the AACM has helped set up concerts, recordings, and teaching sessions, and it has sponsored a free training program for young aspiring musicians in inner-city Chicago. The collective member Joseph Jarman puts it this way: "An organization like the AACM gives a plan, a program, a power, an approach away, not only for black people but for all American people, further all *world* people, to reorient themselves towards social values that can be useful and functional" (qtd. in Mandel, "It *Can* Be Done" 41).

The AACM, in short, is part of a vital history of alternative institution-building strategies that black artists have used to become active subjects of their own histories. Moreover, the improvisatory forms of expression it developed as a function of its relations to its community cannot be dissociated from the rights contexts it was addressing. The discourse of "self-help as fundamental to racial uplift, cultural memory, and spiritual rebirth" that is evident in the organization's mandate "was in accord with many other challenges to traditional notions of order and authority that emerged in the Black Power movement" (G. Lewis, *Power* x). The improvisatory musical practices at the heart of the AACM and the enabling of forms of musical expression not generally encouraged in commercially driven channels of mainstream communication have also been a key part of the organization's ability both to occasion a purposeful disturbance to orthodox assumptions of coherence and judgment and to articulate what Mitchell calls a utopia in sound.

Also key to the organization's critical force has been its explicitly educational mandate. In the fall of 1967, the organization opened the AACM school. Its mission-statement reads as follows: "Our curriculum is so designed as to elicit maximum development of potential within the context of a training program that exposes youngsters to constructive relationships with artistic adults. Widest encouragement is given to music for leisure and educational purposes; and we are continually seeking new ways of relating music to the needs of individuals and the community for increased skills, improved study habits and cultural enrichment" (qtd. in I. Anderson 143). Phrases such as *cultural enrichment* and *constructive relationships* seem particularly germane here. Indeed, these notions significantly informed a roundtable discussion between new and founding AACM members convened as part of the Guelph Jazz Festival of 2005 to mark the occasion of the AACM's fortieth anniversary. The vibrant and myriad perspectives shared at that roundtable make clear the ways the AACM continues to educate younger musicians, who, in turn, represent the best AACM traditions of innovation, social justice, and community-building.

Now if we think of pedagogy in terms of "the complicated processes by which knowledge is produced, skills are learned meaningfully, identities are shaped, desires are mobilized, and critical dialogue becomes a central form of public interaction" (Giroux xi), then to what extent (and in what ways) might improvisational musical practices be understood as vital (and publically resonant) pedagogical acts that generate new forms of knowledge, new understandings of identity and community, new imaginative possibilities with direct implications for social justice outcomes? How do the kinds of cultural (and pedagogical) institutions that present and promote jazz and improvised music shape our understanding of public culture, of memory, of history?

The newer AACM member Matana Roberts provided a compelling context for us to consider some of these issues, when during the 2010 Guelph Jazz Festival roundtable she remarked on "the disconnect between educators and African American students." She explains:

I have sat in music classrooms and listened to teachers speak to African American students about music and . . . there is a disconnect between educators and African American students. I went to a predominantly white college in Chicago but the one thing that saved me creatively was members of the AACM because my particular college program did not care about creative music . . . I was a classically trained person for a while and I had left that behind because I didn't see enough people that looked like me amongst my peers and the history. As beautiful as was Beethoven, Bach, Wagner, all of them . . . I still didn't see anybody that looked like me, so I gravitated more toward jazz music for that reason. ("Power Greater Than Itself")

Roberts's account of this "disconnect" between her African American heritage and the stories and histories promulgated as a valued base of cultural knowledge through her own college education, her account of "how young African American college students are looking for pieces of themselves that you cannot find in white academia," recalls Fanon's argument about how systematized and institutionalized erasures of history have functioned to instill feelings of inferiority in colonized peoples, of how entire histories of knowledge and cultural practice have, in effect, been whitewashed.

But as Ben Okri reminds us, we can change the stories we tell. So here's another: it's a story about the protective and familial bonds of the AACM. Speaking during that same roundtable of her time away from Chicago, faced with new challenges, Roberts states, "It's [membership in the collective] meant a sense of knowing who I am . . . and I was thinking about a good way to describe it. It is like being dangled from a skyscraper but I have a bunch of cords . . . so, I am not going to fall too far even if I fall" ("Power Greater Than Itself"). Nicole Mitchell, also during that roundtable, made a similar observation: "It's important for me to state that the AACM is like a family, it is a mentorship and the beauty of it is, as Roscoe [Mitchell] says, the community." And Wadada Leo Smith echoed that sentiment, claiming, "The most important thing that I would like to relate to you about the AACM is the notion of community. The whole idea that the structure of community is based around not just existence but an ongoing revolution, new ideas, a new way of thinking." For Smith, in other words, the network of social relationships activated through music-making in the AACM has been a vital resource for hope and possibility.

"Where the Music Needs to Be"

A similar set of social and community-based values, and an analogous commitment to "a new way of thinking," are in powerful evidence in another like-minded musicians' organization, the Los Angeles-based Pan Afrikan Peoples Arkestra and the Union of God's Musicians and Artists Ascension (UGMAA), formed in 1961 and led by the pianist Horace Tapscott "to save the music, preserve the music." "We formed UGMAA," Tapscott notes in an interview published in *Revolutionary Worker*, "to preserve music and the arts in the Black community" (Slate). Despite his profound influence, Tapscott remains an unjustly neglected figure in the history of jazz and improvised music, although his autobiography, *Songs of the Unsung: The Musical and Social Journey of Horace Tapscott* and Steven Isoardi's book *The Dark Tree: Jazz and the Community Arts in Los Angeles* should go some distance in redressing this oversight, especially in relation to issues of Tapscott's uncompromising commitment to community-based activism and the transformative power of art (see also Lipsitz, *Footsteps*; Fischlin and Heble, "Other Side"). These accounts, in particular, provide life-affirming examples of how Tapscott, "forged an alternative ethos and aesthetic, forward-looking within the Western world yet also strikingly West African in many respects, that would situate the arts at the center of community development and inspire hundreds of artists to create a remarkable cultural process and body of work" (Isoardi 17).

Key to Tapscott's vision for "preserving the music" (a phrase that the pianist returns to often) was his insistence on the power of the music to bring people together. Indeed, these works are awash with repeated references to his community, to "people coming together" through the UGMAA's work, or to the need to "play for the people" because, as Tapscott liked to put it, "the people needed music," because the community is "where the music needs to be." Formed, in part, as a response to the exploitation and exclusion of black musicians in the Los Angeles community, and closely affiliated with African American struggles for human rights, the UGMAA sought to find work for young black musicians, organized free music workshops for local children, distributed food to families in Watts, and gave free performances on street corners, in parks, schools, hospitals, seniors' homes, and churches.[4] They also gained some notoriety for loading a piano and the Arkestra onto the back of a flatbed truck and playing on the streets during the Watts uprising of 1965, in an effort to curb the violence. In the liner notes to the LP *Live at I.U.C.C.* (1979), Tapscott speaks explicitly about the UGMAA in terms of an ethos of self-determination: "It's a matter of the musicians taking it upon themselves to come together," a sentiment strikingly similar to the AACM's insistence on the right to have control and authority over their music's own histories, identities, and destinies.[5]

In the *Revolutionary Worker* interview, Tapscott is asked to comment specifically on his understanding of the link between the style and content of his music and his social and political mission. Tapscott's response characteristically references his community: "I get inspired for my sounds from the people." He explains:

> I might be lying in the park, watching the rhythms that go down in the community. And from that you apply a sound in your mind of how things are rolling. I look at a scene of people like I might look at poetry. And I can hear lines when I look at certain scenery, when I see certain actions going on, certain smiles on certain people's faces under certain conditions. All of that has a lot to do with how I develop my music . . . That's why the music is like it is because what I'm writing about is this community. (Slate)

Of note here is Tapscott's sense that his music involves (and, in fact, is predicated upon) an ability to adapt and respond via real-time, creative decision-making to the goings-on in his community. It's particularly interesting, especially in light of his focus on preservation, that Tapscott goes on in that interview to insist that improvisation, a form of musical practice that cannot readily be fixed, scripted, or predicted, is what enables him to engage in this model of community-based response:

> Improvisation is in my music because that expresses what happens in the community. I mean, you see a couple of kids walking down the street and one might take off and jump into the street, jump over a couple of cars and come right back in line. So I have to improvise, I have to hook up with that motion, you dig. That movement, that sound, that feeling—this determines how the music is gonna sound in my mind. Improvisation allows you a lot of things. You're able to pick and choose and you can fill in much better. It wasn't like a planned thing to get a particular sound. It was more or less the contributions of different sounds I heard and trying to mesh them together. That's as close as I can get in explaining my music. (Slate)

Tapscott's assertion that improvisation "allows you a lot of things," that it enables him "to pick and choose," and to capture, in music, the rhythms and goings-on in his community is clearly central to his broader social vision.

Some sense of that vision is captured in the title to his first LP, *The Giant Is Awakened*, recorded in 1969 for the Flying Dutchman label. The title, as Tapscott implies in his autobiography, is a kind of call for black consciousness: "I had thought about this sleeping black giant, somewhere, finally waking up and taking care of business and freeing his people. When John Coltrane wrote 'Giant Steps,' the giant was awakened and started taking those steps from Trane's music. Then my sister had an old, old book of black folklore. When I opened it, it fell right to High John the Conqueror, who was a giant, a sleeping giant come to save his people" (*Songs* 113). Indeed, if you listen to the title track on that 1969 recording, there is a determinedly focused sense of urgency in the improvisatory music: it's there in the dark, somewhat ominous, and utterly expressive vamps and ostinati, in the angularity and asymmetricality of its anthemic melodies, in the pounding and propulsive rhythms reinforced by the use of two bassists, in its rousing dissonances and abstractions. Commenting on the politics of the music, Tapscott notes, "Every time we'd play 'The Giant Is Awakened,' the audience would all stand up, salute; some would be crying. If you could have seen how those audiences reacted when we'd play that" (*Songs* 114). The sense of awakening or consciousness-raising, of a people ready to take control of their own destiny, is also reinforced in other Tapscott titles, including, to cite just one salient instance, *Dissent or Descent*, alluding, perhaps, to the choice between a purposeful noncompliance with orthodox habits of coherence and judgment or a downward spiral into the dead zones of conformity and complacency, the former, embodied in Tapscott's improvisatory musical practices, suggestive of what Kelley calls "life as possibility" (*Freedom Dreams* 2).[6]

Life as Possibility: Improvisation and Black Mobility

Again, life as possibility: Kelley's evocative phrase also finds apt expression in Max Roach's oft-quoted insistence that "every new generation of black folks comes up with a new innovation because we're not satisfied with the way the system is economically, politically, sociologically." Roach continues: "Every new generation of black people is going to come

up with something new until things are equitable for black people in society" (qtd. in Owen 60). When asked to riff on "the theory that hip hop
is the new jazz, that there are profound links between what is happening
in rap today and the bebop of the late '40s and '50s," Roach explains that
"hip hop is related to what Louis Armstrong did and Charlie Parker did because here was a group of young people who made something out of very
little" (qtd. in Owen 60). "Hip hop," Roach argues,

> came out of the city's poorest area, out of miserable public education, out
> of miserable housing. They [the artists] didn't have instruments to learn on
> and take home and play, they didn't have rhetoric classes to learn how to
> deal with theatre, they didn't have visual arts classes. And yet these people
> came up with a product of total theatre. On the visual arts side they came up
> with something erroneously called graffiti. On the dance side they came up
> with break-dancing. And on the music side, because they didn't have normal
> instruments, they invented a way to create sounds with turntables . . . They
> joined the ranks of the Louis Armstrongs and Charlie Parkers because they
> created something out of nothing. No one gave them any kind of direction;
> they had to do it themselves with the materials they had available. (qtd. in
> Owen 60)

We've argued elsewhere that such examples attest to the creative and
innovative ways aggrieved peoples have responded to oppression (see
Heble, "Take Two"). Citing Roach's comments, and drawing inspiration
from Paul Robeson's landmark Peace Arch concert, in May 1952—where
the singer and activist, prevented from crossing the American border because of his participation in worldwide struggles for social justice, improvised on a makeshift stage on the back of a flatbed truck and created
a stunningly original document of hope out of what might have seemed
a hopeless situation—we've suggested that improvised forms of creative
practice can enable the profound recognition that social change is possible, that they can sound the possibility of different, and more hopeful,
ways of doing things. And at a time when "advocates and activists for
human rights . . . are often told to resign themselves to the understanding that no other future is possible," improvised music's capacity to sound
other possible futures can be a powerful and a vital social force (Blanco
47–48).

Examples of such capacity to create "something out of nothing," to make
"a way out of no way," abound in the history of African American creative

practice. Here, for instance, is bell hooks writing about African American engagement with the performing arts: "Throughout African American history, performance has been crucial in the struggle for liberation, precisely because it has not required the material resources demanded by other artforms. The voice as instrument could be used by everyone, in any location. In my household, we staged performances in our living room, reciting poetry and acting in written or improvised drama" (211). In such a context of being forced to make do with the materials at hand, to create resources for hope out of seemingly limited or dead-end situations, consider once again the work associated with the AACM. Because extended techniques allow musicians to use familiar instruments to develop new sonic possibilities, the use of what have often been called "little instruments" shows how music can be made from unfamiliar and even everyday objects. These makeshift sound sources and noisemakers are part of a long-standing tradition in aggrieved communities. Max Roach commented that young black people "made something out of very little." These little instruments are also a key feature of the music associated with the Art Ensemble of Chicago, perhaps the most well-known group to emerge out of the AACM. These little instruments are part of a tradition "that started with children banging on washboards and tin-cans, blowing down pieces of rubber-hose and strumming wires stretched between nails on a wall, a tradition deeply rooted in Africa" (Wilmer 112). The jazz scholar Ronald Radano also suggests that these instruments "recall the makeshift sound sources of an earlier time in black history" (107). As such, they function as part of the project of recovering black history that George Lewis identifies as a salient characteristic of experimental musical practices of African Americans.

Such practices are also very much in keeping with arguments that Nathaniel Mackey, a poet and critic, has made in his book *Discrepant Engagement*. Drawing in part on Amiri Baraka's well-known argument in "Swing—from Verb to Noun," on the white appropriation of black music, Mackey argues that improvised music has played a powerful role as an interventionist strategy for black social mobility. He contends, in particular, that a movement from verb to noun (a movement that is played out, for instance, when jazz is canonized or rigidified à la Ken Burns or Wynton Marsalis) "means, on the aesthetic level, a less dynamic, less improvisatory, less blues-inflected music, and, on the political level, a containment of black mobility, a containment of the economic and social advances that might accrue to black artistic innovation" (*Discrepant Engagement* 266). By contrast, he asserts that privileging the verb "linguistically accentuates action among a people whose ability to act is curtailed by racist constraint," a claim that is akin to Nicole Mitchell's argument about African American improvisation as an articulation of utopias in sound (268). Improvisation, we believe, needs to be seen, heard, and understood precisely in the contexts Mackey calls "black linguistic and musical practices that accent variance, variability" (266). Such practices, he tells us, "implicitly react against and reflect critically upon the . . . othering to which their practitioners, denied agency in a society by which they are designated other, have been subjected. The black speaker, writer, or musician whose practice privileges variation subjects the fixed equations that underwrite that denial (including the idea of fixity itself) to an alternative" (267). If one of the most salient and far-reaching lessons of improvised musical practices has to do with shattering what is seen, by way of Mackey, as the deadening and dead-end assumptions of fixity fostered by institutionalized systems of representation, then here's another: what Mackey, writing elsewhere, refers to as improvisation's "discontent with categories and the boundaries they enforce, with the impediment to social and aesthetic mobility such enforcement effects" ("Paracritical Hinge" 368).

History provides no shortage of compelling examples documenting the vital role improvisation has played in African American struggles for mobility and social momentum.[7] In this context, the rising cacophony of horns in John Coltrane's collective improvisation *Ascension* (1965) (and the upward momentum, the social and spiritual uplift, implied by both the music and the title) can be heard as a sonic approximation of the spirit of movement (and the related language of hope) that has historically animated the narratives and struggles of African Americans: "The theme," as John Szwed puts it, "of travel, of journey, of exodus, of escape which dominates African-American narratives: of people who could fly back to Africa, travel in the spirit, visit or be visited by the dead; of chariots and trains to heaven, the Underground Railroad, Marcus Garvey's steamship line" (134).[8]

Indeed, Coltrane's example continues to constitute something of "a life-giving quest for knowledge and excellence that still has much to teach us" (Monson, *Freedom Sounds* 319). There's a wonderfully apt anecdote that's recounted in Steven Isoardi's book on Tapscott and the UGMAA. In Isoardi's book, the writer Sylvia Jarrico tells a story about a time when

Tapscott and some other musicians were rehearsing for an upcoming performance: "As they sat down," she explains to Isoardi, "I moved over to the radio, which was on the jazz station, and turned off the radio. Horace walked out of the group, came past where I was still standing by the radio panel, and as he passed me, he leaned over very tactfully, so that you could hardly see he was leaning toward me, and he said, 'We don't turn off Coltrane'" (129).

The admonition speaks volumes about how Tapscott, too, saw in Coltrane's example a kind of life-giving quest for knowledge. Trane's profound impact and enduring influence on Tapscott's own music and lifework are also notably registered in the nod to Coltrane's landmark recording in the naming of the Union of God's Musicians and Artists Ascension (note, too, the opposition between the uplift—spirtitual, community-based, and musical—implied by the nod to Coltrane's title, and the downward drift associated with the word "descent" in Tapscott's later record, *Dissent or Descent*).[9] But the admonition is also about the urgent need to remain alive to the pattern-shifting impact of Coltrane's oeuvre as both a repository of history and a source of hope and possibility. How, after all, do you "turn off" an artist whose expansiveness of vision remains virtually unmatched in the history of jazz and creative improvised music? "There's nothing else quite like *Ascension* in the history of jazz," says *The Penguin Guide to Jazz on CD* (Cook & Morton). Indeed, there's nothing else quite like Coltrane's career, which itself might be seen, in its exploratory restlessness, its refusal to settle into any kind of orthodoxy, its "discontent," as Mackey would have it, "of categories and the boundaries they enforce," to embody the trope of movement that Szwed characterizes as being so central to African American creative practice ("Paracritical Hinge").

The movement metaphor (Tapscott's comments that the improvisatory nature of his music allows him to "hook up" with the motion and movement in his community) also turns up as a category of analysis in Herman Gray's important book, *Cultural Moves: African Americans and the Politics of Representation*. In a chapter entitled "The Jazz Left," Gray explores an approach to the jazz tradition that draws its sensibilities and practices from what he calls a "road-and-street aesthetic."[10] Here Gray turns his attention to "the fact that the locations and conditions of production where jazz maintains its motion and movement, innovation and expansion, continue in those cultural spaces outside canonical discourses and institutional practices of legitimation" (48). The road and street metaphor, says

Gray, necessitates a conception of the jazz tradition that's very different from the institutionalized hierarchical narratives of jazz history promulgated by Ken Burns, Wynton Marsalis, and others: Gray's metaphor favors constant change, openness, transformation, and an ongoing process of inquiry, rather than stasis, preservation, and a reliance on orthodox habits of response and judgment. Referencing the vital work and alternative institution-building strategies of organizations such as the AACM, the Black Artists' Group, M-BASE, and others who work locally in schools and their communities, and contrasting that work with the canon-building project associated with Marsalis, Gray evinces an interest not just in how jazz is represented (or who gets to represent it), but, perhaps more suggestively, in "how systems of evaluation, assumptions, practices, procedures, and resources authorize and privilege one set of musical practices as against another" (54).

How, that is, do institutions that promote, distribute, teach, market, and present black creative musicking shape the very field of critical understanding, and, in doing so, in what ways (and to what extent) have they promulgated an entire range of assumptions and value judgments (aesthetic, cultural, sociopolitical) about matters as important as nationhood, identity, history, difference, and taste? That this influence is not irreversible and that independent activity, artistic, entrepreneurial, and otherwise, also counts is illustrated by the fact that cultural legitimation comes not only (or even primarily) through affiliation with dominant institutions, but also through social networks and alternative circuits of exchange. Activist disruptions to mainstream, consensual assumptions, in other words, take many trenchant forms in contemporary black culture, as independent artists and networks of practice, like those discussed by Gray in the context of his discussion of the jazz left and those we've discussed here, continue to find innovative strategies to enlarge our base of valued knowledges.

Recent scholarship raises urgent questions about exclusions from the writing of jazz history, insisting that historiography be rendered accountable for what it has systematically repressed. As improvising artists seek to break the tutelage of dominant institutions (and thus of the expressive heritage being shaped by what Gramsci would have called "experts in legitimation" [9–10]), new kinds of organizations have emerged, new forms of dynamism and activity that offer opportunities, especially for artists from historically marginalized or aggrieved communities, to respond to the living and ever-changing experiences of a multicultural and globalized world. The flourishing of independent artist-run organizations such as the Association for the Advancement of Creative Musicians and the Union of God's Musicians and Artists Ascension, dissatisfied with existing structures for producing, promoting, and disseminating their work, have sought to create their own institutions in order to have greater control over the means of production. All these efforts need to be theorized as public programs of action, debate, and criticism in relation to material practices and struggles for institutional authority.

As creative practitioners historically excluded from vital economic resources are redefining the way listeners and critics understand what counts as jazz history, as new initiatives are enabling the development of an infrastructure to support underrepresented and underheard voices (or "unsung," to borrow from Tapscott), the challenge remains for these initiatives not to duplicate—by virtue of being "institutions" and formulating "policies" themselves—the same cultural domination that they seek to abolish. Wadada Leo Smith, in the Guelph Jazz Festival roundtable marking the AACM's fortieth anniversary, alludes to precisely such a challenge when he says that "the biggest problem with [the] AACM and every other kind of artistic community is that they are not privileged with having a consultation amongst themselves about what they're doing. This consultation will not include how to make more money or how to get more personal power and stuff like that. But it would be about how we engage the artistic element to improve and strengthen our communities" ("Power Greater Than Itself"). Smith's insistence that organizations such as the AACM need to engage in a consultative process in order to remain energized by both the realities and possibilities, the histories and hopes, of social transformation is, in part, about the process of resisting the dead-end effects of stasis, rigidity, and fixity; it is also about the urgent need to remain alive to the possibilities for dynamic engagement with the sometimes unexpected opportunities that emerge from the communities in which we live and work. Without such consultation and responsiveness, Smith seems to warn, we remain vulnerable to the rigidities that follow from institutionalization, and we run the attendant risk of settling either for a new kind of orthodoxy or for forms of constrained adaptability.

Smith's insights here are very much akin to one of the central lessons of improvised music. From Nicole Mitchell's attraction to improvisation because it expresses and symbolizes "the greatness of possibility and surprise and spontaneity" to Horace Tapscott's claim that improvisation is the musical form that best enables him to capture the rhythms and goings-on in his community, to Max Roach's argument about improvisation as a form of social mobility (a way out of no way) for black artists, what's key to these arguments is an understanding of the role that creativity and innovation can play as vital tools for building sustainable communities, for promoting social cooperation, and for adapting to unprecedented change.

All of these examples, in short, should make clear that improvisation is about so much more than simply the music itself, that its meanings (and any understanding we might reach about its critical force) are connected in complex, vital ways to broader struggles over resources, legitimation, identity formation, history, power, even, as George Lewis so rightly suggests, "the future of our planet" (Teaching Improvised Music 98).

What, then, about the link to human rights? Who (or what) determines how improvising communities articulate themselves in relation to rights outcomes? And what place do creative practices traditionally marginalized by rights discourses and instruments have in affirming and enacting the historical significance of rights generally as an event-horizon toward which civil society must strive?

As part of that historical process, as the artists we've discussed in this chapter have shown us, improvised music can and does encourage us to reflect on and respond to the situations in which we find ourselves. As a radical practice of alternative forms of encounter via creative means that can, sometimes simultaneously, engage dissonance and consonance, improvisation enacts solutions in the moment to the problem of how to create dialogical relations that respect heterophony and difference. Improvisation engages activism and the responsibilities activism necessitates.

Commenting on the social and political problems facing blacks and on the nine purposes of the AACM, Joseph Jarman suggested in an interview in 1969 in the French journal *Jazz Hot* that "the music is a response to these problems: that means that when people hear it, they can experience a reaction to these problems. Thanks to the music, they can in turn become more active and more responsible" (qtd. in Lewis, *Power* 231). And if the music does spark this kind of response, this kind of taking on of responsibility, then, as Lewis put it during a recent panel discussion celebrating the lifework of the saxophonist Fred Anderson, improvised music-making has the capacity and the power to encourage us to develop options for other ways of living, other ways of thinking about social conditions, other ways to imagine human relations ("Celebrating a Jazz Hero").

William Parker, a free jazz bassist and key catalyzing figure on the contemporary improvised-music scene who, both through his own boundary-shattering music-making and via the organizing role he and his partner, Patricia Nicholson, have played as arts presenters of the New York–based Vision Festival, has worked tirelessly to link music-making with struggles for hope, compassion, and social justice, made a similar point when, during a personal interview, he talked to us about his understanding of the role that improvised music-making, in particular, plays as a vital vehicle for change and transformation.[11] He told us that "improvisation may lead you to open up areas in your life that other musics won't—if you want it to." Improvised music-making, Parker insists, is linked with broader struggles for social justice precisely "because we [as improvising artists] say it is" (Parker, personal interview). Here, then, we return to the life-affirming imperative, evident throughout the history of African American improvised musicking, to "say something," to sound truth to power, to re-cast the identities and histories of aggrieved populations and to promote self-representational counternarratives that enable an enlargement of the base of valued knowledges, in short, to prompt and promote resistance, activism, and mobility in relation to institutions of history-making and knowledge-production.

Mindful of the long and purposeful history of creative resistance by aggrieved peoples against the very assumptions of fixity fostered by dominant epistemic orders, and all too aware of the various kinds of social and institutional forces that too often ask people to resign themselves to an acceptance of the way things are (because no other kind of future is possible), the African American improvising artists we've discussed in this chapter demand, through their cultural practice, that we commit ourselves to other ways of being, knowing, and imagining, that we commit ourselves to seeing and to hearing "life as possibility."[12] Through their improvisatory music-making they insist that they ain't gonna let nobody turn them 'round, turn them 'round, turn them 'round.

CHAPTER 2

IMPROVISATION AND ENCOUNTER
Rights in the Key of Rifference

Improvisation has to do with change, adjustment development, elusive ideas. It isn't any one style of music. It doesn't belong to East or to West . . . But it *is* the creative force in these and many other musics . . . It's [practiced] everywhere in the most complex musical designs and in the earliest attempts at music making.
—Derek Bailey, *On the Edge*

In what is one of the last filmed performances of Coltrane (August 1965), which documents a performance in Comblain-la-Tour, Belgium, by the legendary Classic Quartet, featuring Elvin Jones, Jimmy Garrison, and McCoy Tyner, the camera pans from the stage to the audience and back, capturing coat-clad Belgians amassed before the stage, with its four remarkable, suit-and-tie clad musicians performing at, some might say, the apogee of their powers in this particular grouping.[1]

As wreaths of condensation drift from the musicians in the cold evening air, getting more and more dense as the music intensifies, the camera's gaze on the crowd remains strangely static. As if the intensity of the music being played is somehow in inverse proportion to the reception by the crowd, the musicians' strenuous improvisations in "My Favorite Things" (the 1959 show tune from Rodgers and Hammerstein's *The Sound of Music* that had improbably become the basis of Coltrane's most rarefied improvisations on a well-known tune) are counterposed by the distance that separates the performance from the audience receiving it.

The film frames improvisation as a scene of encounter that stages difference—between the musicians interacting, between the audience and the musicians, between the viewer's gaze and the objects of that gaze, and between the nowness of the moment and the multiple histories that had led up to that moment. The obvious ethnic difference between performers and audience, with cameras zooming in on Elvin Jones's ecstatic, sweat-drenched performance, reinforce tropes of musical difference evident in the film. Similar images of Coltrane's almost impassive focus (he plays with minimal movement) and highly concentrated intensity show off the continuum of cool (ranging from ecstasy to virtuosity) deploying yet another familiar trope of improvised music, especially so-called jazz music, as a site of intercultural encounter, as if to say that all improvised music is always already inherently intercultural, and that this both exoticizes it as a desirable otherness to be staged and makes it impenetrable, forever unknowable because so radically different.

The camera captures the uncanny, radical otherness of the performance, what we call its "rifference," the capacity of improvised music to invoke differential ways of being in the world across multiple contingencies that include politics, ideology, history, spirituality, ethnicity, and alternative forms of social and musical practice. As the music becomes increasingly exploratory, and as the musicians lock in to uncompromised improvisational dialogue, the ethnic differences in the scene are overridden by the aesthetic accomplishment evident in the "riffing" that denotes profound ideological and cultural difference. Improvisation marks its difference rifferentially: the inventiveness and accomplishment shown musically frame how far "outside" the musicians play, but also how other tropes of freedom and difference are implicit in how the riffing is elaborated.

The scene, in short, is one of intercultural presencing. But the degree of interpenetration between the cultures is, as depicted by the camera, at best unknowable and at worst only glancing, there being an undeniable gulf, physical and metaphysical, that separates the audience from the musicians, even as they are brought together by the intensity of the performance. Which is to say that the scene frames encounter and exchange, but in a way that challenges us to rethink what an improvisatory utterance means in relation to how and where it is received. The music underlines the rifference, the ways improvised musicking articulates alterity by destabilizing traditional categories associated with alterity, such as class, race, and gender. Rifference, in this example, underlines the "elusive ideas" (see Bailey's epigraph on previous page) circulating in the performance via improvised musical utterances and the historical contingencies that make those particular utterances possible.

Discourses of improvised musickings must confront how musical forms circulate as a function of intercultural contact in a global economy of such contacts. Improvisation, in its most achieved forms, articulates co-creative sonic shapings that come about as the result of specific communities speaking their voice in multiple, heterophonic ways. Improvisation is, in this sense, a fundamental aspect of jazz consciousness, "a musical manifestation of what W. E. B. Du Bois called 'double consciousness,' the simultaneous African American affiliation with the black in-group and the larger mainstream . . . This inclusivity [in jazz] is based in the syncretic nature of all Afro-diasporic culture" (Austerlitz 184). Voice here can be either a function of self-determination from within a community or of contact with others who are willing to explore through improvisatory discourse the relationship between sound and community formation (both in and across cultures).

But Afrodiasporic musics that found their way to innovative improvised forms did so as a function not only of their underlying syncretism but of persistent historical oppression. Where cultural practices like music are under radical threat, improvisation becomes a mode of survival, a primary response to circumstances in which traditional forms of community have been severely compromised or challenged. Black slave communities in America did not have a choice: they were forced into intercultural hybridization. Too often the term *intercultural* is used to delineate (simplistically) different ethnicities' coming together, or passing exchanges that are strategic or tentatively exploratory. Steve Coleman's attempts to fuse mystical post-bop with animist Afro-Cuban traditionalist forms are an example (as in the album *The Sign and the Seal*, which fuses Coleman's Mystic Rhythm Society with Afrocuba de Matanzas, perhaps Cuba's greatest traditional Afro-Cuban ensemble), as are Don Ellis's big-band experiments played with Indian rhythmic concepts and instrumentations and Arabic scales (especially the Improvisational Workshop Orchestra, formed in 1963).

What if, as a function of how improvised music is made, the problem of difference was no longer reducible to simplistic ways of categorizing complex social practices and affiliations? What if rifference allowed for a more expansive way of thinking through the ways rights discourses can gain amplitude and meaning as a function of what improvisation as a cultural practice can teach? Deep-rooted notions of intercultural exchange underlie improvised music. Those notions have fundamental implications for thinking about rights discourses in relation to improvisation as a model for cocreative ethical engagement, adaptation, and exchange.

To invoke cocreative engagement, adaptation, and exchange is also to invoke stereotypical notions of improvisatory outcomes, as if what some propose as improvisatory ideals are always already outcomes, or indeed features, of improvisatory discourses. The underlying rule of improvisation is that attempts at categorization and definitive renderings of the limitations of improvisation as a discourse are fundamentally antithetical to the core notion of the term, both in theory and in practice. Improvisation can be, and frequently is, the site of disengagement, confrontation, the refusal to adapt (or as some might argue, to be co-opted), and the failure of exchange. The appearance of Sainkho Namtchylak at the Guelph Jazz Festival in 2004, in which the improvising Tuvan singer made a point of inscribing her dissonance publicly and repeatedly (back-dropped by the mercurial effusions of Hamid Drake and William Parker); Michael Snow's appearance at the Resonant Intervals Conference in Calgary (1990), where in addition to giving a parodic history lesson on the evolution of jazz piano, intermixed with autobiographical, shambolic ramblings, he played until no one else (virtually) was left in the room; and the fiasco in Spain (December 2009), where the saxophonist Larry Ochs's performance resulted in the "police decid[ing] to investigate after an angry jazz buff complained that the Larry Ochs Sax and Drumming Core group was on the wrong side of a line dividing jazz from contemporary music" (Tremlett), suggests the buttons that can be pushed by improvising artists. Add to this so-called unlistenable recordings like Pat Metheny's reviled (but sonically and metaphysically provocative) *Zero Tolerance for Silence*; any number of Derek Bailey's recordings in which texture and improbable juxtaposition displace harmony, melody, and rhythm as improvisatory modes; Cecil Taylor's, Don Pullen's, or Matthew Shipp's aggressive, heart-wrenching pianism; the transcendent expressionism of late Coltrane; Coleman's angular, democratizing harmolodics; Ayler's blistering, devastating plastic-reed-induced sound on his tenor. All test the limits of what is deemed acceptable or thinkable musically and improvisationally. Their function is to provoke as much as it is to destabilize. And because they signify at the horizon of musical creation, they represent important interventions—whatever one's take, whatever one's personal aesthetics—on basic rights relating to freedom of expression generally.

Improvisation is one of the few crucial, creative spaces in which the evolution of the discourse in the moment is laid bare, with the outcome being as much a function of the anarchic forces of discourse made manifest (or not) when improvisers play together as it is of contingencies that contribute to the shaping of the discourse that evolves. But even when improvisation is defined as a public contested space in which argument and counterargument are the norm and ideals of community are being challenged in anarchic and highly dissonant ways, even when improvised discourse is far from the model of communitarian ideals (that not all may share), even then, improvisation is a remarkable site for articulating the diversity of discourses as they intermingle and produce consonant and dissonant meanings.

Improvisation, in this sense, can be defined in a number of ways: as a form of asymmetrical engagement between the individual and the community; as a metonymy for the ways larger cultural forms take shape; as a critique of discourses that do not allow for the kinds of anarchic explorations of sonic vocabularies and registers to be found in improvisation at its freest; and as a test of the limits of free speech and free thought, and how that freedom both challenges and establishes a framework for the encounter between the so called individual and the social framework in which she operates. At its most reduced, and knowing how dangerous it is to make these sorts of definitive affirmations, improvisation is a site of encounter. Improvisation restages a vital component of what it means to be human and to have to adapt to social, environmental, and cultural imperatives as a function of being in the world. In this sense improvisation invokes, and is most closely allied to, the defining rights precept "that the capacity to speak to others is a human right, and perhaps the most fundamental human right" (Lyotard 184). As the ur-form of speech, perhaps the very activity that produced human speech, song, and expressive diversity, improvisation reiterates a defining condition for rights: the capacity to freely express oneself, to be heard, to give testimony, to not be forgotten or silenced. These ethical principles lie at the heart of major rights organizations like Amnesty International and Human Rights Watch, whose work derives from testimony and restores "the victim to the community of speakers" (Lyotard 184).

If improvisation is as fundamental to the musical ecosphere as language is to social relations, if indeed it is a primary way of engaging with sounds and adapting creatively to new environments and situations, then the ways improvisation finds its space in the world can reveal some rather interesting things about how we collectively envision and imagine rights discourses. Music is a defining feature of being human, a nonverbal form of signification that adds meaning to existence as a universally created expression of humanity. Musical intelligence is a form of social intelligence and a prototypical form of human communication:

> *synchronous, coordinated song and movement* were what created the strongest bonds between early humans or protohumans, and these allowed for the formation of larger living groups, and eventually of society as we know it . . . Rhythm in music provides the input to the human perceptual system that allows for the prediction and synchronization of different individuals' behaviors. Sound has advantages over vision—it transmits in the dark, travels around corners, can reach people who are visually obscured by trees or caves. Music, as a highly structured form of sound communication, enabled the synchronization of movement even when group members couldn't see each other . . . Singing together releases oxytocin, a neurochemical now known to be involved in establishing bonds of trust between people. (Levitin, *The World in Six Songs* 50–51)[2]

And if what Levitin argues is true or approximates a truth that describes the socioanthropological realities of music's emergence in human community, then improvisation and improvisatory acts of sonic creation must antecede music and the formalized structures that came to be associated with specific cultures, geographies, and peoples. Music in its most inchoate form always emerges from improvised experiments with making sounds with the materials and environments, the material and the imaginative realities, and the survival contingencies and necessities of particular sites and social groupings.

Improvisation underlay the primal ways humans and protohumans engaged with their environments, and they did so in ways that were imitative, pragmatic, imaginative, and dependent on the kinds of materials available in local environments for sonic exploration. Moreover, it is clear that sounds (like language) have a social function related to identity, cultural context, and ability.

Improvisation, then, manifests adaptive and identity markers that are a deeply human aspect of how humans inter-relate with each other and their environments. The Finnish musicologist and semiotician Eero Tarasti argues that improvisation is a "sign of the courage to enter into communication without certainty about whether the improvisation—on any level, be it an action or a particular product of this action—will be received, understood, or accepted. In improvisation the existential, temporal, and spatial situation of the improviser always comes to the fore. Improvisation is a particular way in which signs exist. In linguistic terms, improvisation as an utterance is always deictic, that is, an act that points to the moment and place of uttering. Improvisation is a trace of a performance situation in the performance itself" (185–86). In Tarasti's semiotic terms, improvisation is not only a provisional way of encountering the world in the here and now—a technique that is profoundly rooted in the capacity to read the moment as both provisional and contingent—but also a form of testimonial in which the particulars of encounters that occur under the sign of the contingently provisional are inscribed. The rights implications of such an understanding are significant in that the contexts of improvisation presuppose the freedom to articulate in any given circumstance; they presuppose the recognition that such articulation is provisional and contingent, and thus the recognition of the inherent otherness that is always to be addressed in the improvisatory situation; they presuppose the understanding that improvisation bears testimony, traces, the historicity associated with communicative strategies that are extralinguistic.

Tarasti further argues that "ambiguous musical situations [that is, improvisations], which operate with several superimposed levels of meaning, require the listener to discover or create new codes," and that "all musical interpretation that takes place spontaneously, at the mercy of the situation, is a kind of disturbance" (189). The implication of the actions of the listener or receiver of the improvised performance are every bit as significant here as the performance, for to discern the performance the listener must in a sense cocreate it. The musical "disturbance" of improvisation shakes not only the conventions that have evolved around passive listening and the reduced agency of the listener but also conventions about the one-sided nature of creation.

In these terms the cocreative, interpenetrative engagement of both the agency of the performer and that of the listener signals a potentially productive model of encounter, one in which the rights of both are at stake and coimplicated in ways that enhance (rather than reduce) the mutual responsibility of the one to the other. The reciprocity of this improvised exchange—embodied in both the agency of the player and the agency of the listener, and their respective natures as both provisional and mutually dependent on the many contexts that have produced them, including the environment—lies at the heart of any meaningful discourse of rights. In an article entitled "Improvisation as a Tool for Investigating Reality," Stephen Nachmanovitch, an improvising violinist and music theorist, states, "There is a South African word, *Ubuntu*, which is the same thing as inter-being. Desmond Tutu brought it into currency in the West and it is the opposite of Descartes. Descartes is famous amongst other things for saying, 'I think, therefore I am.' *Ubuntu* means 'I have my being through your having your being.' *Ubuntu* is the territory that we get into as we do our improvisational explorations" (*The Improvisor*).

Does this form of inter-being that Nachmanovitch argues is implicit in improvisation also have rights implications, especially in rethinking the priority given to the individual as the cathexis of all rights discourse?

How might improvisation give us important alternatives to better fulfilling Article 29 of the Universal Declaration of Human Rights (UDHR), which states, "Everyone has duties to the community in which alone the free and full development of his personality is possible"?

Do present-day improvised sonic explorations hint at prototypical community beginnings, negotiations of difference (rifference) through alternative forms of embodied encounter, and if so, are these musical avatars pointing us to ineluctable truths about who and why we are?

If the answer to these questions is even a qualified yes, then the rights implications of improvised musical discourses are profound, as they mark one of the highly achieved and ubiquitous cultural practices of what it means to be human in relation to other beings, other environments, other dimensions of spirit and play.

Being Instrumental: Improvisation and the Ethics of Encounter

Free, creative, improvised music came into its own as a genre in the 1960s, part of the ongoing evolution of so-called jazz discourses and the increased hybridization of those discourses with the European avant-garde. But it also came about as a result of the ways music and civil rights discourses came to share a vocabulary and an ethos. The terms *jazz* and *improvisation* are hopelessly intertwined, the one often a synecdoche for the other. The historical reasons for this have a great deal to do with the contexts that gave birth to the form, especially those rooted in the cultural survival of people who had been uprooted from Africa and enslaved, the kinds of adaptation skills they needed to sustain themselves in new, hostile, and abusive environments, and the resistance they produced to on-going oppression. Because of these contexts, the kinds of improvisatory musical discourses we discuss below are intricately tied with the rights environments (and aspirations of aggrieved communities) out of which they emerged and upon which they comment. In the context of African and Afrodiasporic cultures, it is clear that the music and the social conditions under which it was created have had, and continue to have, profound rights implications. Hotep Idris Galeta, a South African jazz pianist and educator, argues that

> the social conditions [that] spawned this dynamic art form [were] rooted in the human rights abuses and oppressive conditions experienced by Africans captured and uprooted from their traditional cultures then transported in the most barbaric and inhumane conditions to an alien environment as slaves. It is these dynamics coupled over the years with exposure to and assimilation of European arts and cultural forms that gave rise to new modes of musical expression[,] which began to develop within the slave and Creole communities in and around New Orleans as well as other areas in the United States. These were the early embryonic beginnings and early developmental stages of what was to become known as Jazz.

Galeta is a South African musician writing in postapartheid South Africa, an example of the degree to which the discourse of jazz as a form of diasporic cultural practice had, in the course of little over a century, managed to create itself out of enslaved and displaced Africans' responses to historical contingency and then to return to its origins as a global form of music that had passed through the historical contingencies of colonialism, slavery, oppression, segregation, and racism.

Historical contingency, global dissemination, resistance to oppressive and destructive forms of encounter are at the root of this form of improvised musicking. So too are they a cornerstone in articulating rights as a fundamental aspect of being human and being able to resist forces based on injustice and inequity. The historical contexts for both the emergence of the free, improvisational music associated with jazz and the global agreement on notions of universal rights given voice in the UDHR occur in roughly the same historical moment, as if both become thinkable in the specific historical moment to which they were responding, that is, the aftermath of the Second World War (after Auschwitz) and the growing clamor to deal with the insistent problem of racism in America.

The phrase *human rights* retains general currency as a way of addressing rights issues. But *human* can be (and often is) used in a way that only allows for normative conceptions of what and who is human—all too often the frame of reference for defining *human* is a function of institutionalized legal cultures that have emerged from imperial, white culture or from institutional, corporate, technocratic market cultures that have difficulty conceiving of humanity apart from economic function. And the notion of "human rights" excludes all sorts of other formations required to imagine what a more expansive and theoretically informed notion of rights would entail, starting with rights that extend to the biosphere, to all forms of sentience, life (animal and plant rights, seed rights, environmental rights), and to alternative or marginalized expressions of the like.[3]

Moreover, being "human" is a function of multiple heterophonic discourses that contribute to that meaning, not all in agreement. Thus, to imply that there is a normative, shared notion of what it means to be human seems to strike at the logical core of what rights attempt to achieve, that is, to respect the diversity of meanings that accrue to different expressions of humanity in terms that are generally acceptable to all as a function of respect for difference and equity, where the only "purity" and universality entail hybridity and multiplicity.

The concept of "human rights" is most commonly associated with strategic documents, like the UDHR, a product of the global movement to conceive of universally held rights inalienably present in all people. Some might call it the passive or tautological view of human rights: people have rights simply as a function of being people. Coincident with this view is the understanding that the exercise of one's rights is tightly constricted within the legal frameworks by which rights are defined and made possible, necessitating the use of legal resources (and access thereto) in order to guarantee rights. This model sets the stage for neoliberal notions of rights enactment, in which the public commons is displaced as a function of the private sector's engagement in the process of accessing and ensuring rights. And the center point of this equation is the individual "consumer" of rights who embodies the inherent attributes of these universal rights but whose responsibility it is to access these inherent rights within the established legal framework (the so-called negative rights theory) or marketplace of rights. This is in large part the ideological framework for human rights discourses that have come out of post-Enlightenment, Occidental institutional structures: rights inhere in all, but the individual must enact them as a function of access to power and resources that are inequitably distributed in the marketplace. The reality is that negative rights are an artful camouflage of disempowerment and the hard-core allocations of resources that prevent most people from accessing the full range of their rights in practice. How can one think of rights within a framework in which the corrective to inequity is based on the very kind of thinking that produced the inequity?

Even so, with these sorts of limitations, human rights discourses are seen as potentially disruptive to state power. Henry Steiner, a professor of law at Harvard University, argues that the human rights movement "also has a 'utopian' dimension that envisions a vibrant and broadly based political community. Such a vision underscores the potential of the human rights movement for conflict with regimes all over the world. A society honoring the full range of contemporary human rights would be hospitable to many types of pluralism and skeptical about any one final truth, at least to the point of allowing and protecting difference. It would not stop at the protection of negative rights but would encourage citizens to exercise their right to political participation, one path toward enabling peoples to realize the right to self-determination" (qtd. in Mutua 62).

Pluralism, skepticism, the exploration of difference, self-determination and enablement as a function of community empowerment, these tropes affiliate rights discourses with improvising communities in which similar values are at stake. Both rights and improvisatory discourses are frequently belittled as "utopian" or idealized, when the reality is that their potential power lies in the radical, directed criticism of realities other than their own, their acknowledgment of differential relations as a starting point for moving toward something different, their capacity to enact difference constructively.

The great improvising English saxophonist Evan Parker, in commenting on his and Roscoe Mitchell's initiative in cofounding the Transatlantic Art Ensemble, in 2004, states that "learning to live with difference [should be seen], not as a threat but as an opportunity to become wiser." He further associates this sentiment with broader rights contexts: "The politicians will have to learn from the people and develop humility in place of their current arrogance. Science shows that more equal societies are healthier societies. Instead of chasing after the approval of the rich, and because rich powerful, they will need to bring about more justice and decent living conditions for ordinary people. They will need to devise systems that work towards a more equal distribution of wealth" (Parker and Falb 126).

Similarly, the last album by Don Pullen, an improvising pianist, *Sacred Common Ground* (1995), went out of its way to explore cultural and musical difference with Pullen's remarkable grammar of improvisation, bringing together Afro-Brazilian musicians with the Chief Cliff Singers from indigenous Native American communities (the Salish and Kootenai peoples from northwestern Montana). Moved by the force of powwow singing, which he first heard in 1992, and after serious study, Pullen began to hear overlaps with blues, free jazz, shuffle, and gospel music. The hybrid music of *Sacred Common Ground* emerged out of the blend of Pullen's radical improvising aesthetic (its passionate juxtaposition of dissonance and tone clusters with ecstatic melodic playing) and native traditional singing and storytelling. The two groups had to learn cocreatively to accommodate the complexities of each other's styles as the music evolved, and the album clearly makes connections between traditional native songs and rhythms and various elements of African American musicking, as in the almost seamless transition from "River Song" to "Reservation Blues." The project unfolded, not without tensions over traditional native culture's being "improvised," but nonetheless with the approval of the Kootenai elders. And many people in the communities that came together seemed "genuinely surprised by the power of this collaboration between cultures" (liner notes).

As the critic Chris Searle argues, in considerable disagreement with the critical reception of the album, "What [Pullen] achieved no jazz musician has achieved before: to fuse jazz with the music of the USA's indigenous peoples . . . to unite the cry of the black man with the cry of the red man in a nation [that] has scorned both" (247). While it's not entirely the case that Pullen's was the first attempt to bring together elements of jazz and improvised music with Native American musical traditions (listen, for instance, to saxophonist Jim Pepper's brilliant and now oft-covered "Witchi-Tai-To"), Pullen's recording nevertheless, as Searle suggests, marks something of a watershed moment in contemporary jazz. Like Jimi Hendrix, Pullen had mixed-race ancestry (his paternal grandmother was probably half Cherokee), and the evolution of his music toward hybrid forms cannot be simplistically dismissed in relation to larger rights concerns that coincide with that evolution. As Searle argues, "The future of jazz is embedded within its internationalism. Its migratory powers . . . have taken its blue and joyous notes across the world, and they have frequently . . . been welded to a message of peace, justice and political freedom" (18).[4]

Multiple examples of the way improvised musicking takes place within an emerging sense of global contact and interchange exist: Dizzy Gillespie's United Nations Orchestra, formed in 1988, and Charlie Haden's Liberation Music Orchestra, formed in 1969, whose eponymous first album included Ornette Coleman's tune "War Orphans" as well as protest tunes dealing with Vietnam and the Spanish Civil War. There are any number of duos, trios, and other groupings that have come about as a result of a deliberate intent toward border-crossing discourses in the underlying experimentalist and integrationist philosophy driving improvising musicking of this kind. It is important to recognize that this sense of reaching out in the music is itself aligned with early African American understandings about how the music and culture interrelate.

In an essay entitled "Black Internationale," published in *Jazz Planet*, the Berkeley professor Andrew F. Jones, states that

> the domestic parochialism of much current jazz criticism betrays the resolute internationalism of early twentieth-century African-American critical thinking about the relations between culture and music. The black critic J. A. Rogers' "Jazz at Home," an essay anthologized in Alain Locke's epochal 1929 collection of voices from the Harlem Renaissance, *The New Negro*, is a fascinating case in point . . . Rogers locates the "primal" origins of jazz—"nobody's child of the levee and the city slum"—in the "joyous revolt" of African America against "sordidness and sorrow" . . . And it is precisely by virtue of this spirit, he continues, that jazz has become a globalized balm for the suffering and ennui of "modern machine-ridden and convention bound society" the world over. "Jazz," he writes, "is a marvel of paradox: too fundamentally human, at least as modern humanity goes, to be typically racial, too international to be characteristically national, too much abroad in the world to have a special home." (225)

The migratory power of improvised musicking extends into non-jazz worlds too. Take, for instance, the minimalist composer La Monte Young, who played the L.A. jazz scene alongside Ornette Coleman, Billy Higgins, and Don Cherry (not to mention having bested Eric Dolphy in a sax audition for Los Angeles City College). By the early 1960s, Young had "dropped notated composition in favor of evening-length ritual improvisations, which he dubbed the Theatre of Eternal Music . . . Nothing like this had been heard in notated music, because there was no way to notate it. Nothing like it had been heard in jazz, either, although the free jazz of Sun Ra and Albert Ayler came close" (Ross, *The Rest Is Noise* 538–39). The situational fluidity of improvisation as a sociomusical practice gave it great power in bridging difference, even as it articulated radical alternatives to how narratives of traditional encounter were thought to function.

The Transatlantic Art Ensemble and Pullen's African-Brazilian Connection are not the only examples of border-crossing between and across different musical communities, crossings facilitated by improvisatory techniques. The capacity of improvisers to develop such communities as a function of the art form itself hints at much wider rights applications embedded in improvisatory practices, especially in terms of negotiating difference, articulating hybridity as an emblem of the capacity to speak across and between different identities. *Transatlantic Visions*, an album recorded at Vision Festival XIII in 2008 in New York, speaks with the same urgencies to how improvised musicking can generate remarkable artistic expressions that traverse multiple cultural differences. The recording features the French bassist Joëlle Léandre and the American trombonist George Lewis, each with radically different formations.

Perhaps one of the most productive ways of imagining the relationship between rights discourses, defined by the respect for difference, and improvisatory discourses, defined by the production and exploration of difference, is as a potentially exemplary model of encounter. Both rights discourses and improvisatory discourses, in their most achieved forms, get at profound expressions of otherness, even as they integrate those in extraordinarily sophisticated ways with identity and self-expression. The French critic Alexandre Pierrepont explains in his liner notes to *Transatlantic Visions* that "improvisation is the other. It is becoming someone, the other that we are—not the one standing next to you, but the other here awakened by the one who is passing by, passing through you." This view of improvisation necessitates the other, who is in fact standing beside you playing, because the key to self is found through how it encounters difference. Such a narrative points to how identity is a reciprocal relation to otherness, an ethical stance that is at a radical distance from the narratives of the integrated individual who is the focus of traditional human rights discourses.

Improvisation, in the rich context that Pierrepont is trying to get at, troubles reductive notions of the individual even as it reinforces the co-generative elements that produce social relations and cultural practices. Being instrumental in such a context takes on a wider resonance. The core elements of the most achieved improvisers include careful listening, embodied presence, dialogue (even if dissonant or dissident), relational thinking, empathic and intuitive understanding blended with the skillful use of the materials at hand, and the power to awaken others to new possibilities in the improvised soundscape. The qualities required to be instrumental in improvisatory circumstances are also qualities that underlie rights contingencies. And this relation to rights contingencies is especially evident in the ways difference and otherness (both in relation to one's self but also in relation to the others that give that self meaning) are a constant reality of improvisation. Improvisation is a response to a set of basic questions that also arise in, and potentially define, rights contexts:

Who are you here and now?

What do you have to say?

How are you going to join this dialogue?

How will you speak your mind and also listen to how others speak their minds?

How will you contribute to the outcomes of the improvisation?

How far are you prepared to go to experiment with alternative forms of expression that make sense in the particular moment?

How are you going to be instrumental in achieving a meaningful musical dialogue?

Can you integrate your ideas with the larger group in ways that make new meaning?

What resources can you bring to the table to make a difference in the improvisatory moment?

Questions such as these are crucial to any improvised context worth talking about and they show the transposable nature of improvisatory thinking to rights contexts in which similar queries are starting points for meaningful discourse.

Rights and improvisation always begin as an ethics of encounter, moving from there into embodied action, and, sometimes, achievement. The individual and the larger community play a role in that ethics, and the focus is not so much on these component elements as on what unfolds in an aggregate way when encounter happens. In this sense, rights and improvisatory discourses engage with the process and the material outcome of encounter narratives, whether it be aggrieved communities coming together to make music or aggrieved communities coming together to act in the name of their collective interests.

Understood in this way, improvisation destabilizes key elements in the traditional post-Enlightenment narrative of human rights, in which the term *human* is closely linked to normative, hegemonic (and relatively fixed) notions of individuality as the be-all and end-all for determining value in social relations. Improvisation thus brings a more expansive notion of the gathered contingencies that are evident in encounters with difference, with the moment in which potential action is about to erupt. And the marker of value is what is achieved as a result of dynamic interplays that unfold, with singular action associated with the individual a factor that is part of a much bigger picture, a much higher set of stakes that involves far more than individualist-oriented outcomes.

Other Ways of Thinking Rights

Largely excluded from discussions of human rights are peoples and cultures without a specific concept of human rights and without the individual-centered notion of ethical comportment in a rights marketplace, but nonetheless with a concept of relational responsibilities to local communities that require an enacted, quotidian form of dynamic, cocreative ethics — that is, an ethics in constant need of proving and being tested, and an ethics that one acquires as a function of interactions with elders, other community members, family, environment, and so on. Indigenous communities like the Guaraní or the Inuit, large tribal or linguistic groups (such as the Yoruba), and other largely non-Western conglomerations all have highly evolved notions of ethical action that exist apart from Western, post-Enlightenment notions of so-called human rights. For instance, the Guaraní word for *word* also means *soul*: the semiotic relationship denotes a wider ethical relationship well beyond litigious constructions of rights as they are defined by Western legal instruments. Inuit conceptions of rights cannot be dissociated from their relationship to the land and how indigenous populations have adapted to and improvised in a specific set of ecological circumstances that are unique.

These non-Western ethical frames — and improvisational communities can in part embody these same attributes as a function of their emergence from African diasporic histories—involve more active views of a constantly evolving definition of what is right action within a local context that directly affects one's community. Such views do not preclude extending right action to all the contexts that allow the community to exist, that is, its relations with other communities, its dependence on specific environmental contexts, its relation to the land that provides food, its relation to animist beliefs that link humans with the land, with the cosmos, and with a spiritual world, none of which are to be found in Western rights instruments. Important to understand are the extralegal, extrapolitical, and expansive notions (some of which involve spiritual or religious considerations) of what constitutes ethical comportment: reduction to legal frameworks can corrupt the myriad ways *all* actions occur within a sophisticated layering of contexts that require apt consideration in order for ethical action to be taken.

A third view of rights is that of cultural rights, which understands specific cultures and peoples as defined by distinctive practices not to be found elsewhere. These practices are most evident in things that do not have market value per se: one's language, one's music, one's visual and gestural arts, the complex cultural codes that govern behaviors, the foods one eats, one's belief systems, one's approach to health and well-being, to death and memorialization. Cultural rights arise out of the consideration for the preservation of one's way of life, and they are a response to the dramatic eradication of cultural difference via the loss of languages, musical traditions, and so forth, especially in relation to indigenous populations that are forced to acculturate to imperial cultures as a function of militarism, economic pressures, and the like. Cultural rights are essentially a response to the fragility of cultural differences in the face of hegemony, a response to ethnocide and othercide.

A musical example of the kinds of issues addressed by cultural rights involves the Taiwanese ethnic group the Amis, the largest ethnic group in Taiwan, consisting of about 120,000 people from the eastern part of the island. Rosemary Coombe, a Canadian law professor, describes how this tribal group was visited in 1978 by researchers who recorded Amis folk music, ostensibly for archival purposes. The music "made its way into a compilation of Chinese folk music on a record album released in France. Twenty years later a European band [the German pop group Enigma] used a sample of this recording to create a musical composition, which received widespread acclaim. The music performed by the Amis singers was neither individually authored nor fixed in material form. Therefore it was squarely in the public domain, and not eligible for copyright protections. Its use by the band was not in violation of any laws in force. The European composition, 'Return to Innocence,' was a global hit and the Olympic Committee chose it as an anthem for the 1996 Olympic Games in Atlanta" (2–3). Enigma's hit song, some 50 percent of which used the sampled materials from the Amis, remained atop Billboard's top 100 chart for twenty-two consecutive weeks, sold more than eight million copies, and it was the signature theme of the 1996 Olympics; in other words, it was extremely profitable. Yet the elderly indigenous couple that had sung the song, Difang Duana and Guo Xiuzhu, was deemed to have almost no legal rights to the song, and only after an American lawyer brought a suit was an out-of-court settlement achieved in 1999 (Broughton and Ellingham 237–38).

Whereas the human rights discourse of the West relegates the arts and culture to a form of right (a freedom of expression) that one "enjoys," advocates of the cultural-rights perspective see culture as definitive of a dimension of experience that gives specific peoples their unique identity and agency in the world, something that is not necessarily contained within legal discourses of equity or identity. Instead of tropes of enjoyment, which essentially relegate cultural rights to a lesser aspect of humanity, an aspect that is consistent with a kind of capitalized view of what has priority in the marketplace, cultural-rights advocates understand identity in ways that exceed marketplace and economic logics. Cultural rights are a fundamental aspect of the public commons, earned, accessed, and reciprocally shared as a function of belonging to a community. Belonging here implies performance. To belong, one must perform one's role as both oneself and as oneself in relation to others. And this kind of performative relation to a community's comportment plays an important role in improvisatory musickings where self- and community-definition occur as a function of enacted and embodied presencing.

The performative self is a synecdoche for an ethical relationship that defines the community, the public commons—it is not a relationship of property or of copyright, though it speaks to identity and to unique iterations associated with specific cultural formations and social practices. To speak of these sorts of cultural rights from the narrow perspective of "human rights" (in which property, copyright, and intellectual ownership are foregrounded concepts) is to undermine the very different ideological contexts and stakes evident in these different conceptions of rights.[5]

Finally, a fourth kind of rights discourse is that of civil rights, one particularly associated with the struggle to achieve freedom and equity for disenfranchised African Americans and Chicanos (El Movimiento) during the late 1950s and 1960s, though its roots extend well back from these crucible decades. The civil rights movement is related to general principles that give one both the right to be free of excessive government influence and the right to participate in the civil state in an equitable manner. But the specific historical context of the African American civil rights movement was an outcome of the struggle to end racial discrimination, especially in the southern states of the United States, to end segregation, and to gain suffrage and economic, political, and social power. The key trope in the civil rights movement is "freedom," a response to centuries of oppression in the form of slavery and racism and a defining trope in terms of the material outcomes sought by the movement. Music, and especially improvised forms produced by the African American diaspora, played a crucial role in elaborating what freedom meant, in enacting it literally as a form of discursive engagement with the world. The English music critic Robin Denselow describes an encounter with the American civil rights activist Bernice Johnson Reagon in which she describes the function music played in rights struggles:

> "How important were the musicians during the civil rights years?" Bernice Johnson Reagon [member of The Freedom Singers, organized by the Student Nonviolent Coordinating Committee in 1962] looked around the front room of her home in the suburbs of Washington, D.C., and shrugged. "They were crucial. You couldn't call black people together in any committed way without a ritual that involved an enormous amount of singing. The singing was used to create the climate, to get people ready to address the issues. So any statement from lawyers, or a testimony from someone who'd been arrested, was always presented on a bed of song. And the song leaders were absolutely essential." (Denselow 31)

The civil rights movement linked, in extraordinary ways, cultural accomplishment—the fact that in spite of slavery and oppression, African American culture had produced the most invigorated form of new, globalized, and hybridized musical discourse of the twentieth century—with renewed political and rights discourses. Moreover, it linked renewed forms of thinking about rights with direct action.

The freedom to testify meant the freedom to improvise, to enact publicly, with the two forming an indissociable link in the rights and musical discourses of the time. Daniel Belgrad, a scholar of American culture, argues that

> in the 1940s and 1950s, spontaneity had social meaning, both for the artists who used it and for the culture at large . . . Most broadly, spontaneity implied an alternative to the vaunted rational progress of Western civilization, which had succeeded in developing technologies and principles of organization that threatened human life and freedom on an unprecedented scale. In the specific historical context of wartime and postwar America, spontaneity did battle against the culture of corporate liberalism, which was the most recent and local manifestation of these principles. Finally, spontaneity was a means for challenging the cultural hegemony of privileged Anglo-American "insiders," giving voice to artists and writers from different ethnic and social backgrounds remote from the traditional channels of cultural authority. (15)

Here spontaneity is a synecdoche for improvisation, one of the key features associated with improvisatory signifying. Belgrad's argument that the trope had wider cultural meaning, especially as a means of challenging hegemonic structures, is a useful way of thinking about the wider import of improvisation as a social practice. In "Negotiating Freedom: Values and Practices in Contemporary Improvised Music," the improviser and scholar David Borgo notes how

> freedom, in the sense of transcending previous social and cultural restraints, has been an important part of jazz music since its inception. The syncopated rhythms and exploratory improvisations and compositions of jazz have consistently stretched the structures and forms of American music. The music has also provided a symbol and a culture of liberation to several generations of musicians and listeners, both at home and abroad . . . At approximately the same time that "freedom" was becoming a rallying point and a musical goal for many modern jazz musicians, improvisation resurfaced in the Euro-American "classical" tradition—after a century-and-a-half of neglect—in the form of indeterminate, intuitive, and graphically designed pieces. (165–66)

The epigraph before Borgo's essay cites a comment by Davey Williams, the improvisatory guitarist and avant-gardist, in the *Improviser*: "Free improvisation is not an action resulting from freedom; it is an action *directed towards freedom*" ("Towards a Philosophy of Improvisation" 32–34). The same might be said of rights actions most associated with improvised musickings in their highest level of expression, their most accomplished forms. Musical accomplishment was (and continues to be) profoundly tied to alternative forms of social organization driven by creative practices rooted in African American diasporic communities. As the jazz critic Howard Mandel puts it, "The jazz community was in the forefront of the civil rights movement, and remains in the lead for demonstrating how all-inclusive meritocracies look, sound and work" ("Civil Rights-Jazz Document, 1963").

Ralph Ellison's essay "Living with Music" recounts his childhood in Oklahoma City, where he got to know jazz musicians whose

> driving motivation was neither money nor fame, but the will to achieve the most eloquent expression of idea-emotions through the technical mastery of their instruments (which, incidentally, some of them wore as a priest wears the cross) and the give and take, the subtle rhythmical shaping and blending of idea, tone and imagination demanded of group improvisation. The delicate balance struck between strong individual personality and the group during those early jam sessions was a marvel of social organization. I had learned too that the end of all this discipline and technical mastery was the desire to express an affirmative way of life through its musical tradition, and that this tradition insisted that each artist achieve his creativity within its frame. (5–6)

Ellison, who had studied music before becoming a writer (and who was fairly conservative in his jazz tastes), was keenly aware years prior to the civil rights movement of the degree to which improvised musical acts refracted larger social ideals. Improvisation affirmed that alternatives were indeed possible if one were capable of the discipline and focus he saw as a hallmark of the jazz musicians with whom he associated in Oklahoma City. His comments point to an emergent discourse of rights firmly intertwined with musical improvisation.

Ellison's good friend Albert Murray, the African American writer and jazz critic, argues that jazz is the "definitive aesthetic form of American life," and locates this sort of discourse in improvisation: American life "is based on improvisation. The early settlers, the first explorers . . . *that* is based on improvisation. They don't know what's going to happen next, right? But they have aspiration to face the unknown, but they adjust to it, improvise, which means you have to be alert at all times." In these contexts, cultural accomplishment is a marker of freedom, self-mastery, and performative identity within a larger public context. These social practices, while localized in music, point to the more expansive goals of the civil rights movement. Displaying publicly the discipline that produces extraordinary accomplishment, which was the case with the most achieved forms of improvised musicking to come out of the period associated with the civil rights movement, had symbolic import within larger contexts. If largely marginalized musicians could still attain remarkable heights, against all odds, was this not a sign that other forms of social action could produce similar outcomes? Imagining rights, figuring and reconfiguring improvisation, both demand enactment, empowerment, discipline, accomplishment, and the will to experiment with new ways of ordering the world.

What is notable in these varied discourses that have sprung up around rights generally is that rights discourses gather around specific cultural practices. So, in the West, market logic and litigious discourse become a way of codifying rights. In non-Western cultures and communities, processual notions of responsibility that supersede reductive notions are engaged. Cultural rights are all about identity and its preservation, the distinctive features that make a group what it is. And civil rights arose as an enacted practice of freedom-seeking on multiple fronts, fronts that involved elements of the first three forms of rights outlined above. As an expression of cultural practices and formations, rights, then, cannot be separated from other cultural practices to which they relate, and through which they find their expression, their models. And it is in this sense that we situate our discussion of improvisation as a cultural practice that comes to prominence as a genre in itself, in the very historical moment when globally rights discourses and their contestations also begin to emerge.

It may be too easy a comparison to suggest that there are analogues between so-called free jazz and freedom tropes in the African American civil rights movement; that the localized and unique expressions of cultural identity and agency found in improvisatory discourses are a crucial form of asserting cultural rights; that the uncommon gestures that indissolubly link the individual with the community in improvisation are replayed in rights discourses where similar issues are at stake; that the problem of how to address extrainstitutional, nonreductive, processual, and dynamic aspects of being human is modeled in improvisation in ways that challenge received notions of "human" rights as a purely formal legal structure inherent in all, but only claimable if one has adequate access to power and resources.

But there is perhaps a not-so-simple truth at work in these affirmations. And it is largely unexamined or ignored in rights discourses generally, much in the way that arts discourses' contributions to vital aspects of human history and achievement have suffered increasing attack from technocrats who can think only in terms of quantification, output, and commercial value.

The exclusion of clauses dealing directly with the right to a sustainable environment from the UDHR marks perhaps the most notable omission of expanded notions of what a meaningful rights discourse would look like. Similarly, the preamble to that document's affirmation that "human rights should be protected by the rule of law" neglects to address how the rule of law can be perverted (say, under a dictatorship or under a corrupt system of governance) while also legalizing the discourse of rights in ways that neglect other forms of reality that are equally pertinent. Article 27, one of the few to address the arts in general terms, states the following: "Everyone has the right freely to participate in the cultural life of the community, to enjoy the arts and to share in scientific advancement and its benefits." Article 27 cannot be dissociated from article 19: "Everyone has the right to freedom of opinion and expression; this right includes freedom to hold opinions without interference and to seek, receive and impart information and ideas through any media and regardless of frontiers."

As noble and laudable as these assertions sound, the problem remains that they do not provide for contexts wherein "freedom of expression" is dissident expression, punishable by the "rule of law." Nor do they account for the subtle displacement of an arts discourse (to be "enjoyed") by a scientific discourse whose benefits are to be shared, as if to suggest that there is a relative "purely for pleasure" value associated with the arts (they don't advance, nor do they impart information that is beneficial) that doesn't quite merit the same language as the sciences. Nor do they account for the absence of specific language related to creative expression, perhaps the most significant cultural form binding all humanity.

In drafting these articles of the Universal Declaration of Human Rights, the Canadian legal scholar and rights advocate John Peters Humphrey "had almost no clear constitutional precedents before him. The most explicit references were in the draft of the Inter-American Juridical Committee, which had been submitted by the delegation of Chile. It contained a detailed statement on the 'rights to the benefits of science,' as well as rights to 'the use of whatever means of communication are available,' examples of which were 'the freedom to use the graphic arts, the theater, the cinema, and other agencies for the dissemination of ideas'" (Morsink 217–18). It is worth noting how music is marginalized from even being mentioned as part of the cultural matrix informing the drafting of these key articles of the UDHR. Moreover, the relationship between cultural expression and larger rights issues was, at best, in an emergent phase in 1948. This marginalization was a significant flaw in the formulation of these articles, if only because they obscured or ignored the deeply lived historical relation between cultural agency and political agency, the right to express oneself via different art forms being a metonymy for the right to express oneself freely in more expansive political terms, a cornerstone notion underlying advanced and progressive forms of social and political organization.[6]

Hence, expression and opinion slip over into tropes of information and media in article 19 of the UDHR. This slippage is problematic, and has become more so since these words were written, because media and information are defined in strategic ways that are a function of neoliberal thought in which the commercial and market value of these media are the preeminent concern. Considerable resources associated with mainstream media, and determining its content, are a function of advertising and commercial interests, the production of consumption. Information, such as it is information, is often associated with media as a function of the logic of the marketplace and an underlying profit-seeking motive.

Moreover, *media* and *information* are now such problematic and overdetermined terms that imagining them free and clear of the dictates of the marketplace presents an enormous challenge. So what to do with a form of expression that largely stands outside commercial purpose (with Albert Ayler's and John Coltrane's comments on improvised music and spirituality)? Furthermore, article 19 does not address how access to media and information is attained, how there exist fundamental limitations that separate people as a function of questions of access, which ultimately becomes a question of how resources are allocated, often inequitably, on a global level.

Rights language in the UDHR is also driven by less-than-transparent, implicit comparisons between the arts' aestheticization and the sciences' utilitarian benefits. Moreover, the second clause of article 27—"Everyone has the right to the protection of the moral and material interests resulting from any scientific, literary or artistic production of which he is the author"—makes explicit the link between creation and ownership, an ideology driven by capital and how it circulates, rather than by the larger ways artistic production is a crucial form of human activity whose generative, productive effects (and affects) are far more crucial and in need of protection than are localized "moral and material interests" situated in a specific author.[7] The failure of imagination here is in the way the business of authorship and creation preempts the fundamental, underlying, generative aspects of being human that make creation possible.

Improvisatory cultural practices are crucial sources of that sort of activity, and the localized material benefits accruing to authorship (however desirable their protection may be) are a considerable distance in terms of priority for protection from the key elements, like improvisation, that make creation possible. The overt absence of improvisation, an important form of activity through which agency and knowledge are created, from the UDHR is not surprising: it is part of the ecology of being human, a fundamental response and originary gesture in which experimentation and all the aspects of one's environment come together. In fairness, the elaboration of rights instruments is every bit as emergent a form of thinking as the thinking around what it means to improvise. But, that said, improvisation is figured implicitly in the document if one accepts that its universal presence as a form of cultural, adaptive, and experimental practice is a defining element of global musicking, which is also a defining element of being human.

The study *Improvisation in Nine Centuries of Western Music*, by the musicologist Ernest Thomas Ferand, claims that "there is scarcely a single field in music that has remained unaffected by improvisation, scarcely a single musical technique or form of composition that did not originate in improvisatory practice or was not essentially influenced by it. The whole history of the development of music is accompanied by manifestations of the drive to improvise" (qtd. in Bailey, *Improvisation* ix–x). If this is the case, and musical signifying is an accomplished outgrowth of the need to improvise, then as a cultural practice improvisation may have a great deal to teach about fundamental aspects of being human. Improvisation, in this sense, is an alternative narrative to reductive scenarios that limit or restrict the creative and generative expressive powers that are a key to human identity and agency in the world, literally the same area that rights discourses seek to understand and protect.[8]

So how does improvisation fit into these generalist rights constructs?

If improvisation and related tropes like "experimentation" (or even the dismissive "making it up as you go along") are underlying aspects of how human beings achieve new forms of knowledge, how they communicate those new forms, how they participate in the "cultural life of the community," and how they test the limits of "freedom of expression" (by which we also mean they test the limits of what is thinkable within a given set of circumstances), then improvisation is of primary importance in how one defines the rights set out in the UDHR, articles 19 and 27. The UDHR seeks to get at underlying principles that can be applied across all sites and cultures. And, in fact, many of the principles it elaborates are a function of multiple sites of extended, improvisatory community action and cultural practices that have culminated in emergent recognitions about what it means to have rights. But in codifying "universal" rights as it does, the UDHR becomes subject to the forces that have considerable investment in how the code operates, such as legal instruments that are loophole-ridden, that are not necessarily enforceable, and that are not always driven by similar values or outcomes as the UDHR. Moreover the UDHR is subject to how it is interpreted and applied by specific regional or state interests that may not always be coincident with the apparent values it espouses.

The use of music as a form of torture by the United Sates is in direct contravention of the UDHR, article 5, which states, "No one shall be subjected to torture or to cruel, inhuman or degrading treatment or punishment." On October 22, 2009, the National Security Archive (NSA), a nongovernmental, not-for-profit research and archival institution, filed a number of Freedom of Information Act petitions "requesting the full declassification of secret U.S. documentation on the strategy of using music as an interrogation device at Guantanamo and other detention centers" (Blanton and Doyle). The NSA simultaneously made available declassified documents detailing the use of music to "create futility in uncooperative detainees" (Blanton and Doyle), which included playing the music of Metallica, Britney Spears, and various rap musicians, among others.[9]

The petitions were filed on behalf of numerous musicians, known internationally and in the United States, including Prince, Queen, James Taylor, Bruce Springsteen, the Bee Gees, Eminem, Rage Against the Machine, and even the composers of the music behind the Barney theme song (Bob Singleton) and the Sesame Street theme music (Christopher Cerf). The executive director of the NSA, Thomas Blanton, stated that "the U.S. government turned a jukebox into an instrument of torture," arguing that "the musicians and the public have the right to know how an expression of popular culture was transformed into an enhanced interrogation technique" primarily associated with sensory deprivation (Blanton and Doyle). The NSA released excerpts from documents in which music is mentioned in relation to the torture of high-level detainees like Mohammed al-Khatani, who "had . . . been deprived of adequate sleep for weeks on end, stripped naked, subjected to loud music, and made to wear a leash and perform dog tricks," and Mohammad al-Sliha, "who was exposed to variable light patterns and rock music, to the tune of Drowning Pool's 'Let the bodies hit the floor'" (Blanton and Doyle).

The musicologist Suzanne G. Cusick avers that "sound at certain levels creates sensory overload and breaks down subjectivity and can [bring about] a regression to infantile behavior," arguing that music played at a certain volume "simply prevents people from thinking." Cusick further suggests, and this is entirely debatable, that the efficacy of music as torture "depends on the constancy of the sound, not the qualities of the music," but the notable absence of improvising jazz musicians or, for that matter, of classical composers from the list of musicians associated with torture techniques may be as much a function of soldiers' tastes as of which musics are known to cause the most psychological damage. That said, "the idea of using music in psychological warfare goes back to at least the Second World War, when Soviet forces under siege in Leningrad defiantly broadcast Dmitri Shostakovich's Seventh Symphony into no-man's-land and the Office of War Information relayed jazz and other democratic sounds into Nazi-occupied Europe. During the occupation of Germany, from 1945 to 1949, the Office of Military Government, United States (OMGUS), took control of German musical culture, discouraging nationalism and encouraging progressive approaches among younger composers" (Ross, "Futility Music").

To this all, we may add what Jonathan Pieslak describes in his book *Sound Targets: American Soldiers and Music in the Iraq War*: the use of music (primarily heavy metal and rap) by American soldiers as a self-motivational tool, as a mode of indoctrination into specific ideologies with specific focus on recruitment and "inspiration for combat," and as an interrogation tool, though here, as was the NSA, Pieslak is stymied by lack of accessible corroborating evidence due to the classification of documents relating to the torture of detainees (186).[10] Interestingly, Pieslak ends his book by musing about how music may be "more potent in the context of war than in daily life," an observation that says as much about what we don't know about the potency of music in so called daily life as it does about how tropes of militarization seem prepared to co-opt just about any form of discourse (including musical discourse) in their own self-interest (185). Ultimately, music in this context is indicative of a power relation as much as it is of a rights abuse. Cusick asks, "What better medium than music to bring into being (as a felicitous performative) the experience of the West's . . . ubiquitous, irresistible Power?" Cusick's observation is well taken: the perverse use of the transcendent, expressive force of Western music reenacts the West's imagined, transcendent military force and induces a futility response (as in "resistance is futile") in detainees tortured by it.

The examples in the work of Cusick and Pieslak largely involve rock and popular music, but, as Derek Bailey argues, these musics, even though the "instrumentalists and singers . . . have very little concern for the skills of instrumental improvisation nevertheless employ what might be called an improvising principle" (*Improvisation* 39). Furthermore, as Bailey points out, "the derivation of almost all improvisation in rock is the blues" (*Improvisation* 39). But rock is not the only place where improvisatory blues principles are at work. These principles point to the social contexts from which the blues emerged as a defining characteristic of the musical practice. And these are intimately linked with rights concerns.

Clyde Woods, a black studies scholar, reinforces this point when he argues that "attaining human rights is a fundamental category in the blues epistemology, particularly the fate of the incarcerated and the abused, since upon these pillars African American identity was born" ("Do You Know" 1013).[11] Woods makes the keen observation that "the Katrina tragedy was a blues moment . . . The picture of twenty thousand slowly dying African Americans chanting 'we want help' outside of New Orleans's Convention Center was a blues moment. It disrupted the molecular structure of a wide array of carefully constructed social relations and narratives on race, class, progress, competency, and humanity. In the blink of an eye, African Americans, an identity fraught with ambiguity, were transformed back into *black people*, a highly politicized identity" ("Do You Know" 1005).

The transformation recalls Martin Luther King Jr.'s unforgettable comment made to white segregationists: "We will wear you down with our capacity for suffering" (qtd. in McMichael 382). Katrina marked a profound destabilization of illusory rights proclamations associated with the United States as the herald and gatekeeper of democracy. Evidently not everyone is born equal. Nor is everyone treated equally. And deep, endemic, structural racism could not have been exposed more clearly in that "blues" moment.[12] Moreover, the tragedy of Katrina was exacerbated precisely because in so many ways the municipal, state, and federal institutional responses failed to deploy improvisational techniques to cope. Tricia Wachtendorf and James Kendra, a sociologist and a public administration researcher respectively, note, in an extended study of the event, that

> New Orleans is often affectionately referred to as the Birthplace of Jazz. Whether through the city's festivals that attract hundreds of thousands of attendees each year, its legendary musicians, or its dark and smoky clubs, this genre of music that demands both creativity and style—and where the concept of improvisation lies at the core of its successful performance—has become as synonymous with New Orleans as Mardi Gras. It is unfortunate, then, as we consider the loss of life and level of destruction left in the aftermath of Hurricane Katrina in September, 2005, that lack of improvisation at the organizational and multi-organizational level appears to be closely related to some of failures in the overall response.

Wachtendorf and Kendra go on to note that "the very definition of a disaster, that circumstances have exceeded a community's ability to cope, implies that some form(s) of improvisation will be necessary. If initial newspaper accounts prove accurate, the response failures in New Orleans shared inflexibility as an underlying cause. These failures were related to an inability of various government levels to construct a shared vision of what needed to be done. They were related to an inability to communicate effectively across various levels and with community constituents (in part due to the breakdown of communication technology, but also due to breakdown in organizational communication)." Constructing a shared vision, being flexible, effectively communicating among community members: these assets, long a component in improvisatory musical structures that had arisen in New Orleans, were ironically almost wholly absent from the exceptionally inadequate government response to the disaster. In their assessment of how Katrina might have been better handled, Wachtendorf and Kendra also suggest that

> the goal must be to create "learning organizations" that have the collective ability to think about the environment; to pick up signals; compare them with what is known, and then assess what is needed to fill in gaps in knowledge. Structural change is important, but cultural change is important, too.
>
> There are many lessons we should take away from this tragic disaster. Among them, we must outline authority and accountability as well as foster multi-organizational communication, coordination, and improvisation in complex and turbulent environments. We must understand that our interpretation of our social and physical environments can be just as important as the environments themselves.

In short, the very tools that ironically had been deployed by musicians in New Orleans for over a century, tools that involved communication, organization, coordination, culture, and interpretation as mediated through improvisatory practices, were the very tools that might have led to a more effective response to the tragedy. The failure to improvise intensified the tragedy. In this way, Katrina was doubly a blues moment. Not only did Katrina expose deeply racist systemic structures in the United States; it also ignored the very form of post-abyssal thinking that would have introduced improvisation as a valid response, a worthy form of knowledge deployed in a scenario in which the community was overwhelmed by the extent of the disaster. And where improvisation did occur—as it did in the numerous rescuers who risked their lives in small boats to find people trapped in their homes after the storm, and as it did with the local Wal-Mart employees who were "able to improvise on the basis of their tacit and contextual knowledge in the effective ways that they did" to distribute much needed supplies in a timely manner—remarkable interventions were made that diminished suffering in important ways (Horwitz 525).

The blues as a genre inscribes its provenance in oppression and thus marks a profound relation of the music with civil rights abuses. As an important element in improvisatory discourses of various kinds, the blues' presence cannot be denied. Even Albert Ayler's courageous explorations of dissonance and freedom in musical structures were derived from black culture (spirituals, popular music, jazz) and were associated explicitly by

Ayler himself with the blues. In an interview conducted in 1964, Ayler ex-plained: "The music that we're playing now is just a different kind of blues . . . It's the real blues, it's the new blues, and the people must listen to this music, because they'll be hearing it all the time. Because if it's not me, it'll be somebody else that's playing it. Because this is the only way that's left for the musicians to play. All the other ways have been explored" (Mandel, "Albert Ayler's Fiery Sax, Now on Film").

The historical inevitability of new forms that emerge from the old and the need for new articulations is as much a musical issue as it is a chal-lenge to wider culture. Improvisation, as a pervasive musical practice, is always already implicated both in popular culture—the kind discussed above used to torture at Guantánamo—and in new elaborations of social forms yet to be understood or fully appreciated. It is in this sense a deep-rooted social practice found in multiple forms of heterophonic musical expression. The coalition of musicians seeking to control how their music is appropriated to destructive ends by state power and the military is at some level defending general principles of musical creation and expres-sion that transcend genre and get at the fundamental rights principles and values deeply embedded in improvisation as a generative source of musical expression.

So how does improvisation fit more generally into these examples, which juxtapose rights issues with the expressive force of music and sound used in a destructive manner? The capacity to generate affective sounds is an interlinked aspect of an individual's and a community's agency. How those sounds are identified and formulated, made into objects of aesthetic and cultural value (or not) over long historical periods, has a great deal to do with improvisation as a fundamental mode of interacting creatively with one's immediate circumstances. As improvisational practices be-come codified, and they do, whether in harmonic, melodic, rhythmic or generic forms, they represent the outcome of long processes of experi-mentation and development. Their sedimentation, as both methodology (in attaining a particular end) and process (in arriving at new forms of cultural production) is a key aspect of improvisation's hidden history, as is the use of improvisational techniques to produce affective cultural prod-ucts associated with hegemonic outcomes.

Improvised cultural practices make manifest generative, creative power and agency, and the outcomes of such cultural products can be appropri-ated to hegemonic use. Rights discourses are similar, as Fischlin and Nandorfy have argued, in that they can lay the ground for meaningful, lived, cocreative life practices, or they can be appropriated as window dressing for perversions of equity and social justice.[13] Though more needs to be known about the specifics of how music has been used by the United States to torture detainees, the anomaly of one of the key proponents of global rights discourses subverting the UDHR prohibitions against torture through music alerts us to the perils of reductive assertions about any form of cultural practice in which so much is at stake.

What is at stake, both in the moment of improvisation and in the moment when a rights outcome is to be decided through one's own agency, is fundamentally provisional, uncertain, and contingent. The substance of what one decides in that moment becomes the material content of the improvisation, the enactment of agency that has social-justice implications. All such actions are profoundly interconnected and cumulative. Understanding the cultural practices that shape agency in these moments is of critical importance. Thus, the relation between improvisation and rights as cultural practices that test agency in the here and now.

The individual as the focus of rights discourses is highly problematic. Is it too much to argue that the individual is not intrinsically meaningful except in relation to the multiple skeins of relations that define the individual's agency and upon which the individual acts? This is not to say that the individual is unimportant as a component in complex social structures. Though the individual is the preeminent locus of value in Occidental rights discourses, this view is not without problems, especially since individual agency is always relational, a function of acting upon, or acting with, or being enabled through, rather than illusory notions of the individual as wholly self-authorizing and self-defining. All individuals emerge out of group relations (even if they are minimally dyadic, through kinship to parents and family), and all individuals function within environments and collectivities—ecological, social, material, intellectual, and creative—that contribute to their formation and that give them meaning as they act in relation to these over a sustained time.

Improvisation, for all its talk about individual voice, individual technical mastery, originality, and authenticity, cannot be dissociated from the communitarian sources that make music possible, to which music responds, and out of which community is sustained, critiqued, and made anew. David Borgo argues for "*improvising* music" as the appropriate term for the dynamic process of improvisational practices in which the "indissoluble relationship between performances and people, between sounds and society, that is found in every culture and time" is apparent: "While improvising music, individuals balance comfort and caprice, groups enable structure and spontaneity, and traditions become articulated by and respond to both continuity and change. Improvising music is not simply an alternative approach to composition, but rather the ongoing process of internalizing alternative value systems through music" (*Sync or Swarm* 192). In improvising music, individuals also explore their own agency in relation to others, one of the key elements in improvisatory discourses being the way the encounter is negotiated. In short, improvisation provides a significant testing ground for models of encounter that span individual voice and agency, cultural differences and similitudes (each of these presenting their respective challenges), and how to sustain discourse (or not) in the face of the multiple agencies and contingencies that come together as embodied public, performative practice.

It is clear though that in social organizations in which improvisation is seen as a process, a value, and as an important outcome, the civic and social-justice dimensions linked with group identity and group response to conditions of oppression or marginalization are also at stake. Ronald Radano's work on the composer and improviser Anthony Braxton and his cultural critique is instructive, as is George Lewis's remarkable account of the AACM. Radano cites a "special report on the AACM" (90) first published in the literary journal *Black World* (1973), in which the authors Muhal Richard Abrams and John Shenoy Jackson state the following: "The AACM is attempting to precipitate activity geared toward finding a solution to the basic contradictions which face Black people . . . [It] intends to show how the disadvantaged and the disenfranchised can come together and determine their own strategies for political and economic freedom, thereby determining their own destinies. This will not only create a new day for Black artists but for all Third World inhabitants; a new day of not only participation but also of control" (qtd. in Radano 91). The affirmation links the community status of the AACM, as a group in which improvisation is a foundational aesthetic, not only with self-determinative rights outcomes but also with exemplary modes of leadership that extend beyond the local community to the "Third World."

Participatory politics are not enough unless they also generate the "control" that permits the organization to overcome problems of oppression, disadvantage, and disengagement. The parallels between improvisatory musics and civic engagements that actively seek change are compelling. Improvisation plays out the scene of group synthesis and individual voice. But it also plays out the problem of self-determination both for the individual and for the group (the one being a function of the other, the two forever bound by cocreative and codependent circumstances). And it plays out the way participation can mutate into a form of control (over the improvisation's content, over one's contribution to the improvisation, over what the improvising group collectively has to say), even as that control remains liminal and tentative, part of a dynamic, processual response to the multiple contingencies that shape a particular improvised performance.

In both improvisation (as practiced by the AACM) and civic engagement, core values related to change are crucial. These values include the expression of collective identity through the contributory, heterophonic discourses of individuals; the development and testing of solidarity through shared engagement; and the ongoing strategic and critical thinking over how and why one engages with the process. To this may be added how improvisation and civic engagement are geared toward resolving "basic contradictions"; that is, both are dynamic processes that embody and model a form of problem solving that has profound social implications. Radano goes on to note that "the AACM's achievement as a stable, working organization could not have come without a strong commitment from its membership, and that commitment surely would not have developed without inspiration from the black-rights movement. Civil rights initiatives fueled the AACM, providing it with a compelling institutional model consistent with the Association's own social doctrine as well as a framework for voicing that doctrine in public" (91). So the case of the AACM, as an exemplary model for the linkages between rights discourses and improvisatory musickings, brings together community, large-scale social movements borne of the fight against oppression, and the need for public declamation.

Out of these shared qualities, the relations between improvised musical discourses and social-justice outcomes might be more rigorously theorized. Talking about improvisation as if it is the same in all social contexts and histories is widely off the mark, but, in even the most generalized sense of the term, core qualities are apparent. These relate to improvisation because it is processual, experimental, and an embodied performative practice. Though improvisation is marginal in terms of a widely disseminated cultural presencing, it is central in terms of its being a universal form of encounter in and with music, in and with others. Improvisation synthesizes individual and collective (sonic) histories framed as an encounter narrative in which play is a crucial form of engaging in encounter. In this sense, improvisation is a form of problem-solving and of cocreative play. It is also a form of expression in which freedom of speech and of conception are at stake precisely because it deploys powerful means to undermine and challenge conventions and normative, prescriptive, and restrictive ideologies. Improvisation's relation to free speech is even more compelling when one understands it as an expression of identity, self-determination, and agency.

But caution is to be exercised in making such assertions. As Ingrid Monson, the Quincy Jones Professor of African American Music at Harvard University, notes, "The enduring effect of modernism in jazz has always been the deeper presumption that through one's musical and artistic practice it is possible to break beyond the limits of any . . . category. This has also been one of the deepest spiritual messages of the music" (*Freedom Sounds* 317).

Any attempt to reduce improvisation conceptually is problematic: the very nature of it as a form of sonic experimentation precludes easy definitions, and adept improvisers could take any of the descriptors listed above and create an improvisation based on showing them to be inept, too restrictive, or a parody of a category that has always already been subverted by multiple improvisatory practices. And the social pertinence of improvisation, in and of itself, is not solely a function of its aesthetic content and methodologies, though these may well be made amenable to being aligned with political and rights outcomes.

The social pertinence of improvisation is both a function of its aesthetics and the inter-trammeled relation these have to those who choose to use it in relation to their own cultural practices of community and self-determination. It is, in other words, both frustratingly political and not, meaningful politically and not. It is an ideological field where contested politics may be played out and a sonic field in which any ascribed political content is inherently delimiting and reductive. Even its nonmeaning, as pure sound, if such a thing exists, is inherently political, for that points to an extralinguistic, extrainstitutional zone of human activity that, even as an imagined space, presents us with a radical alterity to prescribed conventions about what it means to be human.

That said, the core qualities mentioned above have important implications for any politics associated with them. The myriad examples of how important improvising musicians were made the objects of FBI scrutiny during the Cold War and the civil rights movement attest to this fact. Max Roach's *We Insist! Max Roach's Freedom Now Suite* has a picture on the album cover of black students protesting segregation. His *Speak, Brother, Speak!* articulates a resistant politics. He endured FBI questioning in the summer of 1965. Similarly, Duke Ellington had undergone years of FBI scrutiny dating back to the 1930s, largely for how his music and band leadership advocated for important political causes: the All-Harlem Youth conference of May 1938, the Tribute to Negro Servicemen concert in 1943, Ellington's support of the ban on poll taxes used to prevent African Americans from voting, his support of anti-Franco, anti-fascist freedom fighters in Spain, his support for refugee causes, his appearance in 1966 with James Foreman, then the leader of the Student Nonviolent Coordinating Committee.[14]

And there were others, including Cab Calloway, who supported anti-segregationists, and Charles Mingus, who, though not a "joiner," had been for some time a supporter of the civil rights and antiwar movements. Even Louis Armstrong came under FBI scrutiny because he had been uncharacteristically vocal in calling President Eisenhower "two-faced" for how he had dealt with the Arkansas governor Orval Faubus, who had used the National Guard to prevent nine black students from attending Little Rock's Central High School (Lehren).

Revered practitioners of improvised musicking were frequently associated with political resistance during this period, with the threat they posed seen as a function of their celebrity and public presence, more so than any inherent qualities associated with their music. But what if the reason for this public presence was as a function of what their music represented, the social, political, and aesthetic consciousness that it stood for, the creative challenges to conventional and normative thinking that it posed? This is an unresolved question, but improvisation always already has the potential in it for alignment with liberatory forces that challenge established order. It would be naive to think that this can be its only meaning, its only alignment, the appropriative forces of neoliberal culture being perhaps up to the task of shaping any form of cultural utterance to its ends, the wholesale commodification of rap music into commercial culture being a sad example in point.

Ingrid Monson, in the coda of *Freedom Sounds*, asks the following pertinent question: "But is there anything inherently moral, ethical, progressive, rebellious, or visionary about improvisation per se?" (317). She answers in the negative and then elaborates:

> To argue that improvisation itself—that is, the manipulation of sounds, timbres, rhythms, pitches, and composition in real time—does not guarantee ethical virtue, however, is not to say that jazz improvisers did not play an active role in articulating a social and political vision, but that vision is located in *people* and what they do rather than in the formal properties of improvisation itself. Improvisation, after all, is one of the near universals of music. Virtually all known musical cultures engage in some form of improvisation (yes, even Western classical music), even if some social groups or cultures do not value it very highly . . . The particular resonance of music and politics in jazz history and its progressive ethos comes not from its privileged articulation of freedom in musical form . . . but from the way musicians and their audiences have responded to the juncture of music and larger historical and social forces. How a musician such as John Coltrane, Dave Brubeck, or Max Roach connected them is a matter of both aesthetic agency and historical moment. The musical process of improvisation models the possibility of that engagement but cannot bequeath it alone. The association of freedom and the sounds of jazz is part of a historical process, not only a musical one. (317–18)

Like Archie Shepp's comments cited as the epigraph to this book's introduction, which make no claims for music to be productive of social change but which do make a statement about the importance of the artist's agency and sense of responsibility, Monson is reluctant to align improvised jazz with something that is inherently political, progressive, liberatory, and the like. This is an important move, on both Shepp's and Monson's part, in maintaining the creative freedom associated with the idiom: for if the minute categories of meaning begin to foreclose on the openness of signification that is inherent in improvised expression, the game is lost. But Monson's and Shepp's remarks are an important locus of emergent discussions on what to make of improvisation as both a musical and a cultural practice, inflected by history and its makers, and as a contributory force to history (and to historical agency) when aligned with communities that seize hold of its musical and extramusical signifying powers. Monson's view should be modified: no improvisation, or music generally, for that matter, is ever intrinsically, in and of itself, a guarantor of ethical positioning, visionary comportment, or resistant politics. But music is never anything *in and of itself*. It is always a function of relational identities that are both synchronous and diachronous. It is always in history. It is always located in people—both those who listen and those who play.[15] And the multiple, genre-defying, category-subverting representations that collectively reference what improvisation means, do express a notion of what one might call a formal politics, that is, a politics embedded in form as expressed by historically located musicians. The musician, then, is the ligature between those suppressed or unthought ideologies that reside in form and the historical contingencies that give both meaning.

In short, music cannot be created apart from the historical contingencies out of which it grows and into which it feeds. And, as both Shepp and Monson imply, it is part of a historical process, part of a complex of representations that contribute to a particular moment. Musical process, to borrow from Monson, is always already inherently historical, and cultural critics who step into this terrain need perhaps to reconsider traditional tropes associated with music as a form of pure expression that is inherently ex tempore, extrahistorical, extralinguistic, and beyond any meaning that can be put into words. This is not to say that there are not dimensions of musical experience that are all those things, or that can be perceived to be so.

But even such a perception can be historically grounded, and can find meaning as something that is understood to be more than meaningful. The key in all this is to open the door to modes of inquiry that are not reductive: music's semiotic field is too vast a terrain and improvisation too important a phenomenon for easy conclusions and settled assumptions. Music never was and never will be ahistorical, as much as some might wish it to be. That said, if one accepts this slight adjustment to Monson's argument, is not the next step in any inquiry into the rights content of an improvisation a more rigorous application of theories that make sense of specific improvisatory utterances in relation to specific histories?

A short quote from the *Grove Music Online* article on improvisation, by Barry Kernfeld (also the general editor of *The New Grove Dictionary of Jazz*), addresses its function in relation to jazz: "Improvisation is generally regarded as the principal element of jazz since it offers possibilities of spontaneity, surprise, experiment and discovery, without which most jazz would be devoid of interest." Kernfeld goes on to note, "It is . . . demonstrably untrue that all jazz must involve improvisation. Many pieces that are unquestionably classifiable as jazz are entirely composed before a performance, and take the form of an arrangement, either fixed in notation or thoroughly memorized by the players." These comments betray a particular historical understanding of jazz and improvisation, one in which both terms are perceived to be stable and codependent, something they are not.

Kernfeld's notion that "spontaneity, surprise, experiment and discovery" are key elements of improvisation are no doubt in some general sense true, though with important qualifications about the preparations that go into being spontaneous (as with Coltrane's incessant practicing), the conjunction of high order musicianship and creative imagination that are necessary to produce surprise, and the underlying ideologies that produce experiment and discovery (in both the musician and the audience). Which is to say that none of these terms are ahistorical, without multiple and deep contexts out of which they are produced. To jump from the generalizations about these improvisatory qualities to saying that jazz without them would be "devoid of interest" is an excessively reductive reading of what constitutes jazz as an inherently improvisatory cultural practice (this assuming of course that *jazz* itself has any meaning or coherence as a moniker in these sorts of discussions). One might just as easily say that any music made that does not deploy "spontaneity, surprise, experiment and discovery" would be empty of interest. But what is interesting in Kernfeld's definition is the use of these key terms as synecdoches for jazz. There is no talk of counterpoint, harmony, melody, rhythm, expansive instrumental techniques, or new timbres and sounds brought about by innovative forms of instrumentation, all of which jazz has in abundance, as do most forms of musical improvisation.

Here, jazz is reduced to effects that are extramusical. This slippage is particularly interesting because it covertly diminishes jazz, part of a long trajectory in musicological criticism of doing so (and this has a great deal to do with sublimated, racialized discourses and unfortunate precedents having to do with how musical genres are assigned place within conventional hierarchies of relative value). But it also equates jazz with ontologies (spontaneity, surprise) and epistemologies (experiment, discovery) that give it meaning. Moreover, Kernfeld immediately reverses his own analysis when he argues that not all jazz need be improvisatory, as if to suggest that jazz, seen in this light, derives its value from musical qualities associated with Western art music, a concept Kernfeld associates with nonimprovised jazz.

Kernfeld argues that jazz is jazz because of improvisation, which allows for jazz's only redeeming features, features rooted in spontaneity and experimentation. But jazz can involve nonimprovised forms that are linked to Western art music. So the intrinsic worth of jazz as improvised music, according to Kernfeld, is its reliance on social meanings inherent in improvisation, and not on the musical qualities it manifests, and nonimprovised jazz derives its value from its relation to Western art music. Both views subtly diminish jazz as a musical form while also taking note of how that form encapsulates both forms of social practice that are spontaneous creative acts and experimental practices that lead to new discoveries. So at the same time that Kernfeld repeats historical tropes of musicological value that are familiar and reductive, he does somehow get at how jazz generically allows for multiple forms of representation and is at once a cultural practice and a historicized form of music.

Taking the time to look at these assertions a tad more carefully is important because it shows the degree to which discourses that have authority (the *Grove* being the gold standard for encyclopedic knowledge relating to music generally) can be driven by clichés, themselves driven by historical contingencies that make their power felt as interpretation and as a form of making history.

Again, reductive tropes based on outmoded historical models need to be revised, and emergent forms of discourse thinking through what "improvisation" means in relation to histories of civic engagement, social justice and injustice, and deceptive interpretive tropes that have held sway for too long need to be revivified.

Again, because improvisation is related to modes of civic engagement and rights discourses, it is important to understand how making meaning of improvisation is as much a function of how improvisation makes meaning of the listener as it is of anything else.

The sonic upset, challenges to what is permissible or thinkable in improvised musical discourse, rebellious squawks, itinerant melodies, repeated cyclical patterns that disrupt conventional time, and importune scratchings and whistles, which are all part of improvised music's repertoire, point to how sound can be a force in the world, both consonant and dissonant, both meaningful and more than meaningful. What improvisation theory must grapple with is why and how this cultural form, through which so much music has passed, continues to sustain and make new meaning in spite of its relegation to the margins of normative discourse, even as it survives and thrives in multiple sites where it is compelled into being.

CHAPTER 3

IMPROVISING COMMUNITY

Rights and Improvisation as Encounter Narratives

In discussing the relationship between improvisatory cultural theory and the events of May 1968 in France, George Lewis draws on the work of the Swiss sociologist Alfred Willener, who argues, "Whether collective or individual, improvisation presupposed the dialectical synthesis created by a group or an individual, redefining known elements, elements that have just been played and experienced, while inventing new elements in the course of the activity itself" (qtd. in G. Lewis, *Power* 238). This sociological definition of improvisation points to two fundamental, originary dialectics: the first between the collective and individual, the second between the known and the invention of the new. Both are predicated on encounter models in which improvisation provides the setting and the model for enacting the encounter.

In this context, improvisation can be theorized as a space in which conventions for encounter are modeled, tested, reconceived, critiqued, and renewed or destroyed. Rights discourses, which also are predicated on encounter models, run parallel to improvisatory discourses, with rights norms mediating the way encounters turn out. The encounter parallel to be drawn between improvised performances and rights discourses entails a form of performative embodiment, a material enactment of the encounter that transforms, that reveals intransigence, that ends unsuccessfully.

Improvisation, or rights discourse, for that matter, is not somehow infallibly progressive, inherently positivistic, or even necessarily desirable. Much depends on contexts and contingencies that circumscribe how improvisation and rights discourses are enacted in the public sphere. A dictatorship or a corrupt government that implements human rights tribunals to whitewash human rights abuses erodes the credibility of genuine rights organizations seeking to redress abuses and violations. Rights instruments that have no force in law are similar. Governments that profess to abide by generalized, universal declarations about rights but that fail to ratify those declarations or give them the force of law in their own localized legal contexts undermine the material realities that rights as a form of civic action must acquire to have lived, real consequence. Empty policy declarations against poverty, homelessness, access to adequate food and medicine, meant to produce the illusion of concern under the guise of rights advances, are rife, even among some of the most rights-conscious countries on the planet. The distinction between vacuous talk deployed strategically in the name of rights and embodied rights practices has material outcomes.

Improvised music figures here because, in its most achieved utterances, it is a remarkable embodied cultural practice associated with diasporic black culture's struggle against oppression as a form of resistance, of critical commentary, and of community organization. Improvisation, as an act of artistic freedom that tests our capacity to generate unique performative utterances in the moment, has political meaning in this context, if only as a symbolic staging of the right to speak freely, the capacity to take action. It embodies publicly a basic human right—to make music, to be creative—and is an exemplary way of confronting oppressive realities through sonic dissension generated by and for a community. The artistic statements made by an Ornette Coleman, a John Coltrane, or an Albert Ayler, to mention three musicians whose aesthetics are predicated on improvisation, are remarkable not only for their musical content, but for what that content has to say by way of its exemplary demonstration of creative ingenuity and freedom. The embodied public act of signifying in the ways these three musicians did (and continue to do through their recordings) has profound rights dimensions as enacted practice, one of the few spaces in the public sphere where this sort of exploratory discourse is to be found testing the limits of what is musically thinkable in the moment.

The concept of "freedom" here is paramount. Listening to Albert Ayler describe, in his quietly articulate voice, the enormous sense of freedom he experienced when visiting Scandinavia conveys the stakes for these musicians, for whom acting out artistic and spiritual freedom in ways that commented on their own individuality as part of a larger community was a critical aspect of their performance practice (Collin; Ayler states, "When I come over here, I feel free, quite free, really free, I feel really free"). Ayler's comments reference both his music's underlying aesthetic and philosophical orientations and his identity as a black American. He was, according to the saxophonist Jan Garbarek, in Scandinavia "in search of folk music and shamanistic songs" (Toop 133). In a short, mystical declaration called "To Mr. Jones—I Had a Vision," heavily influenced by the discourse of the Book of Revelation that Ayler published in Amiri Baraka's short-lived arts journal, *The Cricket—Black Music in Evolution*, Ayler writes: "I saw in a vision the new Earth built by God coming out of Heaven. Years ago they called it New Jerusalem. It was a solid foundation built by God himself. It is not like the foundation that we have now where men seek to kill each others' spirit" (29).

Coltrane made enigmatic spiritual declarations that were rooted in his musical and political consciousness. Likewise, Ayler's aesthetics cannot be separated from this sort of declaration, in which he envisions a "new Earth" where "kill[ing] each others' spirit" is no longer the norm. The trope invokes at a distance, and via the language of Revelation, the liberatory discourse that musicians like Ayler were battling to create as a function of the material realities grounded in racism and oppression against which they were struggling. And speaking specifically about music in a *DownBeat* interview in 1966, Ayler averred, "When music changes, people change too. The revolution in jazz took place a long time ago. But, just this year, something happened . . . Today it seems the world is trying to destroy itself . . . unkindness, hypocrisy, injustice, and hard labor that enables a human being to earn very little" (qtd. in Hentoff, "Albert Ayler" 17).

Here Ayler explicitly links music with resistance to and commentary on injustice and poverty, and argues that music is transformative. New forms of musicking allow new forms of thought to emerge. Musical changes have meaning in a wider context, even if only as marginalized or symbolic enactments of alternatives to hegemonic norms. Their value lies not in commerce or in the material resources associated with them but in the resistant symbolic content of generative, creative social practices.

The bassist Ron Carter echoes Ayler's comments about the relation between musical and social change. Carter, in an interview in 1969, stated, "Whenever there has been a major change in jazz, there's been a major change in everything else afterward. It's incredible how it happens. Freedom music to me represents the younger musicians getting tired of the establishment. The establishment to me is chord progressions and a thirty-two bar form. The student radicals are like the freedom jazz players who want to bypass most of the present standards for playing a tune . . . In 1959, when Ornette Coleman hit New York, he predicted the social changes musically" (A. Taylor 63). Carter's comments reveal the degree of self-awareness in the musicians themselves as the new musical forms associated with improvisation fused with the antihegemonic, civil rights discourses of the moment, these musicians aligning themselves, as Ayler indicates, against noncreative, destructive forces loose in the world, forces that black Americans had been confronting for centuries.

Trumpeting Rights: Improvisation and Witnessing

Ayler is not alone in his critique of destructive forces at loose in the world. Nor is he alone in linking music (without idealizing it) with values opposed to those forces. The improvising trumpeter and composer Wadada Leo Smith offers the following analysis, similar in tone to Ayler's:

> We have a world society now that has built a new generation of ideas about solving conflict based off of war, or creating conflict to dominate other societies, based off of war and economics. And it has destroyed the human heart right now. And this repair—and there's a lot to repair and it's going to take a lot of sincere artists to do it—and right now I'm afraid I don't have much trust in what's going to make the repair. And the reason I don't have any trust in it is because art is like every other system right now, and it has become commercial, you see. Now there's an underground, and there's always an underground, but by and large the commercialization of art has taken away the value that art has in society. It has lost that value. (Sumera, "Wadada")

Smith's analysis, coming after 9/11 and during the extended nadir of George W. Bush's presidency, is no naive notion of art as the cure-all. Failed models of conflict resolution tied to interlinked military and economic models that have consistently shown their inability to offer civilized alternatives are rife, and these are tied with the commercialization of art, which inherently diminishes its ethical, and its redemptive, reparative value. The "underground," and by this Smith seems to be referring to the marginal sites in which creative musicking and improvisatory practices that are inherently noncommercial are occurring, is one of the rare sites where this equation is less than stable.

The register in which this sort of thinking operates is wholly concomitant with rights discourses that locate global injustices in relation to state-sanctioned, militarized, violent responses to social and economic inequities as at the root of most of the problems facing "world society." Music is one form of resistance to these, but it too is under attack as a force for change and alternative thinking. In Smith's terms, music is a form of knowledge and communication, and it has a latent power that has nothing to do with its commercial viability. The underground community that nourishes and preserves its ethical value is, in this analysis, culturally significant and meaningful in a broader context that relates to how art and larger social forms and movements seeking rights advances intersect.

The Cricket—Black Music in Evolution, cited earlier, is an interesting case of a community of improvising musicians, a jazz commons, gathering around a clearly articulated idea of music as a political force in the world:

> The editorial in the first issue of *The Cricket* spells out the publication's inspiration: "The true voices of Black Liberation have been the Black musicians. They were the first to free themselves from the concepts and sensibilities of the oppressor." Subtitled *Black Music in Evolution*, the magazine was created by Amiri Baraka (then LeRoi Jones), Larry Neal, and A. B. Spellman in 1968 in the spirit of the hip, improvised come-to-consciousness of Black Nationalism, using the perspective of the music being created within it as a base.
>
> *The Cricket* took its title from a music gossip newspaper printed at the turn of the century by New Orleans cornet master Buddy Bolden [famed for his constant improvising]. Like its namesake it was defiantly street level. Within its visually ascetic, mimeographed pages, it resonated with the same aura of revolutionary spirit, city street authenticity, and inter-artistic collaboration that defined the Black Arts Movement of Harlem in the 1960.
>
> Just consider the names, the conjuring all-star syllables of a revolutionary moment in history: Sun Ra, Milford Graves, James T. Stewart, Sonia Sanchez, Don L. Lee, Clyde Halisi, Stanley Crouch, Cecil Taylor, Mwanafunzi Katibu, Albert Ayler, Willie Kgositile, Aaron Ibn Pori Pitts, Archie Shepp, Stevie Wonder, Ornette Coleman and more—and all that in just four issues published over only two years. (*The Cricket—Black Music in Evolution*)

The *Cricket* editorial specifically links musical concepts tied to black diasporic musics with a liberatory politics: its point of view was heavily inflected by the belief that throwing off the concepts and sensibilities of the "oppressor" can be accomplished through music.

Music is, in the *Cricket*'s estimation, the first cultural form to accomplish this liberation. And the long list of musicians given in the citation were some of the greatest, most radical, improvising musicians alive at the time. In such a context, improvisation, as a form of rights-assertive expression, an affirmation of contrary sensibilities and values, had tremendous symbolic and ideological power associated with it, however marginalized it was in normative musical cultures. The influence of such thinking in a rights context is not to be underestimated. The point is that the *Cricket* was articulating that there were strategies of empowerment available, that emancipation did in fact have a voice (many voices), and that freedom from oppression was achievable.

Gil Scott-Heron's poem "Is That Jazz?" iterates the crucial power of musicians to self-fashion in visionary and politically meaningful and lasting ways, at the same time as he undermines the facile labeling of such musical acts as "jazz":

> *'Trane* struck a vein of laughter and pain
> Adventures the mind could explore.
> *Stevie* and *Bob* talk of freedom and "jam"
> In their own individual ways.
> Playing and singing as long as its [*sic*] bringing
> A message in all that it says.
>
> . . .
>
> I take pride in what's mine—is that really a crime—
> When you know I ain't got nothing else?
> Only millions of sounds pick me up when I'm down;
> Let me salvage a piece of myself.
> What it has will surely last but is that Jazz?

Scott-Heron identifies the key tropes of improvisation as a form of rights discourse here: exploratory expression, freedom, individuality of voice, political content and messaging, and redemption and hope are made possible through sounds. Pride in "what's mine" is associated with musical expression: identity and sound connect to make redemptive meaning. "Freedom" and "jam" (as tropes associated with improvisation) resonate with each other, both as musical strategies and as political and cultural ideals, and they do so even beyond the underground of improvised jazz utterances and are to be found in popular musical practices associated with musicians like Stevie Wonder and Bob Marley.

Musical imagination is a metonymy for other imaginative spaces, other cultural practices that make human potential possible. And making human potential a realizable outcome underpins a profound relation to rights discourses that is inherent in the music. As Sun Ra advised so cogently, "Use your imagination and get out of the most drab places by simply holding on to the imagination and making it real" (Toop 31). Or, as Ra used to declare before he left the planet, "If you find earth boring, just the same old same thing, come on and sign up for Outer Spaceways Incorporated," sounding a profound and salutary commitment to enabling aggrieved peoples to become makers of their own histories and futures.

Scott-Heron's comments are part of a powerfully antireductive stream of critical thinking about the origins of the term *jazz* as a strategy of limiting what it can mean. Archie Shepp's famous comment in *DownBeat*, for instance, argues that "'Jass' is an ofay's [derogatory term of West African origin meaning "white person"] word for a nigger's music . . . Give me leave to state this unequivocal fact: jazz is the product of the whites—the ofays—too often my enemy. It is the progeny of the blacks, my kinsmen" (Shepp). Wadada Leo Smith suggests that from its inception to Ornette Coleman, the music may be designated as jazz, but thereafter it is creative music (Horton). Cecil Taylor avers that "the greatness of jazz occurs because it includes all the *mores* and folkways of Negroes during the last fifty years," going on to suggest that "in particular, the intellectual and revolutionary character of bop was seen as a foundation for this music: 'for jazzmen . . . have come to the beautiful and logical conclusion that bebop was perhaps the most legitimately complex, emotionally rich music to come out of this country . . .' The revolutionary character of this music, therefore, functioned through simultaneous acceptance and rejection of the constructs of jazz history. It was the mainstream conceptions of black music history, not the history itself, which 'anti-jazz' artists sought to debunk" (Goodheart, "Jazz and Society").

Wadada Leo Smith takes these thoughts further in comments from his book *Notes (8 Pieces) Source a New World Music: Creative Music* (1973), when he states, "I, a black man, a creative improviser, strive, through my improvisations and as an improviser to pay homage to the black, the blackness of a people, and that these creations themselves are for all, and the natural laws that are prevailing under these creations are relative as they are interpreted or perceived by beings of other peoples and thus they must extract what is of universality for themselves to each and every individual, but on the level and in the expression that is clothed in the garment of improvisation, and i contend that only the principles underlying these creations are universal to my people" ("Notes on My Music [Part 1]"). The underlying message of identity and communitarian outreach (echoing Gil Scott-Heron's comments) is loud and clear here, with improvisation a fundamental expression of both establishing and paying homage to black identity.

It is useful to remember, as Krin Gabbard does in *Hotter than That: The Trumpet, Jazz, and American Culture*, that improvisation in this context emerges out of the specific histories associated with the "violence and institutionalized racism" that African Americans had faced for centuries. Gabbard notes how "few gestures of resistance were available. Ecstatic worship in the Sanctified Churches was one. Playing the blues was another. It was, after all, the music of an oral, vernacular culture that flourished outside the schools and conservatories of white society and refused to accept the established musical hierarchies. The blues singer would bend notes, cry, moan, and grunt, always in a voice completely unlike any white singer's" (78). These musical gestures, profoundly linked to specific cultural contexts, were, as Gabbard argues, picked up by instrumentalists like the trumpeter Buddy Bolden, from New Orleans, who gave voice to the blues in new instrumental ways that carried forward the improvisations of blues song into new contexts. Such African American musical forms and contexts echoed the antihierarchical, resistant, and vernacular expressions in direct conflict with the injustices of a culture predicated on racist exploitation.

Furthermore, musical improvisation is the conduit through which these cultural values are transmitted as a way of affirming an identity that is both context-specific and universal. It would be a mistake to interpret Smith's comments solely from the perspective of black nationalist discourses. Smith clearly associates black identity with improvisation as a signature cultural strategy (a form of agency, as per Gabbard's arguments about Bolden and the blues) that is nonetheless "for all" and a function of "natural laws" that are "relative" to one's cultural situation. The language, however idealized, is wholly consistent with rights discourses that balance the need to respect independent cultural identities and the specific histories from which they have emerged, while at the same time finding mediating strategies that are common to all. This negotiation is necessary for handling encounter, cultural difference, and conflict. For Smith, then, improvisation figures as an intercultural bridge, whose universalist, co-creative potential makes it useful.

This bridging effect is crucial to understanding the social implications of jazz: "The role of jazz . . . and the reason it is important, is that it has provided, especially since the early 1960s, a site for the production of oppositional identities through its subcultures of integration . . . The connections among jazz, political activism, and racial identity in the early 1960s show that jazz music historically has provided sites of integrationist subcultures in which racial boundaries exist but at moments do not reproduce the same power relations as in mainstream society" (McMichael 381). Though this insight frames integrationist tendencies in terms of white-black divides, it is important to understand that improvisatory contexts also allowed for differing identities not based on ethnic difference to come together to explore musical and social meaning.

In the legal language associated with most rights instruments and paradigms, this sort of an approach is not even close to being on the table as a viable strategy for thinking about achieving rights outcomes. Smith, in a 2003 interview with Howard Mandel some thirty years after his comments above, is frank about the failures of this sort of thinking to affect rights outcomes directly:

> it was exciting at that time [the 1970s], how music interacted in a social way to exact change in society. Freedom is something we were after in both the social and esthetic moment. Musically, freedom served as a model for whoever could grasp it. Of course, socially we failed—most obviously in the area of human rights, because power and wealth still control how people [deal] with each other. Enron is an example of how the old type of culture has prevailed. But artists can use their visions to transform society by getting people to see ordinary stuff anew, and open up. The artist is a mediator who helps people see things in new ways, and can also serve as a moral visionary. ("Yo Wadada!")

In spite of Smith's disillusionment and his open recognition of the limitations of artistic discourse, he maintains that the artist who works out of the context of seeking freedom can be transformative, a "mediator" and a "moral visionary." Exemplarity in the face of a world that does not change is still important; potentially transformative iterations of ideals and visions are necessary even if they do not effect immediate change.

Some eighteen years prior to this statement, Smith had made an album entitled *Human Rights* (released on Kabell), using improvisatory free jazz techniques that frequently take the music in the direction of so-called new music. Among others, Smith deploys reggae heavily influenced by Rastafarian ideals, rock influenced in part by the Mahavishnu Orchestra, which had in its two iterations explored the relations among improvisation, the ethical meaning of music, and world music. And on the album one also finds alternative instrumentations drawn from world music contexts, such as Japanese koto, African mbira, Chinese hand gongs, and synth. Over the course of Smith's lifetime he has consistently attended to the linkages between musical improvisation and social-justice issues, with the release in 2012 of the monumental four-CD album *Ten Freedom Summers*, dedicated to exploring through improvised and composed musicking the resonances of the civil rights movement from 1954 to 1964. A three-night performance event that uses videography (but no spoken word interjections), *Ten Freedom Summers* has a three-part structure grouped around the following rubrics: "Defining Moments in America," "What Is Democracy?" and "Ten Freedom Summers." Titles of the pieces include references to Fannie Lou Hamer and the Mississippi Freedom Democratic Party; Emmett Till, the fourteen-year-old Mississippi boy who was murdered in 1955 for allegedly flirting with a white woman; the Freedom Riders Ride; Medgar Evers, the African American civil rights activist murdered in 1963 by the white supremacist Byron De La Beckwith; Thurgood Marshall; and the Civil Rights Act of 1964, among many others. Both a memorial and an incitement to further reflection, *Ten Freedom Summers* has Smith deploying a lifetime of experience as a creative improvising musician to produce remarkable musical statements about the "movement." In program notes and interviews, Smith explicitly aligns the work with the social, political, and philosophical history of the United States in relation to the civil rights movement, and uses improvisatory techniques to produce startling, affective soundscapes meant to provoke further reflection on the movement as a whole, but also on the creative improvised aesthetic common to both the movement and the music with which it is associated. As Matthew Sumera makes clear in his liner notes to *Ten Freedom Summers*, discussing the connections between music and the civil rights movement, "Too often we think about the two as if they were only tangentially related, as if the latter were simply influenced by the former. But this misses the point. Rather, both were interrelated, each crucial to the development and formation of the other, music influencing the movement as much as the movement influenced the music. Indeed, this has been the traditional role of music in global human rights campaigns throughout history, and especially in the twentieth century." The release of *Ten Freedom Summers* coincided with another Smith composition explicitly tied to the 2011–12 Occupy movement. "Occupy the World for Life, Liberty and Justice" premiered in December of 2011. These works exhibit a consistent trajectory over some thirty-plus years of musical activity tied to a sophisticated practice of thinking improvisation in relation to rights contexts.

The earlier *Human Rights* album, from 1982, is a remarkably proleptic musical and political statement—a synthetic and visionary representation of how rights discourses and improvised music can be aligned. The side-long, thirty-minute improvisation on side two of the recording is entitled "Humanismo justa tutmonda muziko" [Human rights world music] as if to suggest a direct connection between the two. The cut begins with Smith's solo voice stating words originally uttered by Haile Selassie and turned into a song by Bob Marley: "Until the philosophy which holds one race superior and another inferior is finally and permanently discredited and abandoned; that until there are no longer first class and second class citizens of any nation; until the colour of a man's skin is of no more significance than the colour of his eyes; that until basic human rights are equally guaranteed to all without regards to race; that until that day the dream of lasting peace, world citizenship, and the rule of international morality will remain but [an] illusion to be pursued but never attained." These words, which are spoken, are then followed by a short prelude sung by Smith, in which he states:

> People of the world we want to be free
> So let's unite for harmony
> Freedom is yet a liberty
> Human Rights is not a freedom
> We are all one 'cause in JAH's creation
> There is not one thing unconnected
> To that golden cosmic thread
> That fabricates the universe

The musical substance of the improvisation (recorded in 1982 by Tokyo Radio, in Japan, with a remarkable performance by Tadao Sawai on koto and percussion) is clearly framed within this vision of world citizenship and international morality.

Moreover, the album notes clearly show that the spoken and sung words heard at the beginning of the track are to be followed by the musical exposition of the words in the improvisation that follows: in the interpretative framework of the album the two are indissociably linked. In fact, the five lyrics associated with the album ("Freedom Song," "Rastafari #4," "Don't You Remember," "Ethiopia / Africa," and "Humanismo justa tutmonda muziko" [Human rights world music]) elaborate a consistent focus on tropes of freedom, interconnectedness, unity, justice, historical remembrance, and the like—all while placing racial discrimination and hierarchical structures of superiority and inferiority at the ideological center of the rights issues Smith is getting at.

In "Freedom Song" the lyrics make the comparison between freedom as the "eternal emotion of love" and justice as the "intelligence of the great force of the world." Linked to these are images on the *Human Rights* album cover of a "Stop Apartheid" sticker, of Haile Selassie, the emperor of Ethiopia from 1930 to 1974 and a key messianic symbol in Rastafarian belief systems but also a key figure in international movements that promoted internationalism, multilateralism, and notions of collective security, and a quotation from "The Revelation of John." The album cover also prominently features a quote from Bob Marley, and another brief, visionary, ethical statement by Smith: "A time must come, when an African child anywhere on the continent can walk from one end to the other, and never be hungry, never be in any kind of danger. A time must come when that child can walk the breadth of Africa and be protected by every eye that falls upon him."

The integrity of the album, then, as a total musical, ethical concept is clear and purposeful. And the improvisatory aspects of its music-making, not to mention the world-music aspects of its formal content, are not to be separated from its ethical content, its advocacy of a rights worldview that is entirely consistent with other such discourses to be found in other arenas where rights matters were being debated. The specific black-diasporic consciousness associated with the American civil rights movement, contexts active in *Human Rights*, plays a key role in how the album signifies and disseminates its meanings.[1] And the relative obscurity of the *Human Rights* recording, even in jazz and new-music circles, points to both its conceptual marginalization in relation to hegemonic and nonhegemonic circles, and its articulation of uncomfortable truths that mainstream music and culture had little desire to hear.

Human Rights is not an isolated instance of a "free jazz" concept album that uses experimental, hybrid musical techniques and vocalizations in a sophisticated rights context. The trumpeter Freddie Hubbard's collaboration in 1971 on *Sing Me a Song of Songmy: A Fantasy for Electromagnetic Tape* with the Turkish composer and experimentalist İlhan Mimaroğlu (listed as the composer in the album's credits) is another remarkable example of improvised music, blended with composed music, electronic music (analog synth), and musique concrète, extending the musical language of rights discourses. Hybridization and openness to difference are key features of improvisatory musical discourses, and here they are deployed in ways that map onto similar cultural hybrids associated with rights sentiments that extend across multiple cultural sites.

The album protested the torture and mass murder on March 16, 1968, at My Lai (Songmy), in Vietnam, of approximately five hundred people, most of them women, children, and the elderly, conducted by a unit of the U.S. Army led by Lieutenant William Calley, now a disgraced war criminal.[2] Hubbard and Mimaroğlu's collaboration is a stunning example of multiple cultures, musical, ethnic, and political, coming together to make a profound comment on rights abuses. Hubbard appeared on John Coltrane's *Ascension* (1965), Eric Dolphy's *Out to Lunch!* (1964), and Ornette Coleman's *Free Jazz* (1960), albums widely regarded as high-water marks in improvised musicking and as some of the most significant expressions of avant-garde music produced in the twentieth century. And he had replaced Lee Morgan in Art Blakey's Jazz Messengers in 1961, all a testament to his remarkable gifts as an improviser.[3]

Sing Me a Song of Songmy evokes the rights struggles of the 1960s by addressing, among other issues, the Vietnam War, the civil rights movement, student revolt (as at Kent State), the Manson murders and what made them possible, and widespread political oppression. The music is eclectic, with the free jazz of Hubbard and his fellow players a major component of the rich electronic and experimentalist textures created by Mimaroğlu. The texts range from poems by Fazil Hüsnü Dağlarca, a Turkish poet known for his antimilitarist stance, excerpts from Kierkegaard's "On the Dedication to 'That Single Individual,'" Che Guevara, and Susan Atkins (whose grand jury testimony from the Manson Family trials is recited in the disturbing opening track, "Threnody for Sharon Tate").[4]

The album's cover artwork, depicting a group of robotic soldiers about to discharge its weapons on a group of women (some of them pregnant) and children is Pablo Picasso's *Massacre in Korea* (1951), a painting that protested American intervention in Korea and that self-consciously cites other well-known antiwar paintings, especially Francisco Goya's *The*

Third of May, 1808, an influential depiction of the horrors of war. The cover image provides a visual echo of the cut on the album devoted to the Kent State slaughter, on May 4, 1970, of four unarmed students (and the wounding of nine others) protesting the American invasion of Cambodia, "What a Good Time for Kent State." One of the shortest cuts on the album, the piece explodes into a frenzy of improvised playing by Hubbard and his band, a chorus in the background chanting the names of the students killed by the Ohio National Guard: Allison Krause, Jeffrey Miller, Sandra Scheuer, and William Knox Schroeder. The chorus sings, "Flowers are better than bullets, they said," as the piece flows into the next elegiac track "Monodrama," which mixes Hubbard's lyrical, free playing with electronica and haunting textures created by Mimaroğlu.

As a whole, the album makes multiple gestures toward wider political and cultural contexts with significant rights implications. Part of its expressive effect is a function of the musical forms it blends, using improvisatory techniques that seamlessly emerge from more composed moments. In "Black Soldier," for instance, a string quartet provides the disturbing spoken lyrics recited by Hubbard with musical textures that are then picked up by Hubbard and his fellow musicians in "Interlude 1," an extended and blistering improvisation that follows immediately out of the cut imitating impressionistically the sounds of war. The two cuts contrast the challenge to black soldiers not to further enslave themselves through participating in unjust wars. The remarkable musical improvisation that follows is a performance of freedom. Dağlarca's poem "Black Soldier," to which the musicians respond, states,

> You black man,
> U.S. Army
> Private First Class
> For freedom you shoot down
> your own freedom.
> Your body lies crucified on a steel cross.
> The cross is profit and forced slavery too.
> It sells an abuse.
> Your palm bleeds whenever they shake your hand
>
> You black man
> U.S. Army
> Private First Class

You are the night,
which has locked itself into darkness.
(authors' transcription)

On the album, the tracks follow a musical logic that is closely tied with the expressive affect and content of the words spoken. Immediately following these two cuts is a track that opens with the Vietnamese poet Nha-Khe reciting lines from his "Lullabye for a Child in War": "And yet there could be / love and kisses . . . I hope love will never / Never forsake me." A chorus repeats the poem, followed by elegiac music that ends with a postlude played by Hubbard as a solo improvisation that evokes and comments on the sentiment, "And Yet There Could Be Love." Chris Searle summarizes:

> For a jazz tradition that spoke of political realities through implication, code and ambivalence, there had been nothing like this before. Here was an album that was dedicated to absolute cultural resistance and fully explicit anti-government protest, being put into the heart of the market by a major record company [Atlantic], featuring the work of an already established jazz virtuoso who had been given full license to follow his theme through Vietnamese and Turkish poetry, Brahms' *Ein Deutsches Requiem*, Scriabin's "Etude in B flat minor," Hubbard's own lyrics, and an essay by Søren Kierkegaard. All within forty-three minutes. (*Forward Groove* 144)

In short, the album overtly fused aesthetics and explicit rights-oriented sentiment.

The review of the album by the jazz historian and critic Scott Yanow in *All Music Guide* states, "This is a strange LP . . . The thoughts expressed in the music (topical and anti-war messages) are quite sincere but the abstract sounds will only be enjoyed by a limited audience; jazz fans should look elsewhere." This feeble assessment, which pays virtually no attention to the historic contexts out of which the album emerged and which reduces the album's content to the tepid descriptors "strange" and "quite sincere," shows the extent to which so-called abstract music and so-called jazz, especially when linked with the kind of explicit rights commentary found on the album, were frequently marginalized or set aside as generally unpalatable.

And yet, as in Wadada Leo Smith's equally marginalized *Human Rights* album, the association in *Sing Me a Song of Songmy* between rights and improvisatory discourses is clearly an aesthetic context in which the two reinforce each other in compelling, disturbing, and innovative ways. Both albums demonstrate an inherent aesthetic tension with regard to how improvised responses to rights abuses and hegemony are to be framed: either as blatant, combined musical and verbal statements as per Hubbard and Smith; or as radical difference via nonverbal significations that experiment with the limits of improvisatory expression as the prime marker of ideological and aesthetic critique (as in the work of Coltrane and Ayler, for instance).

In 2001 the trumpeter Dave Douglas released *Witness*, shortly before the devastating events of 9/11, which unleashed with renewed energies global conflict and challenges to civil liberties in both the form of terrorism itself and the war on terrorism. The critic Chris Dahlen argues, "*Witness* is the greatest political statement to come from the downtown New York jazz scene since the time John Zorn told loud talkers Madeleine Albright and Václav Havel [and Lou Reed] to 'shut the fuck up [and listen to the music you jive-ass motherfuckers]' during his set [in 1998 at the Knitting Factory]. It's about as specific, too—rather than pushing a cause or specifying issues, Douglas has a broader agenda: 'Each piece is inspired by and dedicated to artists and activists who have creatively challenged authority, sometimes endangering their own lives, but inspiring the rest of us to resist'" (Dahlen).

Douglas notes in an interview,

The music, just like the culture and the society, has retreated from experimentation quite a bit, retreated into entertainment. And yet I think—and I don't want to over-generalize—that in the American improvised idiom there's been a lot of awareness of other art forms—dance, poetry and so on—but also of politics/social justice movements and the like. But that awareness has been muted in the ways it's been able to speak. Over a period of time it became much harder to make any kind of statement in the art itself. While we're seeing things like Ani DiFranco and Steve Earle, and even Springsteen making statements in song, for those of us who are instrumentalists and dancers and even novelists in the United States it's been harder to make any kind of impact. The resurgence of community spirit and activism in the wake of 9/11 has made that easier to do, in some ways." (qtd. in Santoro)

Witness is a complex artistic statement and worth careful attention in relation to rights contexts. The album notes avoid simplistic advocacy: "Enjoy this purely as music. Or find out more about these inspirations and dig into them." The rich geopolitical contexts that played a significant part in the genesis and artistic conception of the album are clearly fore-grounded by Douglas. The album's title, as in "bearing witness," clearly associates the album conceptually with rights organizations founded on similar principles, Amnesty International, Witness for Peace, and Human Rights Watch, to name some of the most prominent. Witnessing, bearing witness, and enacting rights are profoundly related activities, especially when rights violations and abuses often occur under a smokescreen of disinformation in which witnessing is impossible or highly compromised. So the album title evokes notions of testifying (both in the African Ameri-can gospel sense and in the legal sense) as a function of being a wit-ness. Douglas accounts for how the album came about as he traveled in Italy close to the border with Yugoslavia: "I was reading a fairly boring newspaper article on the rising stock of American weapons makers dur-ing the NATO assault on Yugoslavia. Not far away, half a million people were camped in a muddy field without much hope of escaping, or of going home. As usual, some people were making a huge profit . . . Rampant poverty and boundless riches co-exist as the norm. How do you protest a system that co-opts and marginalizes almost every unique and origi-nal thought that confronts it? And how do you stay silent?" (liner notes). Douglas links the arms industry's profit and the enormous inequities that drive that profit in the name of war with the twisted economy of the con-sumer marketplace, which appropriates but also marginalizes differential forms of thinking.

Douglas then locates *Witness* as a "positive response that celebrates art-ists and activists who have persisted in making direct nonviolent state-ments—often in the face of violence and at great personal risk. Each piece is dedicated to those who have creatively challenged authority, sometimes endangering their own lives, but inspiring the rest of us to resist. I see it as proof that we can protest the senselessness with grace and courage—without losing our humanity, our personality, our sense of humor."

The liner notes to the album give further context for each of the pieces and append a short list of activist websites associated with various rights causes and a short bibliography of prominent activist writers, including Arundhati Roy, Eduardo Galeano, Naomi Klein, and Howard Zinn. The album art embeds the Palestinian American scholar Edward Said's affir-mation about freedom of speech, which is "not always a matter of being a critic of government policy, but rather of thinking of the intellectual vocation as maintaining a state of constant alertness, of a perpetual will-ingness not to let half-truths or received ideas steer one along" (*Representations* 17).

Much has been made of Said's influence on Douglas's politics on dis-play in *Witness*, and of the fact that the album draws from Arabic music and Arab cultural influences to underline its globalist rights context. But Douglas had gained important musical experience in John Zorn's Masada project, which intermixed free improvisation with Jewish materials from eastern and central Europe. The Masada Project derived its name from an emblematic moment in the Jewish resistance (by the Sicarii) against the Roman empire in 66 CE, during the first Jewish-Roman war, which ended with a mass suicide of some 960 people. Zorn himself states, "The idea with Masada is to produce a sort of radical Jewish music, a new Jew-ish music which is not the traditional one in a different arrangement, but music for the Jews of today. The idea is to put Ornette Coleman and the Jewish scales together" (qtd. in Maykrantz). Fusing Coleman's free jazz aesthetic with traditional Jewish scalar systems in a politicized context that memorializes struggles for freedom in the Jewish context was, and continues to be, a remarkable gesture, in part made thinkable by analo-gous alignments made between free jazz and the civil rights movement.

In 1994 Zorn had made clear that further rights contexts existed for the Masada project, saying, "Masada continues what was begun in *Kristall-nacht*," an album Zorn released in 1992, a musical allegory of the Night of Broken Glass, the beginning, on November 9–10, 1938, of a German and Austrian pogrom that foreshadowed Nazi Germany's genocide of Euro-pean Jews.[5] Zorn continues, "On *Kristallnacht* a different use was made of Jewish tradition and it had precise references to contemporary music. In Masada I'm using another set of references" (qtd. in Maykrantz). Zorn's Masada project, in other words, was doubly engaged with Jewish history and issues of resistance to empire and injustice, both in ancient and mod-ern terms. So Douglas had already been introduced to how rights issues could be tackled from a musical perspective by his association with Zorn's politicized musicking.

Each of the nine pieces in *Witness* is directly associated with an activ-ist influence. The opening, "Ruckus," is dedicated to the activist group founded in 1996 to provide "environmental, human rights, and social jus-tice organizers with the tools, training, and support needed to achieve their goals" ("Mission").⁶ Douglas's last piece, "Sozaboy," is based on a novel by the executed Nigerian environmental activist and writer Ken Saro-Wiwa. The song describes a young recruit to the Nigerian civil war (also known as the Nigerian-Biafran War, 1967–70) as he moves from idealism to total disillusionment. *Sozaboy* the novel is a profound indictment of war by a writer-activist who was executed in 1995 by the Nigerian government under the military dictatorship of General Sani Abacha. "Sozaboy" the tune is an elegy to Saro-Wiwa, with Douglas's liner notes stating that his work "focused international attention on the complicity of the Nigerian government and multinational oil companies [Shell, in particular] in the rape of a land and its people."

The literariness of Douglas's sources of musical inspiration is remarkable and redefines the notion of a concept album along lines wholly consistent with earlier work by Wadada Leo Smith and Freddie Hubbard. Underlying this form is an expansive notion of the jazz commons, in which overt reference to rights contexts in an improvised aesthetic recapitulates and expands upon crucial relations between improvised musicking and the civil rights movement that is a key part of the history of both forms of social practice. J. A. Rogers sensed that jazz is "too international to be characteristically national, too much abroad in the world to have a special home" (qtd. in Jones 225). Smith, Hubbard, and Douglas exemplify the internationalist political logic embedded in the aesthetics of improvisation. The remarkable intertextuality and range of reference found in all the works discussed here point to how "abroad in the world" the aesthetic form of improvisation is, even as it is aligned with the specific global rights affirmations made transparent by the music and its contexts.

The tune "Child of All Nations" references the banned novel of the same name by the Indonesian writer Pramoedya Ananta Toer, a novel whose "stories were created and recited aloud for his [Toer's] fellow prisoners in exile on the island of Buru" (liner notes). "Mahfouz" references the great Egyptian writer Naguib Mahfouz, who in 1994 had been attacked by religious extremists six years after winning the Nobel Prize for Literature, in 1988 (he became a recluse after the attack). Douglas's notes underline Mahfouz's "appeal to social justice, class equality, and women's rights"— and in his speech to the Swedish Academy, Mahfouz had articulated a comprehensive global view of rights that is very much aligned with the politics on display in *Witness*:

In South Africa millions have been undone with rejection and with deprivation of all human rights in the age of human rights, as though they were not counted among humans. In the West Bank and Gaza there are people who are lost in spite of the fact that they are living on their own land; land of their fathers, grandfathers and great grandfathers. They have risen to demand the first right secured by primitive Man; namely, that they should have their proper place recognized by others as their own. They were paid back for their brave and noble move—men, women, youths and children alike—by the breaking of bones, killing with bullets, destroying of houses and torture in prisons and camps. Surrounding them are 150 million Arabs following what is happening in anger and grief. This threatens the area with a disaster if it is not saved by the wisdom of those desirous of a just and comprehensive peace. (Mahfouz)

"Mahfouz" uses Tom Waits's reading from the work of Mahfouz and the French radical philosopher Gilles Deleuze, as if to emphasize the marriage of words and music that underlies the album's overall concept. The piece is the longest on the album and at twenty-four minutes is the most obviously improvisatory in terms of the space given to the eleven musicians who contributed to the album (including Mark Feldman, Yuka Honda, Chris Speed, and Ikue Mori). Musically, as the jazz critic Doug Ramsey has noted, Douglas "calls on the tradition of his jazz predecessors and contemporaries but also draws from Balinese, African and Middle Eastern forms and, heavily, from modern classical composers like Lutoslawski, Ligeti, Stockhausen and, one suspects, Steve Reich." The richness of the musical influences evident on the album is clearly aligned with the attention Douglas pays to literary and activist influences, making for a remarkably evocative aesthetic context that supports the political content.

The tune "Witness" celebrates Said's work and especially his *Representations of the Intellectual,* which Douglas calls a "guiding light" for the project. "Woman at Point Zero" is inspired by the novel of the same name by the Egyptian novelist and physician Nawal El Saadawi. Published in 1979 and set in contemporary Egypt, the novel is about a psychiatrist's encounter with an imprisoned woman who has killed her pimp and been sentenced to death. It is a disturbing critique of disparate power relations between men and women, and of female genital mutilation and the death penalty. These evocations are part of the challenge Douglas's aesthetics take on: how can music somehow translate the rights contexts of the novel in ways that are profoundly moving (in the sense of being affective in a meaningful way but also in moving one to take action against the rights abuses the album uses as its frame). "Episode for Taslima Nasrin" "was written in reaction to this poet's exile from Bangladesh" (liner notes). Like El Saadawi, Nasrin is an author and a physician who has taken on radical Islam, has critiqued its misogyny, and is someone who, through her experience treating rape victims and working as a gynecologist in family-planning clinics, had seen firsthand the abuse suffered by women. In 1994 she was forced to flee Bangladesh (to Sweden) as a result of her novel *Lajja* (*Shame*, published in 1993), which told of the Muslim persecution of a Hindu family.

All these citations point to a vast context of rights abuses told outside the standard discourses of Western and American culture, an extension to a global context of the civil rights dimensions associated with improvisatory music made in the 1960s (and an inherent continuation of the logic of civil rights social justice affirmations, which had a clear sense of their own global importance). The literariness of Douglas's sources and his self-conscious explication of these sources in the liner notes play a crucial role in the rights pedagogy the album undertakes and in the attack on critical and artistic positions that suggest there is no place for overt politics in making music. The vision is of an expanded jazz commons in which aesthetic and political context have meaning in relation to each other. Recalling Archie Shepp's comments cited at the beginning of the introduction to this book, Douglas, as do Smith and Hubbard, generates a rich and carefully constructed iteration that may not change the world but that does lay out some very clear ideas about the kinds of changes that need to be brought about. As such, *Witness* contributes to notions of jazz citizenry and the instrumentality of that form of civic engagement, activating the affective, pedagogical, aesthetic, and critical powers inherent in what improvisation can contribute to the public commons. Improvisation plays an important role in shaping the iteration, and the album's musical activism is something that *Witness* overtly argues needs to be ported over into democratic and liberatory discourses with renewed vigor and intentionality.[7]

The sort of language associating jazz discourses and the challenges of democratic freedoms is to be found throughout the gamut of jazz discourse. Even the jazz traditionalist Wynton Marsalis argues for the relationship between jazz as a dialogic social discourse and democratic principles, although in ways that are worth thinking through critically:

> Jazz is a music of conversation, and that's what you need in a democracy. You have to be willing to hear another person's point of view and respond to it. Also, jazz requires that you have a lot of on-your-feet information, just like a democracy does. There are a lot of things you simply have to know. In jazz you have the opportunity to establish your equality based on your ability. That's the chance you have in a democracy. It doesn't mean you're going to be even, but you do have an opportunity. And often things won't go your way; they'll go the way the majority takes them. So you'll have to go with them and make the best out of a situation you might not like. The principle of American democracy is that you have freedom. The question is "How will you use it?" which is also the central question in jazz. In democracy, as in jazz, you have freedom with restraint. It's not absolute freedom, it's freedom within a structure. The connection between jazz and the American experience is profound. Believe me, that's the heart and soul of what jazz is. That's why jazz is so important. And that's why the fact that it has not been addressed has resulted in our losing a large portion of our identity as Americans. Because the art form that really gives us a mythic representation of our society has not been taught to the public. (qtd. in Goodheart, part 1)

Marsalis's comments get at the heart of the problem of rights discourses: how to enact individual liberties within reasonable limitations that are equitable (how to achieve "freedom within a structure").

Yet between the socially Darwinist view of democracy, in which competition is the driver of human evolution and social achievement (as opposed to established circumstances like poverty, ethnicity, history, class, and the like), expressed by Marsalis and the idea that "mak[ing] the best of a bad situation" is an adequate response to historic injustices and extreme oppression, there is much that is arguable in how these comments co-opt jazz to democratic discourse. Whose democracy? Whose principles? Which Americans? Equality based on ability is an all-too-easy sound bite but glosses over the complex contexts that go into how ability is achieved and who has access to the means that produce that ability. And the question may well not be "How will you use it [your freedom]?" so much as "What systemic factors put invisible limits on how your freedom can be enacted?"[8]

In October of 2004, just before a presidential election that was to reelect George W. Bush, Marsalis scheduled the "Let Freedom Swing: A Celebration of Human Rights and Social Justice" concerts.[9] These involved six newly commissioned pieces for the Lincoln Center Jazz Orchestra, which played composed settings of "inspirational oratory on liberty and triumph" by the likes of Darin Atwater, Toshiko Akiyoshi, Darius Brubeck, and Zim Ngqawana, using the words of, among others, Nelson Mandela, Archbishop Desmond Tutu, Eleanor Roosevelt, and Martin Luther King Jr., performed by celebrities like Morgan Freeman, Mario Van Peebles, and Alfre Woodard, to name a few.

Marsalis himself framed the event as a "risk," adding, "Could new music in a classic format inspire as much as the words being celebrated? For the most part, the results added up to an uneasy draw" ("Report from the 'Let Freedom Swing' Concert"). The *New York Times* review, by Edward Rothstein, noted how "an attempt to illuminate and expand on the text was missing through much of the concert. Rather as if a trumpeter, called upon to improvise on a motif and to carry forward a musical argument, ended up having very little fresh to add to the argument." The very classicism of the musical format, classicism that reduced the improvisatory significance of the music, also reduced the music's ability to convey the affective power of the words; indeed, it functioned in terms of what Nathaniel Mackey, by way of Amiri Baraka, might call a movement from verb to noun, and a containment of black mobility. Limiting musical structures did not measure up to the expressive significance of the words with which they were aligned, throwing into question the project.

Rothstein writes that the contexts of the performance were contradictory, the setting being the glitzy, new $128 million Time Warner Center, at Columbus Circle, "intended to display jazz's broad range, deep ambition and not incidentally, ready marketability." The use of rights as a tool for increasing marketability by neoconservative discourses that are inherently nonexperimental, inherently opposed to or critical of free improvisatory discourses, and inherently limited in their conception of rights by the contexts in which they choose to operate, is a familiar problem. In September of 2004, just a month before the concert, Time Warner (formerly AOL Time Warner, a company that in 2006 had sales of more than $44 billion) had been deleted from the FTSE4Good Index Series for its "failure to meet the human rights criteria" of the index (Baue). The FTSE4Good Index Series measures corporate social responsibility and is "designed to measure the performance of companies that meet globally

recognized corporate responsibility standards, and to facilitate investment in those companies" that display environmentally and socially responsible behaviors ("FTSE4Good Index Series.").

The extent to which the stream of jazz that foregrounded improvisation
as an expression of social dissonance was inherently ill-at-ease, to say the
least, with the corporate sponsorship of Time Warner can be read into the
description of the Time Warner Center as a "dynamic mix of components
[that] consists of The Shops at Columbus Circle, The Restaurant and Bar
Collection, The Five Star Mandarin Oriental Hotel, Jazz at Lincoln Center, One Central Park Luxury Condominiums, 60 Columbus Circle offices
and Time Warner World Headquarters" ("Overview of Time Warner Center"). The corporatization of jazz in such a context, not to mention its appropriation by luxury living and commodity culture, is highly problematic and dramatically at odds with the realities confronting the diasporic
African communities in which jazz originated (think post-Katrina New
Orleans).[10]

That access to this sort of highly corporatized, bourgeois space is not
even thinkable for anyone other than elite audiences is problematic
(upper-end tickets for the event cost US$150) and contrasts dramatically
with the material circumstances from whence the music originated. Commercialism and experimentalism, corporatization and social dissonance,
do not align easily in this example. In a similar vein, Marsalis's annual
salary of $833,686 as artistic director of Jazz at Lincoln Center attracted
significant criticism in an article in *Reader's Digest* in 2006, because such
a huge salary seemed significantly at odds with the spending limitations
on most nonprofit organizations. This example is important in the larger
discussion of rights and improvisation because it highlights the ways resource allocation can collude with ideology to reinforce limited aesthetic
and rights notions that are dramatically at odds with wider forms of cultural practice, or what we refer to earlier in the book as an "ecology of
knowledges." The Canadian cultural critic Alan Stanbridge argues,

> In the case of the Jazz at Lincoln Center program, a narrowly neo-conservative
> understanding of the "classical" jazz canon has been mobilized in support of
> a high-profile, publicly-funded jazz series within a major American cultural
> institution. In October 2004, the Lincoln Center opened the $131 million US,
> 100,000-square-feet Frederick P. Rose Hall, known as the House of Swing.
> In an early press release, Marsalis was quoted — somewhat ominously per-

haps — as saying that "The whole space is dedicated to the feeling of swing," thereby firmly establishing a stereotypical conceptualization of jazz performance that has been sadly evident in his programming for Jazz at Lincoln Center.

Stanbridge's point is that at Lincoln Center significant wealth is aligned with a very particular ideology of what constitutes jazz, one that wholly ignores the significant debates about the viability of the term *jazz*, a musical form frequently made manifest as a result of diverse improvisatory activities and philosophies. In terms of the rights implications of such a situation, Fischlin and Nandorfy argue that "disproportionate wealth is equivalent to disproportionate power, which can in turn lead to disproportionate allocation of rights" (*The Concise Guide* 33). What does it mean, in short, to set in place at one of the great global centers for improvised musicking such a structure of inequality?

In his book *Who Owns Music?* William Parker, the New York bassist and exponent of creative improvised musicking, argues, "When we play ourselves, the music is always too long or too dissonant or too something. They long for excuses to justify the earth-shaking sound but refuse to recognize it for what it is: America is owned and controlled by a few selected families, jazz is owned and operated by a few critics, producers, record companies, club owners. The jazz life is based off of the plantation system. Because of this, we must drop the term 'jazz' and along with it the accompanying business practices" (41). Centralization and commercialization of the complex aesthetics associated with African diasporic culture are betrayals of that culture in these terms — and betrayals of its improvisatory aesthetics and its liberatory politics:

> Black improvised music has had to fight for its life since the first slaves were brought here in 1619. This fight for survival goes on today and will continue to go on until America is transformed. Too many creative beings have died needlessly throughout the years, simply due to the way America is set up. Systematic lynching went on in America up until 1968. These acts of violence by America against blacks were supported by segregation laws making murder legal . . . White America has set the standard of what life is . . . creating a system based on a lie . . . Progress has become a process of dehumanization. In America, all of life's resources are controlled by those who have no respect for life. The lives of all who live in America are in the hands of monstrous

corporations like AT&T, Coca-Cola, Con Edison, Citibank, Chase Manhattan, General Electric, Mobil Oil, IBM, etc., corporations and gangsters who only wish to make a profit. The neglect of the poor and minorities is no accident. It is a conscious, calculated plan to keep those who control in power . . . To be effective against America's anti-life policies, we have to be radical in every area of our lives. The music we create, how we walk, eat, sleep, breathe, must all be geared to a new aesthetic. (58–59)

Elsewhere, Parker explicitly argues that improvised music, what he calls "free music . . . a musical form that is playing without pre-worked structure without written music or chord changes," must "grow into free spiritual music which is not (shouldn't) be a musical form, it should be based off of a lifeform" (*Document Humanum* 17).

Free music, in other words, tends toward a spiritual recognition and respect for life at a level that gets beyond conventional notions of musical form and conventional notions of the limitations associated with that form. Such an idea is profoundly tied to rights discourses that argue from a basic respect for the dignity of all life and for the spiritual connectedness of all things that provides the grounds for meaningful and full ethical engagement with the world. There's a universal principle at stake here but also multiple specific expressions (musical or otherwise) of that engagement, reiterated as the struggle to enact these universal principles continues.

Parker's insights intertwine improvised musicking, critiques of profound rights abuses that have been sustained over many centuries (including lynching), spirituality struggling against dehumanization, and a call against the corporatization and commercialization that benefits the few and exploits the many.[11]

What might it have meant to have had Parker express these thoughts publicly and musically to the audience for the "Let Freedom Swing" event, hosted in the shining new Lincoln Center with its luxury condos and exclusive shopping, its corporate headquarters and its creation of a putative jazz commons in which only the privileged few could pay entry? Nor is the situation with Jazz at Lincoln Center a recent one. The historian and cultural critic Robin Kelley reminds us of the efforts of the pianist Randy Weston to promote civil rights in the late 1950s through educational programs and the founding of the Afro-American Musicians' Society. Weston's agenda was to confront issues of racism directly faced by fellow jazz performers and "problems ranging from low pay, the poor conditions of jazz clubs, royalties, publishing and recording contracts, the absence of black music at new venues such as Lincoln Center, and the overall concern that 'the music [was] disappearing from the black neighborhoods'" (Kelley, *Africa Speaks, America Answers* 55). Lincoln Center, sadly, has a long history of various forms of exclusionary programming.

The gaping difference between Marsalis and Parker is a function of Marsalis's complicity with a system that Parker judges to be profoundly corrupt (ethically, economically, artistically). But it also arises from Parker's insistence on the ongoing need to radicalize black aesthetics (through improvisation and other ways of being in the world) even as one continues to remember what oppressive systems have done to suppress those aesthetics and how those same systems continue to sustain principles that are profoundly inequitable, unjust—and racist.[12] The contradictory irony here is that the free music Parker sees as one form of response was itself born as a response to massive, unrelenting injustices, and thus its appropriation by (and subsumption within) the very system that has perpetrated those injustices is particularly odious and dangerous.

Marsalis's work over the years, however, has engaged with rights issues arising from the African diaspora, whether it be in the album *From the Plantation to the Penitentiary*, the first CD Marsalis produced after the tragedy of Hurricane Katrina, or the Pulitzer Prize–winning oratorio *Blood on the Fields*, a slave narrative (the first jazz work to be awarded the Pulitzer Prize for Music). Much of the criticism aimed at Marsalis is troubled by the degree to which his standing in corporatized musical structures is at odds with the underlying aesthetic of improvisation as a practice that gains its authenticity and power from its capacity to remain outside (or deeply critical of) such deeply compromising allegiances. Institutional context does matter in relation to how the repertoire is chosen, who plays it, and how it is played. And it does matter if it appropriates notions of where one goes to hear the music, thereby threatening the multiple small clubs and venues where institutional influence is distant and seen as profoundly undercutting the inherent value and freedom of creative expression.

The critique of institutions whose inertia is an impediment to change and experimentation is an inevitable aspect of improvised musicking, which does not stand on stability and institutional investment as driving forces in the music. Any number of improvisers' trajectories, such as those of William Parker, Anthony Braxton, Eddie Prévost, and Evan Parker, attest to this dynamic. Contexts and spaces do matter, and they can play a role in how the music is conceived and disseminated. So too do the social contexts and interrelations among the musicians matter. Marsalis, for instance, has said outrageous things about fellow musicians, including his sulfurous comment on Miles Davis: "'They call Miles's stuff jazz,' said Marsalis. 'That stuff is not jazz, man. Just because somebody played jazz at one time, that doesn't mean they're still playing it'" (qtd. in Byrnes).

The editorialist Sholto Byrnes goes on to note that "the jazz department at New York's Lincoln Center has been lauded for its recreations of the classic music of Armstrong and Duke Ellington—the kind of music liked by Marsalis, who is the department's artistic director. But you won't hear any style originating in the past 30 years there. For good measure, he has also been accused of ageism, sexism and racism" in the years he has run Jazz at Lincoln Center. Marsalis was accused of sexism because the Jazz Orchestra at Lincoln Center had never employed a woman.

And yet as far back as Louis Armstrong, there were examples of female musicians working in a jazz context, as did the trumpeter Valaida Snow, who had played in Armstrong's orchestra in 1928 and who soloed in the band on Armstrong's invitation. (Armstrong referred to her as the world's second best trumpeter, after himself, and she was a prodigious musician who could play some ten instruments fluently by the age of fifteen.) Byrnes also cites the saxophonist David Murray, one of the most recorded artist in jazz history, who states of Marsalis and his neoconservative influence, "We have great jazz musicians out of work because of this stuff . . . It's awful, a whole bunch of musicians who don't play the styles he likes are now totally intimidated."

So the (unfortunately named) "Let Freedom Swing" social-justice event took place on a site funded by a company that had just been singled out for its human rights derogations, especially in the areas of media consolidation and labor practices associated with its overseas suppliers. Swing is not a neutral trope in this context. It implies values associated with a certain conservative view of institutionalized jazz, itself aligned with the corporate values and strategies supporting the event. As the improvising guitar master Pat Metheny says, "You know, that word *swing* is almost a political buzzword. To me, in the language I'm using here, that's the glue I'm talking about. The connection of ideas. To me, the jazz education movement is really interested in qualifying these things, even on a sort of political-cultural spectrum. But to me what's beautiful about this is that it's prequantification. The most abstract thing in the world can swing, in terms of this glue quotient. Cecil Taylor, Derek Bailey—to me, this stuff has got unbelievable glue" (Ratliff 22). Swing, for Metheny, evokes indeterminacy, connectedness, and beauty that evade quantification, evade reductive definition or association with a particular style or musical taste.

The Marsalis event betrays the very term it was advocating for by the series of connections it was making between limiting and imposed notions of what good jazz taste is, and the corporate and institutional resources being aligned paradoxically with the kind of quantification that makes Metheny so uncomfortable. As Bill Ivey, the former chair of the National Endowment for the Arts argues, "Art doesn't find its way to audiences by itself. The gatekeepers—our arts companies—are absolutely essential to creativity and artistry" (187). "Let Freedom Swing" was as much marked by who and what kind of music got excluded from the event as by the munificent corporate resources it utilized.

Moreover, the "Let Freedom Swing" event was not clearly associated with any specific fund-raising targets to support direct rights outcomes, one of the key problems in rights discourses being the gaping distance be- tween the amount of talk about rights (theory) and the actual material resources (practice) used to target a specific problem.[13] And this was so in spite of the phenomenal wealth and privilege brought together to make the "Let Freedom Swing" evening happen. The concert is exemplary of the ways the appropriation of the rights discourses in a privileged musical context can be misleading, wholly or partially undercut by contradictions.

What would it have meant to let freedom "swing" in its most exemplary forms, from a musical and a rights perspective?

To what extent were the considerations of corporations and audiences determinants of what was said that evening and, perhaps, more importantly, how it was said (and of course what was not said)?

Is the underlying clash between artistic conservatism and experimentalist discourse, which is part of the story we outline in this book, also pointing to a larger conflict in which musical aesthetics of improvisation become uncomfortably, and in complicated, salutary ways, politicized?

Improvisation and the Public Commons

The "Let Freedom Swing" event and the ways it envisaged a certain public commons associated with jazz recall the infamous incident in which Max Roach, a former bandmate of Miles Davis in the legendary Charlie Parker Quintet, intervened at an event Davis was playing in support of the African Research Foundation (ARF). The organization was formed in 1957 by three white doctors, to bring primary healthcare services to sub-Saharan countries (by 1961 the organization was multiracial). The story of Roach's intervention at the Davis concert goes as follows:

> One of the most artistically successful concerts of the time was given by Roach's friend Miles Davis at Carnegie Hall with the Gil Evans Orchestra on 19 May 1961. It was a benefit for the African Research Foundation . . . This hugely successful concert was almost spoiled and cut short by a political incident. When Miles was in the middle of "Someday My Prince Will Come," Max Roach, dressed in a white jacket and carrying a placard on which was painted "AFRICA FOR THE AFRICANS! FREEDOM NOW!," walked up and sat down on the stage apron, while Davis and the crowd looked on in amazement. A moment later Roach was joined by another demonstrator. Miles waved his trumpet at Roach in dismay and then stopped the music and walked off stage. Security guards carried off Max Roach and his companion, and backstage people talked Miles into going back on, which he eventually did to prolonged applause. The anger Davis felt expressed itself in the even greater intensity of the music.
>
> When asked later what he thought Roach had been doing, Davis replied, "I don't know . . . Ask him." Carr recounted Roach's explanation . . ."I was told some things about the Foundation that I thought Miles should know. Some people tried to contact him, but they couldn't get to him. I went onstage because I wanted Miles to be aware of these things." Roach was referring to accusations by African nationalists that the Foundation was in league with South African diamond interests who sought to enslave Africans instead of helping them. (Voce)

The concert raised $25,000 for a mobile medical unit but Roach and fellow demonstrators linked the ARF with CIA fronts, saying the foundation played "into the hands of colonialism" (Early 90). As Ingrid Monson explains, Roach had been misled into thinking that the ARF was a white supremacist organization tied to South Africa's apartheid regime, and Roach did apologize for the protest.

Nonetheless the ARF's liberal politics were at a distance from revolutionary African nationalist sentiment that "was at a fever pitch in the spring of 1961 in the wake of the assassination of the Congo's Patrice Lumumba" (Monson, *Freedom Sounds* 189), the only leader of the Congo ever to have been democratically elected, an assassination that took place with the support and involvement of the CIA's Project Wizard. As Monson points out, "Max Roach and Abbey Lincoln had been involved in the demonstrations at the UN that included members of the United African Nationalist Movement, the Liberation Committee for Africa, and On Guard" (*Freedom Sounds* 189).

The incident is instructive of the highly politicized terrain in which improvising jazz musicians were (and continue to be) situated, and the multiple contradictions at work in the historical moments when improvisatory and rights discourses were beginning to fuse. Ironically both Davis and Roach thought they were acting on principle and in the interests of what today might be called the basic rights of Africans to self-determination, to proper medical care, and the like. And yet, the confrontation staged the challenges faced by the musical community in developing a coherent response to the politics with which the music was associated—and of course this was compounded by contradictions in the personal politics that musicians like Davis embodied (as in his domestic violence and abusive relationships). This challenge is, in a sense, inherent in any rights-oriented action, and it complicates both the ideological and the symbolic field of the music. And out of the tension, money was raised, dialogue and some reconciliation emerged, awareness of more expansive issues was necessitated, and the space of improvised musicking was again associated with vigorous debate.

The history of jazz is full of such contradictions. Hotep Idris Galeta, the South African jazz pianist, points out in his essay "The Development of Jazz in South Africa," that the "first contact South Africans had with black Americans and black American music in particular was on the 30th of June in 1889 when the minstrel troupe of Orpheus Myron McAdoo's 'Virginia Jubilee Singers' from Hampton, Virginia, appeared in concert in Cape Town. Their appearance was to have a significant impact upon the music scene as it later influenced the creation and formation of the

'Kaapse Klopse' or 'Coon Carnival' . . . It is not clearly known how such a derogatory racist American term 'Coon' came to be known in Cape Town, however given South Africa's racist colonial past leaves little doubt for speculation as to its origin. The 'Coon carnival's' popularity decreased as the struggle for liberation intensified over the coming years." So jazz music in its initial iteration in South Africa reinforced racist epithets. Galeta also notes how the "first Jazz recording was only made in 1917, and this by the all white New Orleans Band called 'The Original New Orleans Dixieland Band.'" The historical ironies and contradictions of this example are extraordinary, if only for how they show how easily the trope of the "original" can be transmuted to serve particular purposes, and the degree to which, from its inception, jazz has had to grapple with problems of authenticity and appropriation of various sorts.

These examples point to the fraught public commons space in which the political contexts of improvised musickings as a form of social practice are at stake. And it is useful to remember here, as Vijay Iyer points out, that "improvisation takes on a crucial symbolic weight . . . the phrase 'improvised music' suggests not simply that the notes and rhythms are extemporized because of a cultural aesthetic that privileges improvisation . . . but moreover that music is created from a position of disenfranchisement, where sheer survival cannot be taken for granted, where one is perpetually improvising through life by making use of whatever is at hand—especially one's own sensory experience. Hence, it has been suggested that we theorize improvisation as a *condition*, shaped by social, cultural, and economic forces" ("On Improvisation" 286). Not only is improvisation a social practice that has a profound relation to the contexts from which it emerges; it is also an active force in critiquing and providing alternatives to those contexts, even as it is under constant pressure to assimilate to market forces that would neuter its political valences.

In April 2009, in New Orleans, a group of activists launched a mock version of the New Orleans Jazz Fest website called www.ShellJazzFest .com, whose aim was to shed light both on Shell's role as chief sponsor of the enormously popular New Orleans Jazz and Heritage Festival and on Shell's abysmal human rights and environmental record. The mock website was the initial step in an international campaign "coordinated by human rights and environmental groups in Europe, Africa, and North America" and focusing on Shell's historical neglect of linked rights and environmental concerns ("ShellGuilty"). Han Shan, a spokesperson for

ShellGuilty, a coalition initiative of Friends of the Earth, Oil Change International, and Platform / Remember Saro-Wiwa, stated that "in New Orleans, Shell is sponsoring Jazz Fest but in Nigeria, Shell has literally sponsored murder and torture . . . A few weeks after Jazz Fest, Shell will stand trial in federal court in New York for complicity in serious human rights abuses in Nigeria." The case was resolved in an out-of-court settlement in favor of the plaintiffs, who won 15.5 million dollars as part of the agreement in June 2009.

The case was brought to trial by the Center for Constitutional Rights, EarthRights International, human rights attorneys, and the Nigerian writer Ken Wiwa, the son of Ken Saro-Wiwa, mentioned earlier in association with Dave Douglas's tune "Sozaboy." Saro-Wiwa was executed by hanging in 1995 by the Abacha government, along with eight other activists from the Movement for the Survival of the Ogoni People, for their actions in opposing oil development by Shell in traditional Ogoni lands. Saro-Wiwa had spearheaded a campaign focusing on the environmental devastation wrought by Shell's practices and the degree to which there had not been adequate revenue sharing with the Ogoni.

The campaign ended with Shell's temporarily withdrawing from the Niger Delta in 1993, even as it worked with the government to reassert itself in the area, culminating in the activists' executions but also leaving some two thousand dead and thirty thousand homeless. As the journalist Andy Rowell documented in *The Independent,*

> Shell met the director general of the state security services to "reiterate our request for support from the army and police." In a confidential note Shell suggested: "We will have to encourage follow-through into real action preferably on an industry rather than just Shell basis." The Nigerian regime responded by sending in the Internal Security Task Force, a military unit led by Colonel Paul Okuntimo, a brutal soldier, widely condemned by human rights groups, whose men allegedly raped pregnant women and girls and who tortured at will. Okuntimo boasted of knowing more than 200 ways to kill a person.
>
> In October 1993, Okuntimo was sent into Ogoni with Shell personnel to inspect equipment. The stand-off that followed left at least one Ogoni protester dead. A hand-written Shell note talked of "entertaining 26 armed forces personnel for lunch" and preparing "normal special duty allowances" for the soldiers. Shell is also accused of involvement with the MPF, which worked

with Okuntimo. One witness, Eebu Jackson Nwiyon, claimed they were paid and fed by Shell. Nwiyon also recalls being told by Okuntimo to "leave nobody untouched." When asked what was meant by this, Nwiyon replied: "He meant shoot, kill."

Moreover, secret documents Rowell refers to show that Shell actively lobbied the influential newspaper the *Guardian* to limit its support for Saro-Wiwa, with some success: "A Shell executive noted: '*The Guardian* newspaper ran a much more balanced article on the Ogoni issue, with their position moving from apparent support for Saro-Wiwa to the middle ground. There is a slight possibility that this may have been influenced by the meeting we had with *The Guardian*'s editor the week before'" (Rowell).

Though this is an all-too-short account of a much more involved story, the New Orleans Jazz Fest was targeted for its indirect involvement with this sordid history by way of the sponsorship monies it received from Shell (and continues to receive as of this writing), making it complicit in associating the so-called birthplace of jazz, a preeminent form of improvised musicking (and a function of the African diaspora, slavery, and American imperial culture), with rights abuses and violations committed in Africa.[14] This was not the first time New Orleans had figured as a contested site in discourses of rights. The infamous boycott in 1965 of New Orleans by members of the American Football League's all-star game, the first boycott of an entire city by a professional sports league, came about as a response to the fact that numerous black players had been refused service by businesses and institutions in New Orleans.

In the case of Shell's sponsorship role with the jazz festival, activists further localized the issue of sponsorship around the "climate crimes" associated with Shell in Louisiana, this well before the catastrophic oil spill from the BP-owned Deepwater Horizon offshore drilling rig in the Gulf of Mexico, in 2010. Anne Rolfes, the founding director of the Louisiana Bucket Brigade, stated that "from the Niger Delta to the Mississippi Delta, Shell's legacy of destruction belies its professed concern for the environment and local communities where it operates. Here in Louisiana, Shell's refineries pollute local communities and cause massive health problems" ("ShellGuilty").[15] The problem lies in how the status of musicians like Pete Seeger, Etta James, the Ebony Hillbillies, Guitar Slim Jr., Erykah Badu, the reggae group Third World, the Seminole Warriors Mardis Gras

Indians, and the Ladysmith Red Lions of South Africa, with their knowledge and acquiescence or not, all of whom were "presented by" Shell in the 2009 New Orleans Festival, was co-opted to sanitize the public image of a company with this sort of rights abuse and violations record.[16] This sanitizing effect ripples out in all sorts of ways. The HBO TV series *Treme*, about post-Katrina New Orleans, ended its second season in 2011 with an episode entitled "Do Watcha Wanna." The episode shows footage of the New Orleans Jazz Festival of 2011, featuring the Iguanas (a New Orleans–based roots-rock band), Lucinda Williams (the Louisiana-born rock, folk, blues, and country music singer and songwriter), and Donald Harrison (the saxophonist from New Orleans and the so-called King of Nouveau Swing). While obviously making an effort to gesture to a range of Louisiana musical icons, these choices are an odd representation of the so-called face of jazz. The familiar yellow Shell logo is evident in the festival footage, even as the episode explicitly shows the significant pollution occurring in the Gulf as the result of oil leaking from abandoned, and apparently wholly unregulated, wells that dot the coastal horizon.

The mixed messages at work in these scenes are worth highlighting. First, representing jazz for the series' purposes need not include the most experimental and radical improvisatory voices as part of how jazz defines itself. The same episode shows DJ Davis McAlary not even being able to identify the improvisatory music of Kidd Jordan, who is playing as McAlary takes over a late night radio shift. This is followed by the reassuringly affective music of Louis Armstrong, whose music reduces McAlary to tears. Nostalgia here trumps avant-garde experimentalism and the camera's gaze clearly instructs the audience about valuing the former over the latter.

Even more problematically, the Jazz Fest scenes seem to act as a compensatory salve for the scenes of the polluted Gulf waters and for the pollution caused by the very industry (big oil) that supports the festival and that has the logo of one of its major players (Shell) emblazoned on Jazz Fest signage, programs, and so forth. Following the catastrophic Deepwater Horizon oil spill, the federal government awarded Shell Offshore, Inc., the first new deepwater oil exploration plan approved after the BP debacle, for an area near where the BP blowout occurred—this in spite of the fact that "Shell's exploration plan anticipated the company using the same type of blowout preventer that failed at BP's Deepwater Horizon well" ("Enviros Challenge"). The association of the music of the Jazz

Festival with the corporate image of the company is crucial in all sorts of ways, with the prestigious musical event's good vibe an effect that helps greenwash Shell's corporate image as a polluter of consequence. This is far from the localized, independent likes of a Wadada Leo Smith's making improvised music from a context in which such an association would be unthinkable, and, it must be said, unthinkable from the sponsor's point of view, because of Smith's marginal cultural and media presence, whatever his artistic importance.

The pattern to note is that the further one moves away from the scene of improvisation evoked by Smith's album *Human Rights,* the more dangerous are the ways the site of improvisation (and its associations with creative freedom) are put to use in the service of different ideological imperatives. The more corporatized the music, the more it enters the logic of capital and media presence, the less true it is to the improvisatory impulse. That impulse is part of a shared ideological continuum that brings together improvisatory experimentation, its underlying ethics and historical contexts, and rights discourses predicated on similar values. Marketability and commercialization are inherently at odds with improvisational narratives of experiment and autonomy. Furthermore, they are perhaps even more deeply at odds with the visionary, spiritual, and ritualistic moment in which improvised music, in its most achieved form, happens. For all the counterarguments that suggest musicians who get trapped in the marketing machine can somehow function both inside and outside that logic, it is only very rarely that they in fact do so, and usually at tremendous personal cost.

In a wonderfully direct appraisal of Wynton Marsalis's month-long featured performances during the prom season in the U.K. in 1993, the free-improvising percussionist Eddie Prévost got at the ways the bourgeois, classical musical values at work in Marsalis's musical discourse elevate technique over substance, and style over experimentation, at the expense of the ethical and performative logics that underlie improvisational practices:

> Free improvisation is defined by its slipperiness. If it is not constantly reinvented, it fades. It is the only form of musical expression [that] depends on the uniqueness of each performer [and, might we add, of each performance]. The only way to deny the autonomy of this "self-invention"—to dampen down the risk it runs of incomprehensibility or nihilism—is to in-

validate the right of *all* invention. Marsalis calls for historical continuities because he cannot trust the direction that still mobile forms might take (the solos in bebop are now so circumscribed stylistically that it is difficult, if not impossible, to say anything new). (*Minute Particulars* 124)

Prévost continues on to argue that "the focus on Marsalis himself" makes him like

the leader of an emergent nation [who] occupies all media coverage, at the expense of an understanding of his country's post-colonial experience. And, in the fight for freedom, he loses sight of the nature of freedom. Black American culture is important because of the resilience, energy and imagination of a people who have long suffered disadvantages. Their struggle is part of a universal effort. But the narrow focus of the struggle "against" is too often couched entirely in terms of the dominant ideology. Marsalis makes jazz too parochial: it would be more meaningful to develop ideas [that] acknowledge and wrestle with wider realities. In this respect Sun Ra and Cecil Taylor far outclass Marsalis. (*Minute Particulars* 125–26)

The "universal effort" and "wider realities" that form part of Prévost's analysis implicitly link the historical contexts from which improvisatory musical practices emerged as a form of cultural resistance and survival with rights discourses generally. Alignment with dominant ideologies whose interests are not served by such practices, which are inherently disruptive and critical of hegemony, founded on inequity and injustice, is always dangerous and compromising. Improvisation's dominant qualities—mobility of form, cultural reinvention in the moment, unpredictability of invention, and the embodied importance of the performer who can channel these virtues in the here and now—are all profoundly counter to conservative structures that seek stability through repression and hierarchy.

Moreover, because improvisation as a social practice is not fully understood or theorized, all generic forms of jazz are too easily taken to stand in for all improvisatory practices, a profound misperception of the stakes evident in the above examples. The degree to which core discourses of improvised practice are seen to be operative in figures such as Marsalis needs reevaluation. No sound is neutral or innocent, as Prévost has argued, and the full contextual signifying power associated with how, where, and why sounds are made needs careful attention. Though Marsalis is perhaps too easy a target because of his perceived "classicism" and alignment with conservative narratives of jazz, his centrality in popular cultural discourses around jazz diminishes the public musical commons and should not be underestimated.

The discourse of the public commons is rarely applied to music generally and even more rarely to improvisatory music. But if all musical creation has no choice but to pass through improvisation as a fundamental premise of originary musical encounters, then improvisation may in fact be the most important element in musical creation. The child first touching an instrument and experimenting with how to draw sounds from it, the composer not yet a "composer" fiddling with melodies and harmonies, the group of percussionists accompanying a marriage ceremony and evolving a sophisticated polyrhythm as the result of improvised contributions by individuals in the group—all are unthinkable scenarios without the presence of improvisatory strategies. Improvisation, then, is the crucible through which musical creation must pass, the moment when context and history, individual and collective, meld in performative utterance, unleashing the affective signifying power that is sound. Improvisation is perhaps the most important element in the musical commons, across all cultures, for it is the generative space in which new ideas are tried, critiqued, modified, and presented publicly.

A too narrow conception of the musical commons (evident, for instance, in the dominance of Clear Channel or in the classical music circuit, driven largely by a limited repertoire) as determined by salability, marketability, and profit, all of which set limits on experimentation and autonomy, is a constant challenge to the various sites of improvised music. This is so not only as a function of the resources that are drawn away from improvisation but also for the ways improvisation is appropriated to specific musical ends. An important context for situating this sort of thinking does in fact have a strong rights component: as a basic (the most basic?) expression of the creative musical impulse, improvisation is also a dramatic aspect of the larger commons of free speech that is itself an underlying tenet of all rights discourses and instruments. Improvisation is a crucial component in the public expression of autonomy and critique that resides in the individual as a function of community, not in the state or institutional hierarchies in which free speech is frequently converted into moderated speech, heavily mediated speech, or self-censorship.

A remarkable account of the compulsion to find ways to make musical sounds that emerge from improvisations with context, materials available, and personal circumstance is to be found in the altoist Art Pepper's brutal account of his life. While incarcerated (one of many incarcerations throughout his life) at the Los Angeles County jail in the mid-1950s he was placed in the "tanks":

> In the tanks there was no radio, no nothing. I went five or six months without hearing a note of music . . . So if you can imagine, being a musician, or just being any person . . . For most people, music is an important part of their lives, and to be deprived of it completely is terrible. So what I'd do to keep myself from going crazy. I would play my cup. We were all issued one. They give you a tin coffee cup with a little handle on it. I would hold it up to my mouth, leave a little opening at the side, and put my hands over it like you do when you play a harmonica or a Jew's harp. And I found that I could hum into the cup and get a sound sort of like a trumpet. I could do a lot with it. And in the jail, with all the cement and steel, that small sound could really be heard, especially from the corner of the cell. So I'd play to myself, and the guys would hear me. I'd look up and see that there were guys standing all around my cell, just digging. And I found that they got a lot of pleasure out of it, especially at night. We had one guy named Grundig, who had played drums at one time. He'd take the top from a trash can and beat on it with a spoon, and I'd play my cup, and the guys would clap, and we would have, like, a regular session. You'd have to be in that position to realize how much joy you could receive from something as crude as that. (Pepper & Pepper 172)

Pepper's narrative demonstrates the importance of music as a primary form of communication—a primary pleasure. But it also shows how the very act of improvising under extreme duress can produce a version of the public commons that is peaceable, creative, and cogenerative. Improvising music kept him and his fellow inmates human, kept them from "going crazy," gave joy. None of these rights is to be found specifically articulated in rights instruments, a major problem with how they are conceived. And yet here, in Pepper's moving account, improvised music becomes the focus for reattaining a modicum of one's humanity in dehumanized circumstances.

A report for the ACLU on the mental health conditions at the Los Angeles County Jail, authored by the psychiatrist Terry A. Kupers, noted, "Of the 2,088 individuals reported on the mental health caseload, at least 350 are receiving only medications while being subjected to severe crowding or isolation and receiving no mental health programming—this is far from adequate mental health treatment. I would estimate with a high degree of certainty that at least double the number on the current caseload need mental health treatment." The report goes on to document a lack of adequate treatment for inmates suffering from severe disorders like schizophrenia, "disturbing evidence of custodial abuse of prisoners with serious mental illness," and crowding, idleness, and victimization by other prisoners, and so forth, as typifying the facility (45).[17] The just and equitable treatment of the poorest, most disadvantaged, most troubled people in a culture is generally one of the true marks of the material enactment of rights instruments in meaningful ways. Pepper's narrative squarely places music into the rights scenario described by Kupers some fifty years later. However idealized, and Pepper was not one to mince words about his own misbehavior, Pepper's narrative shows the power of music to create peaceful assembly, to generate communication, to express community, however beleaguered, and the crucial contribution that music can make as one aspect of a healthy public commons.

As a marker of the cogenerative power of the public commons, then, improvisation is inherently antineoliberal, an ideology that persistently seeks to transfer public control of shared resources and common needs (water, access to various bandwidths, education, medicine, and the like) to the private sector. Neoliberal discourse has invaded musical spaces to the point that it is hard to imagine the cultural meaning of music apart from its capacity to generate wealth or its part in an economy, rather than a basic human need, resource, and a defining aspect of all humanity. In its marginalization, its often-unseen, intangible presence, which generates new discourses, in its mobility and facility with hybridization, and in its locus, the contestatory space where difference can and is enacted, improvisation's general importance to the underlying health of the musical ecosphere and the public commons must be recognized, valued, and protected.

Improvisation is a fundamental aspect of music as a cultural right, an indelible, universal dimension of being human in all the diverse and specific aspects of what that potentially means. Its intangible, invisible status lies outside increasingly prevalent discourses that trope humanity solely as a quantitative function of economy and wealth, state power and hierarchy, and the media that service these. And it is precisely this status, aligned with the way it is expressive of basic gestures that underlie rights discourses generally, that makes it such a potentially powerful tool for modeling alternatives to these structures.

We say this even as we note how problematic "recognition" is as a desirable outcome for improvisation. All too often recognition is framed as a function of media driven by advertising and dominant corporate ideologies that are largely a perversion of "free" speech for how they narrow the bandwidth of what is thinkable in the space of the public commons. In this sense improvisation needs no recognition, which would inevitably entail co-option. But in the sense of addressing the public commons in ways that challenge improvisation to rethink itself, improvisation offers itself as one model of a social practice for autonomous (within, of course, the limits that anything can truly be so), experimental disturbances that ask what it means to "be" human in relation to the multiple cogenerative contexts in which that meaning is created.

So from Wadada Leo Smith's example through those of Marsalis and the New Orleans Jazz Fest's sponsorship by Shell, another story is told: that of how fragile and tenuous the improvisatory moment is, how easily music can be "dislocated," as Prévost argues, and how "a proper respect for the history of sound and music—as sources for a transformation into music-future"—is necessary (*No Sound Is Innocent* 148). A proper respect for the diverse contextual histories out of which music is made and to which it refers is urgently needed in order to counterbalance how music is so often strategically appropriated by interests whose value systems are deeply at odds with the underlying ethos of improvisation.

CHAPTER 4

IMPROVISATION, SOCIAL MOVEMENTS, AND RIGHTS IN NEW ORLEANS

Poor and Black in the Big Easy

In the face of centuries of systematic rights violations, the mere survival of black people in New Orleans has been nothing short of a miracle. In a city, state, and nation where white property has routinely been valued more highly than black humanity, African Americans have experienced collective, cumulative, and continuing victimization. Systemic forms of segregation, disenfranchisement, and labor exploitation that channeled unfair gains and unjust enrichments to whites over more than a century followed the brutal and exploitative practices of slavery that ended in 1865. Since that time, the twin legacies of slavery and segregation have left blacks in New Orleans with cumulative vulnerabilities. These are presently being exploited ruthlessly by neoliberal programs designed to create new sources of profit for investors, largely through a cruel, calculated, and organized abandonment of the black poor. Economic exploitation, political suppression, and cultural demonization have worked in concert in New Orleans in the past and present to subject blacks disproportionately to economic impoverishment and environmental pollution, to illness, unemployment, and incarceration. The poet, journalist, educator, and community activist Kalamu ya Salaam explains, "Living poor and Black in the Big Easy is never as much fun as our music, food, smiles, and laughter make it seem" (40).

The survival of black people in New Orleans has demanded relentless struggle, suffering, and sacrifice. It has entailed a complex and continuing political project grounded in a creative and collective culture. In the late nineteenth century, the Comité des Citoyens, a group made up of blacks from New Orleans with Haitian ancestry, initiated the first major legal challenge to segregation in 1892 in what became the infamous case of *Plessy v. Ferguson*. In the 1920s, Audley "Queen Mother" Moore mobilized a crowd of armed blacks to encircle the Longshoreman's Hall to defend Marcus Garvey's right to speak in the city. The poet Tom Dent, the art teacher Richard Haley, and the dramatist John O'Neal made New Orleans their base of operations in the 1960s, for mobilizations that blended performances of expressive culture with civil rights organizing.

When police officers in New Orleans attempted to drive the Black Panther Party out of the Desire Housing projects in 1970, thousands of black men, women, and children massed in front of the buildings, preventing the assault. Today, in the wake of the abandonment of the black poor that characterizes plans to rebuild parts of the city from the damage done by the floods that accompanied Hurricane Katrina in 2005, grass roots activist groups have taken the lead in championing human rights for black people in New Orleans. They cite international law and seek help from international agencies in affirming their collective right to return to their homes, rebuild their neighborhoods, and participate meaningfully in deliberations to determine the city's future.

Improvisation and Popular Mobilization

In these battles for survival, improvisation has been an important (if seemingly improbable) weapon. Nurtured and sustained inside alternative academies grounded in many different forms of expressive culture within the black community, improvisation in New Orleans serves political as well as aesthetic functions. Street parades teach musicians, dancers, and spectators to communicate effectively with one another, and to create a common project by building off of each other's energy. The ferocious theatricality of the city's music, dance, dress, song, and speech teaches participants to anticipate dialogue and participate in it. Fused forms of expression and art privilege movement and welcome the unexpected. Collective celebrations emanating from the improvisational creativity of individuals and groups deftly instruct artists and audiences alike to blend sameness and difference, rupture and continuity, speaking and listening, watching and being watched. They function politically as repositories of collective memory, as sites of moral instruction, and as devices for calling communities into being through performance. Improvisation in art necessitates sizing up one's situation, learning to work with others, and making choices swiftly and decisively. The same can be said about improvisation in social movement mobilizations.

Social movements sometimes erupt suddenly out of nowhere, but every social movement has a repertoire of signs, symbols, tactics, and strategies with a long history. New mobilizations rely upon ideas, information, and organizational networks fashioned by previous struggles (V. Taylor 761). Especially under conditions of starkly unequal power, members of aggrieved groups often recognize that voicing their complaints openly runs the risk of provoking retaliation by their oppressors. At these times, when overt rebellion does not seem possible, covert rebellion thrives. Aggrieved groups hold oppositional inclinations, identities, and ideas in "abeyance," inside what Aldon Morris calls "halfway houses," which are institutions and activities that do not seem to have overt political purposes and consequently do not threaten power directly (139–73). Yet these halfway houses promote practices and teach skills that can be applied some time in the future to struggles that can only be envisioned in the present. In New Orleans, improvisational, expressive culture has been a valuable halfway house for social movements. To paraphrase Jason Berry, when politics fails, culture prevails.[1]

An African City in America

In New Orleans, the currents of improvisation that run through musical performances, street parades, dances, dramatic productions, slang expressions, and displays of sartorial style stem from a long history. African cultural influences run deep in a city where elite families fleeing the Haitian revolution brought three thousand slaves with them in 1810, where trade with Caribbean ports and immigration from Caribbean countries over centuries shaped the local economy and demography in definitive ways, where the illegal importation of slaves persisted until the end of the Civil War (Brothers 63). Strong currents of African culture flow through the city's expressive culture. In her study of Yoruba rituals, the performance theorist, dance historian, and ethnographer Margaret Thompson Drewal identifies the important work that improvisation performs in producing transformative power in West African culture. Seemingly spontaneous performances draw on techniques of embodied action learned since childhood. Apparently, isolated and individual expressions actually answer previous moves and shape subsequent gestures by others. Community relations and embodied histories are activated. Transformative power emerges when performances display mastery of the logic of action and demonstrate the capacity to utilize familiar in-body codes for new purposes. Frivolity and fun serve serious purposes. As Drewal explains, "It is indeed the playing, the improvising, that energizes people, drawing them into the action, constructing their relationships, thereby generating multiple simultaneous discourse" (qtd. in Turner 92).

The Plantation Bloc, the Shadow of Slavery, and the Weapons of the Weak

The history of slavery haunts the racial order of New Orleans to this day. After emancipation, whites used Jim Crow segregation, vigilante violence, political suppression, and mass incarceration to reinstitute the exploitative social relations of slavery under a new name. These practices consolidated the power of what the black studies scholar Clyde Woods calls the "plantation bloc" to govern the city of New Orleans and the entire Mississippi Delta region. This elite group institutionalized the regime that Jan Nederveen Pieterse, a scholar of globalization and culture, correctly calls Dixie capitalism. The plantation bloc wields enormous power locally, but it has also used its base to play a decisive role in national politics. As Woods and Pieterse demonstrate, the plantation bloc has made New Orleans into a laboratory for policies designed to exploit the poor, preserve inequality, and protect the privileges of whiteness. Programs originally developed in New Orleans in the shadow of slavery now guide federal policies about welfare, labor, agricultural subsidies, incarceration, reproduction, the environment, and trade.

Yet while New Orleans is the center of Dixie capitalism, it is also the capital of black culture in the United States, a city where the social world that slaves and free blacks created for themselves under dire circumstances remains a powerful and generative force for justice. Slave culture shaped the music, religion, and political mobilizations by freedmen after emancipation. The culture of the black working class and the black poor has held in abeyance African ideas about improvisation and art. In slave communities, stories from Africa and the Caribbean about seemingly weak creatures outwitting more powerful opponents taught lessons about oral performance, collective authorship, and the importance of commitment to a particular course of action, no matter what the costs (Rawick). People who owned no property of their own, who were in fact owned by others as if they were property, created cultural forms that out of necessity did not depend on valuable material possessions. As Thomas Brothers argues in his splendid book on Louis Armstrong's New Orleans, African slaves in America learned to make a way out of no way by improvising, by "taking advantage of the disadvantages." Their emancipated descendants followed in their footsteps. Some of them turned to jazz music and learned how to bend pitch on brass horns and woodwinds, not only to adapt the African pentatonic scale to tonal functional harmony of the European diatonic scale, but sometimes also to compensate for the shortcomings of the inexpensive but antiquated and poorly functioning instruments available to them (53, 63).

Learning to recognize unexpected possibilities on seemingly inadequate instruments functioned to hone and refine musicians' ability to find value in one another as well. Brothers relates a story to that effect, told by Louis Armstrong, about a woman in the sanctified church he attended as a child. When the woman displayed enthusiasm for a substitute preacher who lacked the oratorical skills of the congregation's regular pastor, church members asked the woman why. She replied that whenever she heard a preacher whose sermons did not measure up to what she had become accustomed to in their church, she looked over the speaker's shoulder and saw Jesus there just the same. Armstrong applied this lesson to music, confiding that when he played with musicians lacking in talent but playing as best they could, he could always look over their shoulders and see Joe Oliver and other great musicians from his hometown, and as a result play enthusiastically for them.

In an analysis that applies as much to the work of social movements among aggrieved groups as it does to music, Brothers observes, "It is possible to listen as Armstrong listened, to grant conviction and passion a place in the first line of valuation, with technical sophistication pushed slightly to the rear. One can value *willingness* and learn to hear it, even to think about it as carrying a glimpse of spiritual or artistic purity—at a certain point it does not seem to matter how this is phrased" (47). The history of jazz verifies Brothers's point on the terrain of aesthetics, but these ideas have political import as well. In the African American tradition, cultural performances teach ethical values. Aesthetic principles serve as valuable political resources. Willingness can do important work.

Radical Divisiveness and Radical Solidarity

Members of culturally despised and demonized social groups pay a terrible price for their status. They experience material deprivation, political disenfranchisement, and social ostracism. Even worse, the people they need to ally with in order to fight back have many deficiencies and weaknesses stemming from their subordination. Members of aggrieved communities see a mirror of their own humiliation in each other's eyes. They compete with one another for scarce resources and symbolic prestige. Often they cannot attack their actual enemies, but they can fight with each other. Oppression does not magically unite members of an aggrieved community. More often it exacerbates already existing divisions. As George Rawick, the historian of slave culture, observed many years ago, in its final stages genocide can look very much like suicide. For these reasons, aggrieved groups must create mechanisms of struggle and solidarity. They must fabricate the will and confidence to fight back. They have to see beyond surface appearances to discern not only who they and their neighbors are, but also who they might become. They must listen as Armstrong listened, to appreciate the value of willingness and to learn how to cultivate it. Under these circumstances, creating a collective identity requires a great deal of imagination, effort, and enthusiasm.

The creation of the black community in slavery and in freedom has been a process made possible by imagination and improvisation. Kidnapped Africans arrived in America speaking different languages, worshipping different deities, and practicing different customs. Slave owners established and maintained control over the humans they held as property through radical divisiveness. Slave sales broke up families and communities. Work assignments placed some slaves in the fields and others in the houses of slave owners. Some slaves were ordered to supervise and punish others. Yet in the face of these mechanisms of radical divisiveness, slaves created a unified community. Unable to count on living with blood relatives, they referred to people unrelated to them as "brother" and "sister." They "bargained" with their owners and staged "strikes" by hiding in the woods together until they received promises of better treatment. They helped runaway slaves hide out, and those who escaped to freedom frequently took up the abolitionist cause. Harriet Tubman escaped to the north but returned to slave territory repeatedly to lead others to escape on the Underground Railroad. Secret prayer services, held midweek at midnight, in brush arbors, preserved sacred practices from Africa, while public worship as Christians on Sundays produced a recombinant Christianity made up of both African and Euroamerican elements. The practices of ecstatic praise and worship before and after emancipation served to cement collective solidarity (Rawick 30–52, 125–49). As Melvin Dixon, the brilliant novelist, critic, and essayist, once explained, the slaves were not so much converting themselves to God as they were converting themselves to one another (Brothers 41).

Expressive Culture and Politics

Forms of solidarity and mutuality nurtured and sustained in diverse forms of expressive culture proved easily transferable to collective social action. Within the logic of scholarship and its disciplinary boundaries, struggles for civil rights and performances of improvisational art appear to belong to very different areas of study. Politics and culture are generally studied separately. In most cases, politics is treated as meaningful work in the world, while culture is relegated to the realm of recreation, refinement, and escape. Struggles for human rights and performances of improvisational art voice their claims in different registers and seemingly with different degrees of seriousness. Yet in the world outside the academy and society's dominant cultural institutions, politics and culture are mutually constitutive. Activists, artists, and intellectuals have long recognized affinities between art and social activism. In societies where access to deliberative talk and democratic face-to-face decision-making is blocked, participation in expressive culture plays an especially important role in prefiguring new and better social relations.

Max Roach recognized this link in a conversation with a reporter in 1991. Delineating how jazz musicians have to listen carefully, communicate clearly, and find ways to be in harmony with each other (figuratively and literally), Roach claimed that "a jazz band operates more democratically than a society" (qtd. in Berman and Lee 23). While best known for compositions, performances, and social activism that overtly challenged racism and imperialism, in this interview Roach identifies the very work of making music as political in itself, as prefigurative of new social relations. His observation establishes a connection between the political "matter" of his art and the "manner" in which that art is created.

Improvisation not only teaches new skills; it can also serve as a way of combating the demoralization and fatalism that oppression inculcates in individuals and groups. In "The German Ideology," Karl Marx argues that fundamental social change requires the "alteration of men on a mass scale," and that this alteration can take place only through practical social activity. Oppressed people need a revolution, he claims, not only to seize power from their oppressors but also to change themselves by getting rid of "the muck of the ages" in order to become fit "to found society anew" (193). Marx's argument contains a built-in contradiction, however. Although he calls for revolutionary change as a way for people to rid themselves of the muck of the ages, he also argues that "the class which has the means of material production at its disposal, has control at the same time over the means of mental production, so that generally speaking, the ideas of those who lack the means of mental production are subject to it" (172). Marx seems to present an insolvable dilemma. We cannot rebel unless we become different kinds of people, yet we cannot become different kinds of people unless there is a rebellion. This contradiction does not stem from deficiencies in Marx's analysis, but rather from his accurate recognition of the deep internal conflicts that subordinate social status produces in people. That is one reason why improvisation is important, because it can be one of the activities whereby people break the chains of the past and learn to become fit to found society anew.

In an era when, as Kidd Jordan, the sorely underdocumented, ace improviser and free jazz saxophonist based in New Orleans, has put it, "everybody just wants to play the same stuff that everybody else is playing. Same solos, same licks," improvisation is important because it offers the opportunity to hear the world anew (qtd. in Butters). Jordan, indeed, is forthright in his insistence that the "minute someone pats me on the back about something is the minute I'm ready to leave," suggesting that improvised music-making has enabled him to break with patterns of complacency (qtd. in Butters). But the newness of improvised music, the outness of his own performance practices, as Jordan well knows, comes with no guarantees. As he himself recognizes, "Around New Orleans people been telling me I'm the last free man for the last twenty years. It's not a popular road. You stand a lot of abuse to play this music. But you got to stick to what you want to do" (qtd. in Butters).

Indeed, as the film theorist Laura Mulvey argues, "Moving from oppression and its mythologies to resistance in history" is a difficult process. This movement does not follow a simple and direct path, but instead entails "a detour through a no-man's land or threshold area of counter-myth and symbolisation" (3). Improvisational art has been a site where important social work has taken place in New Orleans. Through expressive culture, black people have turned community-based art-making into art-based community-making. They turn segregation into congregation, transform surveillance into display, combat negative external ascription with internal positive affirmation, replace radical dehumanization with radical rehumanization, and counter the radical divisiveness imposed on them with festive and celebratory solidarity.

Improvisation as Political Training

Improvisation has long served serious political purposes inside black communities. Shortly before his death, in 1965, Malcolm X asked his followers to emulate the improvisational work of jazz musicians. He explained that black musicians do not need sheet music in order to play well, that free from the score they improvise creatively based on their experiences, desires, and imagination. They find freedom by being fully aware and taking actions based on that awareness. "And that is what you and I want," Malcolm declared. "You and I want to create an organization that will give us so much power we can sit and do as we please" (qtd. in G. Lewis, *Power* 97). Seeing improvisation as a source of power, as an efficient and effective way of working, as a road to freedom, as a metaphor for democracy, grows logically out of the lessons that jazz performance imparts. In jazz funerals in New Orleans, for example, music actually rises from the dead to reaffirm the sacredness of life. The somber music that jazz bands play on the way to the cemetery and the rollicking and joyful music they play as they parade back from it bring the community together much in the way that the prophet Ezekiel in the Bible fused together the scattered and shattered bones of a defeated and demoralized people, bringing them back to life (Brothers 86).

The black nationalism at the heart of Malcolm X's politics was itself a kind of ingenious improvisation, a way of changing disadvantage into advantage. Black nationalism turns hegemony on its head by placing the white supremacy of the United States in a global context. It reveals that the same black people who make up a national minority inside the United States, at the same time make up part of a global majority of nonwhite people. They share grievances against racism and imperialism with millions of potential allies around the world. Black nationalism unmasks white supremacy as a local circumstance rather than a universal principle. It uncrowns power by rendering U.S. racism merely a relative, provisional, and contingent local circumstance. It turns a national minority into a global majority. It transforms an isolated and largely powerless population into a node in a network of global struggle.

"Human" Rights and Civil Rights

The improvisations of black nationalism held practical as well as symbolic significance for Malcolm X. At the peak of the civil rights movement, he attempted expressly to shift the frame from civil rights in the context of the United States to global human rights, to move the focal point of struggle from the U.S. Capitol to the United Nations. Tapping into deep, although often submerged, strains of internationalism in the black community, Malcolm X argued, "All of our African brothers and our Latin-American brothers cannot open their mouths and interfere in the domestic affairs of the United States. And as long as it's civil rights, this comes under the jurisdiction of Uncle Sam" (qtd. in Breitman 34). Intervention by foreign allies increased the likelihood of success in Minister Malcolm's judgment, but it also did something about the muck of the ages. Malcolm claimed that seeing the black struggle in the United States as part of the revolutionary, anticolonial struggles then convulsing Vietnam, the Congo, and Latin America would be good for black people because it positioned them to make demands as members of a majority can, instead of begging as a minority is forced to do (qtd. in Breitman 218).

In similar fashion, the citizenship schools in South Carolina organized by the Highlander Folk School and taught by Bernice Robinson in the 1950s also encouraged blacks to make claims as global citizens with inalienable rights. After teaching basic literacy, Robinson immediately had her students read the United Nations Universal Declaration of Human Rights. She discovered that grappling with "big ideas" made her students feel that securing the right to vote in South Carolina made them part of a struggle that extended far beyond the state's borders. The UN declaration enabled the students to view their disenfranchisement in South Carolina as a local aberration out of step with worldwide practices, rather than as a natural, necessary, and permanent condition of their existence (Morris 153). Grappling with "big" ideas also encouraged the students to think of themselves as serious people with important work to do in a society where white supremacists referred to adult black men as "boys," and where black men and women were routinely called by their first names but had to address white children as mister or miss.

Fannie Lou Hamer also improvised the frame of "human" rights as an alternative to the more limited opportunities provided by the frame of civil rights. She remapped the struggle by placing it in an international frame. "Some say that we're fighting for equality," she told a convention of civil rights workers in Mississippi, "but I don't want to be equal to murderers. We're fighting for democracy . . . we want to make Mississippi a democracy where we make our own decision" (qtd. in Lee 117). Especially after visiting the African nation of Guinea in the fall of 1964, Hamer stressed a commitment to seeing all oppressions as connected. She proclaimed to a mostly white audience at a meeting of the National Women's Political Caucus that "nobody's free until everybody is free." She continued, "I've passed equal rights. I'm fighting for human rights" (qtd. in Lee 179).

In the work of Malcolm X and Fannie Lou Hamer, rights served not so much as an abstract legal principle but as an extension of the radical solidarity fused over centuries in the African American community, as a timely tactical move necessitated by the refusal of the U.S. government over nearly an entire century to implement in practice the rights that blacks secured on paper with the passage of the Thirteenth, Fourteenth, and Fifteenth Amendments to the Constitution, in the 1860s. Of course activists from all backgrounds may have to devise strategies in response to new circumstances. The moves made from civil rights to global rights by Malcolm X and Fannie Lou Hamer, however, come from people with direct personal experiences with improvisation in black expressive culture. Malcolm X danced to the music of swing bands, wore zoot suits, and mastered street slang and verbal performance during the 1940s. In his brilliant analysis of this period in Malcolm X's life, the historian Robin Kelley explains how the ability to find oppositional potential in the frivolous, the frowned upon, and the forbidden accounts for much of Minister Malcolm's later appeal and success as an activist (*Race Rebels* 161–81). When speaking to black audiences on street corners and in civic auditoriums, Malcolm X displayed all the skills of an expert improviser as he provoked laughter and applause through playful interactions with listeners, sudden and unexpected changes in register and tone, and rhetoric based on dialogic responses to prevailing wisdom and dialogic provocations for new ways of thinking, speaking, and being.

Fannie Lou Hamer also based her public persona as an activist on improvisational practices, her experiences singing gospel music in church. It was not just that Hamer's strong voice and exemplary pitch control helped give her the confidence to speak in public, but rather that she blended music and movement into a unified totality while at the same time using group singing as a way to enact the radical solidarity that politics generally only envisioned. In group singing in church, on picket lines, and at civil rights meetings, singers produced many different versions of the same melody sung at slightly different tempos, creating slightly different harmonies at each performance. This unity with difference is essential for social movements. Church music (like the blues) is not an autonomous form of art for art's sake. It has concrete work to do in society. Thomas Brothers explains that when people sing together in black churches "the result is a collective rendition of the tune that is both spontaneous and socially organized, coherent yet richly diverse" (41). This singing is also an embodied form of improvisation. As the singer and scholar Bernice Johnson Reagon argues, running a song through the body tampers with a part of people's very being. Singing a song in this tradition requires people to change, to act, to recognize a part of themselves that they otherwise might not know.

The community activist Jerome Smith, from New Orleans, has long recognized the links between improvisational expressive culture and social movement mobilization. As a child, Smith marched in Labor Day parades with his grandfather, a militant member of the local longshoreman's union. He remembers his mother's expressing particular admiration for Paul Robeson and his particular blend of artistry and activism. Smith started blending improvisation and activism at a young age. While riding a streetcar when he was eleven years old, in 1950, Smith pulled down the screen that separated white and black passengers. Whites in the car reacted with hostility to the boy's action and Smith was dismayed when a black woman hit him on the head and dragged him from the car, vowing that she would teach him to show proper respect to white people. Yet when they were a safe distance from the streetcar, the woman hugged him and with tears streaming down her face said, "Never, ever stop. I'm so proud of you. Don't you ever quit" ("A Young Boy's Stand on a New Orleans Streetcar").

During the 1960s, Smith participated in the Consumers League boycott of white-owned businesses on Dryades Street, rode buses as a freedom rider throughout the South, and served on the field staff for the Congress of Racial Equality's campaigns in Mississippi and Louisiana. Today he serves as director of a youth center in the Tremé neighborhood of New Orleans, and as the leader of Tambourine and Fan, an organization he has headed since 1988, dedicated to teaching young people about leadership, political engagement, and civil rights. Among his many influences, Smith lists Allison "Tootie" Montana, the late, legendary chief of the Yellow Pocahontas tribe of Mardi Gras Indians. The Indians are working-class, black fraternal orders that serve as mutual-aid societies. They work all year long sewing costumes to wear on Mardi Gras Day, St. Joseph's Day, and selected other occasions when they parade through the streets and improvise chants, songs, and dances based on patterns from the past. Smith began sewing costumes and marching with the Indians as a child. He derived political lessons from cultural practice, describing Chief Tootie Montana as someone who "unconsciously made statements about black power . . . the whole thing about excellence, about uniqueness, about creativity, about protecting your creativity." He recalls, "I learned that in those houses [of the Indians]. Police would try to run the Indians off the street, but we had a thing. You don't bow, you don't run from 'em, not black or white or grizzley grey" (qtd. in K. L. Rogers 11–12).

Improvisation, Race, and Place

The political culture of black New Orleans, which guides Jerome Smith and so many others, builds on a long history of collective improvisation aimed at creating places of possibility. Even in slavery between 1800 and 1835, slaves gathered in Congo Square for impromptu songs and dances accompanied by drums and horns (Berry, Foose, and Jones 207–8). The creation of black New Orleans itself, in the nineteenth century, was a kind of improvisation. Tens of thousands of blacks fled the hinterlands to gather together for mutual protection in New Orleans when the white supremacist counterrevolution against abolition democracy succeeded in restoring the social relations of slavery in the Louisiana countryside after 1880 through sharecropping and Ku Klux Klan terrorism (Brothers 135). In the late nineteenth century and the early twentieth, street parades and jazz funerals in New Orleans filled functions other than entertainment. At a time when brutal police officers and armed vigilantes generally kept blacks confined in their segregated neighborhoods, street parades and jazz funerals provided a freedom of movement that was otherwise unavailable. As a child, Louis Armstrong begged Bunk Johnson and Joe Oliver to let him carry their horns, so that he could march beside them and get to see other sections of the city. Armstrong credited his subsequent enthusiasm for participation as a player in brass bands with access to a newfound freedom, noting, "I could go into any part of New Orleans without being bothered" (qtd. in Brothers 18). Brothers explains that in a city where neighborhoods and streetcars were segregated, where blacks were expected to step off the sidewalk and move into the street to let white people pass by unimpeded, "parades offered disenfranchised Negroes a chance to assertively move their culture throughout the city's spaces" (21).

The tradition of the "second line" in street parades in New Orleans deploys imagination and improvisation to change the meaning of spaces.[2] Specialist musicians justifiably take pride in their performances, but members of the audience also participate by banging on sticks and bottles, shaking tambourines, waving umbrellas, and improvising dance steps and chants. Thoroughfares designed for commerce become public stages. Music usually available only for purchase inside nightclubs can be consumed for free on the streets. In street parades, the ecstatic frenzy and spirit possession of the sanctified church moves through the streets of the city. Carnival processions defy the standards of proper demeanor and dress that prevail during the rest of the year. They make time stop by honoring the time of play during hours usually reserved for work, by turning weekdays into Sundays, by resuscitating the African and Caribbean pasts as productive parts of the present. As second lines wind their way through black neighborhoods, they cognitively remap the city and challenge its prestige hierarchies. Mardi Gras Indian tribes avoid Canal Street, where the social elite masquerades and parades on carnival day. Instead, they march through black neighborhoods, treating as sacred spaces that are virtually unknown to the rulers of their city, places such as the Dew Drop Inn, at the intersection of Washington Avenue and LaSalle Street, and the median islands, along Claiborne Avenue.

The flamboyant dress and display characteristic of street parades and jazz funerals serves serious purposes for blacks in New Orleans. People who have been systematically denigrated, demeaned, and demonized need to defend themselves and their self-worth. They fight back in the arenas open to them with the tools they have at their disposal. In peak moments, like the years immediately after the Civil War or during the civil rights movement of the 1960s, blacks in New Orleans have organized and mobilized openly and in public. Yet when the opportunity structure has been less favorable, they have been forced to use more covert means. Clyde Woods, whose work in relation to post-Katrina New Orleans was discussed earlier, delineates in detail how blues music emerged in the context of bitter battles for survival, subsistence, resistance, and affirmation, how the pleasure-affirmative aspects of the blues functioned as a form of refusal against what the surrealist writer Franklin Rosemont described "as the shameful limits of unlivable destiny" (qtd. in Woods, *Development Arrested* 38). The costumes, umbrellas, and embodied movements of street parades cry out for attention. They display fashion sense, sewing skill, bodily control, imagination, and the ability to improvise beautifully with whatever resources happen to be at hand. The very excessive nature of these displays affirms emphatically that this community contains what the literary and legal scholar Karla Holloway describes as "lives of importance and substance," showing "these were individuals, no matter their failings or the degree to which their lives were quietly lived, who were loved" (Holloway 181).

These efforts at positive affirmation and self-love have political as well as psychological dimensions. White supremacy has always justified and rationalized its pathologies by projecting fears of nonnormative dysfunction onto black bodies and communities. George Rawick explains that the end of slavery increased rather than decreased anti-black racism. During slavery, the chains and whips of slave owners as well as the full force of federal laws like the Fugitive Slave Act guaranteed that blacks could not compete for jobs with white workers or exercise independent political power. Emancipation and the civil rights measures attendant on it enabled newly freed slaves to form coalitions with poor whites, coalitions that produced the first real democracy the nation had ever known, a democracy propelled by new laws opening up access for poor people to education, voting, health care, and economic opportunities. To combat the threat posed to racialized capitalism by these new developments, former slave owners and their northern capitalist allies abandoned the commitment to equality inscribed in the Thirteenth and Fourteenth Amendments.

Within a few decades, sharecropping re-created the social relations of the slave system, Jim Crow segregation separated free blacks from their poor white allies, and the promise of expanded suffrage inscribed in the Fifteenth Amendment was nullified through the use of voter-suppression strategies such as "grandfather" clauses, poll taxes, voter literacy tests, the White Primary, and of course vigilante violence and lynchings. These undemocratic measures could not be justified as equitable social policy, so they were portrayed as defensive responses against black people, who were collectively judged as unfit for freedom. Rawick shows that this newly energized white supremacy depicted the social taboo of black freedom as a biological transgression through a linked chain of representations of blacks as dirty, lazy, larcenous, and licentious. Minstrel shows, popular "coon" songs, lithographs, and lurid works of fiction and film disseminated these ideas and images widely throughout society.

In an era of rapid industrialization, these racist myths served to channel anxieties among whites about the newly ascendant regimes of time-work discipline into fantasies about the nonnormative behaviors and dispositions of black people. The white social order depended upon a fever pitch of fear about violations of white women by black men, diseases contracted by whites as a result of contact with blacks, or the jeopardy posed to white manhood by the possibility of black self-activity. At the same time, of course, white profits depended on the low wage labor of blacks in the agricultural and industrial sectors of the economy, just as the well-being of the white family rested on the exploited labor of black domestics, nannies, cooks, and laundresses.

The white racial order in New Orleans and the United States has long been legitimated through what the literary scholar Esther Lezra terms monstrous misfigurations of blackness. When confronted with evidence of their own unjust actions, it is always easier for people in power to blame the victims, to claim that people with problems are problems. Confronted with hateful caricatures of themselves, black people have generally followed one of two strategies: the culture of uplift and the culture of solidarity. In the face of the betrayal of radical reconstruction in the nineteenth century, a culture of uplift strategy emerged in the black community. It attempted to render the negative stereotypes about blacks useless through public displays of normativity and accomplishment. Advocates of this position reasoned that if blacks could prove themselves hardworking, sober, thrifty, pious, pure, and dignified, the stereotype would be disproven. High achievement by even a few blacks, it was thought, would prove the worthiness of others.

The culture of uplift remains a powerful current in African American life and culture to this day. Yet by focusing on the behavior of blacks, it makes it seem as if racial subordination is caused by black actions rather than by white supremacist institutions. The culture of uplift has historically been favored by those most likely to benefit from it, by blacks with light skin, education, and assets. They pay a price, however, in volunteering to become race leaders in the eyes of whites. The historian Kevin Gaines explains how the culture of uplift requires black elites to distance themselves from the black poor, to harangue and discipline other blacks in the name of collective uplift (Gaines). Yet rather than uniting the community, the culture of uplift encourages black men to win gains at the expense of black women, counsels prosperous blacks to secure advantages at the expense of the black poor, and promotes disidentification with and separation from members of the community deemed nonnormative because of their marital status, sexuality, or disability.

The culture of solidarity follows a different path. It connects the culture of uplift to the culture of the blues. It speaks to both the chitlin' eaters and the chicken eaters. The black activist newspaper publisher Charlotta Bass, of Los Angeles, exemplified the culture of solidarity from the 1920s through the 1950s as she warned against settling for "dark faces in high places," and instead mobilized collective struggles against housing and employment discrimination (qtd. in Gill 157). The culture of solidarity was exemplified in Ella Baker's challenge to the National Association for the Advancement of Colored People in the 1950s, to defend the rights of the town drunk as zealously as the group defended the rights of the town doctor. It shaped the ways civil rights struggles transformed Martin Luther King Jr. from a model member of the culture of uplift into the leader of the Poor People's March, in 1968. The culture of solidarity set the stage for the success of the Black Power movement of the 1960s and 1970s (as Charles Payne demonstrates) in encouraging blacks to think freely without fear of offending powerful whites, to affirm that black lives were as important as white lives, to insist on the right of self-defense, and to demand freedom and justice now.

The culture of solidarity rejects the idea that blacks are unfit for freedom. Rather than performing normativity in an attempt to please its enemies, the culture of solidarity performs exuberant blackness, encouraging people to live sensuously, passionately, and joyfully, to act as if freedom is already here. Improvised music has provided an important dimension in the culture of solidarity, both in generating performative communities but also in enacting publicly expressive freedoms. Street parades, jazz funerals, and second lines may run the risk of seeming to confirm negative stereotypes about blacks as uninhibited and undisciplined, yet at the same time they do important work affirming the collective worth of the community in its own eyes.

These practices have become even more important to the collective survival of black people in New Orleans since the flooding that accompanied Hurricane Katrina. A key part of the plantation bloc's strategy is to dismiss efforts to rebuild New Orleans by demonizing the city and its black inhabitants. Even as the floodwaters were still rising and creating an enormous human rights crisis, journalists and the governor of Louisiana and the president of the United States worried more about largely nonexistent black looters than about hundreds of thousands of black men, women, and children suffering from hunger, thirst, and lack of medical care. Congressman Richard Baker rejoiced over the destruction, proclaiming that "we" could not get rid of public housing in New Orleans but God got rid of it with the hurricane. Speaker of the House of Representatives Dennis Hastert claimed that New Orleans contained nothing of value and that it would be better to bulldoze the city than to rebuild it. In the face of this vicious propaganda, the ability of New Orleans residents to assert their determination to survive, to return to the city, rebuild it, and participate in democratic deliberations takes on enormous significance. One source of that self-assertion stems from the culture of solidarity fused over centuries, sometimes through collective political mobilization, but always through the messages of creativity and capability communicated through networks of apprenticeship and instruction in improvisational culture. The aggressive festivity of street parades proclaims that New Orleans is a special place, that its unique culture is worth saving and preserving.

Improvisational culture in New Orleans affirms the worthiness of the city, the sacredness of life, and importance of mustering the will to act, create, and struggle. The practice of improvisation also encodes important ways of being and important ways of knowing inside seemingly small practices and gestures. A jazz performer's virtuosity has no once-and-for-all, fixed or final goal. Jazz musicians have to establish their credibility anew with every performance. Jazz music resists the kinds of closure

essential to symphonic works. Jazz has no final chord. Similarly, improvisational practices in New Orleans never seek the last word; instead they
answer the art of those who came before and invite responses from those
who will follow. Street parades do not proceed through established, direct routes, but instead wander unpredictably and circuitously through
neighborhoods. Folk artists turn discarded junk into precious treasures.
They transform stationary tires and hubcaps into metaphorical emblems
of movement and speed.

The clarinetist Bob Wilber remembers that his teacher Sidney Bechet
and other New Orleans musicians dressed oddly, always wearing one item
of clothing that did not match the rest of their outfits. Thomas Brothers
connects this anecdote to African ways of knowing and being by referencing the art historian Robert Farris Thompson's analysis of the asymmetrical patterns characteristic of Afrodiasporic textiles in the southern
states and in Haiti. Thompson notes that a Senegambian proverb holds
that "evil travels in straight lines" and that Senegambian designs stagger
patterns and colors, creating a visual syncopation between strips of cloth
similar to the aural syncopation created by the interplay of musicians
and second liners in street parades (50–51). The improvisations of carnival in New Orleans are not random transgressions giving free reign to impulses repressed during the rest of the year, but rather carefully crafted
performances that demonstrate ways of knowing and ways of being that
are essential for the community's survival. They hold in abeyance dispositions, tools, and skills that can be put in play when needed for political
purposes.

We Know This Place

Improvisation is now needed more than ever in New Orleans. Actions by
city, state, and national authorities in response to the crisis that convulsed
the city in the wake of Hurricane Katrina, in 2005, have posed new threats
to the survival of black people. Cruel, calculated, and organized abandonment of poor and working-class blacks is a central part of the plans being
implemented to reconstruct the city along neoliberal lines for the benefit
of investors and owners. These policies exploit cumulative vulnerabilities
that have built up over decades and centuries, but they also impose new
indignities, injustices, and violations of human rights on people with precious few resources for fighting back. They entail the demolition of thou-

sands of habitable public housing units in a city with a massive home-less population, the removal of basic services from areas inhabited by the poor, the transfer of public schools to private for-profit companies, deliberate dispersal and fragmentation of families, neighborhoods, and social networks, and massive subsidies for commercial projects designed to make the city's population less black and more affluent. Part and parcel of global neoliberalism's approaches to "rebuilding" areas devastated by unusual circumstances like the Iraq war, the Asian tsunami, and the fail-ure of levees to control the floods that followed Hurricane Katrina, this local manifestation of what Naomi Klein calls "predatory disaster capi-talism" seeks to destroy the physical places and social practices that have been central to the survival of black people in New Orleans in the face of centuries of white supremacist rule and systematic violations of human rights.

Although many of the particular mechanisms enabling neoliberal re-construction of New Orleans are new, the general framework follows a pattern that has long prevailed in the city of New Orleans and the state of Louisiana. Since the 1970s, the region has been an experimental labora-tory for neoliberal policies. Dixie capitalists have used the powers of the state to lower taxes for the rich but still provide businesses with lavish subsidies. They have shredded the social safety net by cutting services for the needy while funding a massive increase in incarceration. Wetlands de-velopment and virtually unregulated discharges of toxic materials by the state's petrochemical industry have devastated the natural environment, while educational underfunding, high-stakes testing, and subsidies for charter schools have undermined public schools. Louisiana has the high-est incarceration rate in the world and executes more inmates per capita than any other state. Blacks are less than a third of Louisiana's population but make up 72.1 percent of the state's incarcerated prisoners (Woods, "Les Misérables" 789). Yet in Louisiana, nothing succeeds like failure. While it has become clear that these policies have produced increasing levels of neighborhood decay, homelessness, pauperism, poor health, and outmigration, Dixie capitalists and neoliberals call for more of the same in ever more concentrated and destructive forms (Woods, "Katrina's World" 444). Although there are often small disagreements about details, these policies are supported completely by both major political parties, by black and white elected officials locally and nationally, and are very likely to be upheld by the courts even though their deliberate skewing of life chances and opportunities along racial lines clearly seems to violate the Fourteenth Amendment and the Civil Rights Act of 1866. Black poor and working-class residents of New Orleans are as powerless to participate in the decisions that directly affect their lives with Barack Obama as president as they were when George W. Bush held that office.

Yet armed with the ideas, beliefs, tools, and skills honed inside cultural alternative academies and past political mobilizations, black New Orleans is fighting back. The New Orleans Women's Health Clinic in the Tremé neighborhood not only provides vitally needed reproductive and sexual health care to low-income women of color, but also refuses to separate reproductive freedom from racial, economic, and gender justice. Speaking from and for the experiences of socially marginalized and culturally demonized women, the New Orleans Women's Health Clinic views domestic violence against women as political as well as personal, as one consequence of a sex-race-gender regime that not only condones domestic violence against women, but also enables and excuses state violence against immigrants and people of color as well as street and police violence against transgendered individuals (Luft 504, 512). The frame of human rights has emerged once again as an important focal point of struggle in New Orleans. Activists have invoked international declarations, covenants, treaties, and the United Nations Guiding Principles on Internal Displacement of 1998 to support their claims for housing, safety, medical care, freedom from gender-targeted violence, and family unification. In 2007, the International Tribunal on Hurricanes Katrina and Rita, convened to publicize human rights violations, heard five days of testimony from witnesses about abuses of human rights by state and federal officials (Luft 518–19). The UN's special rapporteur on adequate housing, Miloon Kothari, and the UN's independent expert on minority issues, Gay McDougall, conducted an investigation that found that the demolition of public housing projects and other policies violated internationally recognized legal and moral standards. They asked (unsuccessfully) that local, state, and federal officials immediately cease demolition of public housing units and they called upon officials to "protect the rights of the poorer and predominately African American communities displaced by Katrina" (qtd. in Woods, "Les Misérables" 769).

The Long History of Fighting Back

The nature of power requires activists in New Orleans to embrace improvisational, tactical mobility rather than remain rooted in all-or-nothing commitments to either civil rights or human rights. Freedom for oppressed people does not generally follow a direct path on which incremental gains lead to inevitable victory. Instead, power makes concessions grudgingly and only when absolutely necessary. Aggrieved groups not only have to win victories, but they also have to struggle perpetually to prevent what they have won from being contained, co-opted, and contravened. No one knows this better than black people in New Orleans. When collective struggle created a new era of freedom and democracy sanctioned by the Thirteenth, Fourteenth, and Fifteenth Amendments to the Constitution, former slave owners and their northern allies worked quickly to turn these newfound freedoms into fetters.

In Colfax, Louisiana, in 1873, a white mob murdered more than one hundred blacks because their votes helped pro-black politicians win elective office. White-supremacist state authorities would not prosecute the perpetrators of the riot, so federal officials prosecuted and won convictions of the ringleaders of the mob. The prosecutors argued that the racially motivated massacre was designed to intimidate black voters and therefore violated civil rights laws and the promises of equal rights and equal protection written into the Thirteenth, Fourteenth, and Fifteenth Amendments. The Supreme Court, however, overturned the meaning of these laws by reversing the convictions of the mob leaders. The court held that laws expressly crafted to protect the civil rights of blacks merely prevented the state from taking actions favoring one race over another. The ruling held the civil rights charge brought against whites violated their Constitutional rights, because race relations were considered a private matter. Murder trials were up to the state of Louisiana, the court ruled. Of course the "private" discrimination blacks suffered was their being murdered for trying to exercise their Fifteenth Amendment rights, and the Louisiana authorities did not bring murder charges, because of the respective racial identities of the perpetrators and the victims. But to convict the ringleaders of the Colfax massacre, the court ruled, would mean that the state recognized race and would therefore undermine the equal protection guaranteed by the Fourteenth Amendment. In a bold stroke of hegemonic improvisation, the Supreme Court held that civil rights laws passed to ensure the rights of blacks actually protected the ability of whites to use "private" violence to prevent those rights from being exercised. In subsequent decisions, the court used a variety of subterfuges to outlaw civil rights laws that banned discrimination in public accommodations by private citizens and that prevented state officials from blocking access to voting by blacks. It took these steps not in the name of white supremacy, but by invoking the sanctity of civil rights, contending that the very laws that blacks had succeeded in getting passed mandated their subordination (Newman and Gass).

Similarly, when the Supreme Court issued the 1954 *Brown v. Board of Education* decision, holding that segregated schools violated the Constitutional rights of black children, segregationists in Louisiana viewed the decision as a wedge likely to open the door to black political power in the future. In response, they fabricated a defense of segregation that turned the discourse of injury on its head. Denying that school segregation existed to provide unfair advantages for whites or to impose unjust constraints on blacks, Louisiana's legislators now claimed that segregated schools existed to protect white children (especially innocent white girls) from immoral and unclean blacks. The *Brown* decision expressly rejected that claim in its footnote eleven, which noted that the alleged deficiencies attributed to black children came from poverty, ill health, lack of education, and other aspects of their victimization by southern white oppression, concluding that Louisiana officials could not use the ill effects of segregation on black people as a justification for more segregation.

Elected officials in Louisiana and other southern states attempted to refute this argument by producing evidence of black immorality. They did so by passing laws designed to inflate artificially the numbers of common-law marriages among blacks and the numbers of children born out of wedlock. They changed the requirements to get a marriage license by demanding copies of original birth certificates and health certifications signed by physicians in the previous ten days. One law declared that marriage licenses could be issued only on weekdays, between eight in the morning and noon, hours when working people were at their jobs. These laws also allowed licenses to be issued at the homes of registrars at other times, creating special preferences and opportunities for whites with existing social relations with county officials (who were all white because of segregationist voter suppression). New laws outlawed common law marriages, limited the number of people authorized to perform marriage ceremonies, demanded legal proof that previous marriages had been dissolved and that applicants were free of venereal disease.

At the same time, other statutes insisted that all newborn babies had to have certificates within five days of their birth that indicated if they were born out of wedlock. Armed with the statistics that their policies produced, southern states then began to use "bad moral character" as a reason to deny black citizens the right to vote (Walker 410–16). These measures also functioned to criminalize black poverty. The Louisiana governor, Jimmie Davis, defended depriving more than twenty thousand black children of welfare payments on the grounds that the mothers of these children were "a bunch of professional prostitutes" (Neubeck and Cazenave 72). White supremacists sought to preserve their racial privileges without referring directly to race, to disguise discrimination under the guise of family protection and moral uplift. Anticipating the color-blind racism that prevailed in the courts and society by the 1970s, white supremacists had once again turned an antiracist victory into a defeat by declaring that blacks were unfit for freedom and that race-based policies by private individuals and the state were in fact race-neutral.

Shortly after the assassination of Martin Luther King Jr., in 1968, Congress passed the Fair Housing Act, banning discrimination in home sales and rentals. Deliberately written to be weak and virtually unenforceable, the act nonetheless provoked grassroots activism by civil rights supporters. Their agitation, education, and litigation led to new statutes and a body of case law that made it possible to chip away at segregation. Yet legislators refused to fund fair-housing efforts adequately; state and federal agencies charged with fair-housing enforcement acted timidly and slowly. The National Fair Housing Alliance estimates that despite the law, more than four million acts of illegal housing discrimination take place every year. As has often been the case with civil rights laws and court decisions, declarations of equal rights by no means ensure their implementation. In New Orleans in the years immediately before Hurricane Katrina hit, testers from local fair-housing organizations discovered that black apartment seekers experienced discrimination from landlords and managers seventy-seven percent of the time (N. Wilson 1A, 18A). George W. Bush's secretary of housing and urban development, Alphonso Jackson, did next to nothing to help enforce the Fair Housing Act. Jackson is a black conservative, someone who claims incorrectly that if the government takes note of race in trying to end racial discrimination it violates the principles of the Fourteenth Amendment, *Brown v. Board*, and the Civil Rights Act of 1964. But race was clearly on Jackson's mind as soon as it became clear that the government would have to help New Orleans rebuild after the floods that followed Hurricane Katrina. "New Orleans is not going to be as black as it was for a long time, if ever again," Jackson proclaimed. "I'm telling you," he confided, "as HUD [U.S. Department of Housing and Urban Development] Secretary and having been a developer and a planner, that's how it's going to be" (Rodriguez and Minaya 1). A key part of Jackson's plan to drive blacks from the city entailed destroying the public housing projects in which blacks lived and replacing them with smaller, private developments that would charge rents that the displaced poor would not be able to afford.

Jackson justified this exercise in ethnic cleansing as a civil rights victory. He mimicked the language and arguments used by fair-housing advocates in the *Gautreaux* case, in Chicago, that claimed that concentrated poverty in black neighborhoods constituted a civil rights injury. Yet Jackson's solution to concentrated poverty was to move blacks out of the neighborhood and create subsidized housing in it for middle-income and high-income whites who faced no housing shortage. He "saved" the black poor from concentrated poverty by making them homeless. Jackson echoed the critique of *Gautreaux*, but disdained its remedies. In *Gautreaux*, the courts combated concentrated poverty by assisting inner-city residents in moving to neighborhoods of opportunity, by providing them with financial assistance, counseling, and other forms of social support. Previously white neighborhoods opened up to black residents through this plan (Polikoff). Jackson's scheme, which has been supported by his successors in both the Bush and Obama administrations, does nothing to help inner-city residents, but does a lot to hurt them. The "integration" it creates does not desegregate areas of white privilege, but rather creates new protected zones reserved largely for whites (with a token black presence) in what were once black neighborhoods. In short, it presents gentrification as the solution to the slums, without acknowledging that gentrification creates profitable situations, mostly for whites, by exacerbating an already disastrous housing crisis for blacks. Like the advocates of abolition democracy and school segregation before them, the supporters of fair housing found previous victories used against them by plans to redevelop New Orleans that used the ideas and arguments of previous civil rights victories in support of new forms of white supremacy.

This sad example is not the only one in which rights instruments have been perverted or willfully abused after Katrina. More than half of New Orleans's largely black residents (some 200,000 people) have not returned to the working-class neighborhoods in which they lived: including the Lower Ninth Ward, Gentilly, and Holy Cross, all of which, though poor, were culturally and economically important to the city. This large population of displaced people, spread over some forty-six states, has been systematically denied access to information about their homes, to insurance, and to the kinds of support that would facilitate return and reconstruction. Jeffrey Buchanan, a human rights advocate and activist, notes the hypocrisies and the utter failures of the U.S. government in terms of its application of basic rights principles:

> While America is new to this magnitude of displacement, the fact remains that our government is very familiar with the internationally recognized "playbook" on how to protect the human rights of displaced people before, during and after a humanitarian disaster that forces people to leave their homes but remain within national borders.
>
> The U.N.'s Guiding Principles on Internally Displaced People is endorsed and implemented using US tax dollars by US diplomats, in countries like post-tsunami Sri Lanka and post-war Iraq, as the way to uphold human rights commitments to our allies' displaced citizens. It outlines how to treat displaced people with dignity defining their rights to information, housing, healthcare and food as well as their civil and property rights. The Principles declare that the federal government has a duty to create conditions that allow displaced people to voluntarily return home, giving people a right to return. Governments must allow displaced people to participate in decisions about how their communities are rebuilt and protect their property rights in their absence.
>
> Katrina's survivors have been denied many of the rights outlined in the Guiding Principles but the US sees no harm. Bush Administration officials recently told the UN Human Rights Committee that they do not believe Katrina's displaced survivors, who the administration evasively labels "evacuees," deserve such protections. By some twisted logic, the U.S. government must believe they can ignore the human rights of American citizens by simply re-branding them.

The shockingly cynical response of the federal government to New Orleans in the aftermath of Katrina is indicative of the degree to which rights discourse generally is at the mercy of institutional priorities, and driven by neoliberal profit-seeking. Interestingly, one of the few focused attempts to recuperate from the tragedy involved the New Orleans natives Branford Marsalis and Harry Connick Jr. teaming up with Habitat for Humanity to create the Musicians' Village, in the Upper Ninth Ward:

> The core idea behind Musicians' Village is the establishment of a community for the city's several generations of musicians and other families, many of whom had lived in inadequate housing prior to the catastrophe and remain displaced in its aftermath. A central part of this vision is the establishment of a focal point for teaching, sharing and preserving the rich musical tradition of a city that has done so much to shape the art of the past century. The concept was quickly embraced by NOAHH [New Orleans Area Habitat for Humanity], the organization that has developed a model for building single-family homes that low-income families may purchase with zero-interest financing. In keeping with its commitment to build not just homes but communities, NOAHH has given its support to an effort that redefines neighborhood revitalization. (www.nolamusiciansvillage.org/about)

The initiative recognized both the cultural importance of New Orleans's musicians and the disproportionate poverty that they have faced for generations. Even if only as a drop in the bucket, musicians here showed leadership and took action in meaningful ways that reiterated the connections between social mobilization and improvisation.

Similarly, the trumpeter and New Orleans native Terence Blanchard's score for Spike Lee's devastating critique of America's response to the New Orleans tragedy, *When the Levees Broke: A Requiem in Four Acts* (HBO, 2006), activated his political conscience in ways that have made him an outspoken musical activist, as well as an already distinguished improviser. *A Tale of God's Will (A Requiem for Katrina)* (Blue Note, 2007) is a remarkable blend of improvisation, diasporic African American musicking (especially the tracks "Ghosts of Congo Square," with its dominant Afro-Cuban rhythms, and "Ashé," which references the Afro-Cuban and Yoruban spiritual energy found in all animate and inanimate things), and conventional composition, in the service of artistic and political critique. Blanchard has not minced his words after Katrina, stating in an interview,

> I just want people to reflect on what happened here and what people had to deal with, and how things can go terribly wrong in what is supposed to

be the richest country in the world. The irony of all this stuff, of us fighting for freedom in Iraq and people suffering and dying in their homes in New Orleans, was not lost on me, and I think it's an interesting commentary on the times that we live in. I've been saying for a long time that the country is on the brink of disaster because we've allowed politicians to run amok and we've allowed them to lie to us with no consequence. (qtd. in M. Smith)

Blanchard's status as a musician precedes his activism, and his outspoken critique of rights abuses after Katrina is reinforced by the musical integrity he has established as a respected artist. In this sense, the social practice of improvisation as a form of accomplishment that then gives one the power of critique cannot be neglected. Blanchard's playing, though conventional in many respects, is still highly indebted to improvisational discourse, through his apprenticeship in Art Blakey's Jazz Messengers, and his association as artistic director with the Thelonious Monk Institute of Jazz (which had relocated from the University of Southern California, in Los Angeles, to Loyola University's New Orleans campus after Katrina). The hybrid musical discourses on display in *A Tale of God's Will* recapitulate New Orleans's historical significance as a place where new intercultural formations that have dramatically shaped the musical vision of the twentieth century were made possible, many of these as a direct result of the contingencies that produced improvisatory explorations.

Toward a Critique of "Human" Rights

The freedom dreams of black people cannot be fulfilled by an uncritical embrace of either civil rights or "human" rights frames. Both can be turned into their opposite through the pernicious machinations of people in power. Civil rights laws that seem to ban discrimination may actually proscribe only the most egregious forms of exclusion as a way of legitimating and legalizing many other white supremacist practices. Human rights proclamations and treaties that seem to protect people may actually promote the free movement of capital across national boundaries, by banning extreme acts of torture and brutality while condoning the routine mechanisms of exploitation and inequality that pervade the global economy. Like other aggrieved groups fighting for justice, blacks in New Orleans do not have the luxury of adopting fixed frames or forms of struggle. Their enemies will use even their victories against them. They do, however, possess a rich history of imagination, innovation, and improvisation that has enabled their survival in the past and that will guide their actions in the future. Could it be that improvisation and related forms of community expression hold the key to renewed rights affirmations and practices that New Orleans will yet again be forced to produce? If so, the alternative social practices embedded in improvisation may well provide a way forward into new rights formations and manifest practices that undo the willful neglect New Orleans has suffered for so long.

CHAPTER 5

ART TO FIND THE PULSE OF THE PEOPLE
We Know This Place

Late in the afternoon, on a Thursday early in November 2009, the American Studies Association is holding its annual meeting in an elegant hotel in Washington, D.C. This conference usually consists exclusively of panel presentations by scholars reporting on their research, but one session at this meeting breaks the pattern. Professor Clyde Woods and graduate student Jordan T. Camp, of the University of California, Santa Barbara, have organized a panel featuring the cultural workers and activists Sunni Patterson, Brenda Marie Osbey, Kalamu ya Salaam, and Shana Griffin. The panel members have traveled from New Orleans to present their perspectives on the continuing rights crisis facing working-class black people in that city.[1]

A Community Speaks for Itself

The spoken-word artist and community activist Sunni Patterson begins the session by picking up a hand-held microphone and starting to recite her poem "We Know This Place." Speaking with confidence, clarity, and passion, Patterson describes the deliberate and systematic abandonment of the black working class in New Orleans in the wake of the flooding that accompanied Hurricane Katrina, in 2005. Moreover, she explains, in the four years that have followed the flood, the city, state, and federal government have colluded with developers and investors to prevent the dispersed population of the city's poor and working-class black neighborhoods from returning to New Orleans and participating in projects designed to rebuild it. Her poem revolves around a bitter contradiction: that the seemingly unprecedented abandonment by government agencies of people in need during the Katrina crisis, which shocked many people around the world is part of a pattern that is all too familiar to African Americans in New Orleans. Speaking for and from a black community once again facing displacement and dispossession, Patterson's poem proclaims, "We know this place."

The Ninth Ward neighborhood where Sunni Patterson has lived most of her life was devastated by the waters that burst through poorly constructed and improperly maintained levee walls in 2005. Her closest friends and relatives were among those who suffered from malnutrition, thirst, and inadequate sanitation in the Superdome shelter area. Her former teachers and students were among the people waiting in vain for rescue on rooftops as flood waters rose around them. She knows the names, faces, and personalities of people who fled the floodwaters, those who were forced back into the disaster area by armed police officers and soldiers determined to prevent blacks from entering safer white neighborhoods. Patterson herself lived for a time in exile hundreds of miles away from the Ninth Ward, in Houston, Texas. Her poem describes the "ever changing" but "forever the same" oppression, suppression, marginalization, and exclusion of blacks in New Orleans.

Decrying a world in which "both the prophet and the priest practice deceit," Patterson bitterly connects the Xs marked on the outsides of homes, indicating whether the house had been searched for dead bodies and enduring health hazards, to the death of the Fourteenth Amendment and its guarantees of equal rights to black people. Patterson's poem expresses keen insights about the ways centuries of white supremacy have created cumulative vulnerabilities. The low-lying Ninth Ward is populated largely by black people because housing discrimination has prevented them from residing in homes located on higher ground. When flooding takes place, water flows to the low places. Even gravity works on behalf of white supremacy in New Orleans.

Patterson recites:

So we know this place
for we have glanced more times than we'd like to share
into eyes that stare with nothing there
behind them but an unfilled wish
and an unconscious yearning for life
though death rests comfortably beside us.

As Patterson speaks, her infant son, Jibril, starts to cry. Without missing a breath, a beat, or a word, the poet glides over to where her baby is being held, picks him up, and holds the child with one arm. Still grasping the microphone in her other hand, she continues her recitation. Jibril starts to smile, his eyes fixed on his mother with rapt attention, amusement, and seeming amazement. Patterson seems accustomed to this kind of improvised balancing act. Like many other mothers, she does not have the luxury of keeping the diverse parts of her life in separate compartments, so she blends them together deftly, in this case performing poetry and caring for her child at the same time.

As Patterson holds Jibril, she continues her poem, connecting the problems of the present to the distant past:

And we know this place
It's ever changing, yet forever the same;
Money and power and greed, the game.

The poet invites the audience to think about people who are not present in the room with them. She interpolates snippets of other poems she has written into her recitation of "We Know This Place," poems that honor the men and women "who work 25 hours a day for 24 cents an hour" and who dwell "in a state of lack and limit." Patterson draws connections between "two women in New Orleans shot point-blank in the back of the head" and "two women bombed in their car in Baghdad." Yet while summoning into her presence this roster of people who suffer, Patterson also places them inside a tradition of struggle. "We are people of beginnings," she asserts, "field hands of freedom."

Patterson's improvisation sets the stage for other improvisations to follow. Even though the panelists speak sequentially, in keeping with academic conventions, their words blend together seamlessly. They make references to each other's art and activism, nod knowingly when familiar names are mentioned, and pick up cues from each other's talks in their own presentations. It becomes clear that they know "this place"—the site of oppression and suffering referenced in Patterson's poem and still painfully present in their lives four years after the hurricane. But they also know "this place" that they inhabit on the panel, a place of mutuality and collective struggle, a place where people turn talking back into a form of art, a place where improvisation and imagination demonstrate to themselves and others that they have not yet been defeated. In their presentations, Osbey, Salaam, and Griffin present what Patterson calls an "art to find the pulse of the people"—expressions, images, and actions that "get to the heart of the matter," that awaken and cultivate what she calls the "soul conscience."

Brenda Marie Osbey takes the podium next. The contrast between the first two speakers is significant. Patterson represents the working-class Ninth Ward, but Osbey comes from the city's Seventh Ward, the Faubourg-Tremé, the oldest continuously black neighborhood in North America. Osbey reads and writes in French and English. She is an accomplished historian of the city's intellectual and cultural life, served as Louisiana's first official poet laureate, and teaches literature and writing at Louisiana State University. Her poetry collection *All Saints* won an American Book Award, in 1998. Yet for all her credentials as a traditional intellectual, at this session, Osbey speaks boldly and brilliantly as an organic intellectual as well. She expresses her dismay at the lapel buttons she has seen in New Orleans that designate the wearer as a "New" New Orleanian. Unlike the humorous buttons that read "Make Levees, Not War," or "New Orleans: So Proud to Swim Home," these particular buttons signify to Osbey not pride in the local culture, but rather a commitment to erasing and supplanting it. They relegate the New Orleans Osbey knows and loves to the "past definite" tense. In her judgment, these buttons are worn by people who have come to New Orleans "to save us from ourselves." The buttons symbolize all the plans for redevelopment and gentrification of the city that are premised upon expelling a large part of the black population and disempowering and disenfranchising those who remain. These plans cherish the city's complex culture as a spectacle to attract tourists but not as the basis for an enduring and valuable way of life. Its proponents do not speak from or for the people of New Orleans, in Osbey's estimation. They know nothing "but the lines uttered by the masters and repeated by their henchmen."

Osbey offers art as an antidote to the poison of ethnic cleansing and gentrified redevelopment. She invokes the long legacy of black creativity in the city to justify her stance, connecting herself and the other members of the panel to the black writers and poets of the nineteenth century, whose artistic creations emerged out of fights for freedom in the 1860s and 1890s. She contrasts art that does work inside a community with art that preaches to it from the outside. The exposure of art, for Osbey, entails obligations to the concerns of the community, to reveal what the corporate media, political leaders, and even artists have refused to discuss.

Osbey describes how the logic of neoliberalism that guided government responses to the crisis exhibited callous disregard for human life. She explains that Mayor C. Ray Nagin delayed declaring a state of emergency until it was too late so that the city would not be liable for the expenses that an evacuation would create. Osbey explained that row after row of buses that could have been used to transport people out of the city sat idly while the mayor urged people to leave the city in their private cars. When asked what people who did not own vehicles should do, Nagin simply shrugged his shoulders.

Osbey called attention to the shootings by police officers, on September 4, 2005, of blacks crossing the Danziger Bridge. Six officers and one sheriff's deputy killed nineteen-year-old James Brissette and forty-year-old Ronald Madison, and wounded four other civilians. The officers claimed they had been fired upon first, but all witnesses contradicted their story. To cover up the shootings, the police officers kicked spent shell casings off the bridge and met secretly in a police building to fabricate an official version of events that would exonerate the officers. When the district attorney indicted seven of the officers on charges of murder and attempted murder, a group of their fellow officers and supporters accompanied the accused to court, chanting and carrying signs describing the officers as "heroes." Five of these heroes later pleaded guilty to federal charges of obstructing justice and covering up a felony and agreed to cooperate with a Department of Justice inquiry. A federal jury found five other officers guilty of participating in the shootings and the subsequent cover-up. Yet local officials did not try, and federal officials did not succeed, in securing murder convictions for any of the officers involved in the killings of Brissette and Madison (Kunzelman, "Police Cover-Up Unravels" 1, 6; Kunzelman "1st Member of 'Danziger 7' Charged" 1, 10; Kunzelman, "Former Cop Admits to Danziger Cover-Up" 1, 6; E. W. Lewis, 1, 2, 7).

The veteran activist, poet, and youth worker Kalamu ya Salaam follows Osbey. His presentation focuses on the human costs of displacement, dispersal, and dispossession, on the eerie feeling of walking down familiar streets but no longer knowing if you will see someone you love on your journey. "What we miss most of all is us," he proclaims. "We the people are not there." He translates the coded language of redevelopment, gentrification, and planned shrinkage in the name of an ecologically friendly, smaller carbon footprint. All of these discourses, he notes, simply say "good riddance" to blacks. "Even though we controlled nothing, we were blamed for everything that was wrong," he notes. He improvises a riff on New Orleans's slogan "the city that care forgot" to describe it as the city that forgot to care. He explains how the privatization logic guiding redevelopment in New Orleans after Hurricane Katrina included firing seven thousand teachers and turning the school system over to private entrepreneurs. The firings undercut the financial well-being and social stability of thousands of educated, civic-minded, salary-earning, and property-owning blacks in order to create new opportunities for investors from out of town. Some of the teachers secured new jobs in the new charter schools, schools that spend twice as much per pupil to educate half the number of students that the public schools served and that offer teachers no medical insurance or retirement benefits. Four years after the hurricane, thousands of blighted properties blot the landscape. The city has no funds, or even plans, to renovate or demolish them. Yet the city and the federal government did destroy hundreds of habitable units in public housing projects, an action that exacerbated the city's shortage of affordable housing and increased the number of homeless.

Despite the hard facts his words communicate, Salaam follows the pattern that Patterson and Osbey fashioned in their talks. Like Patterson's poem and Osbey's discussion of the history of art and activism, Salaam's presentation proposes that performance art, poetry, literature, and music are important tools for crafting solutions to the problems facing black people in New Orleans. Coming from a community whose ideas and interests have rarely been recognized or acknowledged in the corridors of power, the panelists deploy speaking, writing, singing, and dancing as ways of using the tools they have to act in the arenas that are open to them. They call communities into being through performance, speaking words that serve as repositories of collective memory and as instruments of moral and political instruction. Through their art, they expand space and time. Patterson repopulates a conference room in an expensive Washington hotel by summoning into her presence the people back home who "work twenty-five hours a day for twenty-four cents an hour." Osbey invokes the experiences of creative ancestors from the nineteenth century and enlists them as allies in the struggles of the present. Salaam uses the panel presentation as an opportunity to start constructing a better future by promoting the writings of the Students at the Center (SAC) program, in New Orleans, especially the book *Men We Love, Men We Hate*, written by students from Douglass, McDonough 35, and McMain High Schools.

The book presents ruminations on masculinity, its many different manifestations, its strengths and its weaknesses. Salaam explains that Students at the Center has a rich history of helping the young learn their history, understand their present circumstances, and develop their voices to become participants in shaping the future. Like earlier books produced by young people working with SAC, including *Sankofa* and *The Long Ride*, *Men We Love, Men We Hate* encourages the community to take stock of itself, to survey where it has been, where it is now, and where it is going in the future. The work that Salaam describes presumes that people have the right to determine their own destiny, even if they are young, poor, and black. The books that he and his fellow teachers in New Orleans have helped bring into existence function as what James C. Scott, the anthropologist and social theorist, calls the weapons of the weak, tools for asserting irrepressible commitments to self-activity and democracy by people who (to borrow the apt phrasing of the historian David Roediger) have been displaced, dispossessed, disinherited, and just plain dissed.

The activities of SAC to which Salaam refers exemplify the aesthetic power and political potential of community-based art-making and art-based community-making in New Orleans. For more than a decade, artists and activists associated with SAC have worked with school children and community groups to stage public performances crafted to promote dialogue and debate about ways of improving local schools and neighborhoods. Here, community improvement and improvisation are instrumental aspects of reconfiguring the rights abuses that have plagued black communities in New Orleans. These interventions connect the rich history of civil rights struggles in New Orleans to stories contemporary residents tell about their own experiences and aspirations. The key mechanism for SAC is the story circle, an activity that uses listening to stories and telling stories as a mechanism for developing participants' capacities for citizenship and leadership. Story circles in New Orleans originated in John O'Neal's Free Southern Theater (FST), an arts auxiliary to the Student Nonviolent Coordinating Committee (SNCC) in the 1960s. The FST evolved into Junebug Productions and further developed the practice of story circles, in collaboration with arts activists from a community-based drama group in Appalachia, the Roadside Theater. Story circles in New Orleans follow the logic and form of jazz improvisation, emerging from dialogues at the time of performance rather than being scripted in advance.

Kalamu ya Salaam began his work with SAC early in its existence, first as a writer-in-residence, and later as codirector. He taught high school students to make films guided by what he calls Neo-Griot principles, a form that deploys modern digital technologies in the service of traditional African storytelling. The story circles, films, and literary publications produced by SAC speak from and for the people of the Ninth Ward and other aggrieved local neighborhoods. Students engaged with SAC go out into the community, knock on doors, start conversations, and invite people to planning meetings and performances. They call a community into being through dialogue and performance, invite spectators to be participants, and help turn bystanders into upstanders. Like the presentations at the panel convened by the American Studies Association, SAC's activities enact the democratic social relations they envision. As Salaam explains, "Our program is based on what can work within the conditions in which we find ourselves . . . That's part of the jazz aesthetic—when it's your turn to take a solo, you can't say, 'Well, wait, that's not the song I wanted to play,' [no], it's *your* turn" (qtd. in Michna 550). Salaam's analysis and pedagogy are clearly rooted in aspects of black diasporic culture that are tied to improvisation as an ethical, social practice of self-enabling agency and identity formation.

The American Studies Association presentations by Patterson, Osbey, and Salaam embody this improvisational ethic of New Orleans. Their words fill the room with voices other than their own. They summon up ancestors and allies. They remap the contours of a physically dispersed but spiritually unified community. They use their places at the podium in the present to help craft a better future. They speak sequentially, but function as an ensemble, playing together while featuring individual solos. They listen attentively to one another, meet each other's gazes, and pick up on each other's ideas in their talks. At one point, Salaam puts his arm around Osbey and expresses his deep respect for her art and her activism. At another moment, Osbey and Patterson nod solemnly as Salaam describes the killing of James Brissette, on Danziger Bridge, as the murder of one of "our" students. Patterson, Osbey, and Salaam blend their own creative work with teaching that helps turn talking back into an art form. Constrained and contained in the present, they reach back into the past and project their work ahead into the future. They train young people to develop the capacity to become voices for change in families, schools, and communities. They view the sharing of stories as a way of helping people heal from their individual and collective injuries and traumas. Perhaps most important, they see resources, knowledge, love, and political potential in places where people with power see only liabilities and problems.

The session's final speaker, Shana Griffin, connects the art presented and described by the other panelists to her own political work as cofounder of the New Orleans Women's Health and Justice Initiative, as executive director of the New Orleans Women's Health Clinic, and as a member of INCITE! Women of Color Against Violence. Griffin's activism challenges the disaggregation of social problems into discrete, atomized activities by blending the provision of reproductive and sexual health care to low-income and no-income women of color with collective mobilizations. These mobilizations proclaim connections that link domestic violence against women to street violence and police violence against transgendered people, and to state violence against other countries, as well as against immigrants and prison inmates at home (Luft 504, 512). Although the poetic flair of Patterson, Osbey, and Salaam is absent from Griffin's presentation, her talk is a virtuoso performance, making unexpected but important connections among seemingly incommensurable realms of experience. Breaking the frames that disaggregate social relations into atomized and discrete sectors, Griffin explains the practices and processes that connect domestic violence, environmental crisis, gender-based inequality, and struggles for reproductive health. Just as inequality and discrimination make floodwaters flow to the low-lying places in New Orleans's Ninth Ward, long histories of racism and sexism compel black women to endure the harshest consequences of privatization, deregulation, and gentrification.

Griffin points out how the city's housing shortage promotes an ecology of sexual violence against women, how militarism overseas exacerbates poverty at home, how restricted access to safe reproductive-health services and treatment compounds the injuries of race and class faced by black women. Griffin's list of the forces working in concert against the interests of working-class black women is a found, improvised poem in itself: images, blame, neglect, abandonment, disinvestment, disenfranchisement, assimilation, heteronormativity, violence, abuse, medical deprivation, and experimentation. Her presentation expresses a holistic, dialogic, and intersectional approach that understands that identity injuries never exist in isolation from other social relations. The full skein of rights abuses unfolding in New Orleans is horizontally and vertically integrated

across a wide range of community interests, institutions, and civil circumstances that affect a widening gyre of constituents. Attacks on the
provision of public housing, for instance, complicate the violations of the
reproductive rights of marginalized women of color. The demonization
of black women's fertility and motherhood serves to criminalize poverty
and legitimize punitive policies that increase gender-related violence,
displacement, and discrimination. Dangerous forms of birth control are
forced on subsidy-dependent black women. When underfunded social service programs fail to meet human needs, the clients who use these services are blamed, rather than the inadequate funding.

Human Rights Crisis as Chronic Condition

Even before the hurricane in 2005, the New Orleans neighborhoods that
formed the focal points for the panel presentations by Patterson, Osbey,
Salaam, and Griffin desperately needed enforcement of basic civil rights.
More than one-fourth of Louisiana's children grow up in poverty. Black
neighborhoods in New Orleans have a greater proportion of their population incarcerated than anywhere else in the world. One-fifth of the population of the city has no health insurance of any kind, and more than one-
third of the population cannot afford basic transportation (C. Anderson
89). The state of Louisiana leads the nation in the number of youths between the ages of fourteen and seventeen serving life sentences in prison
without the chance of parole. Louisiana executes more convicts per capita
than any other state (Woods, "Les Misérables" 790). Nearly 40 percent of
households in the state earn less than $25,000 per year (Wright 89). De-
regulation, lax environmental protection laws, and the defunding of state
services in order to subsidize private wealth combine to produce deadly
consequences. Louisiana leads the nation in waste generation and toxic
environmental discharges (Wright 93). Massive subsidies to corporations
starve the public sector. Between 1988 and 1998, the Industrial Property
Tax Exemption Program let businesses evade $2.5 billion in taxes, money
sorely needed for education, housing, health care, and environmental protection. Beverly Wright, a scholar and environmental justice activist, describes this policy accurately as "a corporate welfare program paid by the
poor of Louisiana" (91).

For racism in New Orleans to "take place," it takes places: segregated
neighborhoods that blacks inhabit but that whites control. The history of

housing segregation confines black people in the Crescent City to an artificially constricted market that compels them to pay exploitatively high rents for cruelly deficient dwellings. Their concentration in areas fouled by polluted air, water, and soil subjects them and their families to premature deaths. They also inhabit these spaces because they have been driven out of other places, out of the plantation lands of rural Louisiana by vigilante violence and police brutality, out of troubled but vibrant neighborhoods that white speculators eyed as sites for new profits. Like the residents of Halifax who were displaced from Africville, an African Canadian settlement in Nova Scotia that was destroyed in the 1960s, the residents of black New Orleans wake up every day with memories of lands and lives that were stolen from them. Like black people in Halifax, they are forced to remember what white people prefer to forget: the enduring legacy of slavery unwilling to die and its cruel self-perpetuating mechanisms of serial displacement.

Nearly every historical center of African American life and culture in New Orleans has been systematically destroyed. Place Congo, where enslaved and free blacks drummed and danced in keeping with African customs and traditions, was renamed Beauregard Square, to honor a Confederate army general in the war to destroy the Union and preserve slavery. The venerable Tremé Market, in the Seventh Ward, was lost to urban renewal in the 1930s. The uptown Dryades Street shopping district was destroyed by white property-owners and merchants who fled the neighborhood in the 1960s to avoid having to employ black workers. The construction of Louis Armstrong Park destroyed much of what had been Place Congo (and Congo Square and Beauregard Square), reconfiguring the street front along Rampart in such a way as to destroy the thriving neighborhood around it. Urban renewal projects destroyed sixteen blocks of historic buildings in the Tremé neighborhood. The construction of the I-10 overpass, enabling commuters to move between white suburbs and downtown businesses without having to drive through black neighborhoods, destroyed some two hundred businesses on the street, and cast a macabre shadow over the grass median neutral ground, one hundred feet wide and 1,600 feet long, that divided the street and previously provided space for picnics, games, and washing cars. Freeway construction killed hundreds of oak trees, divided the neighborhood, marred its appearance, and eliminated twelve blocks of historic homes as well as miles of thriving neighborhoods (Wright 132–33).

The hurricane and its aftermath (and later, the toxic BP oil spill) alerted the world to the continuing rights crisis in New Orleans (and much of the rest of black America). As Carol Anderson, a human rights scholar, observes, "The images of black swollen bodies bobbing in the flood waters, children clinging to rooftops begging for help, and thousands of African Americans trapped in sweltering government-designated evacuation centers with no drinking water, sanitation facilities, or food exposed to the world what America looked like for those without human rights" (90).

Yet if the world looking at New Orleans in the aftermath of Hurricane Katrina saw a profoundly shocking social justice problem, most of the United States saw only a public relations problem. Elected officials, city administrators, and local media ridiculed the findings by international human rights agencies that demolishing public housing units and making decisions about rebuilding the city without meaningful participation by working-class blacks violated fundamental rights principles (Woods, "Les Misérables" 769–70). Instead, both major political parties, the corporate media, private foundations, and investors used the crisis as an excuse for implementing measures designed to redevelop the city at the expense of the black, working-class and poor neighborhoods of the city. As Clyde Woods argues, these policies replicated and intensified all the dynamics that produced the crisis in the first place, a regime of asset stripping, shredding the social safety net, eliminating jobs, demolishing low-cost housing, increasing hunger, closing schools, hospitals, and health clinics, disenfranchising voters, and sending more people to prison (769–70).

These policies carried on the long tradition of perverting civil rights in the United States, of valuing white property more than black humanity, and of turning the antisubjugation principles of the Fourteenth Amendment into principles that prevent the state from protecting the rights of black people. They also affirm American exceptionalism, the idea that the United States is unlike other nations, that its purported innate goodness makes it immune to international law and the principles of civil rights. For nearly a century, the U.S. government has treated rights as a doctrine to be preached to other countries, as a standard by which their worthiness should be judged, yet not as a doctrine applicable to the United States itself. The United States has refused to endorse international prohibitions against genocide, because the nation does not want to be held accountable for its treatment of indigenous people and blacks. It routinely resists the jurisdiction of the World Court and international rights agencies in order to defend capital punishment, torture, and the use of "first strike" military actions.

The political system's response to the crisis in New Orleans demonstrated the costs of not improvising. Problems caused by decades and centuries of exploitation, asset stripping, social-spatial enclosures, joblessness, punitive social welfare policies, food insecurity, housing discrimination, and police brutality came to a crescendo in the wake of the flooding that took place when the levees broke. This could have been an opportunity to make use of the improvisational talents of the local black working class. Yet people in power, accustomed to viewing poor people as passive recipients of state largesse at best and, at worst, as products of a pathological culture that needs to be eradicated, lacked the ability to tap into the resources the community possessed. Private investors and public officials alike immediately embraced plans to shrink the size of the city, to abandon the neighborhoods with the greatest needs, to make it difficult for those forced to flee to other cities to return. As reporters, pundits, and politicians aired largely unfounded or exaggerated alarms about looting, rape, and murder in New Orleans in the aftermath of the hurricane, the longtime local activist and cultural worker Jerome Smith witnessed the workings of improvisation. He saw young men commonly viewed as criminals and thugs by the city's ruling elite repeatedly performing brave acts of love, diving off bridges into deep water to save people from drowning, piloting boats to transport trapped families to safety, collecting information about people in danger, and using their networks to try to help people find refuge. From Smith's perspective, some of the same skills that served these young men in their lives on the street were put to good use in the crisis. Drawing on decades of cultural work with young people in the Tambourine and Fan organization that he started in the Tremé neighborhood, Smith explained, "I have discovered over the years if you give youngsters like the ones coming here the same authority that they give them on the street that they achieve missions that's positive" (qtd. in Woods, "Les Misérables" 792).

Deprived of any meaningful implementation of their civil rights, these youth and their neighbors can understandably wonder if they have any rights as humans. They followed a long tradition in doing so. Frederick Douglass used the term *human rights* in the nineteenth century, as a means of transcending the limits of a society in which the defenders of white supremacy controlled the executive, legislative, and judicial branches of government. During the 1940s, the National Association for the Advancement of Colored People asked the United Nations Commission on Human Rights for an investigation of the conditions confronting African Americans. Systematic segregation in the United States clearly violated international guarantees of access to education, employment, housing, and health without regard to race. Rights discourses became especially important in New Orleans and the entire state of Louisiana during the 1980s and 1990s, in mobilizations against environmental racism. As Monique Darden, an environmental justice activist, explains, "Before we learned about human rights, we looked for laws in the U.S. that could provide protection for people who live, work, play, and worship in places that are also sites for polluting industrial facilities and waste dumps. But we recognized that [U.S.] laws really do not support the fundamental human rights to life, health and non-discrimination" (qtd. in Huang 235).

Once it became clear that civil rights organizations and civil rights laws could not be mobilized on behalf of the black working class in New Orleans, activists raised the language of rights with new fervor. The International Tribunal on Hurricanes Katrina and Rita met for five days in 2007 to hear testimony about human rights abuses by state officials during and after the storm. Subsequent tribunals organized by activists with the People's Hurricane Relief Fund Survivor Councils took testimony from people displaced from New Orleans in Jackson, Mississippi, and Atlanta, Georgia. These hearings focused on the United Nations Guiding Principles on Internal Displacement of 1998, which specify as rights many of the things denied to the black working class of New Orleans during the crisis: housing, safety, medical care, family unification, and freedom from gender violence (Luft 518–19).

The rights frame also exposes white supremacy and neoliberalism as global, rather than purely national, programs. It evokes longstanding identifications among blacks in New Orleans with other oppressed communities around the world. In one of Patterson's poems, rhymes link oppressions overseas to those at home. What's the difference, she asks, between "government sanctioned killings in Kenya and a nigga held hostage in a house in Virginia? Or poverty in Haiti and poverty in Jamaica? Or rape in Rwanda and rape in Somalia? A sweatshop in China or one in Guatemala? Or small pox in blankets [and] syphilis in Tuskegee? Formaldehyde and FEMA? Ethnic cleansing and Katrina? I recall within a speech

Dr. King made us aware . . . that injustice anywhere is injustice everywhere" (qtd. in Camp 706).

Yet, we know this place. Rights proclamations have rarely translated into rights practices for African Americans. Rachel Luft observes rights frameworks are not binding, are not well understood in the United States, and are easier to assert in the abstract than to incorporate into a concrete program (521–22). Moreover, while rights policies do valuable work by proscribing the most egregious forms of inhumane treatment, they do little to challenge the microaggressions and exploitations that work relentlessly to skew opportunities and life chances along racial lines. As with U.S. civil rights law, the focus in rights discourses on abuses and violations works well in extreme cases, but can at the same time unwittingly authorize and support all the smaller injustices that do not rise to the level of the egregious violation.

The New Orleans panel at the American Studies Association deployed frames and formulations from both civil rights and human rights discourses. But the panelists knew from personal and collective experience that no single tool could win their freedom. Civil rights laws and human rights declarations do not erase power imbalances, and those imbalances guarantee that any policy will likely be structured in dominance. The national framework of civil rights contains built-in contradictions for working-class blacks in New Orleans. As Shana Griffin argues, "When you identify the state as the main orchestrator of violence in the lives of many communities, it's hard to make appeals to the state to mitigate the violence the state is committing. Because the state is not going to mitigate itself" (585). Yet the global framework of human rights instruments also entails irresolvable contradictions. Human rights principles do not exist to deliver dignity or democracy to aggrieved populations. Their function is often instead to ensure the smooth flow of capital across international borders by regularizing and standardizing the conduct of states just enough to preserve stability but not so much that moral considerations inhibit the pursuit of material gain.

Activists in New Orleans cannot fully embrace or practically evade appeals to human rights and civil rights. It is not a simple question of "either or" for them, but rather a complex issue of balancing "both and" as well as "neither," according to situational exigencies. This connects them to contemporary activists all around the world. Activists working in the tradition of the Zapatista Army of National Liberation (EZLN), in Mexico, participate in state processes but do not attempt to seize state power. Activists working in the tradition of Okinawa Women Act Against Military Violence (OWAAMV) refuse the legitimacy of the state when it comes to making war or destroying the environment, yet they run candidates for office and try to pressure politicians to take desired actions consistent with their anti-violence ethics. The EZLN does not ask for human rights, but rather for dignity. The OWAAMV does not seek human rights, but rather asks the people of the world to redefine security by elevating the security of women, children, the elderly, and the environment over the security of states and corporations. Like the people of Mexico and the people of Okinawa, and aggrieved populations all around the world, the black working class in New Orleans needs enacted freedom, not merely civil rights or human rights discourses in which that freedom is theoretically (illusorily) mapped out. As "field hands of freedom," they know they need to find different tools for different jobs.

The presentations by Patterson, Osbey, Salaam, and Griffin revolved not so much around *what* they know, but rather around *how* they know. That *how* is intimately related to improvisation, imagination, and invention. It comes from a city where street parades teach musicians, dancers, and spectators to communicate effectively with one another, and to create a common project (a musical commons) by building off each other's energy. The ferocious, brilliant theatricality of the city's music, dance, dress, song, and speech teaches participants to anticipate dialogue and participate in it in ever-evolving, improvised circumstances. Fused forms of expression and art privilege movement and welcome the unexpected. Collective celebrations emanating from the improvisational creativity of individuals and groups deftly instruct artists and audiences alike to blend sameness and difference, rupture and continuity, speaking and listening, watching and being watched. Improvisation in art necessitates sizing up one's situation, learning to work with others, and making choices swiftly and decisively. The same can be said about improvisation in social movement mobilizations. In this respect, the aesthetics of improvisation can pervade and activate other forms of social practice in illuminating, agency-enabling ways.

This form of improvisation is an art that requires doing work in the world, work that makes a difference, that requires reaching across genders and generations to expand space and time, cultivating creative capabilities to prepare for confrontations that may never come. It entails an art that finds the pulse of the people, that mobilizes and organizes them for the struggle. As Patterson calls out in "We Know This Place," this is an art that tells its listeners to

> Hold onto the prize,
> Never put it down.
> Be firm in the stance,
> No break, no bow,
> Got to forward on, Mama,
> Make your move now
> Forward, dear children,
> 'cuz freedom is now.

In going "forward on" and making "your move now" Patterson evokes the restless, steadfast energy of improvisational practices that sustain and enact freedom in the name of those who make it for themselves.

CHAPTER 6

"THE FIERCE URGENCY OF NOW"

Improvisation, Social Practice, and
Togetherness-in-Difference

If one of the most salient and far-reaching lessons of improvised musical practices has to do with shattering the assumptions of fixity fostered by institutionalized systems of representation, then here's another: what the poet and scholar Nathaniel Mackey refers to as improvisation's "discontent with categories and the boundaries they enforce, with the impediment to social and aesthetic mobility such enforcement effects" ("Paracritical Hinge" 368). Now, we have neither the capacity nor the desire in the current context to catalogue the plethora of significant instances of boundary-crossing that have animated the history of jazz and creative improvised music. Mackey, Ingrid Monson, George Lewis, and many others have written wisely and comprehensively about that history, and their work provides a resonant context for our own inquiry into the role that improvised music has played in activating diverse energies of critique, inspiration, and involvement in relation to struggles for rights and social justice.

In the previous two chapters on New Orleans, we've sought to show how our findings about the ways rights discourses might be reconceptualized through an analysis of improvisational practices have real historical and contemporary consequences for material and imagined resources in social spaces and social movements. In turning our attention to musical communities, we would like to build our examples by way of three specific case studies from the Guelph Jazz Festival, a festival with a lengthy history of staging activist forms of insurgent knowledge production, of using boundary-shattering improvisatory interventions and intercultural musical encounters as testing grounds for how people might best get along in the world. As one of the few jazz festivals in North America to host an annual scholarly conference as part of its regular schedule of events, and with an explicit mandate to use its innovative programming and its educational initiatives to reinvigorate public life with alternative visions of community and social cooperation, the festival has been heralded for nearly two decades as a significant agent of cultural change.[1]

Improvisation as Boundary-Blurring Transculturation

Three case studies from a festival with an explicitly activist edge. Three takes on specific instances of musical improvisation pointing to wider forms of social practice in which alternative agencies are activated. Three takes that function, to borrow from the cultural theorist Ien Ang, as registers of "boundary-blurring transculturation" (198). Three takes that enable a consideration of the complex (and often conflicted) ways improvisatory musical practices open up abiding questions of trust, relatedness, responsibility, and social obligation, or what Ang aptly refers to as "togetherness-in-difference" (200). Together these case studies all resonate with the work being done with the larger Improvisation, Community, and Social Practice (ICASP) research project, in particular, with that project's focus on how contemporary improvisational musical practices provide glimpses into unique social formations that have especial pertinence for envisioning and for sounding alternative models for conceptualizing rights.

The ICASP research project is shaping and defining a new field of interdisciplinary inquiry. It brings together an international research team of thirty-five scholars from twenty different institutions around the world, and it fosters partnerships with a range of community-based organizations, including street-level social service organizations working with at-risk and aggrieved populations. Project outcomes range across a wide spectrum of electronic, broadcast, and print media, with a focus on policy-oriented and community-facing impacts. The project seeks to have a significant effect on how research is done and how its results are implemented and disseminated, both within and beyond the academy. As a core objective, the work associated with ICASP models a new paradigm for humanities and social science research, putting into practice the rhetoric of interdisciplinarity systematically throughout every facet of the project:

among scholars from different fields, among theories and methodologies, among academics, artists, and community partners. In addition to public discourse and scholarly publication, ICASP highlights collaboration with arts presenters, educators, social service organizations, and policymakers to ensure the broadest possible impact. Improvisation is, at its core and at its best, a democratic, humane, and emancipatory practice, and securing rights of all sorts requires people to hone their capacities to act in the world, capacities whose origins are in improvisation. We are, both in these pages and in the larger ICASP project, inspired by the wisdom, the creativity, and the deeply relational and profoundly contingent practice of improvising artists.

Research Questions and Hypotheses

The ICASP project's core hypothesis is that musical improvisation is a crucial, largely unexamined model for political, cultural, and ethical dialogue and action. Taking as a point of departure performance practices that cannot readily be scripted, predicted, or compelled into orthodoxy, we argue that the innovative working models of improvisation developed by creative practitioners have helped to promote a dynamic exchange of cultural forms, and to encourage new, socially responsive forms of community-building across national, cultural, and artistic boundaries. Improvisation, in short, has much to tell us, as listeners, scholars, citizens, and activists, about the ways communities based on such forms are politically and materially pertinent to envisioning and sounding alternative ways of knowing and being in the world.

It is the project's contention that there is much to be learned from performance practices, such as those associated with the artists discussed in this book, that accent dialogue, collaboration, inventive flexibility, and creative risk-taking, much to be learned from art forms that disrupt orthodox standards of coherence, judgment, and value with a spirit of experimentation and innovation. To what extent, and in what ways, then, might improvised creative practice foster a commitment to cultural listening, to a widening of the scope of community, and to new relations of trust and social obligation? What role does improvisation play in facilitating global and transcultural conversations, and how (and to what extent) are diverse identities, cultures, and viewpoints being brought together through improvisational music-making? How do artistic and social practices get transformed as they move across cultures? What can improvisation tell us about how communities get organized, how identities get formulated? Who determines how improvising communities articulate themselves in relation to human dignity and human rights? How has the substantial body of cultural practices associated with improvised musics been marginalized as a function of their challenge to orthodoxies? What are the traps in assuming that improvised musics stand for something beyond their musical presencing? What is a meaningful framework for understanding the relationship among intercultural musical practices, improvisation, and the politics of hope associated with positive human rights outcomes?

"Those of us who work, teach, and study as 'traditional intellectuals' in institutions of higher learning have an important role to play in analyzing and interpreting the changes that are taking place around us. We need to develop forms of academic criticism capable of comprehending the theorizing being done at the grassroots level by artists and their audiences, of building bridges between different kinds of theory" (Lipsitz, *American Studies* 229). Our project (both with this book and with the larger ICASP initiative) takes seriously this insistence on building such bridges, on forging innovative alliances among scholars, creative practitioners, and arts presenters. While dominant methodological paradigms have typically been characterized by a separation between theory and practice, our project recognizes the extent to which improvised music-making offers a resonant model for a marriage of the two, and for addressing broad critical, social, cultural, and intellectual issues from a diverse range of perspectives. In drawing our case studies from the Guelph Jazz Festival, we thus take our cue from the assessment by Imani Perry, the scholar of African American studies, that "it sometimes seems that the abstractions allowed for in the arts . . . facilitate a more robust description of race than do the most meticulous academic inquiries" (xiii), as well as from Joseph Slaughter's conclusion in his book *Human Rights, Inc.* that "the texts we read—and how we read, teach, and speak about them—have an effect (however unpredictable) on the possibility that the projection of the world based on human rights might become legible [and] articulable" (328). While neither Perry nor Slaughter is, in these remarks, speaking specifically about improvised music, their comments about the vital role that creative practice and expression can play in enabling scholars to think anew about matters of rights and justice offer an important framework to address the research questions we've inventoried in the above list. The kind of improvised music-making that takes place in the context of a festival such as Guelph's can make imaginable, can, indeed, enact alternative soundings of rights. Furthermore, such performances take place in a context that can productively approximate what Sara Evans and Harry Boyte refer to in their book *Free Spaces* as a vital source for change, a setting that combines "strong communal ties with larger public relationships and aspects. This public dimension," they argue, "involves a mix of people and perspectives beyond one's immediate ties, and also entails norms of egalitarian exchange, debate, dissent, and openness" (ix).

Take One: New Communities of Sound;
Improvising across Borders

As a way of gesturing toward some form of response to the complex research questions we've listed above, we turn to a specific example, taken from the ICASP project (in partnership with the Guelph Jazz Festival), an example that might help us think about what happens when musicians improvise, about why improvisation matters. Now, just to be clear, we're not talking here about the by-now more familiar notion of improvising over a fixed or scripted archive, or of improvising as a practice that commonly takes place among like-minded performers who already share a familiar musical culture or set of assumptions. While the improvisatory flights of Charlie "Bird" Parker, who famously reworked familiar pieces from the American songbook as part of an effort to subvert dominant white culture by mastering its harmonic vocabulary and presenting it in a way that was deliberately bewildering to uninitiated, white listeners, are well documented, as are accounts of Billie Holiday's remarkable ability to transform popular love songs produced by a white-dominated Tin Pan Alley cultural industry, there's another, and equally resilient, set of examples associated with improvisatory musical practices. We're thinking specifically here of improvisation as an embodied, face-to-face interaction among musicians in real-time, an interaction, to borrow again from Evans and Boyte, that "involves a mix of people and perspectives beyond one's immediate ties, and also entails norms of egalitarian exchange, debate, dissent, and openness." Think about what happens in such a context: a group of people who may never have met, who, in many cases, know very little, if anything, about one another, who may not even speak the same language, can create inspired and compelling music. And they can do this on the spot, with no explicit, prearranged musical direction. What makes it work? And what does this tell us? How might such musical examples enable us to think about what it means to negotiate differences within a community, what it means to be living in a multicultural society? What might such musicking tell us about trust, humility, responsibility, critical listening, reciprocity, and social cooperation? As a way of focusing our attention on these questions, we'd like to use as our first case study a performance called "Workshop: New Communities of Sound: Improvising across Borders," held in September 2009 as part of the Guelph Jazz Festival Colloquium.

"New Communities of Sound," like similar workshops held at previous editions of the Guelph Jazz Festival, brought together several musicians from diverse cultural locations, in an ad hoc improvisational setting: Getatchew Mekuria (Ethiopia), Jah Youssouf (Mali), Abdoulaye Koné (Mali), Jane Bunnett (Canada), Brad Muirhead (Canada), Alain Derbez (Mexico), Terrie Hessels (Netherlands), Rob Wallace (United States), and Hamid Drake (United States). Now, we've long been interested in the ways the kind of intercultural collaborations and collisions enacted through the music-making that occurs in such a workshop involves a complex set of strategies that are working outside of and across known paradigms. What's equally revealing, however, is how that very looseness, slipperiness, and inventive flexibility have allowed improvisation to function as a powerful bridge between musicians from such very different cultures. Although specific musical "languages" are indeed at play here, even a quick glance at a short video excerpt from the workshop should make clear that not everyone in the group is using the same one.[2] This excerpt is taken from a much longer and more extended improvisation. The musicians involved were meeting for the very first time, and they were doing so onstage. Also of note is the fact that they came to the workshop with no prearranged plan of action or musical prompts, and there was, literally, no common language between them. In other words, the relationships of communication that emerged did so solely on the basis of their improvised musicking.

In introducing the workshop and its participants, the percussionist and scholar Rob Wallace explained to the audience that this workshop is titled "New Communities of Sound: Improvising across Borders." Improvising across borders implies perhaps two paradoxical things: 1) improvisation might be in some sense a universal musical language that can potentially help us communicate across geographical and cultural differences and 2) there are borders—both self-and-externally-imposed—that might be holding such communication in check. Today's workshop investigates the potentials for cross-cultural improvisation by literally putting us all in the same room and trying to take down some of those borders.

This kind of music-making is sometimes called "jamming," and sometimes it "works" and sometimes it doesn't. It seems that someone is inevitably left out of the communication either because they can't be heard or because they don't hear anyone else. But it can also be a place for what scholar Paul Gilroy calls "strategic universalism," a perhaps temporary but nevertheless valuable state of being where we can come together and talk for a while and feel like a community . . . Even though we don't all speak the same language—literally or musically—we hope that today we can have a provocative and fun conversation. ("Workshop: New Communities of Sound")

Wallace's opening remarks remind the listener, if only implicitly, that there are protocols of engagement at work, between and among the various participants and practices involved in improvised musical encounters such as this one, and that these protocols not only allow particular instances of improvised music to take on a story, and a life, of their own, but they also invite the listener, whether as improvising musicians or as members of the audience, to articulate the basis upon which one might arrive at judgments about what works and what doesn't work in improvised musicking. Moreover, Wallace's invitation for the musicians onstage during the workshop to use those protocols of engagement to participate in the "taking down" of borders is also a prod to find new ways to think together—indeed, to find new ways to travel across vast distances (cultural, geographical, musical, and the like) in an effort to edge us toward—well, yes—who-knows-where.

The who-knows-where of improvisation, its destinations "out," its "other planes of there," as the passage from Mackey with which we began this chapter should remind us, is both a social and a sonic expression of mobility; it's part of the music's resistance to capture, fixity, stasis, and orthodoxy. But the cautions and paradoxes voiced in Wallace's remarks introducing the workshop also remind us that improvisation comes with

no guarantees. It does not necessarily unfold smoothly, unproblemati-
cally, or even coherently. And that productive tension between ideality
and reality is precisely the sonic and ideological space that improvisation
opens up, makes potential. Ingrid Monson hints at a related set of cautions
in *Freedom Sounds*, where she encourages readers to ask several crucial
questions about intercultural contact: "What are the power relations that
shape the contact or cultural overlap? Who profits from the contact? Is an
area of cultural overlap enforced or voluntary for the participants? When
does a borrower have a right to claim ownership? Which set of cultural
values shapes the process by which divergent cultural elements and practices are shared and synthesized? Which values and ideologies, in other
words, are dominant?" (11). Monson's questions (like Wallace's remarks)
make clear that improvisation is about so much more than simply the
music itself, that its meanings (and any provisional understanding about
its critical force) are connected in crucial ways to broader struggles over
resources, recognition, legitimation, identity formation, and power. Like-
wise, Kathryn Sorrells and Gordon Nakagawa, in their work on the connections between intercultural communication and struggles for social
responsibility and social justice, ask a related set of questions: "Who can
speak and who is silenced; whose language is spoken and whose language
is trivialized or denied; whose actions have the power to shape and impact others and whose actions are dismissed, unreported, and marginalized" (29). In the context of such questions, improvised musical practices
might purposefully be considered a testing ground for new visions and
new soundings of how people might best get along in a world in which
one of the key issues entails how to articulate constructively the multiple,
often disjunct communities of interest and practice finding an emergent
sense of collective responsibility and interconnectedness.

Key to such getting along, as any good improviser knows, is, of course,
the ability to listen. Christopher Small argues in his book *Musicking: The
Meanings of Performing and Listening*, "When we perform, we bring into
existence, for the duration of the performance, a set of relationships, between the sounds and between the participants, that model ideal relationships as we imagine them to be and allow us to learn about them by experiencing them" (218). The ability to listen deeply, critically, attentively,
creatively, curiously, and intensively to the others around you is a profoundly sensitive register of a broader set of commitments to social responsibility and cooperation. Improvisation, in this context of emergent

networks of affiliation and community, demands active and responsible listening. It demands shared responsibility for participation in community, as well as an ability to negotiate differences and a willingness to accept the challenges of risk and contingency. Small contends:

> The act of musicking establishes in the place where it is happening a set of relationships, and it is in those relationships that the meaning of the act lies. They are to be found not only between those organized sounds which are conventionally thought of as being the stuff of musical meaning, but also between the people who are taking part, in whatever capacity, in the performance; and they model, or stand as metaphor for, ideal relationships as the participants in the performance imagine them to be: relationships between person and person, between individual and society, between humanity and the natural world and even perhaps the supernatural world. These are important matters, perhaps the most important in human life. (13)

Small goes on to argue that acts of musicking "are to be judged, if they are judged at all, on their success in articulating (affirming, exploring, celebrating) the concepts of relationships of those who are taking part. We may not like those relationships," he tells us, "and we are surely entitled to say so if we wish, but we should understand that our opinions are as much social as they are purely aesthetic . . . That is to say, we are passing an opinion not merely on a musical style but on the whole set of ideal relationships that are being articulated by the musical performance" (213). What kinds of relationships, then, are being articulated through the "New Communities of Sound" workshop?

Well, the short video excerpt from the ICASP website cannot, of course, do justice to (or even begin to reveal the nuances and complexities of) the actual full performance, but there are a few points that, even in the context of that short video clip, ought to command our attention. For one thing, it's important to remember that the short excerpt on the website is part of a much longer performance of improvised music. This particular clip starts about twenty-eight minutes into what turned out to be a performance of just over an hour. When the opening credits for this excerpted video clip are rolling, you hear the musicians freely improvising; that is, they're performing with no tonal center, and there's no regular meter, beat, or pulse. But very quickly (indeed, just a few seconds into this clip), they pick up on a motif repeated by the Malian *kamal n'goni* player Jah Youssouf, and they lock into something of a groove. And if the viewer keeps in mind a point that the communications scholar Kathryn Sorrells has made about how, in intercultural creative practice, "nonverbal modes of communication often bring forth information, perspectives and understanding that might otherwise remain buried" and about how by "gaining access to people's creativity, we tap a remarkable reservoir of potential energy that can be used to facilitate intercultural learning and communication" (qtd. in Lengel 6), then the viewer should notice the visual elements and bodily gestures and movements at work in this short excerpt: how Youssouf, as he's working his way into that repeated motif, turns around to make direct eye contact with drummer Hamid Drake; how several of the artists (especially the guitarist Terrie Hessels and saxophonist Getatchew Mekuria) are nodding heads, moving bodies, stomping feet, and smiling; how several of the audience members are also shaking their heads to the music; how the Mexican soprano saxophonist Alain Derbez walks across the stage at one point to join fellow soprano saxophonist, the Canadian Jane Bunnett, a simple and literal act that neatly encapsulates the mobility at the heart of improvisational practice, while metaphorically suggesting their ability to come together across the distances and borders that separate them. Even the smallest of such gestures plays a role in contributing to the energy, groove, and momentum that's evident in this collaborative act of cocreation in real time.

Improvisation functions here as a model for understanding, and, indeed, for generating an ethics of cocreation. Improvisation accentuates matters of responsibility, interdependence, trust, and social obligation. Through the development of new, unexpected, and productive cocreative relations among people in real time, improvisation aligns with the broader rights project of promoting a culture of collective responsibility, dispersed authority, and self-active democracy.

Improvisational modes of practice and their ability to negotiate across the differences of history, culture, race, ethnicity, and tradition also align with the flexible yet coordinated aspects of the form of action and organization that the sociologist John Brown Childs has called "transcommunality." Childs sees transcommunality as "an important development within which is emerging a twenty-first-century mode of organizing for justice and dignity" (10). Defined as "the constructive and developmental interaction occurring among distinct autonomy-oriented communities and organizations, each with its own particular history, outlook, and agenda," transcommunality, suggests Childs, "emphasizes a constant process of negotiational construction of organization among diverse participants, rather than an imposed monolithic system" (10, 11): "Transcommunality is process—often difficult, slow, and even defeated at certain moments— that constantly creates, and when necessary rebuilds, structures of commonality among diverse peoples" (76). For Childs, the trust that gets built up through the actual experience of shared practical action "results in enhanced awareness of others who were formerly distant and unknown" (64). Although jazz and improvisation aren't at the core of Childs's argument here, they are certainly implicit throughout, and Childs does reference the work of the creative improviser Wadada Leo Smith, an artist whose music and thinking has been consistently engaged with struggles for rights and social justice.

Childs cites the following passage from Wadada Leo Smith's book published in 1973, *Notes (8 Pieces) Source a New World Music: Creative Music*. Like the potential for cross-cultural communication played out in the "New Communities of Sound" workshop, under consideration here, these comments, for Childs, get at Smith's insistence on the need to nurture and to develop "a transcommunal-like set of connections" (71): "It is high time that we begin to help and set up cultural ties with the other more than three-fourths of these Americas (north, central, south) while also seeking other cultures that have improvisation as their classical art music (india, pan-islam, the orient, bali and africa) and make lasting cultural commitments with them. For the days are set in time that this vast world of ours can only survive if we, as humans, become earth-beings committed in our cultural and political aspects to a pan world future" (qtd. in Childs 71).

Furthermore, if the creation of public spaces is vital (as we believe it is) for the articulation of alternative models of relationship-building, vital to the development of a (transcommunal) notion of global citizenship, in which people can learn how best to negotiate differences within the context of a community, then the fact that, with the "New Communities of Sound" workshop, hybridity and cocreation are being staged as public practices during a festival merits our attention. And the fact that audiences are seeing and hearing such creative community-making happen in real time recalls Christopher Small's argument about the "important matters" at stake in an understanding and assessment of the relationships being articulated through the act of musicking. After all, where else does one find these sorts of opportunities to stage (and to witness) such acts of cocreation? Where else do such boundary-shattering acts of transculturation, such opportunities, in effect, to test new soundings of social cooperation, find so apt a setting for their expression and mobilization? Settings that enable this kind of real-time, creative decision-making, risk-taking, and collaboration are, unfortunately, all too rare. With few exceptions, even most jazz festivals (where one might expect, and hope, to find an emphasis on new collaborative opportunities, on creative improvised music-making) tend to avoid taking such risks, instead opting to present more familiar combinations of artists who will guarantee box office success. Functioning akin to what Kay Schaffer and Sidonie Smith, in their book *Human Rights and Narrated Lives*, call scattered sites of rights activism, venues of public culture, such as the one where the "New Communities of Sound" workshop took place, offer a place to "unsettle familiar knowledge frameworks by introducing different interpretations across the boundaries of cultural difference" (51). And such venues, where diverse cultural energies are activated, as Schaffer and Smith maintain, are resources for hope, for they "have the capacity to shatter and transform, to find their way through the cracks and fissures of the dominant culture in unpredictable ways," thus facilitating "new modes of intersubjective exchange that open out rather than foreclose the radical relationalities possible within social life, generating hope and opening new futures" (231, 233).[3]

An analysis of some of the key musical strategies at play in the "New Communities of Sound" workshop can also contribute to our understanding of how improvised musics might help to cultivate resources for hope. If the conventions associated with fixed genres "contribute to an ahistorical view of the world as always the same," and if the "pleasures of predictability encourage an investment in the status quo," then the use of extended techniques in music—the use of unfamiliar performance techniques on familiar musical instruments to expand the sonic vocabularies conventionally associated with those instruments—may be indicative of improvisation's insistence on finding new kinds of solutions to familiar problems and challenges (Lipsitz, *American Studies* 185). And herein, as with so much of the music we are considering, lies a message of hope and resourcefulness, a message about how people choose to work with the situations in which they find themselves. Terrie Hessels provides the most salient example in the current context: listen to how he extends the sonic resources of the guitar by playing it not so much for its notes, but rather as a kind of percussion instrument, how he keeps time by hitting the strings, first with his hand and later with a screwdriver, how he is, in effect, adding a kind of punk-rock energy to the mix, hinting not just, to return to Monson's question, at what a synthesis of divergent cultural forms might sound like, but, perhaps more suggestively, at how the dissonances and boundary shatterings that result when practitioners enter collaboration from different cultural and musical locations can in fact be productive, even exhilarating. Here the sonic explorations map out a form of productive instrumentality that encourages border crossings, while rejecting hegemonic and hierarchical structures that prevent mobility and unpredictability.

And here again it's that ability to adapt, to switch codes—to see things from different perspectives—that gives improvisation its critical force. Sorrells and Nakagawa, writing about intercultural communication, put it this way: "Cognizant of differences and the tensions that emerge from these differences, the process of dialogue invites us to stretch ourselves—to reach across and to exceed our grasp—to imagine, experience, and engage creatively with points of view, ways of thinking, being and doing, and beliefs different from our own while accepting that we many not fully understand or may not come to a common agreement or position" (30). When asked in follow-up interviews what might be learned from such performances of interculturality and about whether they perceive any links between their improvisatory musical practices and questions of human rights and social justice, the musicians involved in the workshop were unequivocal: "Yes, of course, there is a relation" between intercultural improvisation and questions of rights and equality, explains Alain Derbez. "The thing is," he elaborates, "that you have to be aware of it. I think that musicians have to be conscious of what is going on and how music can be a vehicle of changing what is going on, but we fail, probably installed in our everyday life, to gain that consciousness and to spread it with the instruments we have."

When asked a similar question about whether she sees a link between the music she performed in the "New Communities of Sound" workshop and broader questions of rights and justice, Jane Bunnett tells us, "Oh, absolutely." Referencing the ways improvisatory music can help to foster awareness of the vital need to have "a respect for other human beings" by teaching us the importance of "observing and listening," Bunnett goes on to explain. "In a performance like that . . . I think most musicians would agree that . . . what you do is important, and that when you sit down and you're in a collective like that it entails all the things that we as human beings should just be . . . and carry ourselves as human beings in the world. And I think in that way it can teach something to the listener . . . to carry forth too . . . just dealing with all the things that life entails." About the importance of improvisation in particular, Bunnett says: "Well I think it comes down to listening . . . And then reacting . . . And so it's a real give and take. It's a balancing act. It's like going for it and being enthusiastic and joyful on your instrument and doing what you can . . . but it's also holding back, you know? And listening to what's happening around you, and just trying to be in tune—being in tune with the moment, and what's going on around you. And if you think about it, if you could carry that kind of thing with you all day long, you'd be one super enlightened person. But it's not easy." Derbez's remarks make a similar point: "There we were," he says, "to do something, to enjoy something together, not to measure who we were with, not to criticize. Collective music makes that possible. That's an example we have to follow." He adds, "After that [the performance] you go home with the idea of finding, of creating, this kind of momentum everywhere." Now, were people able to mobilize in their everyday lives the momentum, the spirit of dialogue and inquiry, associated with improvised musical performances, both Bunnett and Derbez seem to be suggesting, imagine what could happen.

Yet, as Rob Wallace commented in his follow-up interview, "Sometimes the relationship works musically, sometimes it doesn't. Often this is dependent on whether or not the musicians are interested in expanding their own particular idioms and *listening* rather than necessarily playing." Improvisational intention *does* count for something—and that intention begins with the will to listen to others, to the other. Indeed, all of the musicians interviewed about their participation in the workshop had, perhaps unsurprisingly, a great deal to say about the vital importance in improvised music of curious and responsible listening, and many, as Jane Bunnett's remarks quoted above suggest, were explicit in connecting the kind of listening that goes on in improvised musical encounters such as the workshop with broader questions of social responsibility. In Derbez's words, "You just have to listen, to stay always with your ears wide open." And this, he claims, means that musicians must "be prepared for surprise but never form a prejudice of what surprise is or will be." This focus both on close and careful listening and on the importance of surprise echoes Ingrid Monson's findings in her important ethnomusicological account of jazz musicians' perspectives on the creative processes involved in collective improvisation. Monson writes, "The ongoing process of decision making that takes place in the ensemble perhaps explains why musicians often say that the most important thing is to listen. They mean it in a very active sense: they must listen closely because they are continually called upon to respond to and participate in an ongoing flow of musical action that can change or surprise them at any moment" (*Saying Something* 43). What might it mean for alternative modes of civic engagement to sustain the reciprocal potential of surprise in continuous, responsible listening so evident in the improvisational practices described by these musicians?

Take Two: Sounds of Surprise; Rights, Risks, and Responsibilities in Improvised Music

The sound of surprise: Whitney Balliett's apt coinage for jazz—a music that, in its most provocative historical instances, has celebrated performance practices that cannot readily be scripted, predicted, or compelled into orthodoxy. Admittedly, we're quite drawn to the notion of surprise, of purposeful and innovative ways to confound familiar frameworks of assumption. To be sure, we're attracted to artistic practices that have tried to open new ears, to music that is startlingly and determinedly experimental, music that unsettles comfortable preconceptions, that casts doubt on fixed and static ways of seeing, and hearing, the world. Here's how Mattin, the Basque improvising sound artist and writer, puts it in his essay "Going Fragile":

> To be open, receptive and exposed to the dangers of making improvised music, means exposing yourself to unwanted situations that could break the foundations of your own security. As a player you will bring yourself into situations that ask for total demand. No vision of what could happen is able to bring light to that precise moment. Once you are out, there is no way back . . . You are breaking away from previous restrictions that you have become attached to, creating a unique social space, a space that cannot be transported elsewhere. Now you are building different forms of collaboration, scrapping previous modes of generating relations. (20–21)

What's at stake, then, in an improvised musical performance, and for whom? What kinds of critical questions might the theory and practice of improvised music-making open up about artistic expression and responsi-

bility, about the role of arts presenters and audiences, about intent and interpretation, about histories and communities, about activism and forms
of critical practice, about the ethics and aesthetics of surprise? At its best,
as Mattin's comments would imply, improvisation can encourage people
to take new risks in their relationships and collaborations with others, to
work together across various divides, traditions, styles, and sites, and to
hear (and to see) the world anew. And improvisation provides the crucible in which provisional, fragile experience can be experimented with,
given voice as a fundamental aspect of what makes us most human. As a
fundamental site for the choices made and the challenges emerging out
of social contexts, improvisation can provide a trenchant model for unexpected forms of social mobilization that accent agency, collaboration, and
difference. And as a structured bridge between diverse cultural traditions
and social locations, improvised musical practices can show the audience
what healthy political dialogue might look like in a transcultural society.
But if, as David Borgo suggests in his book *Sync or Swarm: Improvising
Music in a Complex Age*, "improvisers not only welcome but they worship
the sound of surprise," then is it possible, under the definition of improvisation, for things to go "wrong" in an improvised performance? (14).
What's at stake, and for whom? Not every improvisation is successful —
nor does every improvisation provide happy answers to some of the difficult questions we ask in this book. But even in its (oftentimes necessary)
failures does not improvisation actually provide listeners with an important model for rethinking how and why they need to find productive ways
to address encounters with difference, even when these encounters fail?

These are questions fraught with many (and sometimes disturbing) complexities. Much of our own work to date has focused on musical improvisation as a largely uninventoried model form of social behavior. From
the kinds of social relationships envisioned and activated through improvisational music-making, hope (rooted in actual practice and agency)
is derived that will sustain and empower people in their efforts to work
toward a more inclusive vision of community-building and intellectual
stock-taking. These are grand claims, we admit. But grand claims, after
all, are the business of manifestos, which ask to be judged precisely by
the futures they announce.

What happens, though, when those announced futures, those other possible worlds, don't even appear on the horizon of possibility? What hap-

pens when the signposts we have hitherto used to guide our analysis and interpretation of improvisatory musical practices are no longer effective or appropriate? What happens, that is, when improvisation just doesn't work? Despite claims about improvisation's liberatory potential, there are ample instances of improvisational musical practices that don't work in the model ways that we're suggesting they ought to. Furthermore, these instances need to be confronted squarely and honestly. True, listeners will all be familiar with improvisatory musical events where artists have resorted to clichés, where they have failed to surprise us, where they have relied on habitualized gestures, where musicians have been unable or unwilling to listen to one another, where they've deployed authoritarian musical gestures, where they've been more focused on the development of their own virtuoso techniques than with the collective endeavor. But even in so-called failed improvisations there always remains the spark of what might have been: the fact that chances were taken (or not) and that the performative agency enacted, however successfully, can still teach the listener something valuable.

Moreover, when improvisation doesn't work, the tendency of members of the audience, of musicians, and seasoned critics of the music is to think about this in terms of musical failure, as the examples given above (artists who don't listen, and the like) would suggest. But if we're right about the complex ways improvised musical practices inhabit the social landscape, and if we agree with Alan Durant that there's "a correspondence between problem-solving in improvised music and in other areas of human experience which gives improvisation [its] critical power," then the implications and consequences of this failure may be much more far-reaching, much more profound (279). The failure to listen to others represents failure on a musical level. More important, however, it also points to other (perhaps larger) kinds of failure.

Recall Small's argument in *Musicking*: "When we perform, we bring into existence, for the duration of the performance, a set of relationships, between the sounds and between the participants, that model ideal relationships as we imagine them to be and allow us to learn about them by experiencing them" (218). On this view, the failure to listen is symptomatic of a broader failure at the level of social responsibility and cooperation. Improvisation demands shared responsibility for participation in community, as well as an ability to negotiate differences and a willingness to accept the challenges of risk and contingency. And in an era when diverse peoples and communities of interest struggle to forge historically new forms of affiliation across cultural divides, the participatory and civic virtues of engagement, dialogue, respect, and community-building inculcated through improvisatory practices take on a particular urgency.

In considering the question of whether it's possible for things to go "wrong" in an improvised performance, it seems that particular instances of musical "failure"—we use the word *failure* advisedly here—are so controversial, so challenging, so dramatic, and so extreme that they provoke, and indeed insist on, commentary. We would be remiss to ignore the implications of such performances. We have in mind the kind of event that dramatically raises the stakes, the complexity, and the unpredictability of the debate on improvisation.

Our second case study in this chapter offers a particularly striking example. On September 10, 2004, at the eleventh annual Guelph Jazz Festival, a trio performance featuring Sainkho Namtchylak, William Parker, and Hamid Drake sparked debate and controversy in ways that the audience never could have predicted. While Guelph's is a festival that has come to be known for challenging audiences with compelling music and for sparking critical discussion on a range of issues related to innovative jazz and creative improvised music, a festival admired for its ongoing efforts to stage and to showcase the unexpected in music, the performance that took place that evening (and the aftermath of that performance) generated challenges and surprises that festival organizers, even several years later, can barely understand, let alone adequately begin to address. And herein lies a tale fraught with its various twists and turns, its contexts and conflicts, its themes and tensions. Our ways of telling this tale, as one might expect, are shaped and inflected by our own insider knowledges, that is, by our own awareness of, and involvement in, various kinds of extramusical and backstage happenings that aren't (and probably shouldn't be) part of the public record. So, the dilemma: how to write honestly and critically about the music without contravening the ethical principles that guide our practice as arts professionals, primary among them the notion that personal and contractual matters between artists and producers remain confidential, that backstage matters not be offered as part of any kind of public record.

Perhaps the most purposeful way to begin to get at the scope of the controversy that erupted that evening, then, is not to give you our own insider account of what happened, but rather to quote from the press and from others (and, indeed, there were many, including some academic commentators like Borgo) who, in one way or another, have entered the public debate. We start with Mark Miller's description of the concert in his *Globe and Mail* review, entitled "Singer Wails Up a Storm": "Sainkho Namtchylak, a noted singer who improvises in Siberia's Tuvan tradition, was a half-hour into an unhappy, tuneless wail at Chalmers United Church on Friday night. She stood with arms firmly crossed, the picture of defiance, and more than once made a display of consulting her watch, as if to ask, 'How much longer?' At no point did she respond to the tremendous rhythmic undertow generated by the two others on stage, New York bassist William Parker and Chicago drummer Hamid Drake." Miller's *Globe and Mail* colleague, Carl Wilson, in a review entitled "Guelph Fest's Fantastic Fiasco," posted on his *Zoilus* website, refers to the concert as "one of the most memorable, bad-ass improv shows [he has] ever seen." After quoting from sections of Miller's review, Wilson tells us that Namtchylak's

> "wail" was actually a drone, and rather than tuneless it was melodically relentless, the same three notes repeated with little variation. (It even could be defended ethnomusicologically, but that would be disingenuous.) Good portions of the audience were walking out and others were buzz-buzzing in their pews, including some beside me doing so in full speaking voice as if nobody could possibly be listening to this—even though Parker and Drake were turning in, off on their own, one of the best sets I've ever heard them do.
>
> At that point, the hapless MC for the evening, one David Burgess, was sent in by festival staff (and according to fest media liaisons, at the demand of other musicians to bail Hamid and William out) and began waving from the side of the stage. Mark [Miller] was again accurate about what happened next: "After a moment's confusion, she stopped the performance and reluctantly stepped down to shouts of 'Stay, stay, stay' from the audience. She herself could be heard to ask, 'What is freedom then?' In time, the audience prevailed. Back in place, Namtchylak aired her grievances against the festival and against life in general."

Wilson continues:

> Finally, William Parker began playing a golden bowl that produced a calming ring and the focus turned (near unwillingly) back to music. And here's where I differ in the extreme with Mark's account. He says, she "began sing-

ing again, this time a little more tunefully but still with some apparent distraction. It was Parker and Drake who gave the music what contour it had."

Obviously Mark would not have enjoyed Namtchylak's performance no matter what. What she did in the ensuing 45 minutes or so was a textbook case of kicking ass and taking names, Tuvan-shaman style. I have a bunch of recordings of her singing, tho I've never heard her live before, and this show outstripped anything I expected. It was furious, virtuosic and encyclopedic, from screams and overtone sequences that seemed likely to splinter the wood of the church if not cause it to burst into flames, to birdlike fluttering melodies that could have turned your blood to fog, and everywhere in between and sometimes—this being Tuvan throatsinging—simultaneously. An incantatory stream of hyperspeed syllables was perhaps most memorable, partly for its pentecostal fire of labial and glottal cascades and partly for the impression (shared, if conversations after the show are any indication, by the whole crowd) that she was putting one mother of a curse on us all.

(Mark claims that the audience cut her off at the end with its applause, but it seemed clear to me the musicians themselves chose their end point—long after their allotted time ran out.)

Parker and Drake served as able accompaniment at that point but their glory was in the first set, while Namtchylak seemed to be throwing the game. I will maintain to all comers, that first section was worth hearing for the bizarre contrast of her inertia and their dynamism—a supremely interesting combination if you closed your eyes to her scowling and *just listened to the sound*—and I think it's a very weird call to make at any point to decide that an improvisor is doing the "wrong" thing, even if you know that she's doing it to piss you off. That has to be saved for the retrospect.

Still, as Mark said, they were damned if they did stop her and damned if they didn't, and given what we got next, I'm selfishly happy they did.

And here's Josef Woodard writing in *Jazz Times*:

And then there was the memorable Namtchylak evening, which did not proceed without incident (every festival needs at least one incident, to stave off business-as-usual complacency). Apparently perturbed by assorted grievances, the usually captivating Namtchylak proceeded to blandly sing an eight-note motif repeatedly for a good 45 minutes while bandmates William Parker and Hamid Drake rumbled furtively on bass and drums. Perceiving a sham or gesture of protest, a festival official willfully invited her offstage, which drew public criticisms from the performer for disrespectful treatment, transportation woes and unwanted sponsorship issues.

Once she was finally coaxed back into action, Namtchylak eased into an hour-long set. Finally, her magical culture-crossing attributes—including unearthly sonics and throat-singing—emerged, if haltingly, and were allowed to flourish once the musicians toned down their sonic fury.

And, for now, one more commentator. This time, James Hale, on the Jazz Journalists Association website, jazzhouse.org. The subject heading: "To hook or not to hook?"

At the recent 11th annual Guelph Jazz Festival an event seemingly unprecedented since Charles Mingus disavowed responsibility for the onstage behavior of Charlie Parker and Bud Powell at Birdland in 1955 left several JJA [Jazz Journalists Association] members debating when, and if, it's proper for a performer to be removed from the stage.

At the center of the controversy was Siberian-born vocalist Sainkho Namtchylak. Agitated by what she viewed as disrespect on the part of the festival's organizers (she claimed she was not transported promptly from the airport to her hotel) Namtchylak began her performance with bassist William Parker and drummer Hamid Drake by looking at her watch and crossing her arms. She then began repeating a single, braying, phrase. Some 20 minutes later, she was still at it, while Parker and Drake played on, waiting in vain for some melodic variation. Clearly, her intention was to fulfill the contract for a 60-minute performance in as minimal a way as possible.

Numerous audience members began flowing out of the hall, but most stayed.

Eventually, the show's emcee, David Burgess, stepped forward at the direction of festival organizers to stop the show.

Some of the audience members were aghast, loudly expressing their displeasure. Two days later, some who were there continued to express their dissatisfaction with the stoppage.

Although Namtchylak returned to the stage, to launch into a vitriolic attack on the festival's organizers, more droning protest vocalizing and eventually—toward the 80-minute mark, at the coaxing of her rhythm section— some of the actual Tuvan throat singing she was contracted to perform, the debate had been set in motion.

Outside the hall, on the sidewalk, percussionist Famoudou Don Moye opined colorfully that Namtchylak would've received harsher treatment at New York's Apollo Theater, but the "hook" and the Apollo's notorious "Sandman," who used to sweep the stage after a performer had bombed, seem to be anathema for some in the 21st century.

What's your take? Should the festival's organizers have stepped in? Should the decision to stop have been left to Parker and Drake, or to the audience's patience?

Weigh in.

And weigh in people have. Some who were in attendance that evening and others who (like Borgo) weren't; some who commend the festival for being proactive (saying organizers did what they had to do) and others who say that the festival's actions were inexcusable and an affront to any professed notions of free expression. We've quoted at length from the critical response to offer some sense of the debates that emerged from that evening's performance. The turbulence of the event is aptly reflected in the fact that the critics themselves cannot agree on a number of crucial issues: was the singing a tuneless "wail" or was it a "drone"? Were there only three notes being repeated or were there eight? How long did the performance go on before the interruption? Was it twenty minutes, thirty minutes, or even forty-five minutes? Did the audience, as Mark Miller suggests, finally cut Namtchylak off when she paused for breath (and because they had had enough) or did the musicians themselves choose their own endpoint, as Carl Wilson would have it? Was the standing ovation at the end of the show an expression of genuine admiration for the performance or was it part of a concerted effort, on the part of the audience, to get Namtychlak off the stage? Or could it have been both? Was it, to borrow from a headline in *The Globe and Mail,* an example of "fans defend[ing] an artist's right to perform poorly?" Or were the fans, in fact, defending the right of arts presenters to stop the performance? Or could it be that fans were on their feet in support of William Parker and Hamid Drake, who, against all odds (and as some of the commentators have noted) laid down some of their very heaviest grooves in an effort to "save" the performance? Much of the critical discussion focuses, indeed, on Parker and Drake. Should they have been the ones to stop the performance? Why did they feel compelled to play on?

In what is some of the most astute critical writing to emerge in response to the event, Tracey Nicholls, in her McGill University doctoral dissertation, suggests that "audience members seemed of two minds as to how this interruption [of the performance] should be resolved." She continues, "As I recall it, some called for explanation and apology on the part of concert organizers and a resumption of the performance, while others encouraged Parker and Drake to keep playing without Namtchylak" (129). For Nicholls, "Parker and Drake's decision to ignore this encouragement, to not respond to the audience until Namtchylak returned to the stage," is of crucial significance. She interprets "both their musical support of Namtchylak and their silence during the offstage battle over whether she would return or not as modeling a profound ethical commitment to fellow community members. In this instance," she argues, "they had agreed to form a trio with Namtchylak and they were expressing their commitment to it, at least for the lifespan of the concert. Their aesthetic commitment to collaborative music-making appeared to imply an ethical commitment to remaining in community with Namtchylak, to working together as a trio" (129). And then, of course, there are the larger, more provocative questions: Did festival organizers have the right to intervene in the way that they did? Was it their responsibility to do so? In halting the performance, were they, as Borgo asks, "acting under preconceived notions of the types of material and interactions that Ms. Namtchylak would be expected, and therefore allowed, to perform?" (129). Does an artist have the right to do anything, to say anything, onstage as part of a performance? Indeed, the questions have proliferated into something of a seething discordance of unresolved tensions.

For what it's worth, here's what we can fill in about the event. There was a full house that evening, with several hundred people in attendance, everyone from children to seniors. It was a much-anticipated trio collaboration between two longtime friends of the festival and favorites with Guelph Festival audiences, William Parker and Hamid Drake, and the singer Sainkho Namtchylak, who was making her first appearance in Guelph. The show was the first half of a double bill featuring another high-profile act, the Pieces of Time percussion ensemble, led by Andrew Cyrille (and featuring, among others, Famoudou Don Moye, from the Art Ensemble of Chicago). Through no fault of the festival's, the trio set started very late (probably about forty-five minutes late) and there was yet another show scheduled after the performance by Pieces of Time. The event was, in short, well behind schedule. From the very opening notes of Namtchylak's performance (and from her interactions with festival orga-

nizers and fellow artists before the performance), it became clear to festival organizers (and, as the reviews we've quoted above would suggest,
to members of the audience) that there was something seriously amiss.
After singing a repeated, high-pitched, piercing, and "tuneless wail" (to
borrow Mark Miller's words) for about two minutes, Namtchylak looked
at her watch and folded her arms, as if telling her audience that had she
no genuine interest in singing, and that she would continue with the same
repeated wail (which those who know her music immediately recognized
has little resemblance to her art) for the next hour (or longer) in a deliberate gesture of defiance or protest. It was (and is) the belief of festival
organizers that her performance was intended deliberately to discredit
and harm the festival. After about forty minutes of the same wail (with
Parker and Drake doing their very best to save the performance by lay-
ing down some powerfully energetic grooves), festival organizers (who
had met spontaneously in the wings of the hall to discuss the situation—
several actually left the concert after about five minutes) made a difficult
decision to interrupt the concert and to ask Namtchylak what was wrong
and to see if they might be able to rectify the situation. This decision was
made in consultation with festival staff and board members, the artistic director, several artists performing at the festival (including many of
Namtchylak's peers), and other experienced arts presenters.

This decision to interrupt the performance was, of course, one that not
everyone would accept or agree with, and this decision was a complicated one for festival organizers. While organizers acknowledge that they
might have handled the situation differently, in retrospect the festival's
proactive intervention was, in many ways, an important one, for after air-
ing her grievances, ultimately Namtchylak went on (as Wilson and others
have suggested) to deliver a full and genuine performance that revealed
the wonders and intensity of her vocal range and the potency of her voice.

The festival is aware that the decision to interrupt the concert has been
sharply criticized by some and vehemently supported by others. Organizers extended an official apology to anyone who was offended or upset
by any of the circumstances that relate to this event. The incident raised
urgent and not easily resolved questions about artistic expression and responsibility, about the role of presenters and audiences, and about intent
and interpretation—questions with which the festival continues to engage. This chapter is part of an attempt to work through some of these
issues and to open up debate and discussion, in particular, around some

abiding questions: Can things, by definition, go "wrong" in an improvised performance, and on what basis do judgments about a performance such as the one we're describing here occur?

Something did go "wrong" that evening. But what went wrong, in our estimation, wasn't so much about the music. Indeed, we find ourselves thinking that the same music, but performed in another context and under another set of circumstances, might have provoked an entirely different set of responses. Imagine, for instance, if Namtchylak's onstage demeanor had been welcoming, rather than off-putting, if her body language suggested genuine engagement and interaction with the other musicians on the stage rather than projecting an image of defiance, boredom, and ill-will; or what if she had prefaced the concert with some remarks about the music we were about to hear? Obviously, it's impossible to second-guess what might have happened under such circumstances, just as it is impossible to predict the outcome of any improvised musical encounter.

But we do think that any judgments that we make about this event, as indeed about any act of improvised music-making, need to be understood as being not just about the music, but perhaps, more suggestively, about broader social matters. Recall Small's argument that acts of musicking "are to be judged, if they are judged at all, on their success in articulating (affirming, exploring, celebrating) the concepts of relationships of those who are taking part." He continues, "We may not like those relationships, and we are surely entitled to say so if we wish, but we should understand that our opinions are as much social as they are purely aesthetic . . . That is to say, we are passing an opinion not merely on a musical style but on the whole set of ideal relationships that are being articulated by the musical performance" (213). What kinds of relationships, then, were articulated through the concert by Namtchylak, Parker and Drake, and did they justify the festival's heavy-handed intervention? If Small's book is, in the main, concerned with the ways a symphony concert functions "as an instrument for the reassurance of the industrial middle and upper classes, for the presentation to themselves of their values and their sense of ideal relationships, and for persuading those who take part that their values, their concepts of relationship, are true and will last," then, clearly, the relationships articulated and activated during the performance at issue here were far from ideal (193). If Parker and Drake were, as Nicholls would have it, modeling an ethical commitment to remain in community, then what kinds of relationships were modeled through Namtchylak's onstage behavior? Is dissident, discomfiting expression not a key feature, if not always a potential eruption, in any truly improvised context in which the agency of the performer arises from multiple, complex contingencies?

Speaking in another context about her own music, Namtchylak has said, "The shamanistic culture has this art of being in the here and now. My dream is that people will not come up to me after a concert and tell me what a superb singer they think I am, but rather that they found some important meaning in the music. Because I strive on the stage to get so swallowed up by the music that I no longer exist. No 'I,' but something that is no longer discernible from the 'I' of the total ensemble" (qtd. in Heffley 253).

Judged in terms of her own comments about how she would like her music to be assessed, Namtchylak's dogged unresponsiveness to the other players onstage during her Guelph performance might well be heard as a refusal to be part of the total ensemble, a refusal to participate in dialogue or even to try to resolve differences (musical or otherwise). Far from losing herself in the workings of the total ensemble, Namtchylak seemed to be very much center stage that evening: the show foregrounded her self-interest and her authority, this despite the considerable communal efforts and contributions of her bandmates onstage. Moreover, her performance proceeded unhindered for a significant amount of time, during which she was given expressive latitude, an opportunity she took full, unimpeded advantage of, to the point of intruding on the performance time allotted to the next groups waiting to play. And in the words of the scholar and trombonist Scott Thomson, writing in another context, "given the possibility that collective improvisation offers for an ethically responsible reconciliation of musical differences, such insensitivity represents an effectively anti-social negation of the meaningful communitarian space between musicians" (22).

Furthermore, the questions that Small encourages us to ask about the nature of the relationships between those who take part in any musical performance seem particularly germane here. Of the performers, for instance, Small asks, "Do they show outward signs of involvement in their performance, appearing to be moved or excited by it, or do they appear detached?" (195). And, "Is there a leader at all, and if so, what is the nature of his or her authority?" (195). Of the listeners: "Do they talk during the performance or remain silent?" (196). And among the questions to ask about the relationships between listeners and performers: "Who dominates, who controls, how much power do the listeners have over the course of the performance? Can they change it or terminate it, cause it to be lengthened or shortened?" (196).

The media reports from which we quoted earlier should make it clear that these are certainly worthy questions to be asking of Namtchylak's Guelph performance. But they are a reminder that there are no simple, definitive, or necessarily correct answers, especially if one accepts that dissidence and improvisation can take unsettling, sometimes necessary directions that have little to do with fulfilling the expectations of the audience (or even of fellow performers). Recall that critics, for example, strongly disagree over the audience's role, with one commentator suggesting that the audience, in fact, was responsible for ending the concert, while another writer claims that it was the musicians themselves who exercised power and authority by choosing their own endpoint. And Nicholls goes so far as to suggest that if there was any failure that night, it wasn't so much on the part of the musicians or the festival organizers, but on the part of the audience members "who simply could not, or would not, open themselves to the aesthetic possibilities the performance was trying to offer [them]" (133).

Gender issues further complicate questions about power relations and authority, with some commentators pointing to the inappropriateness of the festival's having allowed a white male emcee to interrupt or silence a female Asian improviser. Others argue that the festival would have acted very differently had the offending artist been a high-profile male performer. The power dynamics of the situation were unfortunate and were in a sense laid bare by the tense circumstances of this particular improvisation; and these circumstances raise the question of the ethics of any artist—male or female—who uses a performance situation to engage in behavior that undermines the cocreative aspects of musical dialogue, even if that behavior is enacted in the name of original artistry or freedom of expression.

Our point here is that whether the performing artist is male or female, black or white, young or old, the artist who chooses to do or say whatever he or she likes onstage invites consequences that have a significant ethical dimension. This is, perhaps, a notoriously difficult argument to advance in the context of a festival that prizes improvisatory practices, that accents surprise, that makes a point of unsettling routine expectations. But it's wrong, we believe, to assume that improvisation is in any simplistic way synonymous with freedom from the responsibility of cocreative interplay, wrong to assume "that improvisation involves adherence to neither convention or protocol, that it tolerates no system of constraint . . . that, in both theory and practice, it's best understood, in the words of one writer, as a kind of 'free zone in music where . . . you are responsible only to yourself and to the dictates of your taste'" (Fischlin and Heble 23).

Let us be clear. We intend no disparagement of artists who challenge conventions and protocols, who take risks in their performance practices, artists who, in so many genuinely profound and purposeful ways, have shattered familiar etiquettes of courtesy and complacency, who have pushed the limits of what is thinkable and doable on stage in productively unsettling, discomfiting ways. Improvisation as a genre is replete with artists who have done this over and over during their lifetimes, many of them discussed throughout this book. But there needs to be a more nuanced understanding of (limits to) personal expression as a function of multiple intersecting levels of responsibility and reciprocity that make the ethics of cocreative community possible, indeed thinkable. There is more at stake, as the particular performance we're discussing here makes vividly clear, than the reductive dictates of the performer's own taste, where it's not enough simply to be "responsible to yourself." Rather, we would agree with Edward Said, who is forthright on this matter. "Responsibly," writes Said, "one cannot just say anything one pleases and in whichever way one may wish to say it" (*Humanism and Democratic Criticism* 69).

Perhaps we'll be labeled as defectors—especially in the arts community—for saying so, but we've always had considerable difficulty with the notion of freedom without responsibility, always been troubled by professed expressions of freedom without limits. Recent history, after all, provides no shortage of examples in which various takes on the word *freedom* are used to justify, to provide license for, and to naturalize intolerable behaviors and egregious abuses of rights and power by unaccountable elites. The press toward hope that binds aggrieved communities in their response to such abuses and degradations, it seems to us, is ultimately much more vital, more resilient, more complicated, and more important, than the defense of free expression as a sacrosanct and self-sufficient form of private taste, judgment, and intention. And we note, too, the disturbing link between notions of the private that entail destructive and irresponsible (read: greedy and selfish) agency and neoliberal discourses predicated on a marketplace driven by the will to individual self-interest.

We live in an era when "dominant political institutions encourage us to think of ourselves as atomized citizen-subjects," "as individual consumers, not as members of cultural communities" (Lipsitz, *American Studies* xviii); the consequences, we believe, are quite impoverishing. Hope resides in endeavors that, as we've argued elsewhere, encourage people to seek "social connection as [their] most important life project" (Lipsitz, *American Studies* xviii). Now if we're right in suggesting that improvisational music-making is about more than the sounds themselves, just as it is about more than individual acts of self-expression, if we're right in arguing that the social relationships envisioned and activated in improvisational musical settings demand attention, that responsibility in improvisation is about building cooperation and sustaining public trust, then it seems to us that Sainkho Namtchylak's Guelph performance signals the tense relation between the forces that undermine cocreative acts and the hope that cocreation generates via dialogue in the public commons. The so-called failure relentlessly reinstates the primary questions we've been asking about improvisation as a sonic practice with profound social implications. Such an assessment, of course, cannot in itself justify a decision to interrupt her concert. But we are not so much interested here in any such attempt at justification as we are in trying to understand how the very need to make judgments and to announce commitments that emerged that evening was (and is) grounded in complex patterns of relevance that are worth exploring.

Surprise in improvisation, then, manifests itself not just, as Balliett's coinage would have it, in the sounds, not just in the ability of music to stage the unforeseen or the unexpected (to a certain extent, there's a sense in which, at a festival such as Guelph's, the unexpected in music has almost become the norm). It's also, and perhaps more profoundly, registered in the way improvised music-making forces us to dispense with customary frameworks of assumption, how it eludes any inclusive analysis or interpretation of the effects it produces, how it continually keeps us on edge, how it subjects our assessments to an ongoing process of critical inquiry. Now, were performers and listeners to mobilize the resources, the spirit of inquiry and experimentation, the necessity for robust dialogue associated with improvised musical performances, in the service of sounding new models of social cooperation, imagine the ideals that might be nourished, the relationships that could get fostered, the lessons that might be learned.

Instead, there was rather a different kind of lesson learned that night.

The audience learned how a series of misunderstandings that allowed things to become so explosive could generate an intense crisis of meaning and judgment. The event, clearly, showed neither the Guelph Jazz Festival nor Sainkho Namtchylak at their best. The concert failed, by any standards, to live up to any claims that we, as authors, might like to make for the ability of improvised music-making to inculcate participatory virtues of engagement, dialogue, and tolerance, or to promote socially responsive forms of community-building across cultural boundaries. In retrospect, there's much that festival organizers might have done differently that evening, just as, no doubt, the performers know that they too might have responded to their predicaments in ways that would have significantly altered the outcome of the performance and the assessment of it. Call it taking a stand, call it a kind of act of faith, call it a failure of judgment and imagination: each party to the event responded to the misunderstandings with insufficient and disputable methods of coping.

Living with the consequences of such insufficiencies is not always easy, and it can be tempting to reflect on our decisions with after-the-fact rationalizations that seek stability and security. It would be comforting to say that the festival managed to get through this crisis with generosity, imagination, trust, humility, and with a spirit of cooperation and goodwill. But it did not.

What did happen, though, is that just as the festival issued a public apology, so too did each of the artists involved apologize to the festival. The unforeseen antagonisms that emerged from that act of improvisation gone wrong have generated their own surprising turn of events, out of which new forms of alliance, new and unforeseen kinds of community-building are taking shape. People in attendance that evening recognize that they saw a form of history in the making, and when they discover others who were there, there's a kind of "you were there too" spark of recognition, as if these people have traveled through a storm together, and come out on the other side. The experience of having weathered the storm in itself binds these people together in unexpected ways, almost as if they have discovered solidarity in sharing stories of discomfort. And those who weren't there? Well, we're always surprised when we hear from people who weren't there—as we did just the other day, when we were telling a friend and fellow musician about the subject of this chapter— we're always surprised to hear that they feel somehow left out, that they regret not having been part of what went down on that now fabled, if ill-fated evening in Guelph.

The lesson remains that even in failed instances of improvisation, the social significance of the failure becomes the locus for new dialogue, however tense, that is productive of new forms of engagement, new ways of understanding agency and social practices that test the limits of the listener's ability to interpellate dissidence and difference. Improvisation teaches the listener that in the surprise of the unexpected lies the potential for new understanding, for necessary, though not always easy, self-examination, and for renewed and unrelenting efforts to attempt to negotiate difference.

Take Three: "You Break No Laws by Dreaming": Transculturalizing the Field

Ien Ang has suggested that "one of the most urgent predicaments of our time can be described in deceptively simple terms: how are we to live together in this new century?" (193). She continues:

> "We" and "together" are the key sites of contestation here. In this postmodern world of multiplying claims to particularist identities, any overarching sense of "we" has become fundamentally problematic and contentious . . . In this climate, the very idea of living "together" becomes hugely daunting. Can togetherness be more than a coincidental and involuntary aggregation of groups being thrust into the same space and time, an uneasy and reluctant juxtapositioning of different bodies and identities forced to share a single world even if their respective imaginative worlds are worlds apart? What are the possibilities of constructing transcultural imagined communities in this era of rampant cultural differentiation and fragmentation? How, in short, can we live together-in-difference? (193)

Her fundamental question (how are people to live together in this new century?) finds apt expression in the case studies in this chapter: whether it's the energy, groove, momentum, and resourcefulness so evident in the "New Communities of Sound" workshop or the "unhappy, tuneless wail" of Sainkho Namtchylak, whose own body and identity seemed so insistently, so provocatively, to be not only deliberately unresponsive to, but also "worlds apart" from, her onstage colleagues during her Guelph performance, it's clear that there's something vital at stake in the way improvising musicians interact with one another (and with their listeners) in these transcultural encounters.

How we choose to live (and to do things) together, how we sustain bonds and reclaim history, how we adapt to unprecedented change, how we choose to create a shared future, how we remain attentive to our responsibility to build the world we hope to inhabit: improvised music can be a powerful site for sounding such questions about *how*. And in an era when there is increasing pressure to conform to the narratives promulgated by dominant knowledge-producing elites, and when entrenched positions and settled conditions crowd out alternative visions and opportunities for change, these are, it seems to us, no small matters. Indeed, the musical gestures at work in improvisation are rife with implications about social practice, or, in Monson's words, about "what people choose to do given the particular structural and discursive configurations in which they live" (*Freedom Sounds* 26). "Practice," Monson tells us, "is about agency in everyday life, that is the implementation of cultural ideas, values, and structures through various kinds of social action" (26).

The music functions as a vehicle both for the rehistoricization of minoritized cultures (recall George Lewis's arguments about the AACM) and for the expression of "our as yet unwritten future" (Lipsitz, *Footsteps* 265). This insistence on improvisation's role in the unwritten future is consistent with claims advanced by a number of commentators: Robin Kelley's arguments in *Freedom Dreams*, Paul Gilroy's interest in "black music's obstinate and consistent commitment to the idea of a better future" (36), and bell hooks's assertion that "African American performance has been a site for the imagination of future possibilities" (220) all come to mind.

Enlarging on these claims about black music, the power to dream, and the expression and sounding of future possibilities (as well as on the models of intercultural improvisatory music-making discussed in this chapter), our third case study demonstrates how the improvisative, collaborative, and culturally hybrid practices of so-called hyphenated artists might contribute to the critical discourse on rights and multiculturalism. How might institutions concerned to advance transcultural understanding make use of improvisational practices?

Improvisatory musical practices, as many commentators have noted, have had a long, important history in relation to the formation of hybridized identities. Jason Stanyek's work on the development of a Pan-African intercultural community through forms of musical improvisation, for instance, asserts the central role played in this context by the musical collaborations between Dizzy Gillespie and Chano Pozo:

> What Gillespie and Pozo did was to set a number of precedents for future Pan-African collaborations in jazz; an emphasis on composition with a simultaneous affirmation of improvisation; the insertion of nonjazz repertoires into jazz; the accommodation of instruments not typically found in jazz ensembles; the use of non-English and multilingual texts; the highlighting of African spirituality. But perhaps most important were (1) their ability to juxtapose different histories without sacrificing identity and (2) their reflexive use of notions of cultural difference as a basis for collaboration. (88–89)

Many of the precedents that Stanyek sees as having been established by intercultural collaborations between Gillespie and Pozo continue to inform contemporary music-making. In 2003, as part of its tenth anniversary celebration, the Guelph Jazz Festival premiered a specially commissioned new-jazz opera. Entitled *Québécité*, the opera, with music by D. D. Jackson and a libretto by George Elliott Clarke, explicitly (both in its conceptualization and through its premiere performance) sought to present culturally diverse forms of music, both to new audiences and to aficionados. Here too the insertion, to borrow from Stanyek, of "nonjazz" idioms and repertoires into a "jazz" context, the use of non-English and multilingual texts, and the ability to juxtapose and to negotiate different histories without sacrificing identity all played a vital role. Enlarging, in part, on the success of George Elliott Clarke's previous opera, *Beatrice Chancy*— about slavery in Canada—*Québécité* was, in many ways, an attempt to encourage more artists to base creative projects on themes and subjects of more specific and immediate social and cultural relevance to their audiences.[4]

Québécité is a three-act, multicultural romance set in modern-day Québec City. The plot tells the story of two interracial couples whose developing romances expose the inherent minefield of establishing relationships that cross racial and cultural boundaries. The principal characters are Laxmi Bharati, a student-architect born in Bombay; Ovide Rimbaud, an architect originally from Haiti; Colette Chan, a law student whose parents, avid jazz fans, fled the Tiananmen massacre to find refuge in Canada; and the jazz pianist Malcolm States, a native black Nova Scotian currently playing at the jazz club owned by Colette's parents. As the story unfolds, the couples learn to navigate the stormy waters of gender, race, and culture in order to establish relationships based on love rooted in mutual respect and understanding—relationships strong enough to withstand the trials of opposing parents and clashing cultures. The story, in short, demands involvement from artists who are sensitive to the politics, the pitfalls, and the possibilities of cross-cultural communication. As composer, D. D. Jackson was well positioned to take on such a challenge, not only because of his own mixed-race (African Canadian and Chinese Canadian) background, but also because, as so many of his projects demonstrate, he is a relentless innovator and improviser whose work has always sought to find creative and articulate ways to synthesize a diverse range of influences.

The featured vocalists for the opera included Haydain Neale (the dynamic young African Canadian leader of the popular R&B-acid jazz group JackSOUL, who passed away in 2009 after a battle with lung cancer), the acclaimed Toronto-based Indian Canadian vocalist Kiran Ahluwalia, the African American avant-jazz and gospel singer Dean Bowman, and the New York-based Korean-Canadian experimental jazz and improvising vocalist Yoon Choi. The opera was directed by the African Canadian director Colin Taylor.

From our deliberate emphasis on the diverse and hyphenated identities of the production's principals, you'll recognize that in casting the opera the festival explicitly sought to choose artists (many of whom, including the composer and the librettist, had not previously worked together) who enabled a broadening and diversification of the constituency traditionally defined as a jazz or improvised-music audience. Diverse in cultural backgrounds, and also, in the musical contexts for which they are best known—Punjabi folk songs, acid or hip-hop jazz, classical music, gospel or roots, alternative rock, avant-garde jazz, rhythm 'n' blues, creative improvised music, and so forth—the opera's unique cast played a key role in helping the festival reach out to new target audiences with this production, especially more young people, opera fans (who might not otherwise attend the festival), and audiences associated with the musics of various world-folk traditions. Add to this mix the fact that the libretto was written by African Canadian author George Elliott Clarke, and the result was an explicit broadening and diversifying of the cultural scope of (and subject matter for) new Canadian opera. And this, of course, was in keeping with Canada's stated multicultural objectives: for example, as articulated in the Canadian Multiculturalism Act, to "recognize and promote the understanding that multiculturalism reflects the cultural and racial diversity of Canadian society and acknowledges the freedom of all members of Canadian society to preserve, enhance, and share their cultural heritage," and to "promote the understanding and creativity that arise from the interaction between individuals and communities of different origins." The opera was also very much in keeping with the democratizing impulses that, in its most provocative instances, have shaped so much of the history of jazz and creative improvised music. *Québécité* was, in short, part of an effort to reflect (and to project) a much desired image of Canadian plurality and diversity across the nation, and, indeed, throughout the world.

In thinking about *Québécité*, we're particularly interested in reflecting on the question of how cultural institutions (music festivals, for example) might best play a role in transculturalizing the field, that is, in terms of the range and scope of cultural references that the field takes on, in this case, the field of innovative jazz and creative improvised music. Much of the music at the Guelph Jazz Festival involves precisely such real-time improvisational encounters among artists from diverse cultures.

When asked about what makes these real-time encounters work, Jane Bunnett explained, "I think it has a lot to do with who's curating it." Festival curators and arts presenters are uniquely positioned to radicalize public understanding, to cultivate purposeful resources for listening, to provide audiences and performing musicians alike with encounters that encourage them to hear the world anew. And at issue, if the notion of music curation is taken seriously as an activist practice that can and does lead to social change, is the need to create more equitable structures of inclusion. Answering such a challenge necessitates attending rigorously to matters of diversity (of, for example, race, gender, and sexuality). Indeed, curation itself might be seen as a form of improvisatory practice, one that requires activating new directions (like the jazz-opera hybrid) as part of its social function.

The libretto's title, *Québécité*, is itself deliberately and playfully provocative, especially considering the mixed-race couples at the center of the plot, and in light, too, of the fraught role that ethnicity and race have played in struggles for Québec nationalism.[5] Eschewing the exclusivist, monolithic, and anti-ethnic sentiments that too often attach themselves to expressions of national or cultural identity—think, for example, of Jacques Parizeau's now infamous remarks in October 1995 about how the "ethnic vote" defeated his attempts to win sovereignty for Québec — Clarke's emphasis in the libretto on *le Québec de couleur* is a bold attempt to counter the demonization of the "other" in attempts to fashion homogeneous national communities. With *Québécité*, Clarke seeks to break free from such dangerously monolithic ways of knowing the world.

Clarke's efforts to work toward a more diverse and inclusive understanding of issues such as belonging, identity, and citizenship are, moreover, worth thinking about in relation to comments he has made on the Canada-Québec schism. In the introduction to his anthology of African Canadian writing, *Eyeing the North Star: Directions in African-Canadian Literature* (1997), a text whose own raison d'être Clarke explicitly articulates in terms of an insistence on "new, more inclusive definitions of Canadianness," he writes, "the primacy assigned the Canada-Québec schism marginalizes all other ethnic-racial-linguistic questions" (xxiii, xvii). In this context, Clarke references "the pandemonium that then-Parti Québécois MNA Jean Alfred, a Haitian Canadian, aroused at a National Black Coalition of Canada meeting in Toronto in May 1979, when he declared, before a hundred delegates at the King Edward Hotel, that Québec's 'liberation' was more important than black national unity" (xvii). Clarke's point in recalling this episode is that "language dynamics drive some black francophone intellectuals to prioritize linguistic issues ahead of racial matters" (xvii). Now *Québécité* clearly isn't making a statement about black national unity, and it isn't — as anyone who reckons with the richness, the playfulness, and the extraordinary musicality of Clarke's poetry will immediately recognize — about to pay short shrift to the vitality of language; it does, however, exert a necessary challenge to mainstream assumptions about Québec as white. And in this context, its noncompliance with dominant knowledge-producing elites in Canada seems to us to carry a salutary — indeed an urgent — political force.

That force is perhaps most profoundly registered in the text's insistence on the power to dream. "You break no laws by dreaming," announces one of the opera's characters, Colette Chan, as the libretto draws the audience toward its finale. Colette's remark hastens reflection on the fact that the capacity to dream (as Martin Luther King Jr.'s famous "I Have a Dream" speech so eloquently and so brilliantly made clear) remains an absolute necessity in face of the degradations that beset aggrieved peoples. It is a force registered not only in the opera's dedication to Clarke's mother and to the composer D. D. Jackson's mother—"two dreamers of beauty"—but also in the vision at the opera's end, of a better, more inclusive world, one where "Our children will be / every colour eyes can know," a world, furthermore, where "states, parents, gods / must have no say." The emphasis here on dream puts us in mind of Robin Kelley's *Freedom Dreams*. Addressing "anyone bold enough still to dream" (7), Kelley explains how, from very early in his life, he was taught to "see life as possibility," to imagine "a world where gender and sexual relations could be restructured," or where we could learn to recognize "the poetic and the prophetic in the richness of our daily lives" and "to visualize a more expansive, fluid, 'cosmos-politan' definition of blackness" (2). In like fashion, Clarke's libretto is calling on all dreamers to work toward a more inclusive vision of valued social practices.

Offering an alternative to the doggedly Eurological operatic tradition, *Québécité*, in short, marks something of an unprecedented opportunity on the Canadian operatic stage to generate bold new stagings of identity. Music, like dream, this jazz opera tells us, can empower us not only (to borrow again from Kelley) to hear "life as possibility," but also to foster (and to sustain) vibrant artistic and critical initiatives dedicated to sounding a more inclusive vision of community-building and intellectual stocktaking for the new millennium. And in an era when demands for tighter controls on immigration and border-crossing threaten to put the dreams of aggrieved peoples at risk of being even further abandoned, the structures of hope, possibility, and momentum embodied in Clarke's rainbow quartet of lovers is especially pertinent.

The role of improvisation in *Québécité* commands attention here. On the one hand, D. D. Jackson's music is tightly scripted and composed, and because it's so closely tied to particular movements and developments onstage, it leaves few openings for extended extemporization. On the other hand, many of the musical forms in the opera, including the blues, and call-and-response sections, emerge from improvised and black diasporic musickings. Moreover, Jackson's score, as commentators such as Katherine McLeod and Julia Obert have pointed out, uses improvisatory practices of multivocality to stage cultural and sonic hybridity. McLeod, for instance, points to Kiran Ahluwalia's performance of Laxmi in this context. Ahluwalia herself has noted in an interview, "I am Indian, but I'm Canadian as well so, when I'm improvising, is that Indian music or Canadian music? Well, you know what? It's a bit of both; I'm doing Canadian music even if it sounds foreign to you" (Khanna). In her essay on multi-vocality and improvisation in *Québécité*, McLeod offers this quote to take issue with what she (rightly, we think) sees as a critical misreading of Ahluwalia's performance of Laxmi in the reviews of the opera's premiere performance in Guelph, a misreading and mislabeling, in particular, pro-mulgated by commentators who saw Laxmi as being effective only when relying on her Indianness. In his review for the *Toronto Star*, for instance, Geoff Chapman wrote, "Kiran Ahluwalia was the least effective, except when she could employ her classical Indian style." Countering this as-sessment, McLeod argues that "improvisation provides Ahluwalia with a space for transcultural crossings, which allows her to produce a sound that *subverts* expectations . . . her statement, 'I'm doing Canadian music even if it sounds foreign to you,' speaks back to critics [such as Chap-man] who insist upon labelling her music as other. As Ahluwalia her-self recognizes, blending jazz with Indian styles of music is a significant performative statement, and when the complexities of such a statement are dismissed with an insistence upon hearing her music as 'Indian,' it seems to say more about the listener than about her performance." Ahlu-walia's improvisations as Laxmi, in short, allow different sonic registers to exist simultaneously (an act mirroring the very hybridity at the heart of jazz opera, itself a gumbo concoction), and, in so doing, they not only, as McLeod would have it, unsettle customary assumptions about settled boundaries, but also enable the kind of radicalization of public under-standing that helps the audience think through how best they might live, as Ang puts it, "together-in-difference."

Now lest we seem to be falling back on notions of cultural hybridity or transcultural music-making as automatically, necessarily, or unambigu-ously positive, we need only recall the tensions, the uneasiness, the crises of meaning and judgment associated, for instance, with Namtchylak's Guelph performance. Think also of bassist Joëlle Léandre's comments, cited earlier in our book, about what it means to "be together" via impro-vised music, and all the dissonances and tensions (social as well as musi-cal) that such being together implies. Ang, too, urges her readers to be cautious of reducing hybridity to notions of harmonious amalgamation, or "happy fusion and synthesis." Such reductions, she insists, "are gener-ally conveniently neglectful of the specific power relations and histori-cal conditions configuring the interactions and encounters which induce forced and unforced processes of hybridization" (197). And "any intercultural exchange will always face its moment of incommensurability, which disrupts the smooth creation of a wholesome synthesis" (Ang 198).

In Clarke's libretto, such disruptions are signaled both in the present-tense working out of the storyline (for example, when Colette's parents vehemently denounce Malcolm because of the color of his skin, and refuse to accept his love for their daughter) and in embedded histories involving African diasporic communities responding to change. In canto II, scene 7, confronted with being rejected by Colette's parents, Malcolm recalls one such history when he tells her, "Loving you is like, like, Heaven and a lynching! / Pops abandoned Tennessee to flee such flinching! / For lavish Love, motorcycled to Nova Scotia, / Affianced, married, an Afro-Mi'kmaq madonna" (*Québécité* 70). Malcolm's African American father sought to escape racism and prejudice in the South, in search of a better life in Nova Scotia. Clarke, however, remains fully aware of Nova Scotia's own long, troubled, and complicated history of racism, as several of his other works (including *Beatrice Chancy*) make powerfully clear. He knows that, in the 1960s, the black community of Africville was demolished by the city of Halifax, allegedly as part of a racialized program of urban renewal and "slum clearance." He knows that this history of erasure in response to African diasporic communities, like the shutting down in New Orleans of Storyville as a legal vice district in the early part of the twentieth century, is part of a larger colonial project involving the regulation and management of black bodies, black spaces, black cultures. And he knows that the fight for rights and equality is anything but over. Indeed, as an article about Nova Scotia in the *Globe and Mail*, published in May 2010, soon after an interracial couple in Hants County awoke to the glare of a burning cross on their front lawn, suggests, "No other place in Canada has so many black communities still living in de facto segregation. Nowhere else in Canada does the legacy of slavery remain so tangible, as much as mainstream white society tries to block it out" (Perreaux).

What's interesting about *Québécité* is that such disruptions, what Ang calls moments of incommensurability, the pitfalls of border-crossing, as it were, find expression not just in the storyline, but also, significantly, in the music itself. Both McLeod and Obert are correct to read Ang's sense of uneasiness as being a vital part of *Québécité*'s force. As Obert notes, "The sonic hybridity *Québécite* foregrounds is not unadulteratedly positive; harmony, here, is often offset by acoustic clash." She points, for instance, to the improvisatory dissonance registered in that seventh scene in canto II, in which Malcolm responds to being denounced by Colette's parents: "Its 'funk groove' (D. D. Jackson, CBC interview) is punctuated by screams, howls, irregular rhythms, and interruptions of melodic arc." Again, Ang's comments are worth quoting here: "Rather than seeing hybridity as a synonym for an easy multicultural harmony, or as an instrument for the achievement thereof, I want to suggest that the concept of hybridity should be mobilized to address and analyze the fundamental *uneasiness* inherent in the global condition of togetherness-in-difference . . . In short, hybridity is not only about fusion and synthesis, but also about friction and tension, about ambivalence and incommensurability, about the contestations and interrogations that go hand in hand with the heterogeneity, diversity and multiplicity we have to deal with as we live together-in-difference" (200).

How, then, *do* we live together in the new century? We've seen throughout this book that improvisatory musical practices often respond to this question with an impulse to remember or to bear witness, and that they can also do so by way of an impulse to imagine, to dream, to sound the possibility of another, more hopeful, more just world. In improvised music, of course, these impulses coalesce in the here and now of performance.

Which brings us yet again to the title of our book. *The Fierce Urgency of Now* is a phrase taken from a speech made by Martin Luther King Jr. The speech, entitled "Beyond Vietnam: A Time to Break the Silence," was made on April 4, 1967, before a meeting of Clergy and Laity Concerned at Riverside Church in New York, and is regarded as King's first public statement against the war in Vietnam. In the speech, King sought to make a passionate plea for Americans to "undergo a radical revolution of values" and "to question the fairness and justice of many of [their] past and present policies." King impressed upon Americans that the kind of revolution of values he was advocating—a revolution symbolized by the need for America to withdraw from its involvement in the Vietnam War— was both necessary and urgent: "We are faced with the fact," he told his listeners, "that tomorrow is today. We are faced with the fierce urgency of now. In this unfolding conundrum of life and history there is such a thing as being too late."

King drew significant criticism for this speech: for daring to link white supremacy at home to American imperialism abroad (as Cornel West reminds us, "black folk couldn't take it" [202]); for daring to suggest that sectional loyalties must be replaced by ecumenical ones; for daring to build new coalitions that sought to lift concern "beyond one's tribe, race, class and nation." King's speech compelled his listeners to understand that hope must be seen as an absolute necessity in the face of injustice. Yet hope, like improvisation, comes with no guarantees. Like improvisation, it's sometimes a messy and complicated life-project. In Cornel West's words, "Real hope is grounded in a particularly messy struggle and it can be betrayed by naïve projections of a better future that ignore the necessity of doing the real work" (6). If we're right in suggesting that improvisational music-making is about more than just the sounds themselves, that there are pressing matters at stake in understanding the social relationships envisioned and activated in improvisational musical settings, that such relationships are constitutive of contemporary social life (think of Ang's comment: "This, of course, is what togetherness-in-difference is all about: it is about co-existence in a single world" [200]), then perhaps now is the time to understand that the kind of real work that both West and King are calling for begins only with the recognition that any vision that people might have of a utopia has to do not so much with a "nowhere," but, rather, with little pieces of here and there, in the here and now that they are trying to make to live "together-in-difference."

This insight is what Wallace had in mind when, in introducing the "New Communities of Sound" workshop, he, by way of Gilroy's notion of a "strategic universalism," suggested that listeners learn to hear the improvised encounter as "a perhaps temporary but nevertheless valuable state of being where [participants] can come together and talk for a while and feel like a community." Social change, Wallace seems to be saying, begins with possibility. And the possibilities opened up by boundary-shattering improvisatory musical encounters such as the "New Communities of Sound" workshop entail a shift in the way people listen to one another, in their understanding of relatedness and connection. Indeed, in his book *Community: The Structure of Belonging*, Peter Block reminds the reader that "possibility . . . is a declaration, a declaration of what [people] create in the world each time [they] show up. It is a condition, or value, that [they] want to occur in the world, such as peace, inclusion, relatedness, reconciliation. A possibility is brought into being in the act of declaring it" (16). He continues, using language that aptly echoes Wallace's: "The key . . . is to create in the room a living example of how I want the future to be. Then there is nothing to wait for, because the future begins to show up as we gather. One of the principles is that all voices need to be heard, but not necessarily all at one time or by everybody" (24). Improvisation, as we assert in the prelude, teaches us to enact the possibilities we envision.

Rebecca Solnit, in her account of the improvised, purposeful, and extraordinary communities that arise out of devastation and disaster, makes a related argument. "We speak of self-fulfilling prophecies," she explains, "but any belief that is acted on makes the world in its image. Beliefs matter. And so do the facts behind them" (*Paradise* 3). Think again of comments we've cited earlier from William Parker: "Improvisation may lead you to open up areas in your life that other musics won't—*if you want it to.*" Improvised music-making Parker insists, is linked with broader struggles for social justice precisely "because we say it is" (Parker, personal interview). In the authority of this assertion by one of the greatest living improvisers lies the seed of agency and intention that improvisation deploys as a sonic and social practice anticipating the fullness of what it might mean to be human.

CODA

Listening

Modes of listening and viewing promoted within the Western art tradition assume distinct divisions between performers and audiences. *Listening,* in the sense we intend it, fills the space between with cocreative, cogenerative aspects of both performance and reception. Improvisation asks that the creator listen and the listener create as inseparable aspects of a dialogic, unpredictable process. Art designed to cultivate self-regulating bourgeois subjects disaggregates the social world into putatively autonomous individuals. By contrast, improvisatory art emanating from aggrieved communities tends to be interactive, dialogic, cogenerative, and an evocation of a cocreative form of call and response that defines social practices in which aggregation and contingency coexist. Elevating the creative act over the created object, this kind of art cultivates a taste for the ephemeral, the aleatory, and the unexpected that arise from the full community invoked by performance. Autonomy is provisional and contingent. Improvisation is an aesthetic practice whose underlying values arise from provisional and contingent engagements with the other.

Listening to the improvised music of John Coltrane, Sun Ra, Pauline Oliveros, Horace Tapscott, or the Art Ensemble of Chicago, we are encouraged to hear a compelling and, indeed, an urgent story about the need to learn how to listen, a story about the need, especially in the context of aggrieved populations struggling for access to resources, for rights, and for justice, to cultivate resources for curious, critical, active (and perhaps even radical) listening. Rather than the kind of curious, ear-opening, dialogic, and responsible listening urged by these and other artists, listening, sadly, has too often become a habitualized activity, something we too readily take for granted as a sublimated, passive activity without agency.

In our view, listening is a crucial form of agency that generates ethical and artistic imperatives, like those generated in an improvisation founded on the capacity to hear the other in ways that change one's own contribution to the collective narrative.

Dominant and media-generated ways of hearing the world, we know too well, crowd out alternative perspectives and stifle dissenting voices. Activists working for a better and more just world continue to be confronted with systematic denial and disinterest, with people turning a blind eye (and a deaf ear) to monumental global suffering and abuse. It's all too clear that the world is talking. Is anybody really listening? What improvising artists have succeeded in doing is profoundly and productively unsettling orthodox habits of response and judgment. They've opened our ears to new sounds. They've turned institutionalized versions of music history on their head. Through their use of performance practices that can't readily be scripted, predicted, or compelled into orthodoxy, they've encouraged us, in effect, to hear the world anew, to imagine new forms of relational being that have significant rights implications. Through their radical retreat from conventional sources of musical meaning-making, they've invited us to hear how the mobility of practice associated with musical improvisation is also a story about social mobility for aggrieved peoples. This, we suggest, is no small matter. At a time when egregious abuses of rights continue unchecked (this despite the ratification of various international treaties and covenants), the ability to learn how to listen to others remains absolutely fundamental. If rights are most often centered in legal, judicial, and governmental discourses that summarily tend to exclude marginalized voices and perspectives, then there is much to be learned from the working models of improvisatory music-making (and the attendant notions of critical listening that come out of those models) developed by creative practitioners. How might practices of improvisatory listening that are part of the aesthetic and political realities of African American musicking change the deeply entrenched modes of institutional discourses that have ceased to listen creatively or ethically?

That listening needs to be understood as a vital part of rights discourses, that, as a critical act, it can be a powerful tool both for sounding witness to abuse and for imagining other possible futures, other expressions of social cooperation, has become increasingly evident as various commissions and bodies of inquiry have turned to the use, for example, of nationwide "Listening Tours" or "Human Rights Listening Sessions," in an effort to understand both the challenges and the opportunities around the creation of a fairer, more just, and more equal set of social structures. Imagine, then, what might happen were such commissions and bodies of inquiry to mobilize the resources, the spirit of inquiry and experimentation, and the deep listening strategies promulgated, in particular, by musical improvisers—critical listeners, par excellence—to mobilize them in the service of what we might call a kind of sound knowledge. Imagine the ideals that might be nourished, the relationships that might be fostered, the models of engagement that might be encouraged to flourish.

Learning to listen differently and developing the ability to hear more democratically may be more difficult than we imagine. The aural habits most frequently encouraged by commercial culture, the Western art tradition, and folklore promote a kind of distracted half-hearing that is attentive to formal devices and generic conventions but largely uninterested in the social contexts and power relations that the music shapes and reflects. These habits produce what Jon Cruz, a scholar of black culture, calls "disengaged engagement," a kind of hearing without really listening that leaves all of our preconceptions and assumptions undisturbed (30). Yet the kinds of attentive, empathetic, and interactive skills that deep listening and "sound" knowledge require do not need to be invented anew. They are already present in our everyday lives. Herb Kent, a disc jockey in Chicago, sounded white to station managers and white listeners. When his voice was used to promote products, however, sales immediately jumped in black neighborhoods because black listeners recognized some clue in Kent's voice that marked him as one of their own. In music, Jimi Hendrix turned microphone feedback into a new kind of sonic pleasure. Allen Toussaint and Aaron Neville derived a rhythm 'n' blues rhythm from the pulse of a cement mixer stopped in front of them on a New Orleans street. Miles Davis made cracked and missed notes part of the drama of what he was trying to accomplish in his version of "My Funny Valentine." Distinctions between a work of art and an accident, or between dissonance and harmony, do not come from the sounds themselves but from the modes of hearing applied to them by knowing subjects who then become active agents.

Surprise

The Western art tradition teaches us to expect and savor narrative and aesthetic closure. In contrast, the improvisatory art of aggrieved communities prepares us to resist closures, to enjoy interruption, syncopation, and indeterminacy. Afrodiasporic textile makers fashion asymmetrical patterns of staggered shapes and colors. Jazz musicians compose extended works with no final chord, no predictable cadence. Blues lyricists write open-ended narratives. Painters, sculptors, quilters, and installation artists use improvisation and rhythm in their work. In these arts, interruptions, changes in direction, and unexpected patterns serve as mental training exercises for the aleatory challenges of life.

Romare Bearden, best known as a supremely accomplished painter but also a successful composer and songwriter, recognized the role of improvisation in both his arts. Just as the places where paint initially landed on the canvas set the stage for subsequent decisions about shapes and colors, the place where fingers landed on the piano shaped the nature of the composition to follow. The painter Oliver Jackson created works onstage while Julius Hemphill played the saxophone as part of their work together in the 1960s and 1970s with the St. Louis Black Artists' Group. Jackson felt that working with musicians made him attentive to the importance of "time" in painting, of the need to "grab" viewers' attention and engagement as a musician would.

Struggles for social change often take as one of their most salient manifestations an allegiance to forms of artistic expression, such as musical improvisation, that cannot readily be scripted or accommodated within received, familiar, or habitualized frameworks of assumption. The force of experimental practices associated with aggrieved communities resides in their ability to break out of conventional, recurrent solution-patterns. This kind of opening up, this breaking out of convention, involves risk-taking and unpredictability.

Surprise is the watchword here, and it's registered in how people and communities use improvisatory practices to meet (and adapt to) the needs of the moment, to create a way out of no way, to cultivate profound resources for hope out of seemingly dead-end situations. Improvisation is thus something of a leap of faith, a bet on the future, on the possibility that the unforeseen, the emergent, the adaptive, and the unpredictable might be more vital, more important, more resilient, than certainty, familiarity, or security. What might it mean to imagine surprise as a key aspect of our contingent relation to others, a key aspect of how to resolve seemingly intractable and atrophied responses to complex problems in a new key?

Accompaniment

Accompaniment is an intrinsic part of improvisation. In music, accompaniment makes the parts stronger than the whole. Accompanying another musician entails more than simply adding a new sound. Accompaniment augments, accents, and counters one musical voice with another. Musical works can derive definitive textures from the ways harmonic accompaniments support main melodies, as well as from dialogues between melodies and countermelodies. When an accompanist plays block chords, the primary melody is augmented by chords that move in the same rhythm. A drummer can make improvised bass lines more audible by holding back and playing sparely and simply. Ensembles playing stop time and breaks can make room for the sounds of soloists. Piano accompanists highlight otherwise unheard elements in the music, for example, using "broken octaves," alternating the low and high notes in an octave to underscore its presence. Freddie Green never took a solo during his five decades playing guitar in Count Basie's bands, but his steady rhythms accented by modulating chords helped every other musician sound better. The experience of accompaniment can also set the stage for subsequent virtuosity. Charlie Parker's path to becoming a great soloist on the saxophone included a stint in his high school band playing accompaniment on the baritone horn, as well as hearing chords in a new way while playing dozens of pop songs on his saxophone every night in dime-a-dance venues.

In Central American social movements, the word *accompaniment* (connected to the verb *acompañar*) designates an approach to collective mobilization. In contrast to the atomized individualism of liberal capitalism and the elitist vanguardism of Leninist left-wing parties, the idea of accompaniment envisions political action as a journey taken together, an excursion in which people from different backgrounds and experiences can work together respectfully as equals (Lynd and Lynd). In order to inspire allegiance among impoverished peasants and exploited workers, accompaniment in Central America had to be more than an ideal or a slogan. It emerged organically in El Salvador, Guatemala, and Nicaragua, out of decades of experience in liberation-theology study groups, neighborhood associations, rural collectives, and urban trade unions. Like the musical practice whose name it shares, accompaniment in politics enacts the social relations it envisions. It succeeds best when it engages people in unpredictable and ephemeral yet meaningful acts of listening, speaking, and sharing.

Accompaniment is an important, if underused and undervalued, practice. Conventional categories and practices in performance, politics, and scholarship underestimate the importance of accompaniment. People in this society have been taught to privilege the created object over the creative act, to ignore the collective, cumulative, dialogic, and dialectical dimensions of our existence. We have been taught to elevate individual virtuosity over accompaniment—at the expense of broader conceptions of musical community and social practice. Expressive culture often comes to us in the guise of reparation for the injuries and indignities we suffer routinely. This turns alienation into an aesthetic pleasure and elevates novelty and difference over continuity and connection. A renewed appreciation for accompaniment can lead us in another direction. Cultural gatekeepers and academic experts invite us to look for big achievements and to belittle small ones. Yet a big tree can be felled by a small axe, as the lyrics of a well-known Bob Marley song inform us. Through accompaniment, some of our biggest achievements will come from small acts.

Practice

Practice, in the sense of a discipline to achieve an end, is one sense of the word that matters. Practice, understood this way, is the performance of repetition to acquire a skill that is deployable with consistency in multiple contexts. This understanding of *practice*, the word deriving from Medieval Latin/Late Latin and Middle French, has largely usurped other ways the term is used.

Practice, too, is a crucial form of play, and it is the space in which improvisation is imagined. Improvisation, play, and practice are all aspects of the same confrontation with possibility that defines all forms of human relational activity—whether with other biotic forms, the environment, or other human social formations. Coltrane's infamous (and controversial) approach to practice arose, he said, from the astonishing set of choices he was trying to make to generate his unique sound: "There are some set things I know, some devices, some harmonic devices that I know that will take me out of the ordinary path . . . but I haven't played them enough and I'm not familiar enough with them yet to play the one single line to them, so I play all of them, trying to acclimate my ears" (Coltrane qtd. in L. Porter 158).

Practice in this sense is preparing for possibility, thinking through how to deploy a rich and complex language in ways that lead away from the "ordinary path." Herman Gray's essay on Coltrane and freedom highlights Coltrane's "quest to imagine, practice, and embody a concept of freedom (in his sound and through his social relations) as a better place, one filled with joy, love, community, and possibility" ("John Coltrane" 36). Gray focuses on Coltrane's "professional and personal practice—the literal production and expression of freedom through the formal production of sound (freedom-sound) as much as [on] the social organization and the conditions necessary for those soundings to be generated and produced in the first place" (36).

Practice, in Gray's reading of Coltrane, does not occur in a vacuum but has social ends beyond merely reproducing a set of sounds reliably. Personal practice, here, is the means to achieve a wider social practice with a pointed outcome related to freedom. In short, this is a rights outcome: one that asserts a basic right to speak freely, to create freely, to metonymize social freedom via one's own personal practice of freedom. Practice, insofar as it enables a voice capable of unique declamations, as was the case with Coltrane, and as was the case with so many others addressed in this book, is the means to assert one's voice distinctively and in ways that matter within a larger social sphere.

Practice as play.

Practice as improvisation.

Practice as interplay with others.

Practice as encounter with those who you will accompany, a way into a wider ecology of knowledges that arises from the encounter with difference.

Practice as paradox. The discipline that frees.

Practice as prepared spontaneity.

Practice as process, never-ending: a continual striving to be more capable.

Practice as an embodied assertion of one's capacity to speak in one's own name but also in relation to others.

Practice as social, relational, how we choose to do things with others.

Practice as an encounter with oneself as the other that has yet to be revealed to oneself.

Practice, in Ingrid Monson's words, as "agency in everyday life," as "social action" (*Freedom Sounds* 26).

Practice, in its utilitarian sense, then, is not always necessary for improvisation, which threads the needle between unplanned spontaneity arising from multiple contingencies that allow it to happen and deep forms of disiciplinary engagement with an instrument that, for instance, allow for unthought possibilities to emerge. Practice conceived of as a solitary pursuit by the lone genius deprives the word of its power to signify wider social practices of community engagement that, like accompaniment, point to improvisatory play as a unique form of being in community, of practicing "being with" (*acompañar*), accompanying the other in the collective journey of social encounters that make life what it is. The social practice of improvisation, then, is the space in which collective imaginings encounter the possibilities around which choices get made, the space in which one's agency is given shape in relation to others whose social practices intersect with or diverge from one's own.

In these senses, might the social practice of improvisation play a key role in imagining the social practice of basic rights derived from freedom of speech, freedom to create, freedom to assemble to make decisions based on the interplay between collective and autonomous agencies?

Responsibility

Improvisation is an aesthetic practice with distinct technical properties and parameters, but it is also a social activity that poses enormous moral challenges to both artists and audiences. Vijay Iyer, a pianist, composer, and scholar, reminds us, "Life is a sustained improvisational interaction with the structures of the world, of the body, of culture" ("Improvisation: Terms and Conditions" 171). Improvisation cultivates attentiveness to others and empathy with them as prerequisites for performance. It requires witnesses and listeners to speak, to turn talking back into an art form, to attend carefully to both the things that unite and things that divide. One of the functions that improvisation fulfills for members of aggrieved groups is to provide training for life, to cultivate new kinds of consciousness by honing and refining aesthetic appreciation and creativity, by promoting practical inventiveness to give new meanings to nature, matter, and social relations, and by activating embodied public performances of one's own agency in relation to others. It encourages passive victims to become active victors. Improvisation teaches that the conversations that seem to contain us can also connect us to collective solutions to what may seem like purely personal problems. Improvisation requires giving as well as taking. It compels us to consider our continuing relations with others, to live up to our obligations and responsibilities.

Improvisation is both a response in an ongoing dialogue and a call-out for responses to come. Response figures in all forms of responsibility: and response doesn't happen without listening, without the potential for surprise that listening brings, without trust that listening will result in new forms of affilation, identification, and dialogue. Improvisation calls into being questions of responsibility, rooted etymologically in the word *responsible*, that is, answerable or morally accountable for one's actions, driven by the obligation to respond. Being responsible, as we've intimated earlier, requires deep, careful listening. You need to hear to respond. You need to account for what the other really has to say in order to be responsible, that is, to account morally and ethically for your own actions in relation to others. Improvisation is a key staging ground of this form of encounter, a key crucible through which the event-horizon of infinite possible encounters is addressed, performed, imagined. Responsibility, one's capacity to answer to others for what they have to say and how you have heard it, is implicit in all improvisatory encounters. Where else does the social practice of imagining and experimenting with responsible encounters as both an aesthetics and an ethics find as manifest a staging?

The writer, film maker, and activist Toni Cade Bambara associates responsibility with seeing into the truth of things in discussing the responsibility of arts practitioners: "It's a tremendous responsibility—responsibility and honor—to be a writer, an artist, a cultural worker . . . whatever you call this vocation. One's got to see what the factory worker sees, what the prisoner sees, what the welfare children see, what the scholar sees, got to see what the ruling-class mythmakers see as well, in order to tell the truth and not get trapped" (qtd. in Deck 80). Seeing responsibly—in response to what is seen, being accountable for what is seen, feeling obligated to respond to what is seen—can activate agency. By seeing connections among things responsibly, people can unleash the very ethical imperatives that are the ground of all forms of rights. Responsibility frees people from the trap of dead monologues and myths, the dominant narratives that squelch creative process and empathic affiliations, the lack of dialogue that disaggregates the social practice of being together, in process, in the space of responsible listening that activates our agency in contigent relation to others. Improvisation converts witnessing into agency:

the responsible listener is the listener who responds to what he or she hears. Improvisation is the practice of that response: it is a seeing into what being responsible might mean in the "hear and now." As such, it is a crucial practice of agency in response to a seeing that is also a hearing, a listening to what we see.

Trust

What can be learned about rights from improvised music? How does the way improvising musicians react to one another help the broader project of understanding how people can live together in the new millenium? In an era when the bonds that hold communities together have become enfeebled, when disconnection, self-interest, and individualism have seemingly triumphed over social cooperation, the well-being of the communities in which people live and work depends on trust, on the relationships they establish with one another. While improvisation holds no guarantees, it does bring realities into being through performance. Those realities, when built on trust, teach that collective problems can be solved.

But in politics as in art, no meaningful triumph can come without risk. Improvisation is a defining social practice of risk-taking—learning how to trust via listening, responsibility, surprise—learning how to master unexpected challenges, and to develop the courage to imagine differently. As a practice of performed, embodied public trust, improvisation provides powerful examples of what it means to take risks in a way that is contigent on others.

> What might this dissonance provoke?
> Where might this riff lead?
> Who will take me up on this offer to change the pulse?
> Has anyone heard what I really meant in my last solo intervention?
> How do I surrender to the real-time of here and now and what will that surrender bring to the musical dialogue in which I'm participating?

Improvisatory creation requires cocreative practices of engagement with others, practices that test the degree of trust we have in those others, that test our own trust in ourselves, which also entails trusting that others will respond, will be responsible accordingly, that test the audience's trust in us to experiment, to disagree, to reshape familiar tropes in surprising new ways. The unveiling of this trust in public, embodied performance is one of the key ethical gestures released by improvisatory practices. It is unthinkable without notions of creative possibility, potential, diversity, alternatives, and a deep listening awareness of the other without which any form of ethics is impossible.

Trust is a catalyst of hope, because it provides a consolation from disaggregated, broken forms of social affiliation. In its rudimentary etymological senses, the word *trust* is deeply connected in meaning to concepts of help, confidence, fidelity, agreement, alliance, comfort, and consolation. Publicly enacting trust catalyzes deeply felt, necessary aspects of embodied hope. Improvisation activates the knowledge that within potential and possibility, which are always in process, always in need of making anew, is embedded the cipher of human affiliation, the fidelity to the other that makes explicit our relational contingency, the empathic connection that is the ground for realizing human cocreative expression in its most achieved forms. As an underlying expression of social and musical form, improvisation gives shape to primary ethical imperatives, the hope that these can be made active as embodied visions of human possibility. It is to hope that we now turn, the last of the key concepts we associate with improvisation as a creative practice of ethical engagement with otherness and difference.

Hope

"In order to survive," the free jazz improvising bassist William Parker tells us, "we must keep hope alive" (*Peach Orchard*). Hope, we maintain with Parker and with so many of the other creative practitioners whose work we discuss in this book, is the heartbeat of improvised music. It is, as the philosopher Mary Zournazi writes, the life-giving "force which keeps us moving and changing," and, we would add, dreaming and imagining, "so that the future may be about how we come to live and hope in the present" in the here and now (274). Without the power and the capacity to dream (think, again, of Robin Kelley's work in this context), to imagine, to hope, without the encouragement to take risks in our encounters and relationships with one another, without the opportunities to create spaces and places of possibility, to learn (as in the example we cite from Louis Armstrong) the value of willingness, the ability, that is, to see people not only for who they are but, more suggestively, for who they might become, the rights of aggrieved peoples will continue to be at risk of being abandoned, the struggles for justice, dignity, and equality enshrined in the Universal Declaration of Human Rights will continue to run the risk of being derailed.

Indeed, if we are correct in suggesting that social connection may well be our single most important life project, and if one of the most urgent predicaments of our era, as Ien Ang would have it, has to do with the deceptively simple (yet utterly profound) question, "How are we to live together in this new century" (193), with recognizing, as the words from Archie Shepp we quoted at the very outset of chapter 1 should remind us, that "we're all connected," then the urgency and the social force of improvised music-making resides, at least in part, in how it gets us working together across the divides that separate us, and how, consequently, improvisation allows new ideas, new options, new ways of thinking, to emerge as important aspects of the conversation. Herein, we suggest, lies a message of hope and resourcefulness, of social mobility and momentum, of critical practice for aggrieved peoples responding to oppression.

Improvising musicians, as the examples we document in this book make clear, have played complex and varied historical roles, fashioning alternative institutions and systems of knowledge production, have developed creative and sophisticated responses and solutions to seemingly hopeless, dead-end (and deadening) situations, and, as Wadada Leo Smith puts it in the passage we cited earlier from his interview with Howard Mandel, have transformed society "by getting people to see ordinary stuff anew" ("Yo Wadada!"). Their creative responses and working artistic models, in short, constitute broad outlines, but also historically specific practices, of a vital and enduring project for extending and sustaining social justice. In its capacity to unsettle fixed and rigid systems of knowing, being, and understanding, and in its accenting and embodiment of artistic practices that challenge static orthodoxies, improvised music, at its best, offers us an emergent narrative about hope, resilience, determination, agency, dialogue, and the power of imagination. Whether or not (and the degree to which) musical improvisation plays in to such a narrative depends on multiple overlapping factors and contingencies, including, but not limited to, the affective, sociocultural, historical, and institutional dimensions that activate or fail to activate (in both performers and listeners) such imperatives as trust, critical listening, and responsibility in the unpredictable (and still largely uninventoried) social landscape where music crosses over into ongoing struggles for rights.

Hope, like improvisation, is an irreducible aspect of human interiority that is also outward-facing, capable of producing radical shifts in agency, generating new forms of cocreative affiliation that can have profound ethical implications. Like improvisation, hope is always more than a politics, a practice, a definition that limits what it can become. This being inside but with outward-facing consequences, this refusal of any attempt to make hope and improvisation into one thing is what gives power to both as social practices that feed into the public commons. Both hope and improvisation tend toward, invite, invoke, and imagine the event-horizon of the possible. As such they address the ethics of creation and cocreation that are an underlying aspect of both musical aesthetics as an outcome of improvisatory agencies and of imagining and exercising rights imperatives as an expression of core aspects of human being.

In her book *Hope in the Dark: Untold Histories, Wild Possibilities*, Rebecca Solnit suggests that "hope is not about what we expect. It is an embrace of the essential unknowability of the world, of the breaks with the present, the surprises" (136). Earlier in that book, Solnit makes a passing (but telling) reference to music, riffing on Cornel West's claim in *Race Matters* that jazz is "not so much a term for a musical art form but for a mode of being in the world, an improvisational mode of protean, fluid and flexible disposition toward reality suspicious of 'either/or' viewpoints" (qtd. in Solnit, *Hope in the Dark* 103). Solnit has documented the profound sense of hope that has emerged out of the extraordinary communities and improvised responses found in situations of disaster and devastation, such as those in post-Katrina New Orleans. As a mode of being in the world, improvisation shows us that there are other ways of doing things, that social change is possible, that another world is possible: a world whose hopefulness resides in its destinations out and its freedom dreams, its ascensions and its awakened giants, in a mobility of practice, in a culture of solidarity, and in the who-knows-where of creative response, expression, and participation, in embodied practices that bring together the deep affiliations among listening, surprise, responsibility, trust, and hope.

Listen up. Make your move now. Practice spontaneity. Trust that surprise will teach you something. Respond. Listen again. Accompany yourself and others. Give agency to your hopes. Improvisation matters.

NOTES

PRELUDE: "THE FIERCE URGENCY OF NOW"

1. See Fischlin and Nandorfy, *The Community of Rights—The Rights of Community* (89–106), for a more complete discussion of this term.

2. See de Sousa Santos's "Beyond Abyssal Thinking: From Global Lines to Ecologies of Knowledges."

INTRODUCTION: DISSOLVING DOGMA

1. Marie Korpe, the executive director of Freemuse, notes, "When the first World conference [on music and censorship] was organized in 1998, in collaboration with the Danish Institute for Human Rights, neither the organizers nor the participants of the conference realized what lay ahead of us. Gone was the South African apartheid regime. Censored artists could provide testimony about the repression of their music and talk about it as 'the past.' But 1998 was also the year that Berber-spokesman and musician Lounès Matoub [an Algerian Berber who had protested against the 'arabization' of the Berbers and had vociferously promoted a secular worldview] was killed and the Taliban had established a total ban on music in Afghanistan. So everyone agreed that an organization that could advocate freedom of musical expression was needed. Since the establishment of a Freemuse secretariat in 2000, and the dedicated work of employees and individuals, we have contributed in revealing music censorship through research, reports, conferences, video clips and an offensive media strategy in more than 100 countries" (Korpe, "Human Rights" 9). Freemuse, in addition to documenting abuses of musicians' rights worldwide, also documents how new visa restrictions, as a function of the war on terror, are being used to limit artists' mobility. This is occurring throughout Europe and North America and seems to target especially non-Western musicians (Thomas Mapfumo, various Cuban artists, African and Indian musicians). The hidden censorship that occurs when musicians are turned away from a public because they do not meet excessive and unreasonable requirements (think of the African musician who is required to show a sustained savings of 800 pounds in an account for three months in order to get into the U.K.) limits the kind of diversity of expression and freedom of movement that are core principles of the

UDHR. Article 13's two clauses clearly state: "(1) Everyone has the right to freedom of movement and residence within the borders of each state. (2) Everyone has the right to leave any country, including his own, and to return to his country." For more information on these sorts of visa restrictions that limit artistic movement and freedom of expression, see Josie Appleton's and Manick Govinda's *UK Arts and Culture: Cancelled, by Order of the Home Office* and Freemuse's white paper, "Visas: The Discordant Note," authored by Ole Reitov and Hans Hjorth.

2. Exceptions to these restrictions did exist. The Belgian pianist and bandleader Stan Brenders, for instance, heavily influenced by New Orleans–style jazz, backed manouche-gypsy jazz guitarist Django Reinhardt in 1942 in eight concerts that took place right under the noses of the German censors. Eugene Chadbourne notes, "For the repressive forces of Nazism and the uninhibited creativity of jazz to co-exist may have seemed an impossibility, but jazzmen kept many aspects of their music happening throughout World War II in countries such as Belgium. The resulting gigs, recordings, and performing careers acquired an additional level of interest from intrigue alone. Stan Brenders would stand on-stage in Brussels in the late '30s and announce that the next tune was going to be 'Sept, et avec un combination avec onze,' knowing full well the Nazi censors wouldn't be able to follow the pigeon French reference to the real song title, 'Seven Come Eleven,' which like most swing numbers had been decisively banned from either radio or live airplay. The Nazis had banned jazz itself, but since most of them really didn't know what it was supposed to sound like, the song titles were an all important form of identification, something like the equivalent of a Star of David" (Chadbourne).

3. Henze's musical output, influenced by jazz, has long been distinguished and made controversial for its overt political content. Examples of this include *Das floß der medusa* (The raft of the medusa), a requiem oratorio for Che Guevara that caused a scandal when it was first performed, in Hamburg in 1968, and *El Cimmarón*, a work for voice and small chamber orchestra, based on the Cuban author Miguel Barnet's story of runaway slaves during Cuba's extended colonial history. Henze wrote the piece while living in Cuba (1969–70). Barnet's work is based on autobiographical testimony he gathered in 1963 from a former runaway slave named Esteban Montejo, when Montejo was 103 years old. Montejo was also a veteran of the Cuban War of Independence (1895–98), fought to liberate Cuba from Spanish colonialism, and was an extraordinary example of black diasporic resistance to oppression and colonialism. The link between Henze's politics and his musical influences is not arbitrary. The most explicit of Henze's works to fuse improvisation and politics is *Der langwierige weg in die wohnung der Natascha Ungeheuer* (The tedious way to Natascha Ungeheuer's apartment), premiering at the Deutsche Oper, in Berlin, in 1971. The piece is based on the libretto by Gaston Salvatore, the Chilean poet and 1960s student-movement activist, and deploys a baritone accompanied by an organist, a jazz band, and a chamber ensemble. Henze's piece is an example of Gunther Schuller's so-called third-stream compositional genre, which fuses

classical and jazz and uses improvisation as an important, if not defining, component. The Deutsche Grammophon recording of Henze's piece, made in 1972, included the Gunter Hampel Free Jazz Ensemble and the Japanese percussionist Stomu Yamashta, well known for his exceptional improvisatory skills.

4. Improvisers are keenly aware of how slippery the epithet *free* can be and generally do not use the term naively. Wadada Leo Smith, in an interview, effectively argues that *free jazz* is a misnomer because it too depends on systems and systematized ways of producing the music, whether through conduction, through instrumentation, through specific approaches to harmony, melody, and rhythm, or through more anarchic (but nonetheless) systematized approaches. Even someone as "outside" as Derek Bailey can be seen as functioning systematically through structures of sound and musical gesture. A DVD document of a performance in New York shows Bailey working through sounds generated by harmonics in different positions on his guitar (*Playing for Friends on 5th Street*). An untrained or unsympathetic ear might hear random scratchings and pluckings, but the performance is governed by a structured exploration of where and how harmonic sounds can be produced in different registers on the guitar.

5. The homepage of the Leonard Feather Collection at the University of Idaho has a subdirectory devoted to Feather as a human rights advocate, stating that "he worked his entire life to offset anything that acted to impede originality and inspiration of the art" and citing his participation as the vice president of the NAACP Hollywood–Beverly Hills chapter in 1963 ("Human Rights Advocate"). Rights discourses are full of such contradictions. Feather could effectively compare Coltrane and Dolphy to Hitler as they exercised their right to free speech as African Americans, *and* serve as a member of the NAACP. The example shows how careful one has to be in asking contextual questions about rights proclamations: Whose interests are being served? How does a particular affirmation use rights to advance a specific ideology (that may not be coincident with more expansive notions of rights)? What does *rights* in a particular usage mean? What are the connections between rights discourses and the dominant ideologies they are putatively opposed to?

6. We note the danger in reductive understandings of these complex and nuanced dynamics. And we note, as well, what Clyde Woods points to in his discussion of "cultural imposition" and black musicking: "From their very conception, the blues, jazz, rock and roll, and hip-hop have had to battle two forms of cultural imposition. On the one hand, it was said that they were prima facie evidence of black savagery. On the other hand, it was said that they don't belong to blacks; they're universal. This bit of surrealism gave rise to the observation that 'your blues ain't like mine'" ("Do You Know What It Means to Miss New Orleans?" 1014).

7. "In Louisiana, in 1949, Coleman was summoned from a bandstand and beaten bloody by a mob which also destroyed his saxophone. A decade later, when he arrived in New York to play at the Five Spot, in Cooper Square, the drummer Max Roach came to listen and, as Coleman tells it, ended up punch-

ing him in the mouth" (Giddins 78). Nat Hentoff recalls how the prominent jazz critic Leonard Feather stated, after a concert by Taylor in California before three thousand people, "Anyone working with a jackhammer could have achieved the same results" (Hentoff, "Cecil Taylor" 158).

8. Any number of recordings document the range of improvising musicians making music whose context was firmly embedded in the civil rights movement: "Freedom Sound," by the Jazz Crusaders; Herbie Hancock's *The Prisoner*, with its evocation of Martin Luther King Jr.'s "I Have a Dream" speech; *Percussion Bitter Sweet*, with a feature track entitled "Garvey's Ghost"; and *We Insist*, with its track "Freedom Day," both by Max Roach; *The Festival Album* by the Crusaders, responding in 1966 to the race riots of the previous two summers; Lee Morgan's *Search for the New Land*, which reflected on the pan-African movement; *Power to the People*, by Joe Henderson, with its obvious political thrust; Sonny Criss's *Sonny's Dream (Birth of the New Cool)*, with its track "The Black Apostles," devoted to the civil rights leaders Malcolm X, Martin Luther King Jr., and Medgar Evers; *Byrd in Flight*, by Donald Byrd, with its track "Ghana," celebrating the first sub-Saharan African nation to gain its independence, in 1957; and Art Blakey's *Free for All*, with the key track by Freddie Hubbard, called "The Core," dedicated to the Congress of Racial Equality (CORE), a civil rights organization that played an important role in struggles for equality on behalf of African Americans, and that was later, in 1968, co-opted by members with neoconservative, right-wing political views under Roy Innis (CORE supported Richard Nixon in 1968 and 1972). The blog by Howard Mandel, the jazz critic and historian, makes information available on two specific events, held on the nights of October 20 and 27, 1963, that brought together a plethora of some of the biggest names in jazz in support of CORE. These documents highlight "the conjunction of jazz and the Civil Rights movement . . . programs from two nights in 1963 when major players performed and major jazz journalists emceed in benefit for CORE . . . at New York City's Five Spot Café, plus a letter of thanks to bassist Henry Grimes for his participation. CORE has been one of the most powerful organizations driving the Civil Rights movement from the late 1940s to this day, employing Gandhi's principles of nonviolent civil disobedience with 1950s sit-ins and 1960s' Freedom Rides to combat segregationist policies in the United States. James Farmer was a cofounder of CORE and its first national director. The extraordinary gatherings on October 20 and October 27 of musicians now regarded as jazz giants—among the most recognizable saxophonists Ben Webster (playing tuba? or not the *tenor saxophonist* Ben Webster?), Al Cohn, Zoot Sims, Booker Ervin, Eric Dolphy, guitarist Kenny Burrell, brass-man and composer-arranger Thad Jones, pianists Bill Evans, Paul Bley, Sal Mosca, Horace Parlan, Billy Taylor (now *Dr.* Billy . . .), Don Friedman, Dick Katz, drummers Roy Haynes, Ben Riley (misspelled "Reilly"—and other misspellings abound), Paul Motian, Joe Chambers, bassists Gary Peacock, Ronnie Boykins (of Sun Ra's Arkestra), Ron Carter and vibist Bobby Hutcherson, singers Helen Merrill and Sheila Jordan—were likely prompted by the Civil Rights rally at the Lincoln Memorial on August 28 (occasion of Martin Luther

King Jr.'s "I Have A Dream" speech) and the September 15 bombings by the Ku Klux Klan of Birmingham, Alabama's 16th St. Baptist Church, which targeted churchgoing children and killed four little girls" (Mandel, "Civil Rights-Jazz Document, 1963"). To this listing may be added many other recordings, events, and musicians that directly associated music with the civil rights movement and specific rights outcomes.

9. Charles O. Hartman points to the social situatedness of jazz as a marker of cultural difference and of potential hybridity. Improvisers who aligned themselves with different musical cultures were making important steps in advancing an ideology that had profound implications for rights discourse, especially in terms of opening the doors to alternative and differential experience, a key precondition of making rights thinkable: "The communal music of African peoples from the Shona to the Arabs, with its ties to both mystical trance and tribal conviviality, often goes on for hours without interruption; it does not comprise 'pieces.' Individual musicians pass into and out of the musical ensemble as molecules pass through and constitute a candle flame. The continuousness of the music—linked to a world-view in which historical process means less than cyclical stability—reduces the status of beginnings and endings" (9). Improvisers who made efforts to move their music in these directions were effectively undermining hegemonic notions of musical authority and authorship, the open-endedness, the inventive liberty required to sustain extended playing, and the communitarian aspects of these other forms introducing critical shifts in the ways in which music signified generally as a cultural practice. As Hartman wittily suggests, even the notion of the *concert*, "which originally suggested how the musicians cooperate [not only with themselves but with their audience, their community, as a function of concerted creation], now implies at least as strongly what separates them from an audience of ticketholders" (9).

10. See Fischlin and Heble 14–16.

CHAPTER 1: SOUNDING TRUTH TO POWER

1. On misunderstood improvisation, see, for instance, Derek Bailey's *Improvisation: Its Nature and Practice in Music*.

2. For another take on extended techniques using flute and voice, see Sherrie Tucker's analysis of Janice Misurell-Mitchell's approach to improvising gender (261–62).

3. In recent years, there has been a healthy and growing interest in the intersection of human rights discourses, cultural practices, and neoliberal policies. In March 2007, the Interdisciplinary Humanities Center at the University of California, Santa Barbara, hosted a conference called "Human Rights and Neoliberalism: Universal Standards, Local Practices, and the Role of Culture." And in June 2008, Northwestern University's Center for Global Culture and Communication hosted its Summer Institute in Performance Studies on "Radical Performance, Neoliberalism, and Human Rights."

4. Tapscott's insistence on taking the music "to the people" recalls bell hooks's argument: "When and where institutional structures were not available for individual black folks," she writes, "we used, and still use, street corners, barbershops, beauty parlours, basketball courts and a host of other locations to be in on the live act" (211–12).

5. In an interview published in 1984, the trumpeter Lester Bowie, a member of the Art Ensemble of Chicago, emphasized the fact that the Art Ensemble was "one of the only groups of musicians that labelled [its] own music" (qtd. in Green 17). The ensemble's motto, "Great Black Music: Ancient to the Future," is a key part of the group's efforts to forge an ethos of self-determination, part of their insistence on the right to name their own music.

6. As Willard Jenkins writes in a *Jazz Times* review of the recording, "Clearly, Horace Tapscott in his rich artistic life chose to dissent, never descending to the ordinary or the mundane. His lack of conformity was borne out in a stubborn refusal to forsake the Los Angeles root he steadfastly nurtured and in his lack of pianistic compromise." An ascent-descent motif is pronounced throughout the language and rhetoric that surrounds Tapscott's oeuvre. But descent, of course, can also refer to ancestry, to characteristics that can be traced back to earlier sources. In this context, it's worth noting that this recording finds Tapscott working in collaboration with the bassist and AACM member Fred Hopkins and the drummer Ben Riley (best known for his work with Thelonious Monk), perhaps suggesting a vital form of community extension through music-making.

7. Larry Neal, writing in a *Negro Digest* column in 1968, argued explicitly that art such as the free improvisations of Sun Ra, Albert Ayler, John Coltrane, Cecil Taylor, and Albert Ayler, functioned "to shake us out of our lethargy and free our bodies and minds, opening us to unrealized possibilities" (81).

8. We're drawing here on arguments we've made elsewhere. See Fischlin and Heble, "The Other Side of Nowhere."

9. As Tapscott explains in his autobiography, "I picked [the name] because that was the idea we had in mind, that we were going to ascend through the arts to bring about recognition and understanding of each other" (qtd. in Isoardi 114).

10. The argument here about Herman Gray's *Cultural Moves* was first published in Ajay Heble's review of Gray's book in the *Journal of the Society for American Music*.

11. "Because the world is in constant turmoil," Parker has written, "it is the obligation of the musician to counteract this turmoil like trees and birds anchor the world so it balances again" (*Who Owns Music* 35).

12. On a related note, it remains crucially important to recognize that while policymakers will continue to have a vested interest in seeing rights programs and initiatives as being unequivocally beneficial, recent debates and scholarship on a range of affiliated issues (pedagogy, equity, the regularizing and normalizing effects that accompany the institutionalization of multiculturalism) have made it clear that diversity, equality, and cultural sensitivity cannot be achieved on the basis of legislation alone. Indeed, although human rights may

be a key concept driving much cultural activity, the realities associated with such activities are not always accommodated by the bureaucracy that administers them, or by the complications of internal and international politics.

CHAPTER 2: IMPROVISATION AND ENCOUNTER

1. The performance DVD is available on Jazz Icons, *John Coltrane Live in '60, '61 and '65* (2007).

2. The range of emergent neuroscience and cognitive brain-function research points to improvisation as a unique neural activity: doctors Aaron L. Berkowitz and Daniel Ansari have posited in the journal *NeuroImage* that "the musicians' deactivation of the rTJP [the right temporoparietal junction] during melodic improvisation may present a training-induced shift toward inhibition of stimulus-driven attention, allowing for a more goal-directed performance state that aids in creative thought" abstract). Oliver Sacks, in his book *Musicophilia*, discusses a patient severely afflicted with Tourette's Syndrome, for whom "harnessing his Tourette's and expressing himself in creative, unpredictable musical improvisations seemed to be deeply intertwined" (250). And Daniel Levitin, in *This Is Your Brain on Music*, arguing for the evolutionary importance of music and against the reductive, pleasure-oriented nonadaptive understanding of music's evolutionary role, suggests that "improvisation and novelty in a combined music/dance performance would indicate the cognitive flexibility of the dancer, signaling his potential for cunning and strategizing while on the hunt" (248). Levitin associates these qualities with markers of "sexual fitness" and also with the kind of adaptive social intelligence that is highly prized from an evolutionary point of view. These brief examples point to improvisation's cognitive, evolutionary, and even therapeutic importance, a key element in generating the adaptive, creative qualities and the kinds of generative social intelligence that are linked with survival.

3. The view that sees *human* as too limiting a descriptor for thinking about rights adequately finds musical expression in *Zoochosis*, by Paul Dunmall, Trevor Taylor, and Paul Rogers, a CD project devoted to describing musically, using the language of free jazz and improvisation, "the psychotic behavior . . . animals demonstrate when caged in zoos or other confined spaces" (Labyrinth). In a similar way, evolving notions of sound ecologies (the highly mediated relationships that exist between all beings that create and participate in sonic environments) that need protection and that have significant rights dimensions are almost completely absent from legal discourses and rights instruments.

4. Notions of freedom that are part of the discourse of improvised music are anything but naive and are highly critical of simplistic assumptions about what freedom entails. Sun Ra's poem, "Freedom from Freedom," collected in *Sun Ra: The Immeasurable Equation*, states: "Freedom from freedom / From the liberty / Of the land / Where destruction's light / Is the land. / Freedom from the decree of freedom / From the liberty / Of the land of destruction /

Is the decree / That can truly save / those whose freedom / Is a burden and a shame / What price freedom that despairs? / What glory freedom that destroys?" These poignant and trenchantly ironic lines critique hypocritical freedoms that largely did not apply (or have any utility) to the lived realities of African Americans. The so-called land of the free and the home of the brave announced in the American national anthem (set, ironically, to a well-known Scottish drinking tune) was in fact not so free, from the point of view of its disenfranchised, segregated, and ghettoized populations.

5. Andrew Weintraub argues in his introduction to *Music and Cultural Rights*, "Rights surrounding music fall short . . . by either not accounting for music in all its complexity or by fixing and reducing music to a category that fits current legal frameworks" (15). The full social play of music in culture cannot be reduced to only property and copyright issues, and this agenda is a radical attack on music's expansive significance and meaning to multiple cultures.

6. Micheline Ishay argues that "to destroy the vestiges of Western domination that persisted after independence, many Africans, like the liberal nationalists of the nineteenth century, proposed to develop a genuine national culture freed from Western universal rationalist pretense, while retaining the human rights promises of Western civilization. 'In our return to our cultural roots,' [Léopold Sédar] Senghor suggested, 'and particularly to the Negro-African method of knowledge and comprehension of the world, we can reject European methods, but we also cannot forget Europe's lessons in building a nation, the socialist state'" (196). Senghor was a Senegalese poet, politician, and cultural theorist who served as the president of Senegal for two decades and was also elected to the Académie Française, was one of the key people behind the concept of *négritude* (with Aimé Césaire and Léon Damas), an influential intellectual movement that valorized African culture, knowledge, and perspectives. It is important to remember that one of the key influences behind the concept of négritude lay in the literature of the Harlem Renaissance as well as in jazz from that same period. Cultural expression played a key role in political battles over African self-determination, a very concrete example of how culture and politics cannot easily be dissociated—and a pattern that will repeat itself in the American civil rights movement and its relation to different forms of artistic expression that include improvisation as a form of radical exploration of voice and expressive autonomy.

7. The International Covenant on Economic, Social and Cultural Rights, a multilateral treaty adopted by the United Nations General Assembly in 1966 (and in force since 1976) largely reiterates Article 27 of the UDHR while (in article 15) professing to "respect the freedom indispensable for scientific research and creative activity" and to "recognize the benefits to be derived from the encouragement and development of international contacts and cooperation in the scientific and cultural fields." Loophole terms like *respect* (which means different things under different ideologies and governments), *creative activity* (itself surprisingly undefined for a legal document with implications of this magnitude), and *cooperation* are key areas where the document

fails to guarantee appropriate protections for underlying principles that effect how creative work is generated, disseminated, and received.

8. This is not the only way of seeing improvisation, of course. When asked about jazz and improvisation in American culture, Herbert Brün, a pioneer in the development of electronic and computer music, stated the following: Improvisation "is in keeping and consistency with the growing consciousness among the American people of their state of affairs, of the threatened freedoms, of the lack of personal interaction between the powers and the overpowered. Unfortunately, I find the implementation [of jazz and improvised musicking] led to a decrease of that consciousness which brought it about. My criticism is that the urge was implemented in ways that substituted entertainment for criticism. It is again a success story, and that's one of the negative success stories" (81). For Brün, improvisatory practices that remain acutely critical and outside the paradigm of assimilation into the culture of success, retain their political "consciousness" and cultural relevance as both a musical and a social practice.

9. We note that the basis of much of Metallica's songwriting is improvisational activity: "They also jam and record the results [in the tuning room], improvising rhythms and guitar lines compiled on so-called 'riff tapes,' the traditional raw materials for Metallica's songwriting" (Fricke).

10. The association of music and musical instruments with war is far from new. Adolphe Sax, inventor of the saxophone, played a key role in the reform of the military music corps in France: "In 1845, French military music corps had fallen into disuse. On the proposal of Adolphe Sax, who offered them his instruments [the B-flat and E-flat saxhorns], General de Rumigny, the Minister for War, appointed a study commission, which decided to organise a competition between the traditional system and Sax's configuration.

"A great event was organised on the Champ de Mars (the present location of the Eiffel Tower) on 22 April 1845. The old system was championed by 45 professional musicians directed by [Michele Enrico] Carafa [professor of counterpoint at the Paris Conservatoire, 1840–58]. Sax championed his own with 38 musicians that he was hardly able to gather, since seven of them had failed to turn up. In addition, he himself had to play two instruments alternately, since two performers turned their backs on him at the last minute!

"An audience of twenty thousand applauded Sax! It was a triumph, and on 10 August that year, Sax's organisation was officially adopted, but not without provoking new hostilities on the part of the musicians who had been beaten" ("Adolphe Sax").

As a result, "the saxophone became an integral part of the French Army band and then all other bands," and Sax's desire to improve the tonal merit of all bands was accomplished ("The History of the Saxophone").

11. The improvising trumpeter Wadada Leo Smith, to whom we return later in this book because of the consistent link between rights and improvisation to be found in his work, "a close associate of Anthony Braxton and other jazz avant-gardists, was raised in the Delta by a bluesman, his stepfather Alec

Wallace. 'Growing up in that environment made me feel that whatever I play relates to a gigantic field of feeling,' he says. 'To me, the blues is a literary and musical form and also a basic philosophy. When I get ready to study the mystical aspect of black people, I go to the blues; then I feel that I'm in touch with the root of black people'" (Palmer 276–77). The blues epistemology that is seen to be the root of black experience, and that converts itself into myriad musical energies in which improvisation is a key component, is also a rights epistemology: the blues derive from oppression, injustice, inequality, and how these then feed into daily experience.

12. The example of Katrina recapitulates in some part what the saxophonist Gilad Atzmon has written about the history of postwar jazz in America: "After the Second World War, jazz became hugely popular in western Europe, and jazz giants such as Bird, Dizzy Gillespie, Miles Davis and Dexter Gordon were treated as major cultural figures. At home, those very legends had to enter jazz clubs via back entrances, because the front ones were for the white clients." Atzmon continues on to argue that "while the American ethos is traditionally presented as a celebration of civil freedom, jazz, as it appeared in the late 1950s, laid bare crucial flaws in the American dream. Not only did it expose the fundamental injustice within the capitalistic system; it also valued beauty far higher than money. This was foreign to the American way of thinking." Improvisation played a crucial role in this exposure, because it became a mark of cultural attainment by the musicians practicing it even as it marginalized those same musicians from dominant discourse in ways that attacked the logic of segregation (and the capital structures built on that logic). Chris Searle retells the story of the English jazz critic Geoffrey Haydon's taking a trip with the bop pioneer and civil rights activist Max Roach in the 1980s to his "boyhood home in Dismal Swamp, North Carolina. He tells how they entered a local motel, to be 'met by a wall of white staring faces' and a spokesman who announced to Haydon: 'we don't like your friend and we don't want people like that coming here.' He [Haydon] quotes Roach's words: 'We have proved we're masters of our instruments. Now we have to employ our skill to tell the story of our people and what we've been through'" (88–89).

13. In *The Concise Guide to Global Human Rights*, Fischlin and Nandorfy argue that "rights imply an approach to human identity and agency grounded in principles that are applicable across national and cultural divides. Neither a secular religion nor an ideology that caters to selective, single-state sovereign self-interests, human rights cut across all possible human relations. Rights are based on reciprocal respect, the valuing of all life, the integrity and dignity of all human beings (regardless of religious belief, class status, ethnicity, and sexual orientation, among other characteristics), and the desire to extend those basic values into all areas of human activity" (xvi).

14. Ellington's stock answer when asked if he knew any communists was "the only Communist I know is Jesus Christ," and he argued that, "social protest in the theatre should be made without saying it, and that calls for real craftsmanship." He famously refused to take part in King's March on Washington,

in 1963, claiming, "I'd love to go, but I've got sore feet. I can't walk that far." Within those contexts, he nonetheless supported multiple civil rights causes, including the NAACP, and on the 100th anniversary of the Emancipation Proclamation, in 1963, produced a large-scale composition entitled *My People*, one of whose climactic numbers was called "What Colour Is Virtue?" ("Band of Gold"). As with many artists uncomfortable with reductive analogies between music's meaning being tied solely to complex social movements, Ellington embodied a kind of provocative ambiguity, the kind of ambiguity always already in place in music as a nonverbal form that nonetheless occurs in specific historical and ideological contexts.

15. Derek Bailey, in trying to sort out differences between his style of free improvisation and improvised musics in Africa and South America, argues that the latter are "idiomatic" and that "freely improvised music isn't . . . [Those musics] are the product of a locality and a society . . . improvisation exists in order to serve this central identity. In freely improvised music, its roots are in occasion rather than in place. Maybe improvisation takes the place of idiom" (qtd. in Philip Clark 122). But even so, an occasion also occurs in a place, and even this place of nonidiomatic representation is itself idiomatic. This contradiction gets at the heart of the problem in any definition of *improvisation*: the term escapes reductive meaning and any attempt to reduce it to site, occasion, instrumentation, and the like merely points to its radical ability to shape-shift into something other than what it is proclaimed to be. Nonetheless, there is a nub of truth in what Bailey is trying to get at here: identity, occasion, and the site of production are cocreative, cogenerative aspects of the potential inherent in any improvisation.

CHAPTER 3: IMPROVISING COMMUNITY

1. Cecil Taylor echoes much of what Smith implies about the expansive relations that exist between music and its larger cultural contexts. Taylor contends that those contexts are the meaning of the music: "I'm interested in the cultural importance of the life of the music. The instrument a man uses is only a tool with which he makes his comment on the structure of music. That's why the evaluation of what a cat says about how he plays music is not too far from the non-interesting things he does when he is playing. That person wouldn't have too profound an understanding of what has happened in the music and the culture. We have to define the procedures and examine the aesthetics that have shaped the history of the music. That's much more important than discussing finger dexterity. We might as well discuss basketball or tennis" (qtd. in Goodheart, Part 1).

Taylor goes on to argue for the following: "The history of the people, the culture, even the things they forget consciously. The way they cook, speak, the way they move, dress, how they relate to the pressures around them. What you experience in life informs (in-forms) you. If you work on One Hundred Forty-Fifth Street in Harlem and years later in Tokyo, where you are taken to see the sights, you experience . . . the environment, listen to the sounds, watch the movement. You'll be able to see that there are not these separations between things. There are different aesthetic choices made. What happened in the latter part of the eighteenth century in Africa had a profound effect on painting. The concepts of musical organization now have to be broadened to accommodate the worldwide awareness of music" (qtd. in Goodheart, part 1). Aesthetic choice is informed by historical circumstance and this has play in the global, interconnected discourse of ideas. Improvisation plays a role in this discourse as an aesthetic choice arising out of specific circumstances and contingencies. The ethical, visionary aspects of its historical circumstances in relation to diasporic black histories cannot be revoked or dismissed, however much of a challenge this is to traditional scholarship that is reluctant to move in this direction.

2. *Sing Me a Song of Songmy* takes its place in a range of musical responses to Vietnam, including two remarkable albums by Billy Bang, the American free jazz violinist, *Vietnam: Reflections* (2005) and *Vietnam: The Aftermath* (2001). Bang had served as an infantryman and eventually as a sergeant in Vietnam, beginning with the Tet Offensive in 1968, a particularly bloody phase of the war that produced significant numbers of civilian dead and refugees. After the war, Bang joined the Sun Ra Arkestra and the Vietnam albums were created using other musicians who were veterans of the conflict and also seeking reconciliation with postwar trauma. *Vietnam: Reflection* features two Vietnamese musicians (Co Boi Nguyen and Nhan Thanh Ngo) who play the *đàn tranh* (zither), a traditional Vietnamese instrument, and sing in Vietnamese, referencing traditional Vietnamese songs. Bang's concept was to engage genuine cross-cultural improvisations in order to achieve "resolution, restoration, resurgence" (liner notes).

3. In 1991 Hubbard released *Bolivia*, an album whose track titles (including "Third World" and "Bolivia," the latter written by the pianist Cedar Walton) referenced, as in Gato Barbieri's *The Third World* (1969) and *Chapter Three: Viva Emiliano Zapata* (1974), unjust world orders, the death of Che Guevara, in Bolivia, in 1967, and Hubbard's own ongoing political commitments articulated earlier in *Sing Me a Song of Songmy*.

4. Searle notes that the threnody to Sharon Tate "begins the album, suggesting that the US slaughter and despoliation in My Lai and Vietnam generally, were born of the same demonic and anti-human impulse" (145).

5. In 1998 the French Canadian improvising guitarist and composer, René Lussier, a key participant in the *musique actuelle* scene, which had been heavily influenced by the improvisatory contexts of free jazz, released an album (on Ambiances Magnétiques) called *Chronique d'un génocide annoncé* (Chronicle of a genocide foretold), whose music had been used in a documentary film of the same name produced by Danièle Lacourse and Yvan Patry on the Rwandan genocide in 1994, in which approximately 20 percent of the population (from half a million to a million people) were slaughtered. The film is another example of musicians' consciously choosing to associate improvisatory musical

materials (blended with found sounds from the genocide) with commentary on and witnessing of rights abuses and violations. As in Douglas's *Witness*, the liner notes to the album play a crucial role in contextualizing the music, with actual statements taken from survivors of the genocide (including women and children) cited in the notes. Marceline, an eleven-year-old girl recounts, "They killed my mom before my eyes. They cut off her arms and her legs, which weren't severed from her body right away. I was clubbed on my head. They took me for dead" (liner notes). *Chronique d'un genocide annoncé* asks how, after the Holocaust some fifty years earlier, another one was possible. Claire Julier's brief notes press further: "The genocide is planned, it carries a precise date. The international community owns up to its cowardice, but takes no action. Who is responsible? How should they be punished? How to avoid being betrayed the moment power is regained? Geography, culture and skin colour are incidental. It was children, women and men who were massacred in the name of hate. Were the ghosts of other crimes powerless to prevent it? Are the words of Jean Cayrol and Primo Levi nothing but lies? How can one once again express the inexpressible?" (liner notes). Lussier's music may have no answers to these questions. But it nonetheless articulates some of the affective ground that must be conveyed as crucial information in the form of witnessing itself, a key aspect in developing responses to massive rights abuses and violations. Zorn, Lussier, and Douglas (and Smith and Hubbard, and many others) explicitly place improvisation on the scene of these events as an alternative discourse, a witnessing, and as a resistant ethic and aesthetic.

6. The Ruckus organizers had played a key role in the direct-action protests in Seattle against the World Trade Organization in 1999.

7. Douglas, in a 2003 interview, argues for an antiviolent form of global citizenship, stating, "I'm disturbed by this idea that real politics, that in order to be big boys and understand the ways of the world, we have to be willing to drop some bombs. Because I think that overlooks what really happens when you drop bombs, that a lot of innocent people die . . . Don't get me wrong, I say this in the most patriotic way. I think I am the biggest America lover there is. Any country that gives you Anthony Braxton and Wayne Shorter and Henry Threadgill and Bill Frisell is the best that there is" (Jung). Interestingly, and in spite of the almost obligatory jingoistic rhetoric, the imaginary nation and global citizen that Douglas envisions is one defined by some of its greatest improvisers, not by its trigger-happy politicians.

8. Elsewhere Marsalis argues, in an extended discussion of improvisation, that "jazz also reminds you that you can work things out with other people. It's hard but it can be done. When a group of people try to invent something together, there's bound to be a lot of conflict. Jazz urges you to accept the decisions of others. Sometimes you lead, sometimes you follow—but you can't give up, no matter what. It is the art of negotiating change with style. The aim of every performance is to make something out of whatever happens—to make something together and to *be* together" (12).

9. The title of the 2004 event was later recycled as part of the celebration

of President Barack Obama's inauguration in January 2009, hosted by Justice Sandra Day O'Connor and framed as a tribute to Dr. Martin Luther King Jr.

10. For a more complete discussion of how the term *jazz* has been appropriated, corporatized, and commodified, see Alan Stanbridge's discussion, which is worth quoting at some length, not only for the specific examples of jazz marketing it offers but also for how it associates this form of marketing with dominant modes of discourse that exclude hybrid, free, and avant-garde forms: "In more recent years, jazz has apparently moved even further from its previously marginal social positioning to a considerably more mainstream role in contemporary cultural life. Writing over a decade ago, Krin Gabbard could observe that 'even television commercials testify to the music's rising cultural capital . . . Advertisers no longer use jazz to connote . . . nightlife and slumming . . . jazz can now signify refinement and upper-class status' (*Jazz* 1–2). In some senses, this 'mainstreaming' of jazz is nothing other than a crude marketing exercise, simply exploiting the music's new-found social acceptability, whether by selling condominiums, golf clubs, cars, or airlines.

"On the condominium front, according to Ottawa's Urbandale property developers, 'Word on the street is that Jazz homes are the hottest thing to hit the market in a long time' ('Urbandale'). In its newspaper advertisements, the developer promises to 'Jazz your world' and 'Jazz up your life' with a choice of three exciting models: Acapella, Duet, and Harmony. The Winnipeg-based Jazz Golf company offers Harmony and Melody drivers and irons, alongside the Ensemble and Jazz Festival golf club sets, and the Jazz Boogie set for juniors. Jazz Golf promises to 'help you find your rhythm,' and invited us to 'swing into 2006 with our newly designed Jazz line of clubs' (Jazz Golf).

"Introduced into the European car market in 2002, the Honda Jazz 'continues to perform and bring new, younger customers into Honda's network' (Honda). Honda's marketing strategy is aimed at a primarily younger—but 'mature'—demographic and offers interesting insights into their choice of brand name: 'Key target customers are 20–35 year old males and females without children, particularly early adopters, who are perhaps buying their first car and perhaps their first Honda; young families aged 30–40; and empty nesters aged 55 plus who may well have previously owned a Honda' (Honda). And in his speech launching Air Canada's Jazz subsidiary in March 2002, the President and CEO noted that 'Our new name [Jazz] is a metaphor for who we are and where we are headed. We are an airline that prides itself on its creative spirit, freshness, youthful attitude, and energy . . . The qualities I have mentioned are what define us as an airline, and what makes us different. Our new name, we feel, is the perfect metaphor to reflect who we are and what we want to be. We are a great airline, and a great airline deserves a great name ("Air Canada"). . . .' Such crass marketing aside, there can be little doubt that jazz— or, more accurately, a particularly narrow conceptualization and manifestation of jazz—is now firmly established in the cultural mainstream in a very real and tangible fashion, whether, for example, in Ken Burns's $14-million PBS documentary *Jazz*, or in the heavily-funded Jazz at Lincoln Center program.

These examples serve to illustrate, however, that this mainstream version of jazz simply conforms to dominant cultural ideologies (in which Wynton Marsalis often seems heavily implicated), and has little to say about developments in post-1960s jazz, including free jazz, jazz-rock fusion, free improvisation, and the diversity of hybrid musical forms and styles that have developed in the last twenty years or so. Moreover, these examples also betray a narrowly Americo-centric perspective in which the burgeoning European jazz scene is barely acknowledged."

11. Mark Robert Schneider, in discussing the contexts surrounding the failed Dyer antilynching bill in 1922, notes that "the lynching issue stood at the top of the NAACP's agenda because it was so horrible to contemplate. The threat of terrorism underlay all the other forms of black oppression. Poverty, illiteracy, segregation, and disenfranchisement—these were chronic conditions that remained invisible to white Americans. Lynching, by contrast, was highly visible. Vast crowds attended these ghastly executions, sometimes in a festive spirit as the victim was put to death" (172). Remarkably, though the House of Representatives passed the bill, it was defeated in the Senate, as the result of a filibuster by the white Southern Democratic faction. Only in 2005 did the American Senate formally apologize, in what has been called (shockingly) an unprecedented action, for its failure to enact this and other anti-lynching bills. Schneider notes how there was a decline in the number of lynchings from 1923 on: "In 1922, fifty-one were lynched, then twenty-nine in 1923, and sixteen the following years" (192). The refusal to pass the bill (and others) was another form of state-sanctioned terror directed at blacks in America and a gross human rights failure, one indelibly printed on the historical contexts that led to the civil rights movement.

12. Peter Blecha notes, as have many other critics and historians, "From the time the transatlantic slave industry got rolling in the 1500s, American slave owners forbade the use of 'talking drums' (and other African musical expressions and traditions), fearing that they would be used as communication tools to transmit subversive messages and fuel insurrection" (16).

13. Fischlin and Nandorfy argue that "the pressure to increase meaningful access to rights instruments will require intensifying, especially in the reallocation of resources currently devoted to militarization and the arms trade. Alternatives to the trillion-dollar global expenditure on arms exist, including a budget co-developed by the Stockholm International Peace Research Institute, the World Policy Forum, and the World Game Institute. That budget, in which pressing human needs are addressed over spurious military needs, includes global line items for shelter, the elimination of starvation and malnutrition, safe water, the elimination of nuclear weapons and land mines, refugee relief, literacy, the prevention of soil erosion, and the like. Total cost: $105.5 billion or about one-tenth the cost of total global military spending" (*The Concise Guide* 204). In such a context, "the staggering disproportion between military spending and spending on rights-based resources will thus remain a key struggle for rights activists, recalling Martin Luther King Jr.'s comment that 'A nation that

continues year after year to spend more money on military defense than on programs of social uplift is approaching spiritual death'" (209).

14. New Orleans was the only city in North America to allow slave populations to gather to play music, using a mix of indigenous African and European forms and instruments, usually in Congo Square, now known as Louis Armstrong Park. As a city, it played a key role in the civil rights struggles in the 1960s, and it was the first place in which a black child attended an all-white school in the American South. The city played a key role in mounting an important early challenge to racial segregation. The Southern Christian Leadership Conference, an important American civil rights organization whose first president was Martin Luther King Jr., was founded in the city in 1957, after the Montgomery Bus Boycott.

15. The press release goes on to state that "in addition to causing pollution, coastal scientists estimate that oil companies have caused 40 to 60 percent of the coastal land loss Louisiana is experiencing. The current estimate to restore the Louisiana coast and secure local communities is $50 billion. In Nigeria, where Shell has been operating for over fifty years, Shell has come under fire for gas flaring, a practice which poisons and pollutes the local environment, while also contributing significantly to global warming, which threatens low-lying areas such as the Louisiana coast with rising sea levels. Gas flaring in Nigeria emits more greenhouse gases than all other sources in sub-Saharan Africa combined" ("ShellGuilty").

16. Musicians' association with more than suspect paymasters is not limited to the scenario involving Shell. The scandal from 2011 involving the pop musicians Nelly Furtado, Beyoncé, Mariah Carey, and Lionel Richie, all of whom were paid huge sums of money to play for private functions for Libyan dictator Muammar Qaddafi, is indicative of this relationship, as was the concert by Sting in Tashkent, Uzbekistan, in October 2009, for a putative arts and culture festival ("Furtado to Donate"). Though he claimed he thought the concert was sponsored by UNICEF, Sting was widely criticized for receiving a payment of somewhere between one and two million pounds (between 2 and 4 million U.S. dollars) for his performance from Uzbek president Islam Karimov and his daughter. The UN and Amnesty International have accused Karimov of rights abuses, violations, and torture, and UNICEF unequivocally stated they had no connection with the event. As Amy Davidson, a senior editor at the *New Yorker*, asked, "Why is Sting taking money from a dictator, by way of a dictator's daughter?" (Davidson). Furthermore, "The international community has repeatedly criticized the Karimov administration's record on human rights and press freedom. In particular, Craig Murray, the British ambassador from 2002 to 2004, wrote about financial corruption and human rights abuses during his term in office and later in his memoirs, *Murder in Samarkand*, pointing to reports of boiling people to death. The UN found torture 'institutionalized, systematic, and rampant' in Uzbekistan's judicial system. For several years, *Parade* magazine has selected Karimov as one of the world's worst dictators, citing his

tactics of torture, media censorship, and fake elections" (Wikipedia entry for "Islam Karimov").

17. A more complete account of the ACLU's report on the jail (found in Amit-jha) describes how brutal conditions in Los Angeles County's Central Jail "cause or contribute to violence and serious mental illness" there. The ACLU demanded that Los Angeles County swiftly implement changes to prevent un-necessary deaths or serious injuries in the jail. The report comes as Los Ange-les County investigates the death of John Horton, twenty-two years old, who was found hanging from a noose in his cell on March 30, after spending more than a month in Men's Central Jail, following his arrest on a drug possession charge. The ACLU also released a letter from a witness detailing the events leading up to the death of Horton, who was held in solitary confinement in a dimly lit, windowless, solid-front cell the size of a closet. His body was already stiff by the time security staff discovered it. "Men's Central Jail is so grossly overcrowded, dangerous and dungeon-like that it puts intolerable stress on the jailed as well as the jailers," said Margaret Winter, associate director of the ACLU National Prison Project. Dr. Terry Kupers, a national expert on correc-tional medical health care, detailed intolerable conditions inside Men's Central Jail in a fifty-page report. "A prisoner cannot move more than a few feet away from a neighbor, and lines form at the pay telephones and the urinals. Like-wise, when four men are crowded into the small cells I observed, there is barely enough room for one man to get off his bunk and head for the urinal," Kupers said. "When 150 or more prisoners are crowded into a room that has little space beyond what is taken up by the row of bunk beds they sleep in, there is little room for men to move without bumping into each other, and it is impos-sible for the officer assigned to supervise the dormitories to actually see what is going on," he said. Therefore, he added, beating and raping occurred in the cell. Kupers asserted that idleness and massive overcrowding at the jail leads to violence, victimization, custodial abuse, and ultimately psychotic breakdown even in relatively healthy people, as well as potentially irreversible psychosis in detainees with existing illnesses. With twenty thousand detainees, the Los Angeles County jail system is the largest in the United States. The Los Ange-les County Men's Central Jail is nearly fifty years old and currently houses an average of five thousand detainees, most of whom are awaiting trial and have not been convicted.

CHAPTER 4: IMPROVISATION, SOCIAL MOVEMENTS, AND RIGHTS IN NEW ORLEANS

1. Berry used this phrase differently than we are using it here. In his judg-ment, musicians worked effectively to raise funds for needed redevelopment while elected officials squandered large sums of money on programs that did not help the city. His formulation is that "politics failed, but culture prevailed."

2. "Second line" is an important aspect of traditions associated with brass band parades in New Orleans. The "main line" is the main parade, includ-

ing members of the club with the parade permit. People who follow the main parade to enjoy the music are called the "second line." Second liners walk and dance (using traditional steps) and sometimes twirl parasols or handkerchiefs in the air. Second-lining has been called "the quintessential New Orleans art form—a jazz funeral without a body" (Spitzer 29).

CHAPTER 5: ART TO FIND THE PULSE OF THE PEOPLE

1. All descriptions of and quotations from the American Studies Association session of November 5, 2009, are from the DVD of the event made by the Center for Black Studies Research at the University of California, Santa Barbara, and filed in the center's archives under the title "Poetic Visions."

CHAPTER 6: "THE FIERCE URGENCY OF NOW"

1. The Guelph Jazz Festival is not alone among festivals of innovative music dedicated to issues of rights and justice. New York's artist-run Vision Festival, a festival of innovative African American-inspired music and arts, organized by the dancer-choreographer Patricia Nicholson and the free jazz bassist William Parker, also explicitly articulates its own mandate in the context of broader struggles for social awareness. The theme of the 2004 edition of the Vision Festival, "Vision for a Just World," like the festival's declarations on its website, makes clear the organizers' commitments: "It is imperative," the festival announces on its homepage, "that we respond to the erosion of rights in America and the new and very dangerous Imperialism abroad." In an effort to resist the "deadening effects of fear, conformity and greed," the Vision Festival—which, from its inception has been "committed to combining social awareness and presenting the very best visionary music and art"—seeks to provide a platform for community response and involvement.

2. Videos are available through the ICASP website, www.improvcommunity .ca.

3. See also Heble, *Landing on the Wrong Note*, for a more detailed consideration of arts presentation as an activist endeavor.

4. Although jazz opera is not a particularly well-documented genre, it is worth noting that *Québécité*'s interculturality is part of a longer history in which the genre mix-up of opera and jazz has been attempted. A comprehensive genealogy of jazz operas is beyond the scope of this book but would need to include reference to works by Krenek, Gershwin, and Weill, and, among others, the work of black composers such as William Grant Still, Ulysses Kay, Scott Joplin, and Anthony Davis, whose opera *X: The Life and Times of Malcolm X* remains something of a touchstone, especially in terms of large-scale, hybridized musical forms that address social-justice issues revolving around race.

5. The argument here and in the four paragraphs that follow originally appeared in Ajay Heble's postlude to *Québécité*.

WORKS CITED

"Adolphe Sax." *Dinant.be*. Dinant. n.d. Web. 3 Mar. 2011.

Aidt, Mik, ed. "About Freemuse." *Freemuse*. Freemuse, 2008. Web. 2 Feb. 2011.

Alake, Olu. "A Long Way Gone—Cultural Rights, Identity and Citizenship: How Africa and Europe Are Impacting Each Other in Practice." Campus Euro-Africano de Dooperação Cultural. Maputo, Mozambique, 22–26 June 2009. Paper presentation.

Albisa, Catherine. "Economic and Social Rights in the United States: Six Rights, One Promise." *Bringing Human Rights Home: A History of Human Rights in the United States*. Ed. Cynthia Soohoo, Catherine Albisa, and Martha F. Davis. Philadelphia: University of Pennsylvania Press, 2009. 173–97. Print.

Amitjha. "Los Angeles Jail Overcrowded, Dangerous and Dungeon-like: ACLU." *NowPublic*. Now Public Media, 15 Apr. 2009. Web.

Anderson, Carol. "'A Hollow Mockery': African Americans, White Supremacy, and the Development of Human Rights in the United States." *Bringing Human Rights Home: A History of Human Rights in the United States*. Ed. Cynthia Soohoo, Catherine Albisa, and Martha F. Davis. Philadelphia: University of Pennsylvania Press, 2009. 68–99. Print.

Anderson, Iain. *This Is Our Music: Free Jazz, the Sixties, and American Culture*. Philadelphia: University of Pennsylvania Press, 2007. Print.

Ang, Ien. *On Not Speaking Chinese: Living between Asia and the West*. London: Routledge, 2001. Print.

Appleton, Josie, and Manick Govinda. *UK Arts and Culture: Cancelled, by Order of the Home Office*. London: Manifestoclub, 2009. Print.

Atzmon, Gilad. "Free Jazz." *Guardian* 15 Nov. 2004. Web. 6 Nov. 2012.

Austerlitz, Paul. *Jazz Consciousness: Music, Race, and Humanity*. Middletown: Wesleyan University Press, 2005. Print.

Ayler, Albert. "To Mr. Jones—I Had a Vision." *The Cricket—Black Music in Evolution* (1969): 27–29. Print.

Bailey, Derek. *Improvisation: Its Nature and Practice in Music*. New York: Da Capo, 1992. Print.

———, auth. *On the Edge: Improvisation in Music*. Director's cut. Channel 4 TV, 1992. DVD.

————, perf. "Playing for Friends on 5th Street." Straw2Gold Pictures, 2004. DVD.

Balliett, Whitney. *Collected Works: A Journal of Jazz, 1954–2000*. New York: St Martin's, 2001. Print.

Banfield, William C. *Representing Black Music Culture: Then, Now, and When Again?* Lanham: Scarecrow, 2011. Print.

Barber-Kersovan, Alenka. "Music as a Parallel Power Structure." *Shoot the Singer! Music Censorship Today*. Ed. Marie Korpe. London: Freemuse, 2004. 6–10. Print.

Baue, William. "Apple Added, Time Warner and Petro-Canada Deleted from FTSE4Good Index Series." *Social Funds.com*. SRI World Group, 30 Sept. 2004. Web. 2 Feb. 2011.

Bauer, William R. *Open the Door: The Life and Music of Betty Carter*. Ann Arbor: University of Michigan Press, 2003. Print.

Baxi, Upendra. "From Human Rights to the Right to Be Human: Some Heresies." *The Right to Be Human*. Ed. Upendra Baxi, Geeti Sen, and Jeanette Fernandes. New Delhi: Lancer International, 1987. 185–200. Print.

————. *The Future of Human Rights*. New Delhi: Oxford University Press, 2006. Print.

Belgrad, Daniel. *The Culture of Spontaneity: Improvisation and the Arts in Postwar America*. Chicago: University of Chicago Press, 1998. Print.

Berger, Mark. "Banned Music: Hold That Tune." *Economist* 349 (1998): 91. Print.

Berkowitz, Aaron L., and Daniel Ansari. "Expertise-Related Deactivation of the Right Temporoparietal Junction during Musical Improvisation." *Neuro-Image* 49.1 (2010): 712–19. Print.

Berman, Mitch, and Susanne Wah Lee. "Max: Sticking Power." *Los Angeles Times* 15 Sept. 1991. Print.

Berry, Jason. "Up from the Cradle of Jazz: New Orleans Post-Katrina." University of California, Santa Barbara. 3 Nov. 2009. Presentation.

Berry, Jason, Jonathan Foose, and Tad Jones. *Up from the Cradle of Jazz: New Orleans Music since World War II*. Athens: University of Georgia Press, 1986. Print.

The Black Power Mixtape, 1967–1975. Written and directed by Göran Hugo Olsson. MPI Home Video, Louverture Films, 2011. DVD.

Blake, Felice, and Paula Ioanide. "Color Blindness across the Disciplines." Center for Advanced Study in the Behavioral Sciences Symposium on Color Blindness and the Disciplines. Stanford, Calif., 4 and 5 June 2009. Presentation.

Blanco, Juan Antonio. "Natural History and Social History: Limits and Urgent Priorities Which Condition the Exercise of Human Rights." *The Poverty of Rights: Human Rights and the Eradication of Poverty*. Ed. Willem van Genugten and Camilo Perez-Bustillo. London: Zed, 2001. 40–48. Print.

Blanton, Thomas, and Kate Doyle. "Musicians Seek Secret U.S. Documents on Music-Related Human Rights Abuses at Guantanamo." *The National*

Security Archive. George Washington University, 22 Oct. 2009. Web. 6 Nov. 2012.

Blecha, Peter. *Taboo Tunes: A History of Banned Bands and Censored Songs.* San Francisco: Backbeat, 2004. Print.

Block, Peter. *Community: The Structure of Belonging.* San Francisco: Berrett-Koehler, 2008. Print.

Borgo, David. "Negotiating Freedom: Values and Practices in Contemporary Improvised Music." *Black Music Research Journal* 22.2 (2002): 165–88. Print.

———. *Sync or Swarm: Improvising Music in a Complex Age.* New York: Continuum, 2005. Print.

Breitman, George Ed. *Malcolm X Speaks: Selected Speeeches and Statements.* New York: Grove, 1994. Print.

Brothers, Thomas. *Louis Armstrong's New Orleans.* New York: W.W. Norton, 2006. Print.

Broughton, Simon, and Mark Ellingham, eds. *World Music: The Rough Guide.* 2nd ed. London: Rough Guides, 2000. Print.

Brün, Herbert. "Toward Composition." *When Music Resists Meaning: The Major Writings of Herbert Brün.* Ed. Arun Chandra. Middletown, CT: Wesleyan University Press, 2004. 76–88. Print.

Buchanan, Jeffrey. "Lip Service and Profiteering: Human Rights and the Realities of Returning to New Orleans." *Counterpunch.org.* Counterpunch, 29 Aug. 2006. Web. 2 Feb. 2011.

Bunnett, Jane. Phone interview with Ajay Heble. 16 Mar. 2010.

Butters, Rex. "Kidd Jordan: Messin' with the Kidd." *All about Jazz.* 18 Sept. 2007. Web. 21 Jan. 2011.

Byrnes, Sholto. "Wynton Marsalis: It's Precision Jazz for Non-Smokers." *Independent,* 4 Feb. 2001. Print.

Camp, Jordan T. "'We Know This Place': Neoliberal Racial Regimes and the Katrina Circumstance." *American Quarterly* 61.3 (2009): 706. Print.

Canadian Multiculturalism Act. R.S.C., 1985, c. 24. (4th Supp.). Print.

"Celebrating a Jazz Hero: A Symposium on the Role of Fred Anderson in Chicago's Jazz Legacy." Chicago Cultural Center. 19 Aug. 2009. Presentation.

Chadbourne, Eugene. "Stan Brenders." *Jazz in Belgium.* Lundis d'Hortense, n.d. Web. 2 Feb. 2011.

Chapman, Geoff. "A Bumpy Operatic Ride to Quebec City." *Toronto Star* 8 Sept. 2003. Print.

Childs, John Brown. *Transcommunality: From the Politics of Conversion to the Ethics of Respect.* Philadelphia: Temple University Press, 2003. Print.

Clark, Philip. "Derek Bailey." *The Wire Primers: A Guide to Modern Music.* Ed. Rob Young. London: Verso, 2009. 121–28. Print.

Clarke, George Elliott. Introduction. *Eyeing the North Star: Directions in African-Canadian Literature.* Ed. George Elliott Clarke. Toronto: McClelland and Stewart, 1997. xi–xxviii. Print.

———. *Québécité: A Jazz Fantasia in Three Cantos.* Kentville, Nova Scotia: Gaspereau, 2003. Print.

Cloonan, Martin, and Reebee Garofalo, eds. *Policing Pop*. Philadelphia: Temple University Press, 2003. Print.

Coleman, Jeffrey Lamar. "Michael S. Harper's 'Here Where Coltrane Is' and Coltrane's 'Alabama': The Social/Aesthetic Intersections of Civil Rights Movement Poetry." *J_spot*. York University, n.d. Web. 2 Feb. 2011.

Coleman, Ornette. *Free Jazz: A Collective Improvisation*. Atlantic, 1960. CD.

Collin, Kasper, dir. *My Name Is Albert Ayler*. 2010. DVD.

Coltrane, John. *Ascension*. Impulse! 1965. CD.

Cook, Richard, and Brian Morton. *The Penguin Guide to Jazz on CD: The Comprehensive Critical Guide to Recorded Jazz—From Its Beginnings until the Present*. 5th ed. London: Penguin, 2000. Print.

Coombe, Rosemary. "Cultural Rights and Intellectual Property Debates." *Carnegie Council*. Carnegie Council for Ethics in International Affairs, 2005. Web. 2 Feb. 2011.

"The Cricket—Black Music in Evolution." *Chimurenga Library*. Chimurenga, n.d. Web. 2 Feb. 2011.

Cruz, Jon. *Culture on the Margins: The Black Spiritual and the Rise of American Cultural Interpretation*. Princeton, NJ: Princeton University Press, 1999.

Cusick, Suzanne G. "Music as Torture / Music as Weapon." *Revista transcultural de musica/Transcultural Music Review* 10 (2006): n. pag. Web. 2 Feb. 2011.

Dahlen, Chris. Rev. of *Witness*, by Dave Douglas. *Save the Robot*. N.p., n.d. Web. 2 Feb. 2011.

Davidson, Amy. "Sting in Uzbekistan." *New Yorker*. 1 Mar. 2010. Web. 15 Nov. 2012.

Davis, Angela Y. *Blues Legacies and Black Feminism: Gertrude "Ma" Rainey, Bessie Smith, and Billie Holiday*. New York: Vintage, 1999. Print.

Deck, Alice A. "Toni Cade Bambara (1939–)." *Black Women in America: An Historical Encyclopedia*. Ed. Darlene Clark Hine, Elsa Barkley Brown, and Rosalyn Terborg-Penn. Bloomington: Indiana University Press, 1993. 80. Print.

Denselow, Robin. *When the Music's Over: The Story of Political Pop*. London: Faber and Faber, 1989. Print.

Derbez, Alain. E-mail Interview with Ajay Heble. 25 Mar. 2010.

"The Dizzy Ethos." *Jazz at Lincoln Center*. N.d. Web. 5 May 2012.

"Dizzy Gillespie for President." *Jazz on the Tube*. N.d. Web. 5 May 2012.

Dolphy, Eric. *Out to Lunch!* Blue Note Records, 1964. CD.

Douglas, Dave. Liner notes. *Witness*. Bluebird, 2001. CD.

Drewett, Michael, and Martin Cloonan, eds. *Popular Music Censorship in Africa*. Aldergate, UK: Ashgate, 2006. Print.

Dryden, Ken. *The Game*. Toronto: Wylie, 2005. Print.

Durant, Alan. "Improvisation in the Political Economy of Music." *Music and the Politics of Culture*. Ed. Christopher Norris. New York: St Martin's, 1989. 252–82. Print.

Early, Gerald Lyn, ed. *Miles Davis and American Culture*. St. Louis: Missouri Historical Society Press, 2001. Print.

Ellington, Duke. *Music Is My Mistress*. New York: Da Capo, 1976. Print.

Ellison, Ralph. "Living with Music." *Living with Music*. Ed. Robert G. O'Meally. New York: Modern Library, 2002. 3–33. Print.

"Enviros Challenge Shell's Gulf Deepwater Drilling Permit." *Environment News Service*.13 June 2011. Web. 22 Nov. 2011.

Evans, Sara M., and Harry C. Boyte. *Free Spaces: The Sources of Democratic Change in America*. Chicago: University of Chicago Press, 1992. Print.

Fanon, Frantz. *The Wretched of the Earth*. 1963. Trans. Constance Farrington. New York: Grove, 1968. Print.

Fischlin, Daniel. "'See Clearly . . . Feel Deeply': Improvisation and Transformation. John McLaughlin Interviewed by Daniel Fischlin." *Critical Studies in Improvisation / Études critiques en improvisation* 6.2 (2010): n. pag. Web. 14 Nov. 2012.

———. "Wild Notes . . . Improvisioning." *Critical Studies in Improvisation / Études critiques en improvisation* 6.2 (2010): n. pag. Web. 11 Mar. 2011.

Fischlin, Daniel, and Ajay Heble. "The Other Side of Nowhere: Jazz, Improvisation, and Communities in Dialogue." *The Other Side of Nowhere: Jazz, Improvisation, and Communities in Dialogue*. Ed. Daniel Fischlin and Ajay Heble. Middletown, CT: Wesleyan University Press, 2004. 1–42. Print.

Fischlin, Daniel, and Martha Nandorfy. *The Community of Rights—The Rights of Community*. Montreal: Black Rose, 2011. Print.

———. *The Concise Guide to Global Human Rights*. New Delhi: Oxford University Press, 2007. Print.

Fricke, David. "Louder Faster Stronger." *Rolling Stone* Oct. 2008. Web.

"FTSE4GOOD Index Series." Index. *FTSE.com*. FTSE, n.d. Web. 2 Feb. 2011.

"Furtado to Donate $1M from Gadhafi Gig." *CBC News*. 28 Feb. 2011. Web. 3 Mar. 2011.

Gabbard, Krin. *Hotter than That: The Trumpet, Jazz, and American Culture*. New York: Faber and Faber, 2008. Print.

Gaines, Kevin K. *Uplifting the Race: Black Leadership, Politics, and Culture in the Twentieth Century*. Chapel Hill: University of North Carolina Press, 1996. Print.

Galeta, Hotep Idris. "The Development of Jazz in South Africa." *Jazz Rendezvous*. Western Cape Musician's Association, n.d. Web. 2 Feb. 2011.

"Getting Here." *Jazz at Lincoln Center*. N.d. Web. 5 May 2012.

Giddins, Gary. "Something Else: Ornette Coleman at Town Hall." *New Yorker* 14 Apr. 2008: 78. Print.

Gill, Gerald. "From Progressive Republican to Independent Progressive: The Political Career of Charlotta A. Bass." *African American Women and the Vote, 1837–1965*. Ed. Ann D. Gordon and Betye Collier-Thomas. Amherst: University of Massachusetts Press, 1997. 156–71. Print.

Gilroy, Paul. *The Black Atlantic: Modernity and Double Consciousness*. Cambridge, MA: Harvard University Press, 1993. Print.

Giroux, Henry A. Foreword. *Zones of Contention: Essays on Art, Institutions, Gender, and Anxiety*. Ed. Carol Becker. Albany: State University of New York Press, 1996. ix–xii. Print.

Goodheart, Matthew. "Jazz and Society." "Freedom and Individuality in the Music of Cecil Taylor." Master's thesis. Mills College, 1996. Web. 2 Feb. 2011.

Gramsci, Antonio. *Selections from the Prison Notebooks.* Ed. and trans. Quintin Hoare and Geoffrey Nowell Smith. New York: International, 1971. Print.

Gray, Herman. *Cultural Moves: African Americans and the Politics of Representation.* Berkeley: University of California Press, 2005. Print.

———. "John Coltrane and the Practice of Freedom." *John Coltrane and Black America's Quest for Freedom: Spirtuality and the Music.* Ed. Leonard L. Brown. New York: Oxford University Press, 2010. 33–54. Print.

Green, John. "Interview: Lester Bowie, Don Moye; Two Spirited Forces behind the Art Ensemble of Chicago." *Be-Bop and Beyond* (1984): 16–23. Print.

Griffin, Shana. "The Politics of Reproductive Violence: An Interview with Shana Griffin by Clyde Woods." *American Quarterly* 61.3 (2009): 585. Print.

Hale, James. "To Hook or Not to Hook." *JazzHouse.* phpBB Group, 15 Sept. 2004. Web. 21 Apr. 2010.

Hartman, Charles O. *Jazz Text: Voice and Improvisation in Poetry, Jazz, and Song.* Princeton, NJ: Princeton University Press, 1991. Print.

Heble, Ajay. *Landing on the Wrong Note: Jazz, Dissonance, and Critical Practice.* New York: Routledge, 2000. Print.

———. Rev. of *Cultural Moves: African Americans and the Politics of Representation*, by Herman S. Gray. *Journal of the Society for American Music* 2.2 (May 2008): 265–69. Print.

———. "Take Two / Rebel Musics: Human Rights, Resistant Sounds, and the Politics of Music Making." *Human Rights, Resistant Sounds, and the Politics of Music Making.* Ed. Daniel Fischlin and Ajay Heble. Montreal: Black Rose, 2003. 232–48. Print.

———. "'You Know You Break No Laws by Dreaming': George Elliott Clarke's *Québécité*: A Postlude." *Québécité: A Jazz Fantasia in Three Cantos.* Kentville, Nova Scotia: Gaspereau, 2003. 97–101. Print.

Heffley, Mike. *Northern Sun, Southern Moon: Europe's Reinvention of Jazz.* New Haven, CT: Yale University Press, 2005. Print.

Hegarty, Paul. *Noise / Music: A History.* New York: Continuum, 2007. Print.

Heilbut, Anthony. *The Gospel Sound: Good News and Bad Times.* New York: Limelight Editions, 1992. Print.

Hentoff, Nat. "Albert Ayler: The Truth Is Marching In." *DownBeat* 33.23 (1966): 16–18. Print.

———. "Cecil Taylor: It's about Magic, and Capturing Spirits." *Jazz Times* 32 (2002): 158. Print.

Henze, Hans Werner. "Music as a Means of Resistance." *Music and Politics: Collected Writings 1953–81.* Trans. Peter Labanyi. Ithaca, NY: Cornell University Press, 1982. 123–25. Print.

Herman, Edward S., and Noam Chomsky. *Manufacturing Consent: The Political Economy of the Mass Media.* New York: Pantheon, 1988. Print.

"The History of the Saxophone." *The-Saxophone.com.* N.p., n.d. Web. 2 Feb. 2011.

Holloway, Karla F. C. *Passed On: African American Mourning Stories: A Memorial*. Durham, NC: Duke University Press, 2002. Print.

hooks, bell. "Performance Practice as a Site of Opposition." *Let's Get It On: The Politics of Black Performance*. Ed. Catherine Ugwu. Seattle: Bay, 1995. 210–21. Print.

Horton, Lyn. "Wadada Leo Smith: A Vital Life Force." *AllAboutJazz.com*. 12 May 2010. Web. 1 Dec. 2011.

Horwitz, Steven. "Wal-Mart to the Rescue: Private Enterprise's Reponse to Hurricane Katrina." *Independent Review* 13.4 (spring 2009): 511–28. Print.

Huang, Margaret. "'Going Global': Appeals to International and Regional Human Rights Bodies." *Bringing Human Rights Home: A History of Human Rights in the United States*. Ed. Cynthia Soohoo, Catherine Albisa, and Martha F. Davis. Philadelphia: University of Pennsylvania Press, 2009. 235. Print.

Hubbard, Freddie. *Sing Me a Song of Songmy: A Fantasy for Electromagnetic Tape*. Comp. İlhan Mimaroğlu. Atlantic, 1971. CD.

"Human Rights Advocate." *Leonard Feather Collection*. University of Idaho, n.d. Web. 2 Feb. 2011.

"Improvisation, Community, and Social Practice." *Improv Community*. Improvisation, Community, and Social Practice. n.d. Web. 16 Mar. 2010.

"The International Covenant on Economic, Social and Cultural Rights." *Office of the United Nations High Commissioner for Human Rights*. Office of the High Commissioner for Human Rights, 26 Jan. 2010. Web. 28 Jan. 2011.

Ishay, Micheline R. *The History of Human Rights: From Ancient Times to the Globalization Era*. Berkeley: University of California Press, 2004. Print.

Isoardi, Steven. *The Dark Tree: Jazz and Community Arts in Los Angeles*. Berkeley: University of California Press, 2006. Print.

Ivey, Bill. *Arts, Inc.: How Greed and Neglect Have Destroyed Our Cultural Rights*. Los Angeles: University of California Press, 2008. Print.

Iyer, Vijay. "Improvisation: Terms and Conditions." *Arcana IV: Musicians on Music*. Ed. John Zorn. New York: Hips Road, 2009. 171–75. Print.

———. "On Improvisation, Temporality, and Embodied Experience." *Sound Unbound: Sampling Digital Music and Culture*. Ed. Paul D. Miller. Cambridge, MA: MIT Press, 2008. 273–293. Print.

Jeffries, Hasan Kwame. *Bloody Lowndes: Civil Rights and Black Power in Alabama's Black Belt*. New York: New York University Press. 2009. Print.

Jenkins, Willard. Rev. of *Dissent or Descent*, by Horace Tapscott. *JazzTimes*. Jazz Times, 1999. Web. 2 Feb. 2011.

John Coltrane Live in '60, '61 and '65. Jazz Icons, 2007. DVD.

Jones, Andrew F. "Black Internationale: Notes on the Chinese Jazz Age." *Jazz Planet*. Ed. E. Taylor Atkins. Minneapolis: University of Minnesota Press, 2003. 225–44. Print.

Julier, Claire. Liner notes. *Chronique d'un génocide annoncé*. Music by René Lussier. Ambiances Magnétiques, 1998. CD.

Jung, Fred. "A Fireside Chat with Dave Douglas." *All about Jazz*. All about Jazz, 19 Apr. 2003. Web. 2 Feb. 2011.

Kanellopoulos, Panagiotis A. "Musical Improvisation as Action: An Arendtian Perspective." *Action, Criticism, and Theory for Music Education* 6.3 (2007): 97–127. Print.

Kelley, Robin D. G. *Africa Speaks, America Answers: Modern Jazz in Revolutionary Times.* Cambridge, MA: Harvard University Press, 2012. Print.

———. *Freedom Dreams: The Black Radical Imagination.* Boston: Beacon, 2002. Print.

———. *Race Rebels: Culture, Politics, and the Black Working Class.* New York: Free Press, 1994. Print.

Kernfeld, Barry. "Improvisation III: Jazz." *Grove Music Online.* Oxford Music Online, n.d. Web. 20 Jan. 2011.

Khanna, Vish. "La Belle Québécité: Multiculturalism Examined in Festival's Jazz Opera." *Echo* Sept. 2003: 9, 17. Print.

King, Martin Luther, Jr. "Beyond Vietnam: A Time to Break the Silence." *American Rhetoric.* American Rhetoric, n.d. Web. 20 Jan. 2011.

———. "Conscience for Change." *The Lost Massey Lectures: Recovered Classics from Five Great Thinkers.* Toronto: Anansi, 2007. 163–217. Print.

Klein, Naomi. *The Shock Doctrine: The Rise of Disaster Capitalism.* New York: Metropolitan, 2007. Print.

Kofsky, Frank. "John Coltrane: An Interview." *Black Nationalism and the Revolution in Music.* New York: Pathfinder, 1970. 221–47. Print.

Korpe, Marie. "Human Rights for Musicians: The Freemuse Story." *Freemuse.* Freemuse, n.d. Web. 20 Jan. 2011.

———. *Shoot the Singer! Music Censorship Today.* London: Zed, 2004.

Kunzelman, Michael. "1st Member of 'Danziger 7' Charged." *Louisiana Weekly* 5 Mar. 2010. Print.

———. "Former Cop Admits to Danziger Bridge Cover-Up." *Louisiana Weekly* 1 Mar. 2010. Print.

———. "Police Cover-Up Unravels." *Louisiana Weekly* 15 Mar. 2010. Print.

Kupers, Terry A. "Report on Mental Health Issues at Los Angeles County Jail." *ACLU.* ACLU, 7 July 2008. Web. 20 Jan. 2011.

Labyrinth. "Paul Dunmall / Trevor Taylor / Paul Rogers: *Zoochosis.*" *MusicBox.* Modisti, 19 Oct. 2009. Web. 20 Jan. 2011.

Léandre, Joëlle. *À voix basse: Entretiens avec Franck Médioni.* Paris: MF, 2009. Print.

Lee, Chana Kai. *For Freedom's Sake: The Life of Fannie Lou Hamer.* Urbana: University of Illinois Press, 2000. Print.

Lehren, Andrew W. "Guilty until Proven Innocent." *Jazz Times* 39.3 (2009): 40–45. Print.

Lengel, Laura. *Intercultural Communication and Creative Practice: Music, Dance, and Women's Cultural Identity.* London: Praeger, 2005. Print.

Levitin, Daniel J. *This Is Your Brain on Music: The Science of a Human Obsession.* New York: Dutton, 2006. Print.

———. *The World in Six Songs: How the Musical Brain Created Human Nature.* Toronto: Viking Canada, 2008. Print.

Lewis, Edmund W. "Jury Finds Five Cops Guilty in Danziger Bridge Shootings, Cover-up." *Louisiana Weekly* 8 Aug.–14 Aug. 2011. Print.

Lewis, George E. *A Power Stronger Than Itself: The AACM and American Experimental Music.* Chicago: University of Chicago Press, 2008. Print.

———. "Teaching Improvised Music: An Ethnographic Memoir." *Arcana: Musicians on Music.* Ed. John Zorn. New York: Granary, 2000. 78–109. Print.

Lezra, Esther. "Monsters in Motion: Tracing the Silences in John Gabriel Stedman and William Blake." *Anthurium: A Caribbean Studies Journal* 4.1 (2006). Print.

Lipsitz, George. *American Studies in a Moment of Danger.* Minneapolis: University of Minnesota Press, 2001. Print.

———. *Footsteps in the Dark: The Hidden Histories of Popular Music.* Minneapolis: University of Minnesota Press, 2007. Print.

Luft, Rachel E., "Beyond Disaster Exceptionalism: Social Movement Developments in New Orleans after Hurricane Katrina." *American Quarterly* 61.3 (2009): 499–527. Print.

Lynd, Staughton, and Alice Lynd. *Stepping Stones: Memoir of a Life Together.* Lanham, MD: Lexington. 2009. Print.

Lynskey, Dorian. *33 Revolutions per Minute: A History of Protest Songs, from Billie Holiday to Green Day.* New York: HarperCollins, 2011. Print.

Lyotard, Jean-François. "The Other's Rights." *The Politics of Human Rights.* Ed. Belgrade Circle. London: Verso, 1999: 181–88. Print.

Mackey, Nathaniel. *Discrepant Engagement: Dissonance, Cross-Culturality, and Experimental Writing.* Cambridge: Cambridge University Press. 1993. Print.

———. "Paracritical Hinge." *The Other Side of Nowhere: Jazz, Improvisation, and Communities in Dialogue.* Ed. Daniel Fischlin and Ajay Heble. Middletown, CT: Wesleyan University Press, 2004. 367–86. Print.

Mahfouz, Naguib. "Nobel Lecture." Trans. Mohammed Salmawy. *Nobelprize .org.* Nobel Foundation, 1988. Web. 20 Jan. 2011.

Mandel, Howard. "Albert Ayler's Fiery Sax, Now on Film." *NPR music.* NPR, 7 June 2008. Web. 20 Jan. 2011.

———. "Civil Rights-Jazz Document, 1963." *Jazz beyond Jazz.* ArtsJournal, 17 Jan. 2009. Web. 20 Jan. 2011.

———. "It *Can* Be Done: Why Aren't More Doing It?" *Ear: A Magazine of New Music* 15 (1991): 40–41, 43. Print.

———. "Yo Wadada! Leo Smith's Long Pilgrimage." *JazzHouse.org.* Jazz Journalists Association, 2003. Web. 20 Jan. 2011.

Marsalis, Wynton. *Moving to Higher Ground: How Jazz Can Change Your Life.* New York: Random House, 2009. Print.

Martenson, Jan. "The United Nations and Human Rights Today and Tomorrow." *Human Rights in the Twenty-First Century: A Global Challenge.* Ed. Kathleen E. Mahoney and Paul Mahoney. Dordrecht: Martinus Nijhoff, 1993. 925–36. Print.

Marx, Karl. "The German Ideology." *The Marx-Engels Reader.* Ed. Robert C. Tucker. New York: W. W. Norton, 1978. 146–202. Print.

Mattin. "Going Fragile." *Noise and Capitalism.* Eds. Mattin and Anthony Iles. Donostia San Sebastián: Arteleku Audiolab, 2009. 19–23. Print.

Maykrantz, Scott. "Masada: John Zorn's Jazz Band." *Scott Maykrantz.com.* N.p., n.d. Web. 20 Jan. 2011.

Mazzola, Guerino, and Paul B. Cherlin. *Flow, Gesture, and Spaces in Free Jazz: Towards a Theory of Collaboration.* Berlin: Springer-Verlag, 2009. Print.

McLeod, Katherine. "'Oui, let's scat': Listening to Multi-vocality in George Elliott Clarke's Jazz Opera *Québécité*." *Mosaic* 42.1 (2009): 133–50. Print.

McMichael, Robert K. "'We Insist—Freedom Now!': Black Moral Authority, Jazz, and the Changeable Shape of Whiteness." *American Music* 16.4 (1998): 375–416. Print.

Michna, Catherine. "Stories at the Center: Story Circles, Educational Organizing, and Fate of Neighborhood Public Schools in New Orleans." *American Quarterly* 61.3 (2009): 529–50. Print.

Miller, Mark. "Singer Wails Up a Storm." *Globe and Mail* 13 Sept. 2004. Print.

"Mission." *The Ruckus Society.* The Ruckus Society, n.d. Web. 2 Feb. 2011.

Mitchell, Nicole. "Lex Non Scripta, Ars Non Scripta: Law, Justice, and Improvisation Conference." Improvisation, Community, and Social Practice. McGill University, Montreal. 19 June 2009. Keynote address.

Mitchell, Nicole, and the Black Earth Ensemble. *Black Unstoppable.* Delmark, 2007. CD.

Monson, Ingrid T. *Freedom Sounds: Civil Rights Call Out to Jazz and Africa.* Oxford: Oxford University Press, 2007. Print.

———. *Saying Something: Jazz Improvisation and Interaction.* Chicago: University of Chicago Press, 1996. Print.

Morris, Aldon. "Movement Halfway Houses." *The Origins of the Civil Rights Movement: Black Communities Organizing for Change.* New York: Free Press, 1984. 139–73. Print.

Morrison, Toni. *Playing in the Dark: Whiteness and the Literary Imagination.* New York: Vintage, 1993. Print.

Morsink, Johannes. *The Universal Declaration of Human Rights: Origins, Drafting and Intent.* Philadelphia: University of Pennsylvania Press, 1999. Print.

Mulvey, Laura. "Changes: Thoughts on Myth, Narrative, and Historical Experience." *History Workshop* (1987): 3–19. Print.

Murray, Albert. "Jazz as an Enduring Art Form." *Jerry Jazz Musician.* N.p., n.d. Web. 20 Jan. 2011.

Mutua, Makau. *Human Rights: A Political and Cultural Critique.* Philadelphia: University of Pennsylvania Press, 2002. Print.

Nachmanovitch, Stephen. "Improvisation as a Tool for Investigating Reality." *The Improviser.* N.p., 2006. Web. 20 Jan. 2011.

Neal, Laurence P. Untitled article. *Negro Digest* 17 (1968): 35, 81. Web. 20 Jan. 2011.

Negus, Keith. *Popular Music in Theory: An Introduction.* Middletown, CT: Wesleyan University Press, 1997. Print.

Neubeck, Kenneth J., and Noel A. Cazenave. *Welfare Racism: Playing the Race Card against America's Poor*. New York: Routledge, 2001. Print.

Newman, Nathan, and J. J. Gass. "A New Birth of Freedom: The Forgotten History of the 13th, 14th, and 15th Amendments." *Judicial Independence Series*. Brennan Center for Justice at New York University School of Law, 2004. Web. 20 Feb. 2010.

Nicholls, Tracey. "It Does Too Matter: Aesthetic Value(s), Avant-garde Art, and Problems of Theory Choice." Diss. McGill University, 2005. Print.

Nisenson, Eric. *Ascension: John Coltrane and His Quest*. New York: Da Capo, 1995. Print.

Obert, Julia Catherine. "The Cultural Capital of Sound: *Québécité's* Acoustic Hybridity." *Postcolonial Text* 2.4 (2006): n. pag. Web. 21 Apr. 2010.

Odinkalu, Chidi Anselm. "Why More Africans Don't Use Human Rights Language." *Human Rights Dialogue* 2.1 (1999): n. pag. Web. 11 Jan. 2010.

Okri, Ben. *A Way of Being Free*. London: Phoenix House, 1997. Print.

Oliveros, Pauline. "Harmonic Anatomy: Women in Improvisation." *The Other Side of Nowhere: Jazz, Improvisation, and Communities in Dialogue*. Ed. Daniel Fischlin and Ajay Heble. Middletown, CT: Wesleyan University Press, 2004. 50–70. Print.

"Overview of Time Warner Center." *Shops at Columbus Circle*. Time Warner, n.d. Web. 2 Feb. 2011.

Owen, Frank. "Hip Hop Bebop." *Spin* 4.7 (1988): 60–61, 73. Print.

Palmer, Robert. *Deep Blues: A Musical and Cultural History, from the Mississippi Delta to Chicago's South Side to the World*. New York: Penguin, 1981. Print.

Panish, Jon. *The Color of Jazz: Race and Representation in Postwar American Culture*. Jackson: University Press of Mississippi, 1991. Print.

Parker, Evan, and Hans Falb. "Chasing 'The Pale Fox.'" *Tell No Lies Claim No Easy Victories*. Ed. Philipp Schmickl, Hans Falb, Andrea Mutschlechner, Elvira Faltermeier, Mischa Guttmann. N.p.: Verein Impro, 2000. 114–29. Print.

Parker, William. *Document Humanum 1974–1975*. New York: Centering Music, 1997. Print.

———. Personal interview with Ajay Heble. 22 May 2004.

———. *Who Owns Music?* Köln: Buddy's Knife Jazzedition, 2007. Print.

Parker, William, and In Order to Survive, perfs. *The Peach Orchard*. AUM Fidelity, 1998. CD.

Payne, Charles. *I've Got the Light of Freedom: The Organizing Tradition and the Mississippi Freedom Struggle*. Berkeley: University of California Press, 2007. Print.

Pepper, Art, and Laurie Pepper. *Straight Life: The Story of Art Pepper*. New York: Schirmer, 1979. Print.

Perreaux, Les. "Racism's Long History in Quiet East Coast Towns." *Globe and Mail* 21 May 2010. Print.

Perry, Imani. *More Beautiful and More Terrible: The Embrace and Transcen-*

dence of Racial Inequality in the United States. New York: New York University Press, 2011. Print.

Peters, Gary. *The Philosophy of Improvisation*. Chicago: University of Chicago Press, 2009. Print.

Petti, Robert. "The Control and Dissemination of Music in Corporate Controlled Markets." *McMaster Journal of Communication* 3.1 (2006): 24–29. Print.

Pierrepont, Alexandre. Liner notes. *Transatlantic Visions*. Rogueart, 2009. CD.

Pieslak, Jonathan. *Sound Targets: American Soldiers and Music in the Iraq War*. Indianapolis: Indiana University Press, 2009. Print.

Pieterse, Jan Nederveen. *Globalization or Empire?* New York: Routledge, 2004. Print.

Polikoff, Alexandre. *Waiting for Gautreaux: A Story of Segregation, Housing, and the Black Ghetto*. Evanston, IL: Northwestern University Press, 2006. Print.

Porter, Eric. *What Is This Thing Called Jazz? African American Musicians as Artists, Critics, and Activists*. Berkeley: University of California Press, 2002. Print.

Porter, Lewis. *John Coltrane: His Life and Music*. Ann Arbor: University of Michigan Press, 1998. Print.

"Power Greater Than Itself: Celebrating the AACM in Guelph." *Point of Departure* 3 (Jan. 2006): n. pag. Web. 11 Jan. 2010.

Prévost, Edwin. *Minute Particulars: Meanings in Music-Making in the Wake of Hierarchical Realignments and Other Essays*. Essex, UK: Copula, 2004. Print.

———. *No Sound Is Innocent: AMM and the Practice of Self-Invention; Meta-Musical Narratives*. Essex, UK: Copula, 1995. Print.

Pullen, Don. Liner notes. *Sacred Common Ground*. Blue Note, 1995. CD.

Quinn, Jocey. *Learning Communities and Imagined Social Capital: Learning to Belong*. London: Continuum, 2010. Print.

Radano, Ronald. *New Musical Figurations: Anthony Braxton's Cultural Critique*. Chicago: University of Chicago Press, 1993. Print.

Ramsey, Doug. Rev. of *Witness*, by Dave Douglas. *JazzTimes*. Jazz Times, 2001. Web. 2 Feb. 2011.

Ransby, Barbara. *Ella Baker and the Black Freedom Movement: A Radical Democratic Vision*. Chapel Hill: University of North Carolina Press, 2003. Print.

Ratliff, Ben. *The Jazz Ear: Conversations over Music*. New York: Times, 2008. Print.

Rawick, George. *From Sundown to Sunup: The Making of the Black Community*. Westport, CT: Greenwood, 1973. Print.

Reagon, Bernice Johnson, perf. *The Songs Are Free*. Mystic Fire Videos, 1991.

Reason, Dana. "'Navigable Structures and Transforming Mirrors': Improvisation and Interactivity." *The Other Side of Nowhere: Jazz, Improvisation, and Communities in Dialogue*. Ed. Daniel Fischlin and Ajay Heble. Middletown, CT: Wesleyan University Press, 2004. 71–83. Print.

Reitov, Ole, and Hans Hjorth. *Visas: The Discordant Note*. Copenhagan: Freemuse, 2008. Print.

"Report from the 'Let Freedom Swing' Concert." *Wyntonmarsalis.org*. Wynton
   Marsalis, 2 Nov. 2004. Web. 2 Feb. 2011.

Ro, Sigmund. "'Desercrators' and 'Necromancers': Black American Writers
   and Critics in the Nineteen-Sixties and the Third World Perspective." *Calla-
   loo* 25 (1985): 563–76. Print.

Rodriguez, Lori, and Zeke Minaya. "New Orleans' Racial Makeup Up in Air."
   Houston Chronicle 29 Sept. 2005. Print.

Rogers, Kim Lacy. *Righteous Lives: Narratives of the New Orleans Civil Rights
   Movement*. New York: New York University Press, 1992. Print.

Rose, Tricia. *Black Noise: Rap Music and Black Culture in Contemporary
   America*. Middletown, CT: Wesleyan University Press, 1994. Print.

Ross, Alex. "Futility Music." *New Yorker blog*. N.p., 29 May 2008. Web. 2 Feb.
   2011.

———. *The Rest Is Noise*. New York: Picador, 2007. Print.

Rosselli, John. "Censorship." *Grove Music Online*. Oxford Music Online, n.d.
   Web. 2 Feb. 2011.

Rothstein, Edward. "With Built-In Tension, Jazz Swings to the Past."
   NYTimes. New York Times, 30 Oct. 2004. Web. 2 Feb. 2011.

Rowell, Andy. "Secret Papers 'Show How Shell Targeted Nigeria Oil Protests.'" *Independent*. Independent, 14 June 2009. Web. 2 Feb. 2013.

Sacks, Oliver. *Musicophilia: Tales of Music and the Brain*. New York: Vintage,
   2007. Print.

Said, Edward. *Humanism and Democratic Criticism*. New York: Columbia University Press, 2004. Print.

———. *Representations of the Intellectual: The 1993 Reith Lectures*. London:
   Vintage, 1994. Print.

Salaam, Kalamu ya. "Banana Republic." *Cultural Vistas* 4.3 (1993): 40. Print.

Saldívar, Ramón. *The Borderlands of Culture: Américo Paredes and the Transnational Imaginary*. Durham, NC: Duke University Press. 2006. Print.

Santoro, Gene. "Jazzing Politics." *The Nation*. The Nation, 21 Nov. 2001. Web.
   2 Feb. 2011.

Santos, Boaventura de Sousa. "Beyond Abyssal Thinking: From Global Lines
   to Ecologies of Knowledges." *Review* 30.1 (2007): 45–89. Print.

———. "A Critique of Lazy Reason: Against the Waste of Experience." *The
   Modern World-System in the Longue Durée*. Ed. Immanuel Wallerstein. London: Paradigm, 2004: 157–97. Print.

Saul, Scott. *Freedom Is, Freedom Ain't: Jazz and the Making of the Sixties*. Cambridge, MA: Harvard University Press, 2003. Print.

Schaffer, Kay, and Sidonie Smith. *Human Rights and Narrated Lives: The Ethics
   of Recognition*. New York: Palgrave Macmillan, 2004. Print.

Schneider, Mark Robert. *"We Return Fighting": The Civil Rights Movement in
   the Jazz Age*. Boston: Northeastern University Press, 2002. Print.

Scott-Heron, Gil. "Is That Jazz?" *Now and Then: The Poems of Gil Scott-Heron*. Edinburgh: Canongate, 2000. 44–45. Print.

Searle, Chris. *Forward Groove: Jazz and the Real World from Louis Armstrong to Gilad Atzmon*. London: Northway, 2008. Print.

"ShellGuilty: International Coalition Targets Shell at Jazz Fest for Human Rights and Environmental Wrong Doing." *ShellGuilty.com*. ShellGuilty, 24 Apr. 2009. Web. 20 Jan. 2011.

Shepp, Archie. "An Artist Speaks Bluntly." *Down Beat* 32 (1965): 11. Print.

———. "What Inspires You to Compose/Perform Music That Has Political Overtones?" *Newmusicbox*. American Music Center, 1 Nov. 2003. Web. 20 Jan. 2011.

Slate, Michael. "Jazz Musician Horace Tapscott: Capturing the Rhythms." *Revolutionary Worker* 998 (1999): n. pag. Web. 11 Jan. 2010.

Slaughter, Joseph R. *Human Rights, Inc.: The World Novel, Narrative Form, and International Law*. New York: Fordham University Press, 2007. Print.

Small, Christopher. *Musicking: The Meanings of Performing and Listening*. Middletown, CT: Wesleyan University Press, 1998. Print.

———. *Music of the Common Tongue: Survival and Celebration in African American Music*. Middletown, CT: Wesleyan University Press. 1999. Print.

Smith, Martin. "Band of Gold." *Socialist Review* 228 (Mar. 1999): n. pag. Web. 2 Feb. 2011.

———. Interview. "Terence Blanchard—Full Interview." *Socialist Review* 323 (Mar. 2008): n. pag. Web. 2 Feb. 2011.

Smith, Wadada Leo. *Human Rights*. Kabell / Gramm, 1986. CD.

———. "Notes on My Music (Part 1)." *Notes (8 Pieces) Source a New World Music: Creative Music*. N.p.: Wadada Leo Smith, 1973. Print.

———. *Ten Freedom Summers*. Cuneiform, 2012. CD.

Solnit, Rebecca. *Hope in the Dark: Untold Histories, Wild Possibilities*. New York: Nation, 2004. Print.

———. *A Paradise Built in Hell: The Extraordinary Communities That Arise in Disaster*. New York: Viking, 2009. Print.

Sorrells, Kathryn, and Gordon Nakagawa. "Intercultural Communication Praxis and the Struggle for Social Responsibility and Social Justice." *Transformative Communication Studies: Culture, Hierarchy, and the Human Condition*. Ed. Omar Swartz. Leicester: Troubador, 2008. 17–43. Print.

Spitzer, Nick. "Rebuilding the 'Land of Dreams': Expressive Culture and New Orleans' Authentic Future." *Southern Spaces* (2006): 29. Print.

Stanbridge, Alan. "From the Margins to the Mainstream: Jazz, Social Relations, and Discourses of Value." *Critical Studies in Improvisation / Études critiques en improvisation* 4.1 (2008): n. pag. Web. 14 Nov. 2011.

Stanyek, Jason. "Transmissions of an Interculture: Pan-African Jazz and Intercultural Improvisation." *The Other Side of Nowhere: Jazz, Improvisation, and Communities in Dialogue*. Ed. Daniel Fischlin and Ajay Heble. Middletown, CT: Wesleyan University Press, 2004. 87–130. Print.

Stillman, Nick. "An Ayler in My House." *The Nation*. The Nation, 12 Feb. 2008. Web. 2 Feb. 2011.

Students at the Center. *Men We Love, Men We Hate*. New Orleans: SACNOLA, 2009.

Sumera, Matthew. Liner notes. *Ten Freedom Summers*. Perf. Wadada Leo Smith. Cuneiform, 2012. CD.

———. "Wadada Leo Smith: The OFN Interview [Part 2]." *One Final Note*. N.p., June 2005. Web. 2 Feb. 2011.

Sun Ra. "Freedom from Freedom." *Sun Ra: The Immeasurable Equation*. Ed. James L. Wolfe and Hartmut Geerken. Norderstedt: Books on Demand, 2005. 177. Print.

Szwed, John. *Space Is the Place: The Lives and Times of Sun Ra*. New York: Pantheon, 1997. Print.

Tapscott, Horace. *Dissent or Descent*. Nimbus West, 1998. CD.

———. *The Giant Is Awakened*. Flying Dutchman, 1969. LP.

———. *Horace Tapscott and the Pan-Afrikan Peoples Arkestra—Live at I.U.C.C.* Nimbus, 1979. LP.

———. *Songs of the Unsung: The Musical and Social Journey of Horace Tapscott*. Ed. Steven Isoardi. Durham, NC: Duke University Press, 2001. Print.

Tarasti, Eero. *Signs of Music: A Guide to Musical Semiotics*. New York: Mouton de Gruyter, 2002. Print.

Taylor, Arthur. *Notes and Tones: Musician-to-Musician Interviews*. New York: Da Capo, 1993. 55–65. Print.

Taylor, Verta. "Social Movement Continuity: The Women's Movement in Abeyance." *American Sociological Review* 54 (1989): 761–75. Print.

Thomson, Scott. "The Pedagogy of Community-Based Musical Improvisation." Unpublished paper.

Toop, David. *Ocean of Sound: Aether Talk, Ambient Sound and Imaginary Worlds*. London: Serpent's Tail, 1995. Print.

Tremlett, Giles. "Spanish Fan Calls Police over Saxohone Band Who Were Just Not Jazzy Enough." *Guardian.co.uk*. Guardian News and Media. 9 Dec. 2009. Web. 2 Feb. 2011.

Tucker, Sherrie. "Bordering on Community: Improvising Women Improvising Women in-Jazz." *The Other Side of Nowhere: Jazz, Improvisation, and Communities in Dialogue*. Ed. Daniel Fischlin and Ajay Heble. Middletown, CT: Wesleyan University Press, 2004. 244–67. Print.

Turner, Richard Brent. *Jazz Religion, the Second Line, and Black New Orleans*. Bloomington: Indiana University Press, 2009. Print.

"The Universal Declaration of Human Rights." *United Nations*. United Nations, 26 Jan. 2010. Web. 20 Jan. 2011.

Vision Festival. Arts for Art, Inc. 18 May 2004. Web. 18 May 2004.

Voce, Steve. "Max Roach." *Independent* 18 Aug. 2007. Print.

Von Eschen, Penny M. *Satchmo Blows Up the World: Jazz Ambassadors Play the Cold War*. Cambridge, MA: Harvard University Press, 2004. Print.

Wachtendorf, Tricia, and James M. Kendra. "Improvising Disaster in the City of Jazz: Organizational Response to Hurricane Katrina." *SSRC.org*. Social Science Research Council, 11 June 2006. Web. 14 Nov. 2011.

Walker, Anders. "Legislating Virtue: How Segregations Disguised Racial Discrimination as Moral Reform following Brown v. Board of Education." *Duke Law Journal* 47.2 (1997): 399–424. Print.

Wallace, Rob. E-mail Interview with Ajay Heble. 15 Mar. 2010.

Wallerstein, Immanuel. "Remembering Andre Gunder Frank while Thinking about the Future." *Monthly Review* 60.2 (July): 50–61. 2008. Print.

Warden, William. "From Analysis to Activism." *Human Rights in the Twenty-First Century: A Global Challenge*. Ed. Kathleen E. Mahoney and Paul Mahoney. Dordrecht: Martinus Nijhoff, 1993. 985–90. Print.

Waterman, Ellen. "'I Dreamed of Other Worlds': An Interview with Nicole Mitchell, May 8, 2008." *Critical Studies in Improvisation / Études critiques en improvisation* 4.1 (2008): n. pag. Web. 2 Feb. 2011.

Weintraub, Andrew N. Introduction. *Music and Cultural Rights*. Ed. Andrew N. Weintraub and Bell Yung. Chicago: University of Illinois Press, 2009. 1–18. Print.

West, Cornel. *Hope on a Tightrope: Words and Wisdom*. Carlsbad: Smiley, 2008. Print.

Williams, Davey. "Towards a Philosophy of Improvisation." *Improvisor* 4 (1984): 32–34. Print.

Williams, Raymond. *The Politics of Modernism: Against the New Conformists*. London: Verso. 1989. Print.

Wilmer, Valerie. *As Serious as Your Life: The Story of the New Jazz*. New York: Quartet, 1977. Print.

Wilson, Carl. "Guelph Fest's Fantastic Fiasco." *Zoilus*. Zoilus, 15 Sept. 2004. Web. 21 Apr. 2010.

Wilson, Nayita. "Housing Discrimination Is Significant in New Orleans." *Louisiana Weekly* 7 Mar. 2005. Print.

Woodard, Josef. "Everything's Great in Guelph—Unless You Ask Sainkho Namtchylak." *JazzTimes*. Jazz Times, 10 Sept. 2004. Web. 2 Feb. 2011.

Woods, Clyde. "The Challenges of Blues and Hip Hop Historiography." *Kalfou* (inaugural issue) (2010). Print.

———. *Development Arrested: The Blues and Plantation Power in the Mississippi Delta*. New York: Routledge, 1998. Print.

———. "Do You Know What It Means to Miss New Orleans?" *American Quarterly* 57.4 (2005): 1005–18. Print.

———. "Katrina's World: Blues, Bourbon, and the Return to the Source." *American Quarterly* 61.3 (2009): 444. Print.

———. "Les Misérables of New Orleans: Trap Economics and the Asset Stripping Blues, Part 1." *American Quarterly* 61.3 (2009): 769–96. Print.

"Workshop: New Communities of Sound: Improvising across Borders." Perf. Jane Bunnett et al. *Improv Community*. Improvisation, Community, and Social Practice, 11 Sept. 2009. Web. 22 March 2011.

Wright, Beverly. "Living and Dying in Louisiana's 'Cancer Alley.'" *The Quest for Environmental Justice: Human Rights and the Politics of Pollution*. Ed. Robert D. Bullard. San Francisco: Sierra Club, 2005. Print.

Yanow, Scott. "Sing Me a Song of Songmy: Freddie Hubbard." *All Music Guide*. Artist Direct, 26 Jan. 2010. Web. 2 Feb. 2011.

"A Young Boy's Stand on a New Orleans Streetcar." Prod. Katie Simon. NPR. 1 Dec. 2006. Radio.

Zournazi, Mary. *Hope: New Philosophies for Change*. New York: Routledge, 2003. Print.

INDEX

www.ingramcontent.com/pod-product-compliance
Lightning Source LLC
Chambersburg PA
CBHW071731270326
41928CB00013B/2634